Frommer's®

4TH EDITION

NYC
Free &
dirt cheap

by Ethan Wolff

WILEY

Wiley Publishing, Inc.

Published by:

Wiley Publishing, Inc.
111 River St.
Hoboken, NJ 07030-5774

ISBN: 978-0-470-64374-7 (paper), 978-1-118-00353-4 (ebk), 978-1-118-00354-1 (ebk), 978-1-118-00355-8 (ebk)

Editor: Stephen Bassman
Production Editor: M. Faunette Johnston
Cartographer: Roberta Stockwell
Production by Wiley Indianapolis Composition Services
Interior design by Melissa Auciello-Brogan
Photos on p. 4, p. 80, p. 138, p. 182, p. 222, p. 300, and p. 320 by John Vorwald
Photos on p. xii, p. 24 and p. 46 by Ethan Wolff

For information on our other products and services or to obtain technical support, please contact our Customer Care Department within the U.S. at 877/762-2974, outside the U.S. at 317/572-3993 or fax 317/572-4002.

Wiley also publishes its books in a variety of electronic formats. Some content that appears in print may not be available in electronic formats.

Manufactured in the United States of America

5 4 3 2

CONTENTS

LIST OF MAPS

About the Author

Ethan Wolff is a fourth-generation New Yorker. How he happened to grow up in Virginia is a complete mystery to him. He lives in the heart of the Bargain District on the Lower East Side.

Acknowledgments

Thanks to John Vorwald, who came up with the idea for this book and shepherded it through development; to Stephen Bassman for his stellar editing; and to Evelyn Grollman, Elroy Wolff, Stephanie Kramer, and Anna Sandler for pitching in. Apologies to everyone who has had to put up with my cheapness over the years. It was all just research.

—Ethan Wolff

An Invitation to the Reader

In researching this book, we discovered many wonderful places—hotels, restaurants, shops, and more. We're sure you'll find others. Please tell us about them, so we can share the information with your fellow travelers in upcoming editions. If you were disappointed with a recommendation, we'd love to know that, too. Please write to:

Frommer's NYC Free & Dirt Cheap, 4th Edition
Wiley Publishing, Inc. ● 111 River St. ● Hoboken, NJ 07030-5774
frommersfeedback@wiley.com

An Additional Note

Please be advised that travel information is subject to change at any time—and this is especially true of prices. We therefore suggest that you write or call ahead for confirmation when making your travel plans. The authors, editors, and publisher cannot be held responsible for the experiences of readers while traveling. Your safety is important to us, however, so we encourage you to stay alert and be aware of your surroundings. Keep a close eye on cameras, purses, and wallets, all favorite targets of thieves and pickpockets.

Free & Dirt Cheap Icons & Abbreviations

We also use **four feature icons** that point you to the great deals, in-the-know advice, and unique experiences that separate urban adventurers from tourists. Throughout the book, look for:

FREE   Events, attractions, or experiences that cost no more than your time and a swipe of your Metrocard.

FINE PRINT   The unspoken conditions or necessary prepartations to experience certain free and dirt cheap events.

★   The best free and dirt cheap events, dining, shopping, living, and exploring in the city.

🖼   Special events worth marking in your calendar.

Frommers.com

Frommer's travel resources don't end with this guide. Frommer's website, **www.frommers.com**, has travel information on more than 4,000 destinations. We update features regularly, giving you access to the most current trip-planning information and the best airfare, lodging, and car-rental bargains. You can also listen to podcasts, connect with other Frommers.com members through our active-reader forums, share your travel photos, read blogs from guidebook editors and fellow travelers, and much more.

Priceless views of the Manhattan skyline and New York Harbor are yours for the taking, courtesy of the Governors Island ferry. See p. 113 for more information.

THE BEST THINGS IN LIFE ARE FREE

t's no secret that NYC costs are out of control. Great Recession or no, there remain plenty of local prices steep enough to make a Park Avenue plutocrat wince. We've got $1,000 pizzas (topped with lobster and six kinds of caviar at Nino's Bellissima), $1,000 omelets (more lobster and caviar, from Norma's at the Parker Meridian), and $1,000 sundaes (even more caviar, on top of Tahitian ice cream, Amedei Porcelana chocolate, and edible gold at Serendipity 3). For more prosaic tastes, New York City will serve you a $12 cup of coffee (Café Grumpy), a $14 hot dog (Eleven Madison Park, and it's only big enough for a single bite), or a $36 salad (the Cobb at Michael's).

Extremes aside, prices are up all across the city. The subway has gone to $2.25, accompanied by cutbacks in service. Slices follow fares, and the average piece of pizza is approaching $2.50. Even the humble bagel has jumped 65% in recent years. The national housing market may be in the tank, but you'd never know it in Manhattan. One-point-four million is the latest figure. That's the *average*. So, in a town with $12 coffees and $1,000 plates of eggs, where an apartment that would make a convict feel claustrophobic costs almost a million and a half, a book on living on the cheap must be a pretty slim volume, right?

Wrong.

New York takes a lot of pride in being the cultural capital of the world, and to maintain that reputation we let many of the goods go for free. Art, music, dance, and drama can all be found for simply the price of showing up, and there's plenty of it to go around. When I visit another city and see that they're putting on a production of alfresco Shakespeare I think, "How sweet." This book lists *seven* of them. We've got another 13 spots that host free outdoor films. Over 30 cultural institutions are always free, and most of our top-tier museums set aside several hours a week where you pay what you wish to enter. The best work of the world's emerging artists hangs in our galleries, which never charge for entry. New York's libraries circulate thousands of books, videos, and albums, in addition to offering us free films, classes, and lectures. From La MaMa to the MoMA, you don't need to be a millionaire to cash in on great culture here.

When it comes time to eat, New Yorkers are blessed with incredible ethnic food, which also doubles as some of the city's cheapest. Chinatown serves up savory dumplings for a buck, Peking duck sandwiches for $2.25, and four-course buffets for $3.50. My favorite New York tacos are only $2.50 a pop, and for $4.50 you can dig into humanity's greatest achievement, the bánh mì sandwich.

Between these pages, I show you how to catch a free cruise through New York Harbor to the city's most scenic picnic grounds, on top of dirt-cheap walking tours covering downtown to DUMBO to the Atlantic Ocean. I give you some great cheap date ideas, like "First Saturdays" in Brooklyn, the Rubin Museum of Art's "Cabaret Cinema," and a whole passel of restaurants that will have you looking good without draining your wallet. I also reveal some of the city's secret stashes, like Frank Serpico's guns, George Washington's desk, and the original Winnie-the-Pooh.

In the post-9/11 era, we appreciate the city in new ways, but it's easy enough to forget that New York is not an inevitability; it's a rare phenomenon. Taking advantage of all the amazing resources here is practically a civic duty. When you catch on with a big New York giveaway, you get the bonus of free camaraderie. There's nothing better than sharing the knowledge that you're in on something amazing, like a band playing its heart out in front of sunset on the Hudson, or the group spirit of a Bryant Park film, or the feeling of wending your way out of Central Park at night after a world-class Joseph Papp production. Even little everyday moments can inspire. How many years has it been since Hollywood made a movie half as entertaining as a couple of hours sitting on the steps of the New York Public Library, or Federal Hall, or the Met?

These experiences are literally priceless—gifts bestowed by the city that can make parsimony feel like one of humanity's crowning virtues. Whether you've checked this book out of the library or picked it up from the bargain bin, you should revel in your cheapness. What feels better than beating the system? Just because you don't have the cash flow for $50 cocktails doesn't mean New York has to feel like someone else's party. When you walk across the Brooklyn Bridge on a sunny afternoon, park yourself by the waters of the Temple of Dendur, or cruise by the Statue of Liberty, you own them as much as anyone else does. The city's great charm is that it's available to anybody, at any time.

Every day in New York is an adventure. For better and for worse. Make the most of it, even if you're not sitting on a hoard of gold.

Not NYC's most famous freebie, but with a jaw-dropping view and great flicks, the Brooklyn Bridge Movies With a View film series is one of the city's treasures. See p. 258.

BEST OF THE FREE & DIRT CHEAP APPLE

A lot of great bargains in this world don't withstand close scrutiny. Anyone who's ever "won" a free weekend at a North Carolina timeshare can attest to that. New Yorkers are lucky, however, in having a menu of freebies and cheapies that aren't just discards or traps. From Shakespeare in the Park to car-less drive-in movies to kayaking along the Hudson, there's a host of remarkable activities here that can't be had in other cities at any price. Sleeping for cheap may be notoriously difficult in NYC, but there are some great exceptions. When it comes to stocking up, the Big Apple's big volumes make for unexpectedly great bargain-hunting. Add in cheap ethnic food and giveaway avant-garde theater, and an urban adventurer can go very far on very little. What follows is the best of the best.

1 Best Entertainment Bets

- 🎭 **Best Manhattan Parade:** New Yorkers are pros at assembling en masse. My favorite pageant is one of the city's most inclusive, the **Greenwich Village Halloween Parade,** with elaborate costumes and a healthy dose of gallows humor making the festive spirit infectious. See p. 21.

- 🎭 **Best Outer-Borough Parade:** As New York events become more and more commercialized, it's nice to have one occasion that's defiantly do-it-yourself. Coney Island's **Mermaid Parade** brings low-budget finery to the Atlantic shore. Classic cars serve as the chariots for a procession of mermaids and Neptunes who will never stand accused of being overdressed. See p. 18.

- 🎭 **Best Festival: Harlem Week** began as a single day 30 years ago and now stretches across the month of August. Film, jazz, and food festivals are among the highlights to be found along lovely brownstone blocks Uptown. See p. 19.

- **Best DIY Rock Show:** Why trek out to the Nassau Coliseum to watch some aging monsters of rock, when the Lower East Side offers up the same three chords for free? **Arlene's Grocery** (95 Stanton St.; ℂ 212/358-1633) is the tri-state's best place to play rock star, with a real-live rock band standing in for soulless laser discs. See p. 276.

- **Best Cultural Center with Beer: Pete's Candy Store** (709 Lorimer St.; ℂ 718/302-3770) does its part to keep Williamsburg elevated and enlightened, bringing in a bushel of live music and readings. Quiz, spelling, and Scrabble nights round out a full schedule of free diversions. See p. 280.

- **Best New York Studio-Sized Music Venue:** The stage is tiny and the seats are few, but the back room of **The Lakeside Lounge** (162 Ave. B; ℂ 212/529-8463) brings in improbably big acts. Rock and rock tributaries can be found on most nights, and there's never a cover. See p. 225.

- **Best Jazzy Venue:** Low-pretense Brooklyn meets Euro sophistication over pints of Hoegaarden at Williamsburg's

Zebulon (258 Wythe Ave.; ✆ **718/218-6934**). Afrobeat, funk, and improv jazz can be heard here for no cover. See p. 236.

- **Best Concerts for Skipping Out on the Office:** The worker bees of the Financial District have long taken advantage of the great classical performances heard during the **"Concerts at One"** series at **Trinity Church** (74 Trinity Place; ✆ **212/602-0747**) and **St. Paul's Chapel** (Broadway and Fulton St.). St. Paul's hosts lunchtime Mondays, and Trinity handles Thursdays. The acoustics are great in both churches and the $2 suggested donation doesn't begin to reflect the caliber of talent. See p. 316.

- **Best Summer Music Festival:** Every year **SummerStage** (Central Park; ✆ **212/360-2777**) seems to get better organized, channeling music fans by the truckload into a small arena in the middle of Central Park. Though several shows a year are benefit performances with steep ticket prices, the calendar is still littered with huge names playing for free. See p. 250.

- **Best Summer Music Festival That's Not SummerStage:** The massive **Lincoln Center Out of**

Doors (70 Lincoln Center Plaza; ✆ **212/546-2656**) festival presents hundreds of acts every August. The range is staggering, covering jazz and dance and opera and everything in between. See p. 247.

- **Best Movie Screenings with a Roof:** Spring for a membership at **MoMA** (11 W. 53rd St.; ✆ **212/708-9400**) and not only will you get free museum admission, you'll also have the run of the institution's three theaters. The fare tends to be arty, but the range of offerings is stunning, and $75 is a great price for a year's worth of flicks. See p. 252.

- **Best Movie Screenings Without a Roof:** Forty-Second Street welcomes movie fans with an eclectic selection of classics during the **HBO Bryant Park Summer Film Festival** (✆ **212/512-5700**). The lawn crowds up quickly, but that only enhances the festive atmosphere. See p. 257.

- **Best Movie Screenings on a Roof:** Come summer nights, God dims the overheads, and indie films play on rooftops (and in parks and schoolyards) across Brooklyn, Manhattan, and Queens. **Rooftop Films** (✆ **718/417-7362**) has fast become a local institution, with original, well-selected fare. See p. 255.

● **Best Movie Date Night:** Friday nights the **Rubin Museum of Art** (150 W. 17th St.; ℂ **212/620-5000**) throws open its doors. You can tour intriguing Himalayan art for free, and for $7 you can treat yourself to a martini and a movie. The **Cabaret Cinema** series brings an eclectic selection of films, along with the occasional related celebrity, for just the price of a tipple or a snack at the bar. See p. 251.

● **Best Outdoor Summer Theater:** Forsooth, New York's greatest summer asset is no secret. **Shakespeare in the Park** (ℂ **212/539-8750**) hooks up tens of thousands of bard hounds with the best in Elizabethan drama (using some of today's best actors and directors). The Delacorte Theater's site in the middle of Central Park is well nigh enchanted. See p. 263.

● **Best Outdoor Summer Theater That Isn't Shakespeare in the Park:** Energetic performances substitute for big names and big budgets in downtown's alternative **Shakespeare in the Park(ing) Lot** (ℂ **212/877-0099**). The setting couldn't be less formal, but somehow the troupe manages to cast its spell. See p. 264.

● **Best Free Dance:** Modern and experimental dance has a home during **Movement Research** at the Judson Church (55 Washington Sq. S.; ℂ **212/539-2611**). Dancers and choreographers vary from week to week, but the talent level stays consistently high. The series only seems to be getting better, especially now that the Judson Church has installed its lovely new dance floor. See p. 274.

● **Best Comedy Troupe:** The founders of **The Upright Citizens Brigade** (307 W. 26th St.; ℂ **212/366-9176**) have gone on to movie and television fortune and fame, but the institution's classes continue to crank out rapier wits. Improv nights here are cheap when they're not free, and the legendary ASSSSCAT 3000 is not to be missed. See p. 279.

● **Best Readings:** The great writerly look of **KGB Bar** (85 E. 4th St.; ℂ **212/505-3360**) is well matched by the great writers who come through almost every night of the week. Enough quality words have been spilled beneath the Soviet-kitsch furnishings to justify the publishing of KGB anthologies, in addition to a journal. See p. 288.

- **Best Readings in a Bookstore:** New York has many great literary events at its mom-and-pop shops, but the little players don't have quite the juice to bring in huge names every time. The **Union Square branch of Barnes & Noble** (33 E. 17th St.; ℂ **212/253-0810**) has no difficulty booking the literati glitterati—check out their calendar for a steady stream of famous scribes. See p. 285.

2 Best Cheap Eats

- **Best Investment of $1 (Bagel):** New York exported the bagel to the four corners of America, but after the indignities that have been performed (piña colada bagels?) we should ask for them back. Fortunately, New York still has the best, and a single bill will let you sample one at **Absolute Bagel** (2788 Broadway; ℂ **212/932-2052**). With flavor and texture honed to perfection, you can't make a better carb investment. See p. 73.

- **Best Investment of $1.50 (Hot Dog):** For cheap protein and quick bursts of patriotic fervor, New York's dogs can't be beat. **Gray's Papaya** (2090 Broadway; ℂ **212/799-0243;** plus other locations) is the best of the fruit-drink-and-wiener purveyors, with flavorful, lightly charred links that'll only set you back a buck and a half. See p. 66.

- **Best Investment of $2 (Pizza Bread):** The pizza bianca at the **Sullivan St. Bakery** (533 W. 47th St.; ℂ **212/265-5580**) is closer to a piece of bread than a *Noo Yawk* slice, but it's long on old-world charm. Subtly flavored with rosemary and olive oil (no tomato or cheese), the dough manages to be simultaneously fluffy and chewy. See p. 72.

- **Best Investment of $2.25 (Sesame Pancake):** The dumplings at **Vanessa's Dumpling House** (118a Eldridge St.; ℂ **212/625-8008**) are justly famous and a total steal at four for $1. Less publicized but equally delicious are the sandwiches, which go gourmet by packing a big wedge of sesame pancake with fresh cilantro, carrot, and tender Peking duck. See p. 53.

- **Best Investment of $2.50 (Tacos):** Served in a double layer of supple corn tortillas and topped with fresh tomatillo sauce, the tacos at **Zaragoza** (215 Ave. A; ℂ **212/780-9204**) burst with flavor. At just $2.50 for standouts like beef tongue and buttery roast pork, they're the cheapest way to get south of the border without leaving NYC. See p. 62.

- **Best Investment of $3 (New York Slice):** First-time visitors to **Sal's & Carmine's Pizza** (2671 Broadway; ✆ **212/663-7651**), spurred to spontaneous compliments by the spectacular pies, can expect to hear back "Well, where the hell you been this whole time?" One taste of the crispy crust and character-full sauce and you'll be asking yourself the same question. See p. 75.

- **Best Investment of $3.50 (Buffet):** The competition between two Chinatown buffet restaurants has driven prices into the ground. An almost comical price of $3.50 covers four fresh, tasty Chinese entrees over rice at my favorite, **Yi Mei Gourmet Food** (51 Division St.; ✆ **212/925-1921**). See p. 53.

- **Best Investment of $4.50 (Sandwich):** For me, the bánh mì sandwich (pork pâté, pickled carrots, daikon, onion, and cilantro on a baguette) is more than just an ingenious blending of European and Asian flavors—it's one of the apexes of human civilization. You'll find my favorite at **Saigon Vietnamese Sandwich Deli** (369 Broome St.; ✆ **212/219-8341**). See p. 56.

- **Best Dirt Cheap Sit-Down Meal with Atmosphere:** Cheap Asian too often means over-lit, dingy cafeteria settings. Not so at **Galanga** (149 W. 4th St.; ✆ **212/228-4267**), and **Galanga Garden** (136 Ninth Ave.; ✆ **212/675-3330**). Stylish, modern interiors make for great date atmospheres—enough that the spicy, fresh Thai food seems almost a lagniappe. See p. 62.

- **Best Burger:** New Yorkers have voted with their palates by keeping the **Corner Bistro** (331 W. 4th St.; ✆ **212/242-9502**) busy at every hour. With the succulent, unpretentious $5.75 burgers here, it's no wonder. The city's expense-account $18 rivals at the fancy-shmancy places don't even come close. See p. 62.

3 Best Living Bets

- **Best Free School:** With college tuitions spiking endlessly upward, **Cooper Union** (Cooper Sq.; ✆ **212/353-4120**) is a definite anomaly: The 1,000 students here get their education for exactly $0 and 0¢. The rest of us are invited in for exhibitions, readings, and lectures. See p. 141.

- **Best Free Smarts:** The **Graduate Center at the City University of New York (CUNY)** (365 Fifth Ave.; ℂ **212/817-8215**) keeps adults educated with a terrific selection of lectures, seminars, and panel discussions. Fees are reasonable, and big chunks of the program are on the house. See p. 148.

- **Best Gyms:** Stay thin without a fat wallet. For less than 14¢ a day, 29 gyms and rec centers can belong to you. The facilities of the **Department of Parks and Recreation** (ℂ **212/360-8222**) include tracks, weight rooms, dance studios, and boxing rings. For $75 a year ($25 more), you get access to the swimming pools, too. See p. 170.

- **Best Grooming:** Style-conscious New Yorkers flock to Bumble and bumble salon for the latest looks. Savvier souls sign up for the model calls at their school, **Bumble and bumble.University** (415 W. 13th St.; ℂ **866/7-BUMBLE** [728-6253]). If you're selected for the stylist training program, you'll get a free cut, a head full of styling products, and an invitation to call back in a few months to do it all over again. See p. 165.

- **Best Boat Ride:** Transform yourself into river traffic through the programs at the **Downtown Boathouse** (Pier 40, Pier 96, and at 72nd St.; ℂ **646/613-0375**). They'll loan you a kayak and let you paddle around their west side piers. If you get your strength up, you'll be eligible for a longer ride into New York Harbor. See p. 176.

4 Best Shopping Bets

- **Best Thrift Shopping: Housing Works Thrift Shop** (143 W. 17th St.; ℂ **212/366-0820,** plus other locations) brings fashionable clothes and furniture down to prices real people can afford. The inventory is lightly used and quick to turn over, and the money you spend goes to support a great cause (housing, services, and advocacy for peo-

ple living with HIV and AIDS). See p. 194.

- **Best Department Store: Century 21** (22 Cortlandt St.; ℂ **212/227-9092**) is the Shakespeare in the Park of shopping—everybody knows about it, it's in great demand, and despite New Yorkers' high expectations it rarely comes up short. Amazing selection and equally amazing

FREE **New York's Top Five Best-Kept Free Secrets**

1 The former military base that is **Governors Island** (✆ 212/440-2202) opens up to the public in summer months, with picturesque free ferry rides through New York Harbor leading to the city's best picnic grounds. Programming has been quickly metastasizing—music, art, and even an auto show have been added to the existing roster of historical tours. See p. 113.

2 Three gallery spaces at the **National Museum of the American Indian** (1 Bowling Green; ✆ 212/514-3700) host well-curated exhibits of contemporary and historic Native American art. The building itself, a magnificent Beaux Arts customs house, is worthy of a visit of its own. See p. 94.

3 The **New York Earth Room** (141 Wooster St.; ✆ 212/989-5566) is just that: 140 tons of soil hidden away in a SoHo loft. Even after multiple visits it's a completely unexpected sight, and a few whiffs of the earthy scent can be oddly rejuvenating. See p. 120.

4 For more than a hint of the natural world, light out for **Green-Wood Cemetery** (✆ 718/768-7300; www.green-wood.com) in Brooklyn. Almost 500 acres of ancient trees and glacial ponds are interspersed with the graves of New York celebrities and Revolutionary War history. There are also wild parrots.

5 Malcolm Forbes' affection for his idiosyncratic collections is obvious from the well-crafted displays at the **Forbes Magazine Galleries** (62 Fifth Ave.; ✆ 212/206-5548). As you wind through model boats, toy soldiers, Monopoly boards, and trophies, you just may find Forbes' enthusiasm rubbing off on you. See p. 91.

prices draw in the crowds 7 days a week. See p. 202.

- **Best Gourmet Food Shop for Tightwads:** Tracking down fancy fromage is not a difficult task in NYC, but to actually pur-

chase a wedge without emptying your purse is another issue. Thank the cheese gods then for the **East Village Cheese Store** (40 Third Ave.; ✆ 212/477-2601), which has refrigerator shelves full of $1 and $2 specials up front, and $2.99 per pound bargains at the counter. This is the ideal place for cock-

tail party hosts and hostesses to stock up for next to nothing. See p. 209.

5 Best Exploring Bets

- **Best Exhibits:** The main branch of the **Stephen A. Schwarzman Building** (Fifth Ave. and 42nd St.; ✆ **212/869-8089**), formerly the Humanities and Social Sciences Library, puts on terrific shows in the hushed interiors behind the lions. Rare editions and manuscripts are often on display, accompanied by thoughtful captions that make equally illuminating reading. This is also the home of the original Winnie-the-Pooh. See p. 114.

- **Best Tour:** The mayor and the city council still have their offices in graceful old **City Hall** (Broadway, at Murray St.; ✆ **212/788-2170**). An underpublicized free tour of the premises allows you to catch glimpses of NYC politico celebs, while admiring gorgeous portraiture, architecture, and George Washington's desk. See p. 127.

- **Best New Art Giveaway:** The recently constructed home of the **New Museum** (235 Bowery; ✆ **212/219-1222**) may scream maximum security prison, but the free Thursday

nights are a liberating scene. Contemporary artwork that skews low-fi, playful, and international fills the upstairs galleries, and the LES comes out to mingle. See p. 106.

- **Best Art Museum: MoMA PS1** (22–25 Jackson Ave.; ✆ **718/784-2084**) puts on great art shows just a stop away from Manhattan in Long Island City. The museum is housed in a beautiful conversion of a Renaissance Revival public school, and the interior spaces have been inventively redone to complement the cutting-edge art displayed here. Entrance is by suggested donation. See p. 111.

- **Best Dirt Cheap Date Night: First Saturdays** at the **Brooklyn Museum of Art** (200 Eastern Pkwy.; ✆ **718/638-5000**) are among the best parties of the year. You can generate conversation fodder at exhibits, films, and lectures. You'll also find live music, should all that talk lead to a little dancing. See p. 99.

- **Best Natural Oasis:** Visions of rhododendron valleys, waterfalls, and wetlands conjure up only one place in New York: the Bronx. If you've never seen the **New York Botanical Garden** (200th St. and Southern Blvd.; ℂ **718/817-8700**), you'll be amazed at the biological diversity here. It's arguably the country's greatest public garden. See p. 131.

● 🏅 **Best Elephant Procession:** Forget Republican conventions—New York's best elephant show occurs when the **Ringling Brothers and Barnum & Bailey** circus (ℂ **212/465-6741**) comes to town. Once a year around midnight, the elephants (sometimes accompanied by zebras and camels) stroll through the Queens–Midtown Tunnel and across town to Madison Square Garden. As far as New York wildlife goes, this spectacle is hard to beat. See p. 134.

6 Best Sleeping Bets

● **Best $25 Night in Manhattan:** The sleek lobby of the **Broadway Hotel & Hostel** (230 W. 101st St.; ℂ **212/865-7710**) belies the backpacker-friendly pricing. Unlike other local hostels, this one limits its dorm rooms to just two guests. Share a bunk room with a buddy and you'll each be overnighting for just $25. See p. 42.

● **Best $45 Shared Night in Manhattan:** If you're traveling with your entourage, check out the **Off Soho Suites Hotel** (11 Rivington St.; ℂ **800/633-7646**), a converted tenement in the middle of downtown. The house specialty is apartment-like suites. Low season rates drop to $179, or around $45 per person if you're with three fellow travelers. See p. 30.

● **Best Stay with Free Parking and Swimming Pool:** Enjoy interstate amenities right in the heart of the city at the **Travel Inn** (515 W. 42nd St.; ℂ **888/HOTEL58**). The sun deck, outdoor pool, and parking spaces all come for free. A double starts around $140, which isn't all that much more than it would cost just to park. See p. 38.

● **Best Taste of West Village Brownstone Life:** The **Larchmont Hotel** (27 W. 11th St.; ℂ **212/989-9333**) has as prime a location as you could wish for at any price. The accommodations here come with shared bathrooms, which knocks the rates down to very affordable territory (a single can be as low as $90). See p. 31.

- **Best Taste of East Village Townhouse Life:** Avenue C may be party central these days, but the quirky themed rooms at **East Village Bed & Coffee** (110 Ave. C; ℂ **212/533-4175**) reflect the neighborhood's old-time arty charm. Sound-proof windows in front ensure you get no more of nightlife than you want. Singles start at $120 and doubles aren't much more. See p. 29.

- **Best Taste of Cotton Club-Era Harlem Life:** Don't be scared off by the name; the **Harlem Flophouse** (242 W. 123rd St.; ℂ **212/662-0678**) isn't about mattresses on a basement floor, it's an homage to the musicians and artists who stayed here during the last Harlem Renaissance. Tasteful antiques add to the atmosphere of a restored 1890s row house, which hosts doubles for around $125 a night. See p. 43.

FREE & DIRT CHEAP CALENDAR OF EVENTS

New York knows how to throw a party. Throughout the year, you can find massive celebrations of ancient tribal affiliations, sexual orientations, and pagan holidays. Most of these celebrations come free.

In addition to the numbers listed below, NYC Visit, the city's convention and visitor's bureau, has the lowdown on most events (ℂ 212/484-1222; www.nycvisit.com).

JANUARY

Midnight Run in Central Park `FREE`   For a saner New Year's night than the Times Square hell, one option is to hook up with the New York Road Runners Club. Their annual 4-mile Midnight Run takes racers from 72nd Street to 102nd, and back around. The registration fee will set you back between $30 and $55, but if you don't feel an absolute need to get winded in the small hours, you can enjoy the pre-run dancing, costume show, and fireworks display for free. Dancing begins around 10pm and the parade starts an hour later. Gather near the Central Park Bandshell, just south of the 72nd Street Transverse. ℂ **212/860-4455,** www.nyrr.org. Subway: B/C to 72nd St.; 6 to 68th St. Midnight December 31 (Jan 1).

Brooklyn New Year's Prospect `FREE`   There's no borough envy in Brooklyn as rival pyrotechnics welcome the new year above Prospect Park. Enjoy the fresh air as the embers cascade above the Grand Army Plaza at the stroke of midnight. Prime viewing areas include West Drive and along Prospect Park West, between Grand Army Plaza and 9th Street. ✆ **718/965-8999,** www.prospectpark. org. Subway: 2/3 to Grand Army Plaza; B/Q to Seventh Ave. December 31 (Jan 1).

Idiotarod   Late January and Brooklyn's brains turn to mushing. The plan: to replace lovable blue-eyed sled dogs with teams of liquored-up bipeds, and have them drag shopping carts instead of sleds. The result is more *Cannonball Run* than athletic exposition, with a secret starting point in Brooklyn (to stay one step ahead of Johnny Law). Some years there's a registration fee to participate, but the event is free to watch. www.cartsofbrooklyn.com. Last Saturday in January.

FEBRUARY

Chinese New Year `FREE`   Come February, Chinatown will be par-tying like it's 4709, in honor of the lunar new year. The annual parade sees a firecracker celebration and dragon and lion dancers winding through Mott, East Broadway, and the Bowery. ✆ **917/660-2402,** www.betterchinatown.com. Subway: J/M/N/Q/R/Z/6 to Canal St. Late January or early February.

MARCH

Saint Patrick's Day Parade `FREE`   The green wave gathers momentum through Midtown and converges on Fifth Avenue, where 150,000 marchers (and at least that many spectators) cele-brate Ireland's patron saint. Much of the crowd arrives well before the 11am start time. The entertainment continues with live music and drunken shenanigans at New York's thousand-plus Irish pubs. Wear green or risk pinchery. The parade runs from 44th up to 86th streets, right past Patrick's own cathedral. ✆ **718/231-4400,** www. nyc-st-patrick-day-parade.org. Subway: N/Q/R or E/M to Fifth Ave. March 17.

APRIL

Easter Parade `FREE`   More an informal procession than a parade, people join and leave this Easter Sunday tradition as they please. Expect amazing hats and plenty of pastels. The stroll runs from 10am until 3 or 4pm, along Fifth Avenue between 49th and 57th streets. ✆ **212/484-1222.** Subway: E/M to Fifth Ave.; B/D/F to 47th–50th sts.–Rockefeller Center. Easter Sunday.

MAY

Ninth Avenue International Food Festival FREE
If some huma. in an obscure corner of the globe will shove it in his mouth and call it a comestible, odds are you can find it at this festival. Come mid-May, street-fair staples like Italian sausages and mozzerapa mingle with barbecued whole pigs, empanadas, and soy cupcakes from Ninth Avenue's indigenous roster. Do not miss the hot-from-the-oven Greek pastries from Poseidon Bakery, between 44th and 45th streets. Ninth Avenue, from West 37th to 57th streets. ℂ **212/581-7217,** www.hellskitchen.bz. Subway: A/C/E/7 to 42nd St./Port Authority. From 9:30am to 6:30pm, Saturday and Sunday in mid-May.

NYC Dance Parade FREE
From the cross-pollination of African and Irish tap dances in the Five Points slum to an impressive 20th-century run of ballet, ballrooms, and breakdancing, New York's dance legacy runs deep. In mid-May all of it goes on parade at once, a 6-hour affair with 10,000 dancers, many sporting elaborate getups. The parade boogies from 28th Street and Broadway down to St. Marks Place, where a wrap-up festival goes off in Tompkins Square Park. Free lessons are thrown in as well. ℂ **267/350-9213,** www.danceparade.org. Saturday, mid-May, rain or shine.

Fleet Week FREE
One week a year, New Yorkers get nostalgic over the sight of thousands of sailors on the make in the port of Manhattan. Squint and pretend it's V-E Day. Along the west-side piers you can get an even closer look: Navy, Coast Guard, and Marine reps will let you tour some of the floating behemoths you spent all those tax dollars on. Demonstrations, tug of war competitions, and a ship parade are also on offer. ℂ **212/245-0072,** www. intrepidmuseum.org. Last week in May.

JUNE

Museum Mile Festival FREE
The classiest fair in New York sees Fifth Avenue closed to car traffic so 50,000 culture vultures can take in Manhattan's Gold Coast to the sounds of string quartets. Kids get live performances and special arts and crafts opportunities. Nine of the museums that give the mile its moniker offer free admissions. And the classiest part of all? No vendors. Fifth Avenue, from 82nd to 105th streets. ℂ **212/606-2296,** www.museummilefestival. org. Subway: 4/5/6 to 86th St.; 6 to 77th, 96th, or 103rd St. From 6pm to 9pm, usually the first Tuesday in June.

The Street Fair Sham

It takes less than a New York minute for a newcomer's excitement about "street fairs" and "block parties" to fizzle into the reality of another traffic-clogged exercise in low-end commerce. For two exceptions to the rule, see the Ninth Avenue International Food Festival, above, and The Feast of San Gennaro, below.

Lesbian and Gay Pride Week and March `FREE` The city bursts with Pride every June in a week that begins with rallies and protests and ends in a dance, fireworks, and a parade. Pride commemorates the June 27, 1969, Stonewall Rebellion, where gay men first stood against police harassment outside the Stonewall Inn in the West Village. Just standing on a street corner downtown can be almost as entertaining as the parade, especially the spectacle of drag queens teetering on high heels as they rush across multiple lanes of traffic. ✆ **212/807-7433,** www. hopinc.org. Mid- to late June.

Puerto Rico Day Parade `FREE` Fifth Avenue's staid character goes into remission for the Puerto Rico Day parade. There's salsa music and festive floats and millions of spectators lining the way. The parade has been running annually since 1958, and despite some ugly incidents, it remains a quality spectacle. Fifth Avenue, from 44th to 86th streets. ✆ **718/401-0404,** www.nationalpuertorican dayparade.org. From 11am to 6pm, the second Sunday in June.

Make Music New York! `FREE` The longest day of the year begets this citywide musical celebration. Inspired by the French Fête de la Musique, thousands of musicians take to the sidewalks of New York (as well as the parks, community gardens, and clubs) to play just for the sake of playing. Although only a few years old, this summer solstice event is quickly gathering momentum. ✆ **917/779-9709,** www.makemusicny.org. June 21.

Mermaid Parade `FREE` This moving freak show recalls the glory days of Coney Island. See p. 306 for more details. ✆ **718/372-5159,** www.coneyisland.com/mermaid.shtml. Subway: D/F/N/Q to Coney Island/Stillwell Ave., then walk toward the Atlantic. Saturday, near the summer solstice, 2 to 6pm.

JULY

Battery Park 4th of July Concert `FREE`   New York puts the free back in freedom with an outdoor concert in Battery Park, featuring the likes of Emmylou Harris and The New Pornographers. There's a festive, laid-back vibe, with blankets spread on the grass and New York Harbor in the background. Gates usually open at 1pm and the show starts around 3:30pm. `FINE PRINT` Some years require tickets, which are free, but must be reserved in advance online; make sure you log in when they become available in June, and stay persistent. ✆ **212/835-2789,** www.downtownny.com. Subway: R to White-hall St.; 1 to S. Ferry. July 4.

Fourth of July Fireworks `FREE`   In New York's previous incarna-tion, you knew July 4th was coming because starting mid-June your sleep was interrupted by nightly amateur firework shows. With quality-of-life crackdowns, however, The Man has taken up a monopoly on the summer eye-candy. Fortunately, The Man does a nice job of blowing up stuff for our entertainment. Macy's explodes 120,000 shells into the air from barges docked on the East River in the 20s and 30s or the Hudson. For East River years, try Hunter's Point in Long Island City, Queens, or Greenpoint in Brooklyn. ✆ **212/494-2922,** www.macys.com. July 4.

AUGUST

Harlem Week `FREE`   Harlem Day was first celebrated in 1975, and over the subsequent 3 decades it has grown from a day to a week to over a month of cultural celebration. Auto shows, film festivals, Uptown Saturday Nite, and Harlem Day are among the 150-plus events. ✆ **212/862-8477,** www.harlemweek.com. Sub-way: B/C to 135th St.; 1 to 137th St.

The Hong Kong Dragon Boat Festival in New York `FREE`   Dragon boats date back thousands of years, to races conducted during celebra-tions of the fifth lunar month of the Chinese calendar. The boats' appearance on Meadow Lake in Queens is a little more recent (1990), with a racing roster growing from four original teak specimens to doz-ens of sleek fiberglass models. Bands, theatrical and dance perfor-mances, and dumpling eating contests augment the races. Flushing Meadows Park, Flushing, Queens. ✆ **718/767-1776,** www.hkdbf-ny. org. Subway: 7 to Willets Point/Shea Stadium, transfer to the special event bus. Saturday and Sunday, 9am to 5pm, usually in early August.

SEPTEMBER

Howl! Festival of East Village Arts FREE   Though the East Village's legendary artistic past is increasingly obscured by layers of gentrifying paint, early September sees a return of the old contrarian spirit. The Howl! Festival serves up theater, live music, and art. Although there's an admission charge for some events (usually reasonable, in the $5–$10 range), many are free, like the Allen Ginsberg Poetry Festival in Tompkins Square Park. Avenue A, between 7th and 10th streets. ✆ **212/673-5433,** www.howlfestival.com. Subway: L to First Ave.; 6 to Astor Place; N/Q/R to 8th St. Early September.

West Indian–American Day Parade FREE   New York's biggest parade takes place a long way from Fifth Avenue, along Eastern Parkway in Brooklyn. Two million revelers (yup, *2,000,000*) come together on Labor Day to move to Caribbean rhythms and dine on jerk chicken, oxtail, and roti. The route varies, but generally follows Eastern Parkway at Utica Avenue in Crown Heights down to the arch at Grand Army Plaza in Prospect Heights. ✆ **718/467-1797,** www.wiadca.com. Subway: 2/3 to Grand Army Plaza. From 11am to 6pm, Labor Day.

September Concert FREE   Under any other circumstances, a day bringing hundreds of performers to dozens of venues across all five boroughs would be cause for upbeat excitement, but the context of the September Concert is a somber one. To commemorate the World Trade Center attacks, the city fills with the healing sounds of music. Throughout the day, find free sounds in the city's cafes, bars, libraries, squares, and parks. It's a perfect excuse for people to be together. ✆ **212/333-3399,** www.septemberconcert.org. Multiple venues; check the website. From noon to 10pm, September 11.

The Feast of San Gennaro FREE   This is New York's oldest and biggest street fair—11 days of zeppoles, pork braciole, and deep-fried Oreos in honor of the patron saint of Naples. Little Italy main drag Mulberry Street becomes an extremely narrow small-town carnival. There are rides for the kids, cannoli-eating contests for the adults, and an abusive clown in a dunking booth that's discomfiting for everybody. With the heavy emphasis on commerce and the beer-addled crowds, the fair gets old fairly quickly. Mulberry Street, between Canal and Houston, with runoff on Hester and Grand. ✆ **212/768-9320,** www.sangennaro.org. Subway: N/Q/R to Prince

St.; 6 to Spring St. or Canal St. Starts the second Thursday in September, from 11:30am to 11:30pm (to midnight Fri–Sat).

OCTOBER

New York's Great Halloween Party FREE   The hobgoblins of little minds can be found in haunted sites across 40 of the city's back acres come Halloween. Central Park fills with excitable costumed children, looking for the perfect pumpkin among the 7,500 scattered among the straw at the Bethesda Fountain. Once the little demons have made their incisions they take the resulting jack-o'-lanterns north, to the Charles A. Dana Discovery Center, mid-park at 110th Street. A parade is followed by an annual pumpkin sail, where the jack-o'-lanterns glow on the Harlem Meer as they float gently away. © **212/860-1370,** www.centralparknyc.org. Subway: 6 to 68th or 77th St.; 1/2/3 or B/C to 72nd St. Saturday, a few days before Halloween (date varies).

Greenwich Village Halloween Parade FREE   For many New Yorkers, every day feels like Halloween. Come late October, the last thing we need to wade through is another crowd of freaks. Fight this instinct, however, and you will enjoy New Yorkers' legendary gallows humor at the annual Halloween parade. This parade is one of New York's most participatory events (anyone costumed can join); no one will think any less of you for not being covered in body paint or latex, but you run the risk of feeling like you're in a wet-blanket minority. Parade runs up Sixth Avenue from Spring to 21st Street. www.halloween-nyc.com. Subway: C/E to Spring St.; A/B/C/D/E/F to W. 4th St./Washington Sq.; F to 14th St.; L to Sixth Ave. October 31, with the coming of night.

NOVEMBER

The New York Marathon   The race ends in Central Park near Tavern on the Green, where you can watch the survivors, adorned in the glory of heat-retaining silver blankets, as they walk it off. The race begins in the morning, with the elite runners getting off around 11am. © **212/423-2249,** www.ingnycmarathon.org. Subway (to Central Park): B/C to 72nd St. First Sunday in November.

Macy's Thanksgiving Day Parade FREE   New York's favorite excuse for dragging bloated floating cartoon characters down the west side of the city comes with the Macy's Thanksgiving Day Parade. Rocky, Bullwinkle, and Garfield join slightly-less-inflated celebrities to march down Central Park West and Seventh Avenue from 77th Street to the Mothership (Macy's in Herald Sq.). *Tip:* Balloon fanatics can get a head start on the action the night before, when the balloons get their helium fixes on the broad sidewalks around the Natural History Museum from 3–10pm. ℰ **212/494-4495,** www.macysparade.com. Subway: B/C to 72nd St.; A/B/C/D/1 to Columbus Circle. From 9am to noon, Thanksgiving morning.

DECEMBER

Lighting of the Christmas Tree at Rockefeller Center FREE
Professional ice-skaters make graceful turns, live music plays, and Hizzonner throws the switch on 30,000 bulbs strung along 5 miles of wire. Rock Center's overflow crowd, many of whom have been waiting in the cold for 4 or 5 hours, cheer with relief. Even for grinches like myself, watching the tree come alive is a pretty cool moment, but they'd have to make the spruce levitate while spouting a fountain of $50 bills for me to want to weather that crowd twice. Better to come back at a more mellow time, especially if you can visit at dusk, when the tree is at its most quietly dramatic. ℰ **212/332-6868,** www.rockefellercenter.com. B/D/F to 47th–50th sts.–Rockefeller Center. At 9pm, the Wednesday after Thanksgiving.

Alternatives to the Rockefeller Tree Lighting FREE
It's not like Rock Center has the only Christmas tree in New York City. The Winter Garden at the World Financial Center sets 100,000 lights softly glowing. More elaborate rites can be found at Lincoln Center's Christmas celebration, usually held on the Monday after Thanksgiving. A tree lighting supplements crafts booths and live music along Broadway from 61st to 68th streets. You'll find plenty for the kids, and the crowds are a fraction of Rock Center's. World Financial Center: ℰ **212/945-0505,** www.worldfinancialcenter.com. Subway: 1/2/3/A/C to Chambers St. Lincoln Center BID: ℰ **212/581-3774,** www.winterseve.org. Subway: 1 to 66th St./Lincoln Center.

Festival of Lights FREE
If you want to celebrate the other half of the Judeo–Christian cultural tradition, you can attend the lighting of Midtown's menorah. This skyscraping candle-holder (at 32 ft., it's the world's largest) shines at sunset on the first night of Hanukkah, gaining another light on each of the following 7 days. Grand Army Plaza on Fifth Avenue, at 59th Street. ℰ **917/287-7770.** Subway: N/R/Q to Fifth Ave.; F to 57th St. During Hanukkah.

The Station at Citigroup Center FREE Most New Yorkers don't have the surplus square footage for obsessive train sets, but the Citigroup Center does. Thirty-two rail and trolley lines ply the byways for the holiday month between Thanksgiving and New Year's. Visiting is free, but the show is popular, so expect plenty of company. FINE PRINT Check in advance to make sure they have a sponsor—the trains don't always run during a soft economy. Citigroup Center, 153 E. 53rd Street at Lexington Avenue. ✆ **212/559-1747,** www.dunham studios.com/cititour.htm. Subway: E/M to Lexington Ave.; 6 to 51st St. Monday to Saturday 10am to 6pm; Sunday noon to 5pm.

New Year's Concert for Peace at the Cathedral of St. John the Divine FREE Leonard Bernstein inaugurated this event, and in the subsequent decades, it's become a beautifully honed candlelit legend.

FREE **A Brooklyn Christmas**

The big department stores offer the sidewalks plenty of entertainment with elaborate window displays, but for my money, New York's best free Christmas show is in Brooklyn. Homeowners from Bay Ridge to Bensonhurst run up the Keyspan bills to bring bulb envy to their neighbors. Dyker Heights is "Christmas Central," with 100,000 tourists drawn every year to the blocks around 80th and 86th streets, between Tenth and Thirteenth avenues. Unbelievably elaborate choruses of mechanical Santas and snowmen compete to prove the lights are always brighter on the other side of the fence. Take the D to 79th Street or the R to 86th Street and walk toward the lines of wide-eyed-munchkin-packed minivans. Between Thanksgiving and New Year's.

Pop stars like Judy Collins join opera greats and world-class conductors in headlining the bills. The best seats are reserved and come with steep price tags, but general seating is free. Cathedral of St. John the Divine. 1047 Amsterdam Ave., at 112th Street. ✆ **212/ 316-7490,** www.stjohndivine.org. Subway: 1 or B/C to Cathedral Parkway/110th St. December 31, 7pm.

At the Marrakech Hotel, stylish rooms with a private bath run as low as $99, a bargain in what Hotel.com ranks as the third most expensive city for hotels in the world. See p. 42.

CHEAP SLEEPS

New York is the city that never sleeps. At these prices, who can afford to? The city plays host to some 45 million guests a year, and we'd be overcrowded even without them. Hotel occupancy rates top 80%, meaning most of the time it's a seller's market. Interested in a night at the Mandarin Oriental? An executive suite is a mere $1,695 a month. Err, night. Even the Holiday Inn Express by the Gowanus Canal in Brooklyn doesn't get much below $200 a night (and that's a good $40 off the overall city average). That said, there are plenty of ways to evade New York's steep hotel tariffs. In the pages below, I show you a night at a boutique-style hostel for

$25, a 4-way downtown share for $45 a head, and enough sub-$100 singles to get you through a major blowout with your spouse.

Shared bathrooms are one way to knock a digit off your hotel tab. Sacrificing views, elevators, and frills are others. Giving up on space is already a given; but you didn't come to New York City to hang out in a hotel room, did you? Just because you're saving sawbucks doesn't mean you can't be in the thick of things—some of the city's best bargains come in prime locations. Time of year is the biggest factor in determining the severity of your lodging pain. If you arrive in January or February, you'll find tons of options and be all but able to name your price. Sure, you'll be running into some weather, but you'll see an authentic New York, with folks getting back to their business after the December holidays. Those December holidays are about the worst time to visit, at least cost-wise, with hotels doubling their prices, and really gouging guests the closer it gets to New Year's Eve. Summers are a lull, as is the November gap between autumn leaves and Thanksgiving crowds. If your timing is right, you'll also fare better on bidding sites like Priceline, which will release rooms at half the price of advertised "rack rates" (the prices I use in the listings below). You might also consider alternatives to conventional hotel rooms, like temporarily swapping your digs for a local's, renting an apartment, or even staying in the spare bedroom of a real, live New Yorker.

Note that price categories ("Under $150," "Under $100," and "Under $50") are determined according to cheapest available rate and are simply rough guidelines. All accommodations are subject to additional city and state taxes of 14.75%, plus a $3.50 occupancy fee per room per night. I hate to even mention it, but at press time we're dealing with bedbugs in New York City. If you're anxious, have a look at www.bed bugregistry.com/metro/nyc before you book. For more on the world of New York accommodations, consult Pauline Frommer (*Pauline Frommer's New York City*) and Brian Silverman (*Frommer's New York City*), both of whom provided helpful groundwork for this chapter.

1 TriBeCa

UNDER $150

Cosmopolitan Hotel–Tribeca This is the longest continuously operated hotel in the city, although you'd never know it by the standard-issue furnishings (the cafe retains some historic details). Rooms are

CHEAP SLEEPS DOWNTOWN

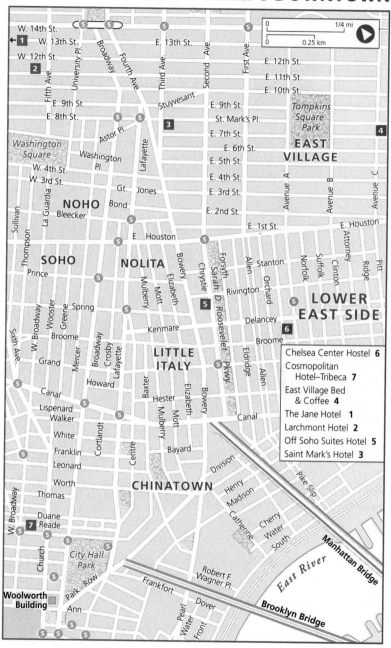

W. 14th St.
W. 13th St.
W. 12th St.
E. 13th St.
E. 12th St.
E. 11th St.
E. 10th St.

Broadway
University Pl.
Fourth Ave.
Third Ave.
Second Ave.
First Ave.

Fifth Ave.
E. 9th St.
E. 8th St.
Stuyvesant
E. 9th St.
St. Mark's Pl.
E. 7th St.

Tompkins
Square
Park

Washington
Square

Astor Pl.
Washington
Pl.
W. 4th St.
W. 3rd St.

Lafayette

E. 6th St.
E. 5th St.
E. 4th St.
E. 3rd St.
E. 2nd St.

EAST
VILLAGE

Avenue A
Avenue B
Avenue C

La Guardia
Sullivan
Thompson

NOHO
Bleecker
Gt. Jones
Bond

E. Houston

E. 1st St.

E. Houston

SOHO
Prince

NOLITA

Bowery
Elizabeth
Mulberry
Mott

Chrystie
Forsyth
Sarah D. Roosevelt Pkwy.

Rivington
Stanton
Allen
Orchard

Norfolk
Suffolk
Clinton
Ridge
Pitt

Attorney

LOWER
EAST SIDE

Sixth Ave.
W. Broadway
Wooster
Greene
Spring
Broome
Grand

Mercer
Broadway
Crosby
Lafayette

Kenmare

LITTLE
ITALY

Delancey

Broome

Eldridge
Allen

Howard
Canal
Lispenard
Walker

Baxter
Hester
Elizabeth
Mott
Mulberry
Bowery

Canal

Chelsea Center Hostel **6**
Cosmopolitan
  Hotel–Tribeca **7**
East Village Bed
  & Coffee **4**
The Jane Hotel **1**
Larchmont Hotel **2**
Off Soho Suites Hotel **5**
Saint Mark's Hotel **3**

White
Franklin
Leonard
Worth
Thomas

Cortlandt
Centre

Bayard

CHINATOWN

Division
Henry
Madison
Catherine
Cherry
Water
South

Pike Slip

Duane
Reade

W. Broadway
Church

City Hall
Park
Park Row

Robert F.
Wagner Pl.
Frankfort

Manhattan Bridge

East River

Woolworth
Building
Ann

Pearl
Water
Front

Dover

Brooklyn Bridge

27

The Shadow Universe of Vacation Apartment Rentals

Given the scarcity of real estate in NYC, it makes sense that the city would develop a shadow universe of less formal accommodations. Even in my own apartment building, I see strangers tramping up the stairs with luggage every other week or so. Somebody on the third floor is obviously renting out a room short-term, which is one way New Yorkers close the gap between income and ungodly rents.

There are several ways to connect with non-traditional sleeping arrangements (I'd put you up at my place, but I can't reveal my priceless collection of Hummel figurines to the public just yet). **Craigslist. org** is an obvious starting point. Beyond short-term rentals, you can work out swaps where you trade time in your apartment for time in someone else's. A more formal version of this cheap vacationing is **Home Exchange** (✆ **310/798-3864;** www.homeexchange.com). As the name suggests, you're swapping houses (or maybe second houses), and the company claims that in 14 years of business they've never had vandalism, theft, or folks showing up to a vacant, windswept lot. Membership starts at $15.95 a month for three months, or $9.95 a month for a year; swaps are free.

If you want to stay in New York without putting up your own home as collateral, there are several services that help with rentals. Costs can be slightly higher than a Craigslist hookup, but it's nice to know your rental has been vetted and inspected. **NY Habitat** (✆ **212/255-8018;** www.nyhabitat.com) specializes in unhosted stays. They work only

small, but lofts are ingeniously designed to maximize limited space, just so long as you don't mind ducking to get into bed. The property is very clean, and the location is excellent. Prices for mini-lofts run $139–$210, with space enough for a couple to share.

95 W. Broadway at Chambers St. ✆ **888/895-9400** or 212/566-1900. Fax 212/566-6909. www.cosmohotel.com. 150 units. $175–$250 double. AE, DC, MC, V. Subway: 1/2/3 or A/C to Chambers St. **Amenities:** Cafe. *In room:* A/C, TV, Wi-Fi.

with buildings that allow boarders, so you'll never have to stammer in a hallway and say that you're somebody's cousin. Much of their stock is corporate apartments, so digs can be bland, but there are a lot of large-size units should you be looking to settle in with the whole family. A studio is $115 to $225, a one-bedroom is $155 to $325, and prices go up from there. For both hosted and unhosted stays, **Affordable New York City** (© **212/533-4001;** www.affordablenewyorkcity.com) has a large stock of Manhattan units. A shared bathroom set up runs $95–$120, and a shared apartment with your own private bathroom is $125 to $150. A studio apartment all to yourself starts at $150. Another well-curated list of rentals is carried by **City Sonnet** (© **212/614-3034;** www.citysonnet.com). Their website offers specials like a one-bedroom in Long Island City, capable of sleeping four, for $105. Generally, hosted stays in Brooklyn are $95 to $125 for singles and another $20 a night for doubles. Their Manhattan hosted doubles run $120 to $175. Unhosted "artist's lofts" start at $215. To enjoy the residential charms of uptown neighborhoods, look to **At Home in New York** (© **800/692-4262** or 212/956-3125; www.athomeny.com), which represents a lot of stock in prime locations. Their prices start at $100 to $160 for hosted singles and $135 to $200 for hosted doubles. Private apartment rentals start at $175, with discounts available for longer term stays.

2 Lower East Side/East Village/SoHo

UNDER $150

East Village Bed & Coffee   Although the area's become more of a destination for partying of late, this little town house retains a lot of downtown's old-time arty charm. Quirky one-off accommodations range from the sunny French Room to the tiny Van Gogh–accented Dutch Room. Singles start at $120 and doubles aren't much more.

Bathrooms are shared and there's no elevator (the building is only three stories, so you won't have far to climb.)

110 Ave. C, btw. 7th and 8th sts. ✆ **212/533-4175.** Fax 212/979-9743. www.bedand coffee.com. 11 units, all with shared bathroom. $135–$155 double. AE, DC, MC, V. Subway: L to First Ave. **Amenities:** Common kitchens; living room with a TV; Wi-Fi. *In room:* A/C.

Off Soho Suites Hotel If you're traveling with a posse, this converted tenement is a great option. The specialty here is suites, designed for two or four guests. The smaller iteration shares a bathroom and kitchen with the next suite over; the larger has its own living room on top of a kitchen, bathroom, and master bedroom. The result is spacious miniapartments, ideal for a group of friends (or a band gigging in one of the many nearby venues). Low season rates drop down as far as $179, or around $45 per person if you have three fellow travelers. Staff is chill, and for exploring downtown neighborhoods you won't beat this off-Bowery location.

11 Rivington St., btw. Chrystie and Bowery. ✆ **800/633-7646** or 212/979-9815. Fax 212/979-9801. www.offsoho.com. 38 units. Double with shared bathroom, $129–$199. AE, MC, V. Subway: J/Z to Bowery; F to Second Ave. **Amenities:** Fitness center. *In room:* A/C, TV, hair dryer, kitchenette, Wi-Fi.

Saint Mark's Hotel This is not the place to put the 'rents when they come in for your NYU graduation—this corner of the city is as youthful and bustling as New York gets. The young and budget-minded fare best here, not least because they won't be deterred by the walkup to the rooms. (They're also better primed to take advantage of the lively cheap eats right outside the door; see p. 53). FINE PRINT No credit cards accepted, just cash or traveler's checks.

2 St. Marks Place, at Third Ave. ✆ **212/674-0100.** Fax 212/420-0854. www.stmarks hotel.net. 70 units. $102–$170 double. Cash or traveler's checks only. Subway: 6 to Astor Place; N/Q/R to 9th St. **Amenities:** Restaurant; bar. *In room:* A/C, TV, Wi-Fi ($9.95).

3 West Village

UNDER $150

The Jane Hotel If you're looking for a mix of trendy style and local color, the Jane's your place. This riverfront hotel was built in 1908 to house sailors, with tiny cabinlike rooms designed to ease the transition from cramped seaboard quarters. A century later the square footage isn't any bigger, but the closetlike interiors have been decked out with lux wood, marble, and 300-count cotton sheets. Since bathrooms are shared in the hallways, prices here are well within the grasp of steerage passengers: $99 for singles, and $125 for bunk bed cabins. Prior to being taken over by nightlife hotshots, the Jane was a single room occupancy hotel, and there are still several tenants from that era in residency.

113 Jane St., at the West Side Hwy. © **212/924-6700.** Fax 212/924-6705. www.the janenyc.com. 200 units. Cabins for two, $125. AE, DC, MC, V. Subway: A/C/E to 14th St.; L to Eighth Ave. **Amenities:** Restaurant; bar; concierge. *In room:* A/C, TV, hair dryer, MP3 docking station, Wi-Fi.

Larchmont Hotel   Without laying out serious cash, it's pretty much impossible to get closer to brownstone Village life than this small, aging hotel. You will be sharing a bathroom, but for that moderate inconvenience, you'll save a bundle: The small singles are $90 to $125, doubles run $119 to $145, and hefty queen-bed spaces are $149 to $165. (The higher end of the range comes on the weekends; prices include a continental breakfast.) It's also hard to find a more central location than this, no matter how much money you're dropping.

27 W. 11th St., btw. Fifth and Sixth aves. © **212/989-9333.** Fax 212/989-9496. www. larchmonthotel.com. 62 units, all with shared bathrooms. Double, $119–$145. AE, MC, V. Subway: F to 14th St.; L to Sixth Ave. **Amenities:** Common kitchenette, Wi-Fi. *In room:* A/C, TV, hair dryer.

4 Chelsea/Flatiron/Union Square

UNDER $150

Chelsea Inn   Dual Queen Anne-style town houses from 1880 do the hosting at this central spot. Interiors are homey, with a feel more like an apartment than a hotel. There's no elevator, but staff will book you in a ground floor unit if stairs are an issue. Some units have shared bathrooms (it's a two to one ratio), but those rooms start at only $89 a night.

46 W. 17th St., btw. Fifth and Sixth aves. © **800/640-6469** or 212/645-8989. Fax 212/ 645-1093. www.chelseainn.com. 26 units, 18 with private bathroom. Double, $159– $189. Subway: F to 14th St.; L to Sixth Ave. *In room:* A/C, TV, fridge, hair dryer, Wi-Fi.

Chelsea Lodge   The town house blocks near the General Theological Seminary are as quaint as any in New York, and this brownstone hotel will help you feel like a local traversing them. The building's original woodwork has been impressively restored and the full-size beds are comfortable. Rooms have their own sinks and shower stalls, although toilets are shared out in the hallway. For that privation, you'll get a deep discount on a night in a prime location (a single is $119, and a double only $10 more). FINE PRINT Tight quarters make this better for couples than shares.

318 W. 20th St., btw. Eighth and Ninth aves. ☎ **800/373-1116** or 212/243-4499. Fax 212/243-7852. www.chelsealodge.com. 22 units, all with semiprivate bathroom. $129 double. AE, DC, DISC, MC, V. Subway: 1 to 18th St.; C/E to 23rd St. *In room:* A/C, TV, Wi-Fi.

Chelsea Savoy Hotel Built from scratch just 15 years ago, the Chelsea Savoy lacks the quirks of most of its budget brethren, which is in many ways a good thing. The hotel is clean, modern, and rooms were designed to be rooms, not odd crannies carried over from antediluvian layouts. That said, those rooms are small, the decor is blah, and the staff is brusque. All of which you'll forgive when it comes time to settle up: Singles are just $99–$125, and all units have private baths. Free continental breakfast is provided as well.

204 W. 23rd St., at Seventh Ave. ☎ **866/929-9353** or 212/929-9353. Fax 212/741-6309. www.chelseasavoynyc.com. 89 rooms. $145–$375 double. AE, DC, MC, V. 1 to 23rd St. *In room:* A/C, TV, fridge, hair dryer, Wi-Fi.

Hotel 17 This Victorian-accented spot is a pocket of affordability well-situated between the East Village, Union Square, and Gramercy. Big with the Euro backpacking crew, there's a hostel-like energy, but the rooms are modern, and fresh off a recent renovation. Singles with shared baths go as low as $69, and there are triples and quads if you traveling with a crew (a low-season quad can be as cheap as $119). If the place looks familiar, perhaps you've seen its starring role in Woody Allen's *Manhattan Murder Mystery*.

255 E. 17th St., btw. Second and Third aves. ☎ **212/475-2845.** Fax 212/677-8178. www.hotel17ny.com. 120 units. $79–$250 double with shared bathroom; $115–$325 double with private bathroom. MC, V. Subway: L to Third Ave. *In room:* A/C, TV, Wi-Fi.

UNDER $50
Chelsea Center Hostel This small hostel on two floors of a Chelsea brownstone provides a laid-back alternative to its bustling competitors. A pleasant garden and continental breakfast add to the charms. Accommodations are bunk beds in clean, bright rooms (although it's 6–12 people per room). If you'd rather stay on the Lower East Side, request a dorm bed there upon booking.

313 W. 29th St., just west of Eighth Ave. ℂ **212/643-0214.** www.chelseacenter hostel.com. 20 dorm beds. $35 per night, includes continental breakfast and tax. Cash only. Subway: C/E to 23rd St. **Amenities:** Shared kitchen, garden. Other location: *Lower East Side,* 83 Essex St., btw. Broome and Delancey sts. ℂ **212/260-0961.** Subway: F to Delancey St.; J/M/Z to Essex St.

Chelsea International Hostel   You can't do much better location-wise than these typical hostel rooms clustered around a courtyard right in the heart of Chelsea. International travelers love this well-managed place. Your $38 to $48 includes lounge areas, self-service laundry, and linens. Bring your own towel, though.

251 W. 20th St., btw. Seventh and Eighth aves. ℂ **212/647-0010.** www.chelsea hostel.com. 288 dorm beds. $38–$48 per night. AE, DISC, MC, V. Subway: 1 to 18th St. **Amenities:** Shared kitchen; courtyard; Wi-Fi.

5 Midtown East

UNDER $150

Hotel 31   Like its southern cousin Hotel 17 (p. 32), there's not much that distinguishes this serviceable hotel besides the great prices. Which is distinction enough in New York City: Shared bathroom doubles start at just $85, and private-bath accommodations begin at $120. You won't get those prices in the fall (UN folks take over pretty much the whole place then), but this is a great central location if you're in town at a down time.

120 E. 31st St., Lexington Ave. and Park Ave. S. ℂ **212/685-3060.** Fax 212/532-1232. www.hotel31.com. 100 units. $85–$195 double with shared bathroom; $120–$220 double with private bathroom. AE, DC, MC, V. *In room:* A/C, TV, hair dryer, Wi-Fi.

Hotel Thirty Thirty   Just remember the hotel name and you can work your way back to the address, which is right in the heart of Midtown. This circa-1920 structure has been stylishly updated, with a lofty lobby and contemporary neutral-toned rooms. Spaces are small, but no worries, there's more than enough to keep you amused right outside the front door. A low-season double is just $129.

30 E. 30th St., btw. Madison and Park aves. ℂ **800/804-4480** or 212/689-1900. Fax 212/689-0023. www.thirtythirty-nyc.com. 255 units. $129–$389 double. AE, DC, DISC, MC, V. Subway: 6 to 28th St. **Amenities:** Restaurant; concierge. *In room:* A/C, TV, hair dryer, Wi-Fi ($14).

Murray Hill Inn   This is a basic budget spot, which is fitting given the often utilitarian nature of the neighborhood. Rooms are clean, small,

CHEAP SLEEPS IN MIDTOWN

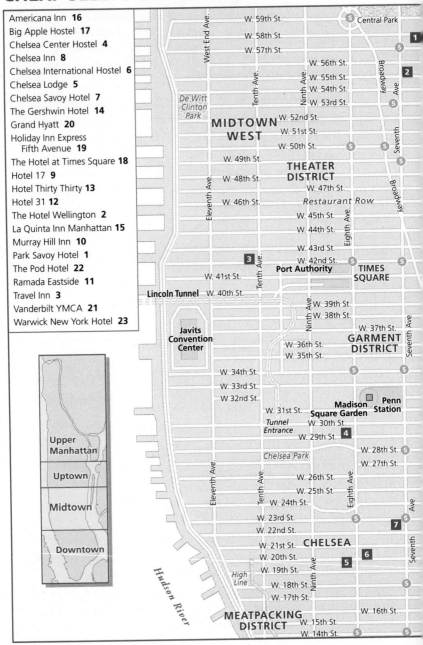

Americana Inn **16**
Big Apple Hostel **17**
Chelsea Center Hostel **4**
Chelsea Inn **8**
Chelsea International Hostel **6**
Chelsea Lodge **5**
Chelsea Savoy Hotel **7**
The Gershwin Hotel **14**
Grand Hyatt **20**
Holiday Inn Express
   Fifth Avenue **19**
The Hotel at Times Square **18**
Hotel 17 **9**
Hotel Thirty Thirty **13**
Hotel 31 **12**
The Hotel Wellington **2**
La Quinta Inn Manhattan **15**
Murray Hill Inn **10**
Park Savoy Hotel **1**
The Pod Hotel **22**
Ramada Eastside **11**
Travel Inn **3**
Vanderbilt YMCA **21**
Warwick New York Hotel **23**

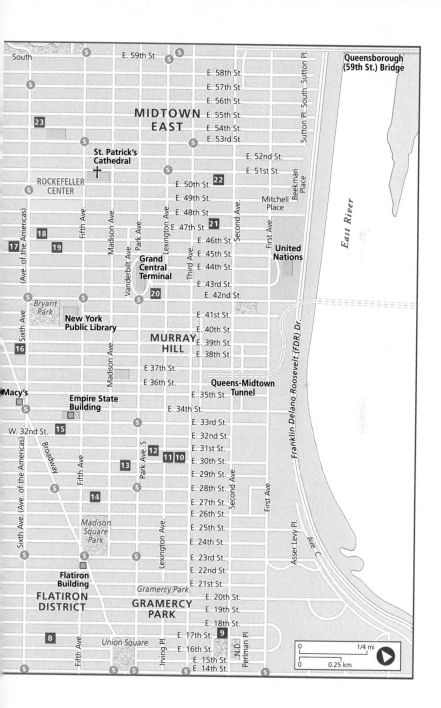

South

E. 59th St.

Queensborough
(59th St.) Bridge

E. 58th St.
E. 57th St.
E. 56th St.

MIDTOWN E. 55th St.
EAST E. 54th St.
E. 53rd St.

23

E. 52nd St.
E. 51st St.

**St. Patrick's
Cathedral**

E. 50th St. **22**

**ROCKEFELLER
CENTER**

E. 49th St.
E. 48th St.

Mitchell
Place

E. 47th St. **21**

18

E. 46th St.

17 **19**

E. 45th St.
E. 44th St.

**United
Nations**

**Grand
Central
Terminal**

E. 43rd St.
E. 42nd St.

East River

20

*Bryant
Park*

E. 41st St.

**New York
Public Library**

E. 40th St.
E. 39th St.
E. 38th St.

**MURRAY
HILL**

16

E 37th St.
E 36th St.

**Queens-Midtown
Tunnel**

E. 35th St.

**Empire State
Building**

E. 34th St.

Macy's

E. 33rd St.
E. 32nd St.

W. 32nd St. **15**

E. 31st St.

12 **11** **10**

E. 30th St.
E. 29th St.

13

E. 28th St.
E. 27th St.

14

E. 26th St.

*Madison
Square
Park*

E. 25th St.
E. 24th St.
E. 23rd St.
E. 22nd St.

**Flatiron
Building**

E. 21st St.

**FLATIRON
DISTRICT**

Gramercy Park

E. 20th St.

**GRAMERCY
PARK**

E. 19th St.
E. 18th St.

8

E. 17th St. **9**

Union Square

E. 16th St.
E. 15th St.
E. 14th St.

0   1/4 mi

0   0.25 km

Franklin-Delano Roosevelt (FDR) Dr.

and not entirely immune to the sounds of the city. Prices start at just $79 for shared-bathroom accommodations. There is, of course, a catch: No elevator, which means you could be facing as much as a five-story walk-up. Then again, aren't flights of stairs part of the authentic New York experience? The rooms with private baths are considerably nicer, although you do pay a premium for them.

143 E. 30th St., btw. Lexington and Third aves. ℂ **888/996-6376** or 212/545-0879. Fax 212/545-0103. www.murrayhillinn.com. 45 units, 3 with shared bathroom. $79–$139 double with shared bathroom; $139–$229 double with private bathroom. AE, MC, V. Subway: 6 to 28th St. *In room:* A/C, TV, Wi-Fi ($7).

The Pod Hotel   Big-time design meets small-time prices at this Midtown economy hotel. Super-modern rooms reflect a Scandinavian influence, with light wood and brushed metal. The latest electronics—LCD TVs, MP3 docking stations, and Wi-Fi—are all within easy reach, and you definitely won't feel overwhelmed by excesses of space. Bunk bed arrangements go for $99 in the low seasons, and a single with a shared bathroom is $89. The Pod's lobby bar has become a hip gathering place for bloggers.

230 E. 51st St., btw. Second and Third aves. ℂ **800/742-5945** or 212/355-0300. Fax 212/755-5029. www.thepodhotel.com. 345 units, 152 with shared baths. $119–$299 double. AE, DC, MC, V. Subway: 6 to 51st St.; E/M to Lexington Ave./53rd St. **Amenities:** Bar; concierge. *In room:* A/C, TV, MP3 docking station, Wi-Fi.

Ramada Eastside   Ramada Inns originated in 1954 on Route 66, but like many folks, they've made an easy transition to Manhattan. The chain's east side hotel is clean and functional, with cozy rooms distinguished by Tempur-Pedic DreamSpa mattresses. There's also free breakfast, Wi-Fi, and a tiny gym.

161 Lexington Ave., at 30th St. ℂ **800/567-7720** or 212/545-1800. Fax 212/679-9146. www.ramada.com. 101 units. $119–$269 double. AE, DC, MC, V. Subway: 6 to 28th St. **Amenities:** Breakfast room; fitness center. *In room:* A/C, TV, hair dryer, Wi-Fi.

UNDER $100

The Gershwin Hotel   This hotel's high design, arty flair, and central location would seem to put it way out of budget reaches, but a semi-secret cache of dorm spaces makes it quite accessible. The six-person Fabuloso room is $49 a night per person, with a bathroom inside the room. The Auberge is even cheaper ($39), but then you're sharing your ceiling with nine other souls. Real rooms here start at about

$185. [FINE PRINT] Linens are provided, but bring your own towel for the Auberge. Lockers are not provided.

7 E. 27th St., btw. Madison and Fifth aves. ✆ **212/545-8000.** Fax 212/684-5546. www.gershwinhotel.com. 150 units, 60 dorm beds. Double, $185–$345. AE, MC, V. Subway: 6 or N/Q/R to 28th St. **Amenities:** Restaurant; bar; babysitting. *In room:* A/C, TV, hair dryer, Wi-Fi.

Vanderbilt YMCA   The Young Men's Christian Association has sheltered many a newly minted New Yorker on the hunt for more permanent housing. For city visitors, low prices and free access to two swimming pools and a massive fitness center make this a tempting option as well. Of course, the Y is not the Ritz: Digs are institutional, and not exactly long on charm. Of the several city Y's, the Vanderbilt is the best managed, and $89–$105 single room rates are hard to beat in this central location.

224 E. 47th St., btw. Second and Third aves. ✆ **212/912-2500.** Fax 212/752-0210. www.ymcanyc.org. 370 units. $115 bunk bed double with shared bath; $160 private bath double. AE, MC, V. Subway: 4/5/6/7/S to 42nd St./Grand Central. **Amenities:** Gym; 2 pools. *In room:* A/C, TV, Wi-Fi.

6 Midtown West

UNDER $150

Americana Inn   The roadside motel-style name here signals the utilitarian accommodations. Despite a lack of frills, the place is clean and well-run, and pretty hard to beat for the price. Singles start at around $115. There are sinks in the rooms, but bathrooms are shared for all units. The ratio is three or so rooms per bathroom. Ask for a room in the back, as there's street noise up front.

69 W. 38th St., at Sixth Ave. ✆ **888/HOTEL-58** or 212/840-6700. Fax 212/840-1830. www.theamericanainn.com. 50 units, all with shared bathroom. $130–$160 double. AE, MC, V. Subway: B/D/F/N/Q/R to 34th St./Herald Sq. **Amenities:** Common kitchen. *In room:* A/C, TV, hair dryer (ask reception).

The Hotel at Times Square   The savvy marketers at Apple Core have rebranded this former Super 8. It still has a chain feel, but remodeling has injected a little more style, and there's nothing generic about the building's ornate, bowed facade. The location is impressively close to Rockefeller Center, and they throw in breakfast for you, too. Prices start at $102, but get pretty gouge-y at peak times.

59 W. 46th St., btw. Fifth and Sixth aves. ℭ **800/567-7720** or 212/719-2300. Fax 212/921-8929. www.applecorehotels.com. 209 units. $134–$269 double. AE, DC, MC, V. Subway: B/D/F to 47th–50th sts.–Rockefeller Center. **Amenities:** Breakfast room; concierge; exercise room. *In room:* A/C, TV, hair dryer, Wi-Fi.

La Quinta Inn Manhattan   This chain hotel is housed in an ornate 1904 Beaux Arts building, although the street is so busy hardly anybody ever notices the architecture. Korean Town is a great neighborhood for affordable feasting, and the streets are lively without being as annoying as Times Square's. Like its sibling Red Roof Inn across the street, La Quinta is friendly, competent, and throws in a free breakfast. Also like its sibling, prices veer wildly depending on the time of year. There's a laid-back bar up on the roof, with killer Empire State Building views.

17 W. 32nd St., btw. Fifth and Sixth aves. ℭ **800/551-2303** or 212/736-1600. www. lq.com. 182 units. $119–$329 double (usually less than $199). Rates include continental breakfast. AE, DC, DISC, MC, V. Subway: B/D/F/N/Q/R to 34th St./Herald Sq. **Amenities:** Bar; breakfast room; concierge; exercise room. *In room:* A/C, TV w/pay movies and video games, Wi-Fi.

Park Savoy Hotel   Most stays this close to Central Park come with an extra digit on the tab. Somehow this hotel in the center of everything charges just $106 for a single with a private bathroom. Doubles are only a little more, and while rooms are small, they're plenty serviceable. (If you need more space, the Great Lawn is just a little ways away.)

158 W. 58th St., btwn Sixth and Seventh aves. ℭ **212/245-5755.** Fax 212/765-0668. www.parksavoyhotel.com. 80 units. $141–$155 double, $106 single. AE, MC, V. Subway: N/Q/R or F to 57th St. *In room:* A/C, TV, Wi-Fi ($10).

Travel Inn   Despite a 42nd Street location, this hotel has some definitely un-Manhattan amenities, like an outdoor pool, sun deck, and free parking. There's a chain hotel feel here, but rooms are decent sized and a renovation has the place fully updated. The location is a little west of the beaten path, but that's a good thing when it comes time to lay down your head in a city that never sleeps. Doubles start at $140—heck, you could spend that much just parking.

515 W. 42nd St., near Tenth Ave. ℭ **888/HOTEL58**, 800/869-4630, or 212/695-7171. Fax 212/967-5025. www.thetravelinnhotel.com. 160 units. $140–$250 double. AE, DC, DISC, MC, V. Subway: A/C/E/7 to 42nd St./Port Authority. **Amenities:** Coffee shop; fitness center; outdoor pool w/deck chairs and lifeguard in season; room service. *In room:* A/C, TV, hair dryer, Wi-Fi.

Doing Your Bidding

Even if Captain James T. Kirk wasn't the face of the operation, I'd still be a huge fan of the budget travel site **Priceline**. A quick perusal of their offerings pops up discounted rates on a bevy of New York bargain hotel mainstays (many of which I list here, albeit at slightly higher "rack rates"). But that's not the fun part. Playing eBay with your stay and outwitting the virtual auctioneer is where the action's at. Hotels, just like airlines, hate to see space go unsold. When underbooking beckons, they release swaths of rooms to price-slashers like Priceline (**Hotwire.com** is another good option for similar bargaining). You can easily pay 50%, or even 70%, off the regular published rate if you sync your bid up right. To get a little more insight into plausible ranges, check out **www.biddingfortravel.com**, which allows folks to trade notes on recent wins. There are usual suspects in the city, mostly hotels so large that they almost always end up releasing rooms to discounters. Places like the **Warwick New York Hotel** (65 W. 54th St.; ✆ 212/247-2700; www.warwickhotelny.com), **The Hotel Wellington** (871 Seventh Ave.; ✆ 212/347-3900; www.wellingtonhotel.com), **Holiday Inn Express Fifth Avenue** (15 W. 45th St.; ✆ 800/465-4329; www.ichotelsgroup.com), and the **Grand Hyatt** (109 E. 42nd St.; ✆ 212/883-1234; www.grandnewyork.hyatt.com) are frequent names accompanying "congratulations, your bid was accepted" messages.

When you do get accepted, that's it, you're locked in and your credit card has been charged, so make sure you're ready to commit.

Tip: Make your first bid with only your main target neighborhood included. When your lowball gets negged, you can bid again at a slightly higher price without the 24-hour wait, just so long as you expand your area search. When that bid fails, expand and bid again.

UNDER $50

Big Apple Hostel   A primo near–Times Square location makes this the most central dirt-cheap sleep you'll find. Rooms are clean, folks are friendly, and there's a sharable kitchen and a backyard with a barbecue. Bunk beds sleep four people per room. There are shared-bathroom doubles as well, but the bunks are the deals here. Dorm guests should bring their own towels.

119 W. 45th St., btw. Sixth and Seventh aves. ℂ **212/302-2603.** www.bigapple hostel.com. 112 dorm beds. Dorms, $36–$54. Subway: 1/2/3/7/N/Q/R to Times Sq./42nd St. **Amenities:** Shared kitchen; Wi-Fi. *In room:* A/C.

7 Upper West Side

UNDER $150

Hotel Belleclaire   This Art Nouveau hotel, designed by legendary architect Emery Roth, was about as luxurious as New York City got when it opened in 1903. The exterior is stunning, and after years of decline the interior is finally catching back up. New management has done a major renovation, making for a great bargain in the heart of the Upper West Side. To really bring down costs, opt for one of the shared bathroom units (three to a floor, in a segregated section; rates start at $109). The rooms with private bathrooms go at prices more consistent with the rest of an upscale neighborhood.

250 W. 77th St. at Broadway. ℂ **877/HOTEL-BC** [468-3522] or 212/362-7700. Fax 212/362-1004. www.hotelbelleclaire.com. 189 units, 39 with shared bathroom. $109–$269 double with shared bathroom; $169–$569 double with private bathroom. AE, DC, DISC, MC, V. Subway: 1 to 79th St. **Amenities:** Access to nearby health club. *In room:* A/C, TV w/pay movies and games, fridge, hair dryer, Wi-Fi.

Hotel Newton   An attentive, uniformed staff makes a warm welcome at this Uptown bargain spot. Rooms are on the large side (for the city), with firm beds and a rosy color scheme to match cherrywood furnishings. A standard double with a shared bath drops as low as $75 in the January lull (it'll be double that at peak times). The range for a standard single with its own bathroom is $100 to $185.

2528 Broadway, btw. 94th and 95th sts. ℂ **800/643-5553** or 212/678-6500. Fax 212/678-6758. www.thehotelnewton.com. 117 units. $75–$185 double with shared bathroom; $95–$300 double with private bathroom. AE, DC, DISC, MC, V. Subway: 1/2/3 to 96th St. **Amenities:** Room service. *In room:* A/C, TV, hair dryer, Wi-Fi ($4.95).

Hotel 99   The newest entry into the burgeoning Upper West Side bargain hotel scene, this friendly spot has air conditioning and an elevator and not much more when it comes to frills. Rooms are small and trim, most utilizing shared bathrooms down the hall. There are 32" flatscreen TVs for end of day winding down. Nearby express trains make it quick and easy to access the rest of the city.

CHEAP SLEEPS ON THE UPPER WEST SIDE

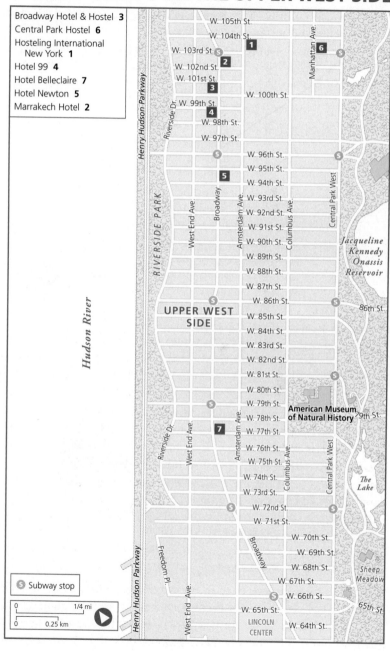

Broadway Hotel & Hostel **3**
Central Park Hostel **6**
Hosteling International
  New York **1**
Hotel 99 **4**
Hotel Belleclaire **7**
Hotel Newton **5**
Marrakech Hotel **2**

W. 105th St.
W. 104th St.
W. 103rd St.
W. 102nd St.
W. 101st St.
W. 100th St.
W. 99th St.
W. 98th St.
W. 97th St.
W. 96th St.
W. 95th St.
W. 94th St.
W. 93rd St.
W. 92nd St.
W. 91st St.
W. 90th St.
W. 89th St.
W. 88th St.
W. 87th St.
W. 86th St.
W. 85th St.
W. 84th St.
W. 83rd St.
W. 82nd St.
W. 81st St.
W. 80th St.
W. 79th St.
W. 78th St.
W. 77th St.
W. 76th St.
W. 75th St.
W. 74th St.
W. 73rd St.
W. 72nd St.
W. 71st St.
W. 70th St.
W. 69th St.
W. 68th St.
W. 67th St.
W. 66th St.
W. 65th St.
W. 64th St.

Manhattan Ave.
Henry Hudson Parkway
Riverside Dr.
RIVERSIDE PARK
West End Ave.
Broadway
Amsterdam Ave.
Columbus Ave.
Central Park West

Hudson River

UPPER WEST SIDE

Jacqueline Kennedy Onassis Reservoir

86th St.

American Museum of Natural History
79th St.

The Lake

Sheep Meadow
65th St.

Riverside Dr.
West End Ave.
Amsterdam Ave.
Columbus Ave.
Central Park West

Henry Hudson Parkway
Freedom Pl.
West End Ave.
Broadway

LINCOLN CENTER

Ⓢ Subway stop

0   1/4 mi
0   0.25 km

41

244 W. 99th St., near Broadway. ℂ 877/249-9INN or 212/222-3799. Fax 212/678-4445. www.hotel99.com. 99 units. $99–$229 double with shared bathroom; $139–$269 double with private bathroom. AE, MC, V. Subway: 1/2/3 to 96th St. *In room:* A/C, TV, MP3 docking station, Wi-Fi.

Marrakech Hotel   For a budget property, the Marrakech pays a lot of attention to detail, with a stylish Moroccan-themed lobby and accent walls complementing exposed brick up in the rooms. A social lounge lets guests mingle over cocktails and *American Idol*. The building itself dates to 1911 and is missing one key modern component: an elevator. There are stairs up to the front desk (staff is there to help with luggage), but you may face another four flights to your room. In exchange for bonus toning of your leg muscles, you'll get a chic, private-bathroom unit for as low as $99 a night.

2688 Broadway, btw. 102nd and 103rd sts. ℂ **212/222-2954.** Fax 212/678-6842. www.marrakechhotelnyc.com. 127 units. $99–$279 double. AE, DC, DISC, MC, V. Subway: 1 to 103rd St. **Amenities:** Restaurant; concierge; coffee shop; lounge; spa; Wi-Fi. *In room:* A/C, TV, MP3 docking station.

UNDER $50

Broadway Hotel & Hostel   The approach here is "boutique hostel," lending a cosmopolitan touch to backpacker-friendly rates. Sleek design and a social, international crowd mark the lobby and nearby common space. Upstairs is a mix of hostel bunk beds and sedate private-bath rooms. The former is a great deal—there are only two berths to a room, meaning you can double up with a friend for $50 a night, or take a chance on a share for just $25. The communal bathrooms are clean and modern, and the hotel provides both linens and daily housekeeping.

230 W. 101st St., at Broadway. ℂ **212/865-7710.** Fax 212/865-2993. www.broadway hotelnyc.com. 60 dorm rooms, 50 doubles. $25 per dorm bed; $89–$129 double with shared bathroom; $119–$169 double with private bathroom. AE, DC, DISC, MC, V. Subway: 1 to 103rd St. **Amenities:** Wi-Fi. *In room:* A/C, TV.

Central Park Hostel   Unlike so many New York accommodations, this hostel comes by its name honestly: It really is just a few steps from the park. (It's also close to subway trains, for easy access to the rest of the city). The clientele here tends to be young, and undaunted by the lack of elevators. There are several dorm arrangements, with up to eight beds per room ($34–$55 per night, depending on the season). A private room with a shared bathroom starts around $89. FINE PRINT Credit cards are required to hold rooms, but settling up is by cash only.

19 W. 103rd St., btw. Central Park W. and Manhattan Ave. ℂ **212/678-0491.** Fax 212/ 678-0453. www.centralparkhostel.com. 202 dorm beds, 21 private rooms, 7 studios. $89–$135 double with shared bathroom; $109–$179 studio apartment. Cash only. Subway: B/C to 103rd St. **Amenities:** Lounge; common kitchen; Wi-Fi. *In room:* A/C.

Hosteling International New York The largest hostel in the United States occupies this block-long Victorian-Gothic institution, originally built in 1883 for the Association for Relief of Respectable Aged Indigent Females. With 624 beds, there's a lot of room at the inn, divided into male, female, and coed dorm spaces. Rooms sleep 6, 8, 10, or 12, with discounts on overnights for the larger spaces. A night starts at $30 and goes up to $49, with an extra $3 charged if you're not a member of Hostelling International (an annual membership can be purchased on the spot for $28). With hundreds of youthful guests around, there's a ton of social potential, some of it facilitated by the hostel itself. Free or inexpensive city tours run daily, and there are pub crawls and nightclub visits at night. Linens are provided.

891 Amsterdam Ave., btw. 103rd and 104th sts. ℂ **212/932-2300.** Fax 212/932-2574. www.hinewyork.org. 624 beds. $30–$49 per bed. AE, DC, MC, V. Subway: 1 to 103rd St. **Amenities:** Cafe; shared kitchen; 2 game rooms; common space; Wi-Fi. *In room:* A/C.

8 Harlem

UNDER $150

Harlem Flophouse Harlem is experiencing another renaissance, and if you'd like to spend the night just a couple of blocks from Bill Clinton's office, this 1890s row house is a great pick. The flophouse name refers to the musicians and artists who crashed here back in the day, not to mattresses on the floor (rooms are very comfortable, furnished with tasteful antiques). Bathrooms are shared between two rooms, and if you're booking in summer, keep in mind this place was built long before the advent of air conditioning.

242 W. 123rd St., btw. Adam Clayton Powell and Frederick Douglass blvds. ℂ **212/662-0678.** www.harlemflophouse.com. 4 rooms. $100 per room; $25–$35 for additional person; weekends $25 higher. MC, V. Subway: 2/3 or A/B/C/D to 125th St. *In room:* TV, Wi-Fi.

9 Brooklyn

UNDER $150

Super 8 Brooklyn Yes, New York City has Super 8s, just like a regular old interstate. This one is located in a no man's land between Park

Slope and Carroll Gardens, which is actually convenient for Brooklyn exploring (the subway back to Manhattan is close by, too). Interiors are chain standard, but the building is new, and they'll lay out a complimentary continental breakfast for you.

265 Third Ave., btw. President and Union sts., Park Slope, Brooklyn. ℂ **718/534-0451.** Fax 718/534-0455. www.super8motel.com. 57 units. $119–$169 double. AE, DC, DISC, MC, V. Subway: R to Union St. **Amenities:** Breakfast room. *In room:* A/C, TV, hair dryer, Wi-Fi.

UNDER $50

The New York Loft Hostel   Bushwick's blend of young, arty energy and run-down streets is about as close as you can get to the East Village of the '80s. (There's even an offshoot of the original Life Café immortalized in *Rent*.) An early-20th-century loft building hosts this hostel, with exposed brick walls and industrial-chic steel bunks. Rooms sleep up to 12, and a communal scene carries over to the backyard and the big hot tub. Dorm beds start at just $45 and come with a free continental breakfast.

249 Varet St., btw. Bogart and White sts., Bushwick, Brooklyn. ℂ **718/366-1351** or 800/780-5733. www.nylofthostel,com. 30 beds. $45–$64 dorm. Subway: L to Morgan Ave. **Amenities:** Shared kitchen; outdoor space; hot tub; Wi-Fi. *In room:* A/C.

ZIP112   Williamsburg's youthful nightlife scene more than rivals Manhattan's: You could spend an entire vacation in this part of Brooklyn and be more than sated with all your options for food, drink, music, and art. (For Manhattan fixes, it's an easy trip in on the L train, not to mention amazing skyline views from the dorms and balcony.) The dorm beds are female-only, starting at $45 a night (four beds to a room). Those traveling in two's can book the private double (shared bathroom). FINE PRINT Note that the rooms are on the fifth floor and there is no elevator.

112 N. 6th St., btw. Berry St. and Wythe Ave., Williamsburg, Brooklyn. ℂ **347/403-0577.** www.zip112.com. 8 dorm beds, 1 double. $110–$140 double. Subway: L to Bedford Ave. **Amenities:** Shared kitchen; outdoor space. *In room:* A/C, hair dryer, Wi-Fi.

10 Queens

UNDER $150

Verve Hotel   One of the city's newest hotels (built in 2007), this boutique accommodation is made affordable by an industrial Queens

FREE Nights Without Roofs

You don't have to be on the tail-end of a nasty bender to find yourself spending the night under the stars in New York City. Parks offer family camping nights in all five boroughs, even Manhattan (Central Park and Inwood Hill Nature Center do the hosting there). Knowing that urbanites are light on tents and portable stoves, the city provides all the equipment save sleeping bags. They even throw in dinner, s'mores, and breakfast the next morning. It's all free, although you will have to get lucky with a lottery to nail down a space. Usually 30 spots are available for each camp night; the nights come on 30 different dates in summer, 6 nights per borough. Check with the Urban Park Rangers (www.nycgovparks.org) for exact times and dates, and to take your shot at the online registration lottery.

If you're looking to camp sans kids, there is one overnight spot in the city, **Floyd Bennett Field** (www.nps.gov; ✆ **718/338-3799**). On the edge of Jamaica Bay, and close to Riis Beach, this former airport offers four sites for year-round tenting. A registration is $50, but covers three nights. You can access the park by taking the 2 train to Flatbush Avenue and then the Q35 bus.

location. Nearby subway lines make for a quick and easy trip into Manhattan. The larger suites are reasonably priced and come with hot tubs, and many rooms have sweeping skyline views. To help seal the deal, they'll throw in a free continental breakfast.

40–03 29th St., btw. 40th Rd. and 40th Ave., Long Island City, Queens. ✆ **718/786-4545.** Fax 718/786-4554. www.vervehotel.com. 87 units. $119–$299 double. AE, DC, DISC, MC, V. Subway: N/Q/R to 39th Ave. **Amenities:** Breakfast room; fitness room; discount parking. *In room:* A/C, TV, hair dryer, Wi-Fi.

Selective diners can find cheap eats all over Gotham; the Lower East Side's Tiengarden serves refined vegan fare at affordable prices. See p. 54 for a review.

CHEAP EATS

New Yorkers speak over 130 languages, and we eat at least that many different cuisines. Many of the ethnic superstars are hidden away in low-rent corners of the boroughs, but plenty of spectacular cheap eats can be found even in the high-rent districts of Manhattan. Being selective about price doesn't necessarily mean sacrificing quality. Some of my favorite cooking just happens to be some of the city's cheapest. The island tilts toward downtown when it comes to budget grazing—Chinatown and the East Village dominate. Across the rest of the city, Asian eateries offer the most for the least, with some solid backing from Latino and Indian contenders. Culinary trends of late have been favoring the low end, meaning new purvey-ors of cheap burgers; hot dogs; fried chicken; and pizza now dot the city. Lunch specials are a great way to sample the city's harvest with a minimal investment, but for all meals, I'm constantly surprised by how far $6 or $7 or even $3 can take me in NYC. Leave the Jacksons in the wallet and *bon appétit*.

1 Financial District

Bennie's Thai Café *THAI* This unprepossessing basement spot serves authentic Thai food that bursts with flavor. Worker bees stream in for the $5.95 lunch specials, served over rice on weekdays from 11am to 3pm. Red, yellow, and green curries are the highlights. The dishes are pork, chicken, and beef, so vegetarians have to order off the regular menu. Helpfully, vegetarian entrees, including an awe-some pad thai, average $8.95.

88 Fulton St., at Gold St. ℂ **212/587-8930.** www.benniesthaicafenyc.com. Mon–Fri 11am–9pm; Sat–Sun noon–9pm. Subway: A/C/J/Z/2/3/4/5 to Fulton St./Broadway Nassau.

Carl's Steaks *CHEESESTEAKS* City of Brotherly Love transplants have long looked down their noses at New York's feeble attempts at the cheesesteak. A slew of hopefuls have stepped up, but only Carl's delivers a sandwich with the potential to hold its own in South Philly. The shaved sirloin melts on the tongue, while taut hoagie rolls make the meal substantial. Choose American or provolone, but connois-seurs know Cheese Whiz is the only way to go. A steak sandwich alone is $6.25, with cheese $6.75; $2.25 for a side of fries.

79 Chambers St., btw. Broadway and Church St. ℂ **212/566-2828.** www.carlssteaks. com. Mon–Tues 11am–9:30pm; Wed–Fri 10:30am–9:30pm; Sat–Sun noon–9:30pm. Subway: A/C or 1/2/3 to Chambers St.; Q/R to City Hall. Other location: *Midtown*, 507 Third Ave., at 34th St. ℂ **212/696-5336.** Subway: 6 to 33rd St.

L & L Hawaiian Barbecue *HAWAIIAN* For most New Yorkers, the *katsus, loco mocos,* and *lau lau* combos here will be unfamiliar. The tangy Asian-inflected flavors make quick converts, though. Plates come with creamy macaroni salad and scooped rice. Short ribs in black pepper sauce are $6.69; a mixed barbecue combo that could feed a family for a week is $9.99. (Manhattan is blessed with the only version of this franchise east of Texas.)

64 Fulton St., btw. Cliff and Gold sts. ✆ **212/577-8888.** www.hawaiianbarbecue. com. Mon–Fri 10:30am–11pm; Sat–Sun 11am–11pm. Subway: A/C/J/Z/2/3/4/5 to Fulton St./Broadway Nassau.

2 Chinatown

Bánh Mì Saigon Bakery *VIETNAMESE* If you ask me, bánh mì sandwiches are up there with penicillin as far as human achievements go. Layers of cilantro, carrot, cucumber, and a creamy dressing top a crusty baguette. Beyond the bread, French influence can also be found in the thinly sliced pâté that accompanies crumbled pork sausage in the classic version ($3.75 here). This purveyor's tiny counter in the back of a jewelry shop reinforces a sensation that anything this delicious must be illegal.

138–01 Mott St., btw. Grand and Hester sts. ✆ **212/941-1541.** Tues–Sun, 10am–7pm. Subway: B/D to Grand St.; J/Z to Bowery.

Dragon Land Bakery *BAKERY* Bakeries litter the landscape in Chinatown, all of them offering up fresh goods at ridiculous prices. The differences between any two shops are subtle, but Dragon Land does a particularly good job. In addition to baked goods, the mango and green tea flavored puddings are delicious. Prices range from 75¢ to $4.

125 Walker St., btw. Centre and Baxter sts. ✆ **212/219-2012.** Daily 7:30am–8pm. Subway: J/N/Q/R/Z/6 to Canal St.

Hong Kong Station *CHINESE* DIY soup-designing saves you money! Less labor-intensive than shabu shabu, Hong Kong Station does the work once you've selected a noodle, a broth, and fillings. The usual Chinatown body parts (that is, pig's blood, beef shin, and chicken gizzards) are joined by greens, tofu, and taut fish balls. Garlic and hot sauces top it all off, along with scallions and "parsley" (well, cilantro actually—somebody fire the translator). A noodle soup with one topping is $3; additional toppings are just $1.25 each.

128 Hester St., btw. Chrystie St. and the Bowery. ✆ **212/966-9382.** Sun–Thurs 7am–8:30pm; Fri–Sat 7am–9:30pm. Subway: B/D to Grand St. *Also in Chinatown,* 45 Bayard St., at Elizabeth St. ✆ **212/233-0288.** Subway: J/M/N/R/Q/Z/6 to Canal St. *Also in Chinatown,* 45 Division St., btw. Market and Catherine sts. ✆ **212/966-9682.** Subway: F to E. Broadway; J/M/N/R/Q/Z/6 to Canal St.

Pho Grand *VIETNAMESE* Pho Grand is a contender for the best Vietnamese food in the city, and it's just a little added bonus that it's

CHEAP EATS DOWNTOWN

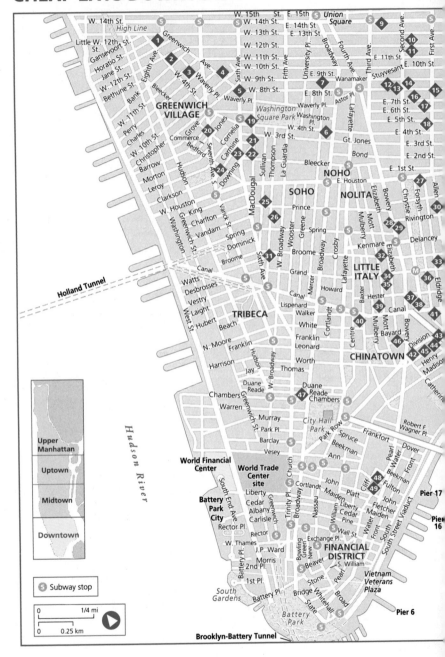

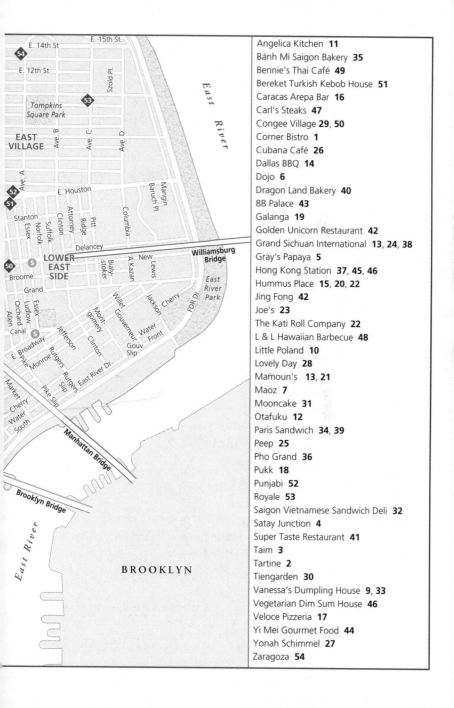

Angelica Kitchen **11**
Bánh Mì Saigon Bakery **35**
Bennie's Thai Café **49**
Bereket Turkish Kebob House **51**
Caracas Arepa Bar **16**
Carl's Steaks **47**
Congee Village **29, 50**
Corner Bistro **1**
Cubana Café **26**
Dallas BBQ **14**
Dojo **6**
Dragon Land Bakery **40**
88 Palace **43**
Galanga **19**
Golden Unicorn Restaurant **42**
Grand Sichuan International **13, 24, 38**
Gray's Papaya **5**
Hong Kong Station **37, 45, 46**
Hummus Place **15, 20, 22**
Jing Fong **42**
Joe's **23**
The Kati Roll Company **22**
L & L Hawaiian Barbecue **48**
Little Poland **10**
Lovely Day **28**
Mamoun's **13, 21**
Maoz **7**
Mooncake **31**
Otafuku **12**
Paris Sandwich **34, 39**
Peep **25**
Pho Grand **36**
Pukk **18**
Punjabi **52**
Royale **53**
Saigon Vietnamese Sandwich Deli **32**
Satay Junction **4**
Super Taste Restaurant **41**
Taim **3**
Tartine **2**
Tiengarden **30**
Vanessa's Dumpling House **9, 33**
Vegetarian Dim Sum House **46**
Veloce Pizzeria **17**
Yi Mei Gourmet Food **44**
Yonah Schimmel **27**
Zaragoza **54**

Dirt Cheap Brunch: Dim Sum

A typical New York brunch is $20 to $30 per person, but you can feast like royalty for $10 to $15 a head at a Chinese brunch, or *dim sum*—Cantonese for "touch the heart," which refers to the small dishes that are usually pushed around on carts. You point to the dishes you want, the waitstaff stamps your card, you eat entirely more than you planned, then marvel at how cheap the bill is. Fill up on everything from steamed pork buns, shrimp shumai, and fried taro balls (one of my favorites) to chicken feet and jellied pig's blood.

For the full effect, you'll want a large dining hall with the carts, and **Jing Fong,** 20 Elizabeth St. (⌀ **212/964-5256**), is still the place I take my visiting guests. Watching the hustle and bustle of this football-field sized space filled with Chinese families is an experience in itself. But the secret's out on this place, and you may wait 30 minutes or more on a weekend. You'll have a similarly grand experience at **Golden Unicorn,** 18 E. Broadway, at Catherine St. (⌀ **212/941-0911**), though you'll pay a few bucks extra per person. I also like **88 Palace,** 88 East Broadway, 2nd floor (⌀ **212/941-8886**), in the Chinese mall under the Manhattan Bridge, and it's one of the cheapest dim sums (a huge feast including beers for three people came to $34 before tip). Even carnivores will enjoy **The Vegetarian Dim Sum House,** which does satisfying mock-meat versions of all the traditional dishes, minus the carts.

—*Stephen Bassman*

also among the cheapest. Huge bowls of rich, complex *pho* (beef noodle soup) are only $5.25. Vermicelli noodle and rice dishes come in under $6. Most entrees top out well before $10 and are routinely delicious. A lodgelike interior with wooden panels underscores the homey quality of the food.

277C Grand St., btw. Forsyth and Eldridge sts. ⌀ **212/965-5366.** www.phograndny.com. Daily 10:30am–10:30pm. Subway: B/D to Grand St.

Super Taste Restaurant *CHINESE*   In the back of this barebones little soup shop you can see the noodle-maker at work, stretching dough as ritualistically as a pizza maker. The noodles themselves are taut and flavorful, dunked into a rich beef broth that originated along the

Silk Road. Soups average $4. Steamed dumplings with silky wrappings make a great side at $3.

26 N. Eldridge St., btw. Canal and Division sts. © **212/625-1198.** Daily 10am–11pm. Subway: F to E. Broadway; B/D to Grand St.

Vanessa's Dumpling House *CHINESE/DUMPLINGS*   If they tripled their prices, this little shop on the Lower East Side–end of Chinatown would still be laughably cheap. They offer an amazing $2 sandwich, a big wedge of sesame pancake with roasted beef or pork in a fresh cilantro and carrot dressing. Add 25¢ and go full-on gourmet with Peking duck. Dumplings make a great side, four for $1 and cooked in a thick, flavorful wrapping. Soups start at $1 and buns at 3/$1. A major overhaul doubled the size of the space and made things less chaotic, with some decent tables for sit-down dining. FINE PRINT There's a satellite location on 14th Street, but its prices are higher and the food's not quite as good.

118 Eldridge St., btw. Broome and Grand sts. © **212/625-8008.** Daily 7:30am–10:30pm. Subway: B/D to Grand St. *East Village,* 220 E. 14th St., btw. Second and Third aves. © **212/529-1329.** Subway: L to Third Ave.

Yi Mei Gourmet Food *CHINESE*   I'm all for capitalism if it means that two tasty buffets will set up side-by-side shops and battle it out for the cheapest, freshest food around. Yi Mei and its neighbor Golden Bowl both put out a dozen-plus daily entrees, from salt-and-pepper shrimp to century eggs to baby bok choy. Choose any four items and it's only $3.50 ($3.25 at Golden Bowl), and that includes a cup of soup (which resembles bathwater and should be skipped). Both restaurants are good, but for my (almost no) money, Yi Mei's got the edge.

51 Division St., btw. Market and Catherine sts. © **212/925-1921.** Subway: F to E. Broadway; J/N/Q/R/Z/6 to Canal St.

3 Lower East Side

Bereket Turkish Kebob House *TURKISH*   The guys working here clearly never got the memo that fast food doesn't require four-star taste. The $3.50 falafel is crispy, served up in a flavorful pita with farm-fresh tomatoes and lettuce. As good as the falafel is, the rest of the menu is even better. My own personal addiction is the adana kabob, a spicy blend of lamb and beef, available as a $6 pita sandwich.

187 E. Houston St., at Orchard St. © **212/475-7700.** Daily 24 hr. Subway: F to Second Ave.

Congee Village *CHINESE* The Chinese–Disney–acid trip interior here has recently been scaled back, resulting in a marble and brick expanse that could almost pass for classy. The house specialty is congee, a hearty rice porridge that starts at $2 and comes in multiple combinations. My favorite is squid with ginger, for $2.95. For sharing, try the house special chicken, a banquet plate of garlicky delight at $9 for a half. Lunch specials, served over rice, average $3.50. FINE PRINT The original space is wildly popular; for shorter waits try the Bowery satellite location. Don't let them shove you into an empty first-floor corner—ask to sit with the cool kids on the upper floor.

100 Allen St., btw. Delancey and Broome sts. ✆ 212/941-1818. www.congeevillage restaurants.com. Daily 10:30am–2am. Subway: F to Delancey St.; J/M/Z to Essex St. Other location: *Bowery*, 207 Bowery, btw. Spring and Rivington sts. ✆ 212/766-2828. Subway: J/Z to Bowery; 6 to Spring St.

Tiengarden *VEGETARIAN* A mix of pencil-thin model types and local hard-core vegans frequent this quirky little storefront for some of the healthiest food around. The Chinese-inspired menu is prepared without dairy, onion, or garlic, but somehow manages to be packed with flavor. Prices have gone up some, but it's still cheap for such wholesome offerings—noodle dishes and oversized soups start at $9, and entrees hover around $11.

170 Allen St., btw. Stanton and Rivington sts. ✆ 212/388-1364. www.tiengardener. com. Daily noon–10pm. Subway: F to Second Ave.; J/M/Z to Essex St.

Yonah Schimmel *KNISHES* The knish is a New York classic and can be found everywhere from delis to hot dog stands, but for the best in gut bombs you have to go to the source, the Lower East Side. Yonah Schimmel offers up flavors traditional (potato, mushroom, kasha) and sacrilegious (pizza), cooked with a generations-old recipe. For $3.50, it's hard to get more filled up. The rich cheese versions are less cost conscious ($4), but equally delicious.

137 E. Houston St., btw. First and Second aves. ✆ 212/477-2858. www.yonah schimmel.com. Mon–Thurs 9am–7pm; Fri–Sun 9am–11pm. Subway: F to Second Ave.

4 SoHo/Nolita

Cubana Café *CUBAN* In its quick trip to becoming New York's outdoor answer to the Mall of America, SoHo has managed to squeeze out most of its low-rent neighbors. At this quaint Cuban boutique restaurant, however, plenty of offerings remain under $9. Spicy huevos rancheros are only $6.50 and are served all day, along with a host of other breakfast items. A hearty Cuban sandwich is $8.50. Strong flavors help to compensate for portions on the small side.

110 Thompson St., btw. Prince and Spring sts. ℂ **212/966-5366.** Mon–Thurs 11:30am–11pm; Fri–Sat 11:30am–midnight. Subway: C/E to Spring St. Other locations: *Carroll Gardens, Brooklyn,* 272 Smith St., btw. Sackett and Degraw sts. ℂ **718/858-3980.** Subway: F/G to Carroll St. *Park Slope, Brooklyn,* 80 Sixth Ave., at St. Marks Ave. ℂ **718/398-9818.** Subway: 2/3 to Bergen St. Also Habana Outpost, see p. 256.

Lovely Day *JAPANESE/THAI* This little cafe is as hip as affordable gets, and they've bounced back admirably from a bad fire. The menu features creative takes on Thai and Japanese dishes, with noodles coming in at $8.50. A plate of meat and pineapple fried rice is $8. Red or green curries and pineapple cashew plates are all under $10. The seasonings are a little on the sweet side, but the fun, bustling room quickly puts a diner in a forgiving mood.

196 Elizabeth St., btw. Prince and Spring sts. ℂ **212/925-3310.** Daily 11am–11pm. Subway: 6 to Spring St.

Mooncake *PAN-ASIAN* This cheerful little family-run shop serves up fresh food with Asian accents. Portions are decent for such small prices. A pork chop sandwich with mango chutney is $7.75, as is a steak and pepper sandwich. For $2 more, you can get a big salad bowl with lemongrass shrimp and Vietnamese-style vermicelli noodles. The biggest seller here is the miso-glazed salmon, a plate of which is $9.75.

28 Watts St., near Sixth Ave. ℂ **212/219-8888.** www.mooncakefoods.com. Mon–Sat 11am–11pm. Subway: A/C/E to Canal St. Other location: *Midtown West,* 263 W. 30th St., btw. Seventh and Eighth aves. ℂ **212/268-2888.** Subway: 1/2/3 or A/C/E to Penn Station.

Paris Sandwich *VIETNAMESE* Fresh baguettes are the innovation here, cooked on site, and then transformed into hearty Vietnamese heroes ($4 for most). Although I prefer the *bánh mì* elsewhere, the grilled pork is spectacular, caramelly meat sunk deep into the pores of the bread. Cheap fresh-roasted Vietnamese coffee, soups, noodles, and curries are also for sale.

213 Grand St., btw. Elizabeth and Mott sts. ℂ **212/226-3828.** www.parissandwiches. com. Mon–Thurs 8am–8pm; Fri–Sun 9am–9pm. Subway: B/D to Grand St.; J/Z to Bowery. Other location: *Chinatown,* 113 Mott St., btw. Hester and Canal sts. ℂ **212/ 226-7221.** Subway: J/N/Q/R/Z/6 to Canal St.; B/D to Grand St.

Peep *THAI*   Peep proves that an upscale, modern decor and central location don't require exorbitant prices. Dinners are reasonable ($10 pad Thai and sautéed entrees), though the real deal comes at lunch. For $7 to $8.50 you get an appetizer and an entree, with a large selection of Thai favorites to pick through. Presentation is as attractive as the crowd. Though the neighborhood's discovered this place, it's usually not so crowded that you can't get a seat. FINE PRINT Don't miss the bathrooms.

177 Prince St., btw. Sullivan and Thompson sts. ✆ **212/254-PEEP** [7337]. www.peepsoho.net. Sun–Thurs 11am–midnight; Fri–Sat 11am–1am. Subway: C/E to Spring St.

Saigon Vietnamese Sandwich Deli *VIETNAMESE*   The bánh mì craze is still raging on. A recent spruce up of this little takeaway shop has resulted in slightly raised prices, but the quality is up as well—substantial baguettes are packed dense with fresh, top-quality cilantro, radish, carrots, and homemade pâté. $4.50 covers the house special (there are a dozen or so sandwiches available in all.)

369 Broome St., near Mott St. ✆ **212/219-8341**. www.vietnamese-sandwich.com. Daily, 7am–7pm. Subway: J/Z to Bowery; B/D to Grand St.

5 East Village

Caracas Arepa Bar *VENEZUELAN*   An arepa is a Venezuelan improvement on bread, with flavorful corn standing in for wheat flour. The small arepa sandwiches at this East Village shop start at $4.75 with plain white cheese and top out around $7.50. The selections are varied for such a small place, with ingredients changing with the seasons.

91 E. 7th St., btw. First and Second aves. ✆ **212/529-2314**. www.caracasarepabar. com. Daily, noon–11pm. Subway: F to Second Ave. Other location: *Williamsburg, Brooklyn*, 291 Grand St., btw. Hevemeyer and Roebling sts. ✆ **718/218-6050**. Subway: L to Lorimer St.; G to Metropolitan Ave.; J/M/Z to Marcy Ave.

Little Poland *DINER/POLISH*   The old-time Eastern European flavor of the East Village is fading fast, but fortunately this greasy-spoon stalwart is still hanging on. Some dozen hearty soups are less than $4 a bowl, and pierogi are $7.95 for eight. For dinner, a breaded pork chop bigger than a serving plate is $10.50, and if you're in before noon you can get a full array of breakfast specials (starting with two

BYOB, Baby!

BYOB occupies a gray area legally, but several spots are famed for letting you brown bag your way in. Most every address on Curry Row (6th Street btw. First and Second aves. in the East Village) will wave you right in if you're toting a bottle (or perhaps a sixer from Dowel Quality Products; see p. 209).

Looking to impress the militant vegan in your life? Hit up the long-running **Angelica Kitchen** (300 E. 12th St.; ℂ **212/228-2909**)—the original '70s crunchy charm is still intact, and the food remains creative after all these years.

There's no irony in **Nook**'s (746 Ninth Ave.; ℂ **212/247-5500**) name, with tiny tables shoehorned into a cramped space. Fortunately the crowd is friendly, happy to be digging into hearty roast chicken and peppercorn steak.

Shade trees and an inevitable line adorn **Tartine** (253 W. 11th St.; ℂ **212/229-2611**), a tiny Village cafe known for *croque monsieurs* at lunch and tasty namesake tartes.

Hot Thai curries headline the offerings at **Wondee Siam** (792 Ninth Ave.; ℂ **212/459-9057**), which has spawned a handful of popular offshoots. To enjoy the pleasures of BYOB, stick with the Hell's Kitchen original. Also in Hell's Kitchen is NYC's only outpost for Druse cuisine. **Gazala Place** (709 Ninth Ave.; ℂ **212/245-0709**) serves up variations on Middle Eastern classics, highlighted by a supple bread fresh-cooked on what looks like an upside-down wok in front.

I was a fan of Ivo & Lulu for a long time, but that legacy is better carried out in Brooklyn now. Ivo & Lulu's original former owners have opened **Kaz An Nou** (53 Sixth Ave.; ℂ **718/938-3235**) in Prospect Heights. The name translates to "our house," and hospitality informs the friendly service, laid-back room, and home-cooked West Indian delicacies. For stocking up on the bottles themselves, see "Free Wine Tastings" (p. 292)—pricewise, it's hard to beat Astor Wines (p. 292) and Trader Joe's (p. 210).

eggs, potatoes, toast, juice, and coffee for $4.25). If you can't fill your stomach here for $10, consult your physician about the possibility of a tapeworm.

THE BEST DEALS ON ST. MARKS PLACE

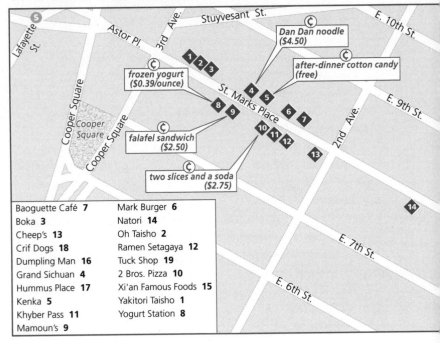

Baoguette Café **7**
Boka **3**
Cheep's **13**
Crif Dogs **18**
Dumpling Man **16**
Grand Sichuan **4**
Hummus Place **17**
Kenka **5**
Khyber Pass **11**
Mamoun's **9**

Mark Burger **6**
Natori **14**
Oh Taisho **2**
Ramen Setagaya **12**
Tuck Shop **19**
2 Bros. Pizza **10**
Xi'an Famous Foods **15**
Yakitori Taisho **1**
Yogurt Station **8**

200 Second Ave., btw. 12th and 13th sts. ℂ **212/777-9728.** Daily 7am–11pm. Subway: L to First or Third Ave.

Otafuku *JAPANESE*   Ideal drunk food can be found at this tiny takeout in the East Village—though the sober will be equally sated. The dishes are hot, flavorful, filling, and decidedly odd. The mainstays are *okonomiyaki,* a pizza-shaped pancake fried up with shredded cabbage, bonito flakes, and a choice of meat; and *takoyaki,* dumplings made of batter and octopus, topped with some of the above pancake fixin's. At $3 to $8, everything's cheap and large enough to share. *Yakisoba* (fried noodles with squid and shrimp) is only $7. FINE PRINT This is sidewalk food. The place is the size of a closet, and aside from a bench in front, there's no seating.

236 E. 9th St., btw. Second and Third aves. ℂ **212/353-8503.** Mon–Thurs 1–10pm; Fri–Sat noon–11pm; Sun noon–10pm. Subway: 6 to Astor Place; N/Q/R to 8th St.

Pukk *THAI*   Don't be intimidated by the over-designed interior of this narrow restaurant. The food here transcends the trends to deliver inventive meat-free soups, curries, and tofus. Among the fake flesh, duck is the standout. Entrees and noodle dishes start at $7 (the spicy

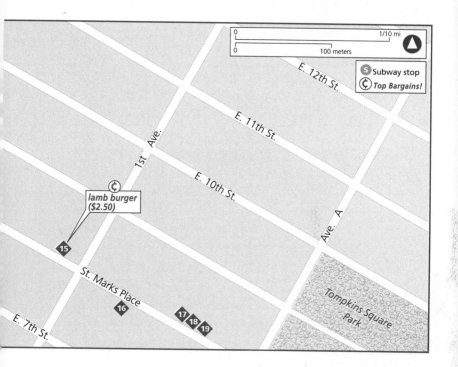

eggplant tofu comes in a huge, delicious portion), and two-course lunches are $6.

71 First Ave., btw. 4th and 5th sts. (?) **212/253-2741.** www.pukknyc.com. Sun–Thurs 11:30am–11pm; Fri–Sat 11:30am–midnight. Subway: F to Second Ave.

Punjab *INDIAN*   Local hipsters have discovered this Sikh taxi stand, which serves its dual constituencies with equal cordiality. Choose from six daily veggie entries, which are then microwaved and served over rice. Have two on a small plate for $3, or splurge for three over a big plate for $5. The food is fresh and tasty, and you can throw in two samosas for only $2 more.

114 E. 1st St., btw. First Ave. and Ave. A. (?) **212/533-9048.** Subway: F to Second Ave.

Royale *BURGERS*   Though it's short on history (and the TVs undermine its character), this bar's deft burger execution reflects the ambitions of a place targeting classic status. Big patties full of Black Angus flavor rest on brioche buns ($6.50), cooked to order and served fresh. (Add $1 for cheese.) In the warmer months, the garden in back makes for a laid-back scene. To maximize your savings, come at happy hour (weeknights from 4–7pm) and enjoy two for one drafts and well drinks.

Meal Deal-ing on St. Marks Place

St. Marks Place runs from Avenue A to Third Avenue. Somehow in just three short blocks, over five dozen affordable restaurants are packed in. Highlights follow, listed from west to east within each section.

North Side

Yakitori Taisho. This tavern's perennially overflowing crowds attest to the down-home goodness of the Japanese cooking. (Sister spot **Oh! Taisho** is two doors down.) ✆ **212/228-5086.** 5 St. Marks Place.

Bokā. Fine moderately priced Korean, but most folks are here for legendary BonChon Chicken—take your pick of spicy hot or garlicky soy. ✆ **212/228-2887.** 9 St. Marks Place.

Grand Sichuan. Best. Restaurant. Ever. See p. 65.

Kenka. Perhaps the most transporting restaurant in New York, this rollicking izakaya feels just like a Japanese beer hall. Cheap eats, bright flavors, and free DIY cotton candy for dessert. ✆ **212/254-6363.** 25 St. Marks Place.

Mark Burger. Sliders with a rich porterhouse, chuck, and short rib blend are just $2 each. ✆ **212/677-3132.** 33 St. Marks Place.

Baoguette Café. A "gourmet" spin on Asian street food, with some hits (classic bánh mì, $5.75) and some misses (bizarrely spiced catfish sandwich, $7.25). ✆ **347-892-2614.** 37 St. Marks Place.

Xi'an Famous Foods. Flushing favorite introduces New Yorkers to Silk Road–influenced Chinese cuisine. Lamb "burgers" equal instant New York classics. No phone. 81 St. Marks Place.

Hummus Place. Imported white tahini is the key ingredient to this rich hummus (around $7). See www.hummusplace.com for other locations. ✆ **212/529-9198.** 109 St. Marks Place.

157 Ave. C, btw. 9th and 10th sts. ✆ **212/254-6600.** www.royalenyc.com. Sun–Thurs 4pm–2am; Fri–Sat 4pm–4am. Subway: L to First Ave.

Veloce Pizzeria *ITALIAN*   Pizzeria doesn't do this place justice, with its dim lighting and stylish modern furnishings. A margherita pie, sized right for splitting, is $15. If you sit at the bar you can take advantage of

Crif Dogs. Renowned refueling spot with tasty hot dogs. Unassuming telephone booth leads to hidden, pricey cocktail den. ℂ **212/614-2728.** 113 St. Marks Place.

Tuck Shop. This "canteen" specializes in savory, flaky pies, running from Aussie traditional to Thai-influenced gourmet ($5.50–$6). ℂ **212/979-5200.** 115 St. Marks Place.

South Side

Yogurt Station. Yogurt here is just 39¢ an ounce. DIY toppings ensure you're getting all the mochi cubes you're craving. ℂ **212/677-5017.** 18 ½ St. Marks Place.

Mamoun's. Mamoun's $2.50 falafel is legendary. See p. 63. (The area's cheapest pita is **Cheep**'s $2 hummus, at 129 Second Ave. Falafel $2.50.)

2 Bros. Pizza. Not the world's greatest pie, but at just $1 for a fresh slice, pretty hard to beat. (There's an affordable-artisanal spinoff called **Totale** at #36). ℂ **212/777-0600.** 32 St. Marks Place.

Khyber Pass. The decor here may be a little tired, but if you're looking to expand your palate, you'll find intriguing Afghan at moderate prices. ℂ **212/473-0989.** 34 St. Marks Place.

Ramen Setagaya. This is not the ramen you lived off of in college: Homemade broth combines clams, scallops, lemon peel, and pork for amazing, addictive soups ($10–$11.75). ℂ **212/387-7959.** 34½ St. Marks Place.

Natori. Don't be deterred by the ragged exterior; this East Village pioneer serves fresh fish, available as a $14 early bird special. ℂ **212/533-7711.** 58 St. Marks Place.

Dumpling Man. Handmade numbers here start at $3.95 for six. ℂ **212/505-2121.** 100 St. Marks Place.

the weeknight special. Just $10 nets you a slice of pizza (or sometimes a plate of pasta), salad, and a glass of wine, beer, or soda. You'll also get free expertise if you chat up your server, which may extend to a sample pour or two.

103 First Ave., btw. 6th and 7th sts. ℂ **212/777-6677.** www.velocepizzeria.com. Mon–Fri 5pm–1am; Sat–Sun 3pm–1am. Subway: F to Second Ave.

Zaragoza *MEXICAN*   A renowned late-night fortification stop, this run-down deli's food tastes just as good *before* a four-hour East Village bender. You can't go wrong with roast pork, chipotle chicken, *lengua* (beef tongue, but trust me), and enchilada with hints of pineapple. The friendly counterfolk will stuff your meat of choice in a double corn tortilla and top it with an addictive tomatillo sauce for just $2.50. They also serve top-rate tostadas, tamales, and under-$10 entrees, all of which justify my somewhat obsessive relationship with this place.

215 Ave. A, btw. 13th and 14th sts. ✆ **212/780-9204.** Mon–Thurs 9:30am–midnight; Fri–Sat 9:30am–4am; Sun 11am–midnight. Subway: L to First Ave.

6 West Village

Corner Bistro *AMERICAN/BURGERS*   Inside this dark, worn West Village bar you'll find one of the best burgers in the city. The no-frills regular is $5.75, while $6.75 adds decadent layers of cheese, bacon, and onions. This place is a well-guarded local secret, known only to you and the 10,000 other people waiting beside you at the bar. (Weekday afternoons are the least-crowded times.) A mug of beer to wash it down will only set you back $2.50.

331 W. 4th St., btw. Jane St. and Eighth Ave. ✆ **212/242-9502.** www.cornerbistro. ypguides.net. Mon–Sat 11:30am–4am; Sun noon–4am. Subway: 1/2/3 or A/C/E to 14th St.; L to Eighth Ave.

Dojo *HEALTH/JAPANESE*   As any NYU student will tell you, the cheapest sit-down meals can be found at Dojo. The menu is Japanese-inspired, but the restaurant serves a full array of healthy-ish food for reasonable fees. A soy burger goes for $3.95, salads start at $5.95, and a big plate of veggie don noodles is $5.95.

14 W. 4th St., btw. Broadway and Mercer St. ✆ **212/505-8934.** Mon–Thurs, Sun 11am–1am; Fri–Sat 11am–2am. Subway: B/D/F to Broadway/Lafayette; 6 to Bleecker St.

Galanga *THAI*   Although this place scores high style points with its refined decor, there's no tradeoff in substance. Witness good-size portions, exquisite seasoning, and more authenticity than one usually finds this side of distant boroughs. Curries and wok concoctions start at $9, and noodles are even less. I have difficulty getting the tangy taste of the charcoal beef salad ($9) out of my head. The weekday lunch special comes with soup or salad and starts at $7.50. FINE PRINT The new Chelsea offshoot, Galanga Garden, is bigger and even more elegant, with a fountain and bamboo garden in back.

149 W. 4th St., btw. MacDougal St. and Sixth Ave. ℂ **212/228-4267.** Mon–Thurs 11:30am–11pm; Fri–Sat 11:30am–11:30pm; Sun 11:30am–10:30pm. Subway: A/B/C/ D/E/F to W. 4th St./Washington Sq. Other location: *Chelsea*, 136 Ninth Ave., btw. 18th and 19th sts. ℂ **212/675-3330.** Subway: C/E to 23rd St.

Joe's *PIZZA*   In the art of laying out consistently fresh slices, Joe's has it down (as it has since 1975). Village tourists, locals, and drunk- ards alike are drawn to the $2.75 beauties here, turned out piping hot from the gas-fired oven. Tangy sauce and thick cheese complement the character in the crust.

7 Carmine St., btw. Sixth Ave. and Bleecker St. ℂ **212/255-3946.** www.joespizza. com. Daily 9am–5am. Subway: A/B/C/D/E/F to W. 4th St./Washington Sq.

Mamoun's *MIDDLE EASTERN/FALAFEL*   This NYU favorite opened in 1971 and they've been so busy serving up Middle Eastern delicacies that they haven't had the chance to revise their prices much. At $2.50, the falafel sandwich here is one of the city's best buys. The balls are small, dense, and packed with nutty flavor. Other veggie pitas, like the baba ghanouj, are also $2.50. The chicken kabob, a mix of savory, seared meat and lightly sweet tahini, is a highlight of the $4 meat sand- wiches. Several competitors have hung their shingles on the block, but Mamoun's is still the best. Seating is limited; in nice weather Washing- ton Square Park serves as Mamoun's back garden.

119 MacDougal St., btw. Minetta Lane and W. 3rd St. ℂ **212/674-8685.** www. mamounsfalafel.com. Daily 11am–5am. Subway: A/B/C/D/E/F to W. 4th St./Washing- ton Sq. Other location: *East Village*, 22 St. Marks Place. btw. Second and Third aves. ℂ **212/387-7747.** Subway: 6 to Astor Place; N/Q/R to 8th St.

Satay Junction *INDONESIAN*   Street food is the focus of this sliver of a restaurant. The house specialty is the skewer, and it comes in options as varied as tofu, veggie, fish, shrimp, and four kinds of meat. Pick any three for $5, or any five for $9. Veggie rice and noodle dishes start at $4, and you can wash it all down with a surreal glass of choc- olate and avocado juice.

28 Greenwich Ave., btw. Charles and W. 10th sts. ℂ **212/929-9400.** www.satayjunction. com. Sun–Thurs noon–11pm, Fri–Sat noon–1am. Subway: 1 to Christopher St.

Taim *ISRAELI/FALAFEL*   Though Taim takes a gourmet approach to its Middle Eastern cooking, it's barely reflected in the prices. Falafel is the specialty here, balled into small and taut bites. The options are varied: green, with mint, parsley, and cilantro; roasted red pepper; and *harissa*, a Tunisian version spiced up with paprika and garlic. A

Food Trucks & Street Meat

Street carts are classic icons of New York City, although many still specialize in the dirty water hot dogs and day glo-orange empanadas of Gotham's last incarnation. For a new city era, purveyors have gotten much more sophisticated, adding elaborate truck setups to the mix. There's even an annual award show, The Vendys (www. streetvendor. org), that recognizes the city's finest street meat chefs.

The Biryani Cart (southwest corner, 46th St. and Sixth Ave.) won the '08 People's Choice Award for its fresh and flavorful Indian cuisine. Namesake chicken biryani is $6 for a huge portion, and kati rolls ($6 for two) are a midtown cult favorite.

Just a half a block away is another crowd-pleaser, **Kim's Aunt Kitchen** (46th St., btw. Fifth and Sixth aves.) The awesome whiting sandwich (fish, fried on the spot) is just $3.50; order it on a hero with plenty of tartar and hot sauce.

Have a jones for authentic Taiwanese cooking? Look no further than the **NYC Cravings** (www.nyccravings.com) truck, which is minting

sandwich is $5.25 and comes dressed with tahini and homemade hummus. Everything is made fresh daily, more than justifying this carryout's name (Hebrew for "delicious"). FINE PRINT Seating is limited.

222 Waverly Place, btw. Perry and W. 11th sts. ℂ **212/691-1287.** www.taimfalafel. com. Daily 11am–10pm. Subway: 1/2/3 to 14th St.

7 Chelsea/Union Square

Big Booty Bread Co. *BAKERY* All risk to expanding posteriors aside, the $1.75 "cheese rock" here is worthy of obsession. Like a dinner roll of Olympian aspirations, the rock is taut on the outside, protecting a savory, Latin-tinged queso blanco and yucca flour interior. Oven-baked empanadas are huge and flavorful as well, for just a little more. Cupcake fans can gorge on red velvet and dulce de leche cupcakes.

261 W. 23rd St., btw. Seventh and Eighth aves. ℂ **212/414-3056.** www.bigbooty breadco.com. Mon–Fri 8am–8pm; Sat, 8am–6pm. Subway: C/E or 1 to 23rd St.

addicts all across the city. Two huge pieces of chicken, rice, and pickled veggies are just $7. For the same price you can get the diabolically tasty fried pork chop, served with pork sauce! Check the website or Twitter feed, as the truck rotates between several parking spaces.

The city's most famous cart is **53rd and Sixth** (www.53rdand6th.com), named for the Midtown corner it holds down from 7:30pm until 4am. Tourists are regularly flummoxed by the length of the line, but it's no mystery to the regulars—the $6 platters and $4 sandwiches here combine flavorful chicken and a legendary white sauce with a recipe guarded more tightly than Fort Knox. (The daytime "imposter" cart on the same corner has become almost as good as the original.)

If you want to taste the top prize winner at the 2009 Vendys, head to Brooklyn near Red Hook park to Country Boys, a.k.a. the Martinez Taco Truck parked near the corner of Bay and Clinton streets (www.redhookfoodvendors.com).

Grand Sichuan International *CHINESE* Don't be fooled by the average decor or below-average prices—this place serves the best Chinese food in the city. The menu is thick, but it's hard to make a bad pick here. Orange beef, sautéed string beans, and General Tso's chicken are three normal-sounding dishes that get reworked into Szechuan gems. You can splurge on more expensive items like the amazing $16.95 smoked tea duck, but if you limit your ordering to the many under-$10 entrees you won't be disappointed. The soup dumplings ($5.75–$6.75) are legendary, and I am obsessed with the dan dan noodles ($4.50). Lunches are not heavily attended, despite the $5.95 specials. At dinner time arrive early or arrive patient. FINE PRINT The other locations are good, but only St. Marks brings the same magic as Chelsea.

229 Ninth Ave., at 24th St. © **212/620-5200.** www.thegrandsichuan.com. Daily 11:30am–11pm. Subway: C/E to 23rd St. Other locations: *East Village,* 19–23 St. Marks Place. btw. Second and Third aves. © **212/529-4800.** Subway: 6 to Astor Place; N/Q/R to 8th St. *West Village,* 15 Seventh Ave. S., btw. Carmine and Leroy sts. © **212/645-0222.** Subway: 1 to Houston St. *Midtown East,* 1049 Second Ave., btw. 55th and

Hot Dog Days

Papaya King was the original, but time has not been kind to this chain. Knockoff **Papaya Dog** holds down the middle of the pack, leaving **Gray's Papaya** as New York's top dog. The meat is flavorful, finished with a light char, and kept fresh thanks to quickly moving queues. Long live the recession—as long as Gray's continues to offer their classic hard times special (two hot dogs and a drink for $4.45). FINE PRINT Standing room only here. 2090 Broadway, at 72nd St. ℂ **212/799-0243.** www.grays papaya.com. Daily 24 hr. Subway: 1/2/3 to 72nd St. Other locations: *West Village,* 402 Sixth Ave., at 8th St. ℂ **212/260-3532.** Subway: A/B/C/D/E/F to W. 4th St. *Midtown,* 539 Eighth Ave., at 37th St. ℂ **212/904-1588.** Subway: A/C/E to 34th St.

56th sts. ℂ **212/355-5855.** Subway: E/M to Lexington Ave./53rd St.; 4/5/6 to Lexington Ave./59th St. *Midtown West,* 368 W. 46th St., btw. Eighth and Ninth aves. ℂ **212/969-9001.** Subway: A/C/E/7 to 42nd St./Port Authority. *Chinatown,* 125 Canal St., at Chrystie St. ℂ **212/625-9212.** Subway: B/D to Grand St. *Flushing, Queens,* 42–47 Main St., btw. Franklin and Blossom aves. ℂ **718/888-0553.** Subway: 7 to Main St./Flushing.

Kofoo *KOREAN* Where students congregate, cheap food cannot be far away. An F.I.T. clientele flocks to nearby Kofoo, for a wide selection of Korean delights. *Kim bop,* Korean sushi, comes in 10 varieties, for $5 to $6.50. Korean rice classics are also served, including sliced-beef *bulgogi* and *bibim bop* for $7.50 each. Fresh, crisp kimchi on the side stands out, too. FINE PRINT There are just a couple of seats; most business is takeout.

334 Eighth Ave., btw. 26th and 27th sts. ℂ **212/675-5277.** Mon–Sat 11am–10pm. Subway: C/E to 23rd St.

La Taza de Oro *PUERTO RICAN* The daily specials at this classic greasy spoon make it easy to get filled up for under $8. My favorites are bacalao (stewed codfish), *ropa vieja* ("old clothes"—a stew made with shredded beef), and roast chicken, which average $8 or so, including knock-out rice and beans.

96 Eighth Ave., btw. 14th and 15th sts. ℂ **212/243-9946.** Mon–Sat 6am–10:30pm. Subway: A/C/E to 14th St.; L to Eighth Ave.

Maoz *FALAFEL* I've never understood how a little ball of shredded chickpea can come out tasting so meaty and delicious. Somehow falafel satisfies in a way other vegetables can't. (The deep-frying probably doesn't hurt any.) Maoz makes some of the best falafel in town, and they'll let you customize your sandwich with toppings from their exten-sive salad bar. A sandwich, three toppings, and two sauces costs $4.95. Meal deals, which go over well will the local worker bees, are $8.75.

38 Union Sq. E., btw. 16th and 17th sts. ℂ **212/260-1988.** www.maozusa.com. Mon–Thurs 7:30am–11pm, Fri 7:30am–midnight, Sat 11am–midnight, Sun 11am–10pm. Subway: L/N/Q/R/4/5/6 to 14th St./Union Sq. Other locations: *West Village*, 59 E. 8th St., btw. Broadway and University Place. ℂ **212/420-5999.** Subway: N/Q/R to 8th St.; 6 to Astor Place. *Midtown West*, 558 Seventh Ave., at 40th St. ℂ **212/777-0820.** Sub-way: 1/2/3/7/N/Q/R/S to 42nd St./Times Sq. *Upper West Side*, 2047A Broadway, btw. 70th and 71st sts. ℂ **212/362-2622.** Subway: 1/2/3 to 72nd St. *Upper West Side*, 2857 Broadway, btw. 110th and 111th sts. ℂ **212/222-6464.** Subway: 1 to 110th St.

Tebaya *CHICKEN WINGS*   All the way from Nagoya, Japan, comes this recipe for extraordinary chicken. I had no idea wings could taste this good. City of Buffalo, hang your head in shame. The chicken here is double fried to burn off the fat, and then basted in a savory garlic sauce. Eight pieces are $5.75. For your next Super Bowl party, vol-ume discounts bring the price of each wing as low as 65¢. Japanese fast food items like teriyaki chicken sandwiches and fried potato cakes fill up the rest of the menu. FINE PRINT Seating is limited.

144 W. 19th St., btw. Sixth and Seventh aves. ℂ **212/924-3335.** www.goojapan. com/tebaya/index.htm. Mon–Fri 11:30am–9:45pm; Sat noon–9:45pm. Subway: 1 to 18th St.

8 Midtown East

Barros Luco *CHILEAN*   Chilean food mixes Spanish and other Euro accents (French, German, Italian) with indigenous flavors. Accordingly, the fast food standards here—hot dogs, sandwiches, fries—end up with intriguing twists. String beans and banana peppers dress up classic steak sammies ($6.49), franks get topped with avocado ($3.50), and fries are of the sweet potato persuasion ($3.19, served with ranch dress-ing). For sit-down dining, there's a nicely appointed room upstairs.

300½ E. 52nd St., btw. First and Second aves. ℂ **212/371-0100.** www.barrosluco. com. Mon–Fri 11am–10pm; Sat 11:30am–10pm; Sun 11:30am–8pm. Subway: 6 to 51st St.

Bhojan *INDIAN*   I am a fascist about Downtown being better at all things, but when it comes to Indian, the East Village's Curry Row lags miles behind Midtown's Curry Hill. One of the best spots in the neigh-borhood is one of the newest, an elegant all-vegetarian paradise that highlights the cuisine of Gujrat and Punjab. "Thali" platters allow you to sample a range of delicacies, and they're just $8 for weekday lunches.

102 Lexington Ave., near 27th St. ℂ **212/213-9615.** www.bhojanny.com. Daily 11:30am–10pm. Subway: 6 to 28th St.

Chennai Garden *INDIAN*   Vegetarians can relax in this Indian legend, as the long list of *dosai, utthappam,* and curries here doesn't contain a scrap of meat. Entrees are under $10, and portions are substantial. Despite the prices, mint-colored walls under decent lighting make for a date-suitable atmosphere. FINE PRINT The weekday lunch buffet is a steal at $6.95.

129 E. 27th St., btw. Park and Lexington aves. ℂ **212/689-1999.** Mon–Fri buffet 11:30–3pm, dinner 5pm–10pm; Sat–Sun noon–10pm. Subway: 6 to 28th St.

Ess-A-Bagel *BAGELS*   The huge bagels here won't win any points with purists, but they make an already good deal even better at $1, or $2.25 with a surplus helping of cream cheese. The bustling full-service shop has several tables for your savoring pleasure.

831 Third Ave., btw. 50th and 51st sts. ℂ **212/980-1010.** www.ess-a-bagel.com. Mon–Fri 6am to around 9pm; Sat–Sun 6am–5pm. Subway: 6 to 51st St. Other location: *Gramercy*, 359 First Ave., at 21st St. ℂ **212/260-2252.** Subway: 6 to 23rd St.

57 Napoli Pizza e Vino *ITALIAN*   I am a groupie for pizzaiolo Salvatore Olivella, having followed his classic Neapolitan pies from L'Asso to No. 28 to his latest wood-burning oven on 57th Street. Top-quality ingredients make for stellar pizzas, with tangy sauce topping well-structured, lightly singed crusts. $20 or so gets you a skateboard-shaped pizza that'll be hard for three people to finish, although specials bring tabs down even further. On the weekends, brunch is served all day and night and comes with bottomless mimosas. Worker bees can flit in for $6 cheese pizettas until 3pm on weekdays, and they can stick around for half-price beer and wine (off an already bargain-basement $5 regular price) from 3 to 7pm. Take advantage of a rare slot of affordability on one of the city's toniest blocks, made possible only by the eccentric location, up a flight of stairs from C'est Bon Café.

120 E. 57th St., btw. Park and Lexington aves. ℂ **212/750-4586.** www.57napoli.com. Mon–Thurs 11am–11pm; Fri 11am–midnight; Sat 10am–midnight; Sun 10am–11pm. Subway: 4/5/6 or N/Q/R to 59th St./Lexington Ave.; E/M to 53rd St./Lexington Ave.

Oms/b *JAPANESE*   This little expat shop puts rice balls together with whimsy and creativity. Strong flavors like burdock, wasabi shrimp, and plum are in effect, executed with artistic flair. Although this is probably closer to snack food than meal fodder, balls start at only $1.50 a piece, with set menus starting at $7.25.

156 E. 45th St., btw. Third and Lexington aves. ℂ **212/922-9788.** www.riceball-omsb.com. Mon–Fri 8am–7:30pm; Sat 11:30am–5pm. Subway: 4/5/6/S to 42nd St./ Grand Central.

9 Midtown West

The Burger Joint at the Parker Meridian *BURGERS*   One of the city's best burgers hides behind curtains inside the lobby of a fancy Midtown hotel. The Burger Joint is as unpretentious and inexpensive as its name, and the burger is a delicious instant classic, juicy and not too greasy. Buy one for $7, add 50¢ for cheese. FINE PRINT Though the entrance is hidden (look for the neon arrow by the check-in desk), the local businessfolk and tourist trade have discovered the place, and it's mobbed at lunch.

118 W. 57th St., btw. Sixth and Seventh aves. ℂ **212/245-5000.** www.parkermeridien. com/eat4.php. Sun–Thurs 11am–11:30pm; Fri–Sat 11am–midnight. Subway: N/Q/R or F to 57th St.

Empanada Mama *LATINO*   This Queens transplant is a patty pro, offering up over two dozen takes on this humble Latin pocket. I prefer the tried and true to exotics like the Polish (kielbasa and sauerkraut) or the Elvis (peanut butter and bananas.) Wheat-wrapped rascals average $2.50, and triangular corn flour versions are $2.35. Beef in the latter form is a can't miss. A pleasant, colorful shop rounds out the eating experience.

763 Ninth Ave., btw. 51st and 52nd sts. ℂ **212/698-9008.** www.empmamanyc.com. Mon–Fri 10am–1:30pm, Sat–Sun 10:30am–1:30pm. Subway: C/E to 50th St.

The Kati Roll Company *INDIAN*   These aren't your bland Midtown deli wraps. Here, flaky, flavorful paratha bread envelops grilled meat and veggies that pop with exotic spicing. On the downside, the rolls ($3.25–$6.25) fall somewhere between snack and meal (on the upside, there's a discount when you buy two). Bollywood posters amplify the authenticity of a small, well-used space.

49 W. 39th St., btw. Fifth and Sixth aves. ℂ **212/730-4280.** www.thekatirollcompany. com. Mon–Thurs 11am–11pm; Fri 11am–5am; Sat noon–5am; Sun noon–ppm.

CHEAP EATS IN MIDTOWN

Barros Luco **35**
Bhojan **26**
The Biryani Cart **33**
The Burger Joint at the Parker
   Meridian **40**
Carl's Steaks **28**
Chennai Garden **26**
Dallas BBQ **11**, **18**
East Japanese
   Restaurant **1**, **25**, **30**
Empanada Mama **3**
Ess-A-Bagel **24**, **36**
57 Napoli Pizza e Vino **38**
53rd and Sixth **39**
Galanga Garden **19**
Gazala Place **5**
Grand Sichuan
   International **9**, **16**, **37**
Gray's Papaya **13**
The Kati Roll Company **29**
Kim's Aunt Kitchen **32**
Kofoo **15**
La Taza de Oro **21**
Maoz **12**, **23**
Margon **34**
Mooncake **14**
Nook **4**
Oms/b **31**
Pio Pio **10**, **28**
Sullivan St. Bakery **7**, **17**
Tebaya **22**
Tehuitzingo Mexican Deli **6**
Tulcingo Del Valle
   Restaurant **8**
Wondee Siam **2**
Woorijip **27**

South E. 59th St.

Queensborough
(59th St.) Bridge

**MIDTOWN
EAST**

E. 58th St.
E. 57th St.
E. 56th St.
E. 55th St.
E. 54th St.
E. 53rd St.
E. 52nd St.
E. 51st St.
E. 50th St.
E. 49th St.
E. 48th St
E. 47th St.
E. 46th St.
E. 45th St.
E. 44th St.
E. 43rd St.
E. 42nd St.

St. Patrick's
Cathedral

ROCKEFELLER
CENTER

Sixth Ave.
Fifth Ave.
Madison Ave.
Park Ave.
Vanderbilt Ave.
Lexington Ave.
Third Ave.
Second Ave.
First Ave.
Ave. of the Americas

Mitchell
Place

Beekman
Place

Sutton Pl. South / Sutton Pl.

United
Nations

East River

Grand
Central
Terminal

*Bryant
Park*

New York
Public Library

**MURRAY
HILL**

E. 41st St.
E. 40th St.
E. 39th St.
E. 38th St.
E. 37th St.
E. 36th St.
E. 35th St.
E. 34th St.
E. 33rd St.
E. 32nd St.
E. 31st St.
E. 30th St.
E. 29th St.
E. 28th St.
E. 27th St.
E. 26th St.
E. 25th St.
E. 24th St.
E. 23rd St.
E. 22nd St.
E. 21st St.
E. 20th St.
E. 19th St.
E. 18th St.
E. 17th St.
E. 16th St.
E. 15th St.
E. 14th St.

**Queens-Midtown
Tunnel**

Franklin Delano Roosevelt (FDR) Dr.

Macy's

**Empire State
Building**

W. 32nd St.

Broadway

Madison Ave.
Fifth Ave.
Park Ave. S.
Lexington Ave.
Second Ave.
First Ave.

Sixth Ave. (Ave. of the Americas)

*Madison
Square
Park*

**Flatiron
Building**

**FLATIRON
DISTRICT**

Gramercy Park

**GRAMERCY
PARK**

*Union
Square*

Irving Pl.

Asser Levy Pl.

Ave. C

N.D. Perlman Pl.

**Upper
Manhattan**

Uptown

Midtown

Downtown

Subway: B/D/F to 42nd St.; 7 to Fifth Ave. Other location: *West Village,* 99 MacDougal St., btw. Bleecker and W. 3rd sts. ℂ **212/420-6517.** Subway: A/B/C/D/E/F to W. 4th St./Washington Sq.; 1 to Houston St.

Margon *CUBAN*   This diner's delicious Caribbean fare, low prices, and central location keep it packed with Midtown lunchers. Order a Cuban sandwich up front ($5.50), or choose from to-stay steam-table selections in the middle and to-go from the line in back. Chicken fricassee is a top seller, served with rice and beans and just $7.75 for a plate.

136 W. 46th St., btw. Sixth and Seventh aves. ℂ **212/354-5013.** Mon–Fri 6am–4:45pm; Sat 7am–2:30pm. Subway: B/D/F to 47th–50th sts.–Rockefeller Center; N/Q/R to 49th St.

Pio Pio *PERUVIAN*   The small corporate front desk here gives no indication of the cavernous bi-level dining room in back, finished in rustic wood and an intricate thatch of branches. Pio Pio has come a long way from its humble Queens storefront beginnings, but it still leans on its original specialty: Golden rotisserie chicken marinated in Peruvian beer and a secret blend of spices. A whole chicken is just $14, or add avocado, rice, beans, and french fries with hot dogs (!) for a $32 Matador Combo feast, which is enough to put three people in a food coma. FINE PRINT This is a date-worthy spot for pre-theater fuel ups, although note that the rest of the menu is pricier than the chicken specials.

604 Tenth Ave., btw. 43rd and 44th sts. ℂ **212/459-2929.** www.piopionyc.com. Sun–Thurs 11am–11pm, Fri–Sat 11am–midnight. Subway: A/C/E/7 to Port Authority. Other locations: *Upper East Side,* 1746 First Ave., btw. 90th and 91st sts. ℂ **212/426-5800.** Subway: 4/5/6 to 86th St. *Upper West Side,* 702 Amsterdam Ave., at 94th St. ℂ **212/665-3000.** Subway: 1/2/3 to 96th St. *Midtown East,* 210 E. 34th St., btw. Second and Third aves. ℂ **212/481-0034.** Subway: 6 to 33rd St. Also three locations in Queens, and one in the Bronx.

Sullivan St. Bakery *BAKERY*   One of the best pizzas in town is the bianca at this upscale bakery. The bread is fluffy and lightly seasoned with rosemary, olive oil, and a little salt. It's an Old Country slice—rectangular instead of triangular and lacking red sauce—and it's served at an old economy price. $2 gets you a doughy length 4½ inches long.

533 W. 47th St., btw. Tenth and Eleventh aves. ℂ **212/265-5580.** www.sullivanstreet bakery.com. Mon–Sat 8am–7pm, Sun 8am–4pm. Subway: C/E to 50th St. Other location (anticipated): *Chelsea,* 236 Ninth Ave., btw. 24th and 25th sts. Subway: C/E to 23rd St.

Tehuitzingo Mexican Deli *MEXICAN* A ramshackle counter area that could be a rest stop on a Mexican highway is the setting for this clandestine *taquería*. Über-authentic tacos are $2.50, generously piled with meat, from juicy pork carnitas to slow-cooked *lengua* to succulent chicken. Equally good are the Mexican sandwiches, *tortas,* which are $6 meals unto themselves. The deli refrigerators stock Mexican beers, for refreshment on the side.

695 Tenth Ave., btw. 47th and 48th sts. ℂ **212/397-5956.** Daily 8am–11:30pm. Subway: C/E to 50th St.

Tulcingo Del Valle Restaurant *MEXICAN* This mom-and-pop spot is every bit as authentic as Tehuitzingo above, but with more of a sit-down scene. The specials board (most everything is under $10) lists fresh-made entree platters, like chicken in a green pumpkin-seed sauce. Chilaquiles, fried tortillas in red or green salsa, are a very tasty $6.95. I'm a big fan of the tacos, too, especially the carne asada, at $2.75 a pop.

655 Tenth Ave., btw. 46th and 47th sts. ℂ **212/262-5510.** www.tulcingorestaurant. com. Mon–Sat 8am–10pm; Sun 10am–10pm.

Woorijip *KOREAN* Korean delis are ubiquitous in New York, but most serve up bland, mainstream cafeteria fare. To find real Korean dishes, the natural destination is 32nd Street in Midtown, where a delicious by-the-pound deli is hidden among pricier Korean restaurants. Bulgogi, squid, tofu, jellyfish, Korean pancakes, and, of course, kimchi, can be found on the serve-yourself buffet line ($6.49 per pound). You can also get pre-made snacks and meals, like filling kimbap veggie rolls for under $5.

12 W. 32nd St., btw. Broadway and Fifth Ave. ℂ **212/244-1115.** Daily 6am–3am. Subway: B/D/F/N/Q/R to 34th St./Herald Sq.

10 Upper West Side

Absolute Bagel *BAGELS* The absolutely fabulous bagels here are a little too puffy to be traditional, but the extra air doesn't hinder the taste. For $1.95 you get a bagel loaded with cream cheese. Opt for butter and it's just $1.25. Don't let the lines deter you—that's a sign of the quality, and the cheerful staff works fast.

2788 Broadway, btw. 107th and 108th sts. ℂ **212/932-2052.** www.absolutebagels. com. Daily 6am–9pm. Subway: 1 to 110th St.

Big Nick's Burger Joint/Pizza Joint *AMERICAN/BURGERS*   When your menu serves every dish ever thought of, you're bound to have a few items that seem a little overpriced. For the most part, though, this Upper West Side joint has great values on big portions. The options are endless—with burgers alone, there are over three dozen choices. Prices start at $6.30 and go to $9.40 for the heart-unfriendly hollandaise and Canadian bacon Benedict Burger.

2175 Broadway, at 77th St. ✆ **212/362-9238.** www.bignicksnyc.com. Daily 24 hr. Subway: 1 to 79th St.

Land Thai Kitchen *THAI*   Mercer Kitchen alum David Bank presents the flavors of his native Bangkok inside the brick, tin, and mesh confines of this Uptown charmer. Seared mains from the wok top out at $11, while noodle dishes hover in the $9 to $10 range. The prix-fixe lunch, which includes papaya salad and basil and beef, proffers two courses for $8. FINE PRINT Small place plus rabid popularity equals potentially long waits.

480 Amsterdam Ave., btw. 81st and 82nd sts. ✆ **212/501-8121.** www.landthai kitchen.com. Sun–Thurs noon–10:45pm; Fri–Sat noon–11pm. Subway: 1 to 79th St.; B/C to 81st St. Other location: *Upper East Side,* 1565 Second Ave., btw. 81st and 82nd sts. ✆ **212/439-1847.** Subway: 4/5/6 to 86th St.

Noche Mexicana *MEXICAN*   Authentic Mexican food was long a void in the New York gastronomic scene, but mom-and-pop places like Noche are rapidly raising standards. Choose a savory red or green salsa to top your enchilada platter ($9), or opt for a triple order of tamales ($7) or corn-tortilla chicken chilaquiles ($8.50). Tacos are excellent ($2.50 for most) and a glass of wine on the side is but $4.50.

852 Amsterdam Ave., btw. 101st and 102nd sts. ✆ **212/662-6900.** www.noche-mexicana.com. Daily, noon–10pm. Subway: 1 to 103rd St. Other location: *Upper West Side,* 842 Amsterdam Ave., at 101st St. ✆ **212/662-7400.** Subway: 1 to 103rd St.

Roti Roll Bombay Frankie *INDIAN*   A little grill annexed to a bar and open until the wee hours, this is a convenient spot to get your fortification during an UWS debauch. The specialty is *roti,* chewy wraps packed up with spicy fillings, somewhat like an Indian burrito. Spiced potato and pea or egg ($2.75 each) occupy the low end, working up to shrimp with sour cream and fenugreek ($6). Buy two and get a discount ($4.50 for the cheapest). And you don't have to be sloshed to enjoy this fare—it works equally well for lunch.

994 Amsterdam Ave., btw. 109th and 110th sts. ✆ **212/666-1500.** www.bombay frankie.com. Sun–Mon 11am–2am, Tues–Wed 11am–3am, Thurs–Sat 11am–4am. Subway: 1 to 110th St.

Sal's & Carmine's Pizza *PIZZA*   At your first taste of the pizza here, you will realize what your previous 10,000 New York slices were supposed to taste like. Creamy mozzarella syncs with a tangy sauce and crispy crust to achieve perfection. Although Sal has passed on, Carmine or family members will be on hand to ensure both quality control and a curmudgeonly atmosphere. Each pie is a work of art and cannot be expected to endure the indignity of a ride in an insulated plastic carrier: No delivery here. A regular slice is $3; add a buck for toppings.

2671 Broadway, btw. 101st and 102nd sts. ✆ **212/663-7651.** Daily 11am–11pm. Subway: 1 to 103rd St.

11 Upper East Side

Dallas BBQ *BARBECUE*   This local chain won't win any prizes for authenticity, but they do a decent take on comfort food. Ribs, pulled pork, and beef brisket highlight the menu. For cheapskates, the early bird special is not to be missed—two full meals for $9.99. You'll get double soups, double servings of rotisserie chicken, cornbread, and a choice of potatoes or rice. It's as filling as New York gets for less than $5. FINE PRINT Available weekdays from 11am to noon, and again from 2 to 5:30pm; weekends 11am to 4pm; not available on holidays. Dine-in only.

1265 Third Ave., at 73rd St. ✆ **212/772-9393.** www.dallasbbq.com. Sun–Thurs 11am–midnight; Fri–Sat 11am–1am. Subway: 6 to 77th St. Other locations: *Chelsea*, 261 Eighth Ave., at 23rd St. ✆ **212/462-0001.** Subway: C/E to 23rd St. Other locations: *Upper West Side*, 27 W. 72nd St., near Central Park W. ✆ **212/873-2004.** Subway: B/C to 72nd St. *Washington Heights*, 3956 Broadway, at 166th St. ✆ **212/ 568-3700.** Subway: A/C/1 to 168th St. *East Village*, 132 Second Ave., at St. Marks Place. ✆ **212/777-5574.** Subway: 6 to Astor Place. *Times Square*, 241 W. 42nd St., btw. Seventh and Eighth aves. ✆ **212/221-9000.** Subway: 1/2/3/7/N/Q/R/S to 42nd St./Times Sq.; A/C/E to 42nd St./Port Authority. *The Bronx*: 281 W. Fordham Rd., at Cedar Ave. ✆ **718/220-2822.** Subway: 4 to Fordham Rd. *Brooklyn*: 180 Livingston St., ✆ **718/643-5700.** Subway: A/C/F to Jay St./Borough Hall; 2/3 to Hoyt St.

East Japanese Restaurant *JAPANESE*   This sit-down minichain was a New York pioneer in *yakitori,* or grilled skewers. The prices are moderate to begin with, but hit them at the right time and they get

CHEAP EATS UPTOWN

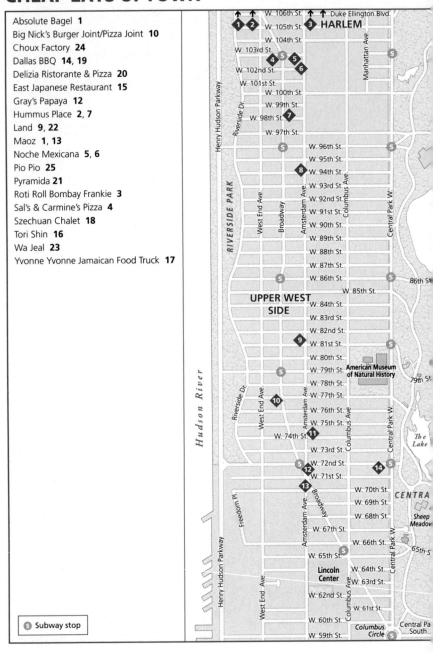

S Subway stop

Eat Like the Rich: Upper East Side Bargains

As a ritzy neighborhood in a city already famous for being expensive, the Upper East Side is a true cheap eats challenge. After all, this is the playground of blue bloods and old money. Fortunately, the last few years has seen an influx of 20-somethings, due to relatively decent rents. To satisfy this thriftier subsection of the 10021, a number of affordable options are staking claim.

I'm a big fan of the **Yvonne Yvonne Jamaican Food Truck** (71st St. and York Ave.), home of silky braised oxtail ($6.50), and a Thursday $7 special of stewed peas and pig tails.

The chicken roll ($4.69) at **Delizia Ristorante & Pizza** (1374 First Ave.; ✆ **212/517-8888**) is a hybrid meal of chicken parmigiana wrapped in pizza dough. Sweet marinara (for dipping) completes the picture; ask for it well done.

For affordable pitas, check out the lamb shish kebab ($6.75) at **Pyramida** (401 E. 78th St.; ✆ **212/472-5855**).

Yakitori shrine **Tori Shin** (1193 First Ave.; ✆ **212/988-8408**) is famous for its omakase sets, but for a fraction of the price order a la carte—don't miss *kubi kawa* (crispy neck skin skewer, $3.50) and *tsukune* (chicken meatball skewer, $7).

Wa Jeal (1588 Second Ave.; ✆ **212/396-3339**), has the best spicy sesame noodles in the city (sorry, Chinatown). A deft hand with the chili oil and springy noodles that have heft meet vinegar and crisp scallions, all cleaving through a creamy coating of peanut and fiery oil. The result ($4.70) hits all the right notes—spicy, sweet, salty, and sour—as good Sichuan food does.

For dessert? It's off to the **Choux Factory** (1685 First Ave.; ✆ **212/289-2023**), with its rich creampuffs at just $2 a pop.

—*Zachary Feldman*

downright cheap. Discounts and hours vary by location, but you're looking at deep cuts in skewers, sushi, and sashimi. Both lunch and dinner see great deals.

Upper East Side, 354 E. 66th St., btw. First and Second aves. © **212/734-5270.** Mon–Thurs noon–2:30pm and 5–10pm; Fri noon–2:30pm and 5–10:30pm; Sat 5–10:30pm; Sun 5–10pm. Subway: F to 63rd St. Other locations: *Midtown East,* 210 E. 44th St., near Third Ave. © **212/687-5075.** Subway: 4/5/6/7/S to Grand Central. *Gramercy,* 366 Third Ave., btw. 26th and 27th sts. © **212/889-2326.** Subway: 6 to 28th St. Midtown West, 253 W. 55th St., btw. Broadway and Eighth Ave. © **212/581-2240.** Subway: N/Q/R to 57th St.

Szechuan Chalet *CHINESE*   There's nothing very alpine about this standard-looking Chinese restaurant, but the dishes here climb to culinary heights. Items with chili oil and scallion "pesto" are good bets, as are noodles and dumplings. Entrees, like the standout double-cooked bacon with capsicum, manage to stay under $14. Lunch specials come with soup or soda and stick to the $7 to $8 range.

1395 Second Ave., btw. 72nd and 73rd sts. © **212/737-1838.** www. szechuanchalet nyc.com. Mon–Thurs 11:30am–10:30pm; Fri 11:30am–11pm; Sat noon–11pm; Sun noon–10pm. Subway: 6 to 77th St.

A haven of elegant Beaux Arts architecture, the Stephen A. Schwarzman Building (formerly the Humanities and Social Sciences Library) offers a host of free exhibits. See p. 114.

EXPLORING
NEW YORK

When it comes to culture, New Yorkers have so many amazing options it's probably inevitable that we start taking our bounty for granted. We sometimes forget that many of the world's great treasures have found their way to our little island and its surrounding boroughs. New York is in a constant state of transformation, but miraculously a lot of history has survived, too, in houses, churches, and museums. Foundations and galleries protect New York's cutting-edge reputation, putting on thousands of risk-taking avant-garde art shows every year. What's most amazing, given the out-of-control nature of New York rents, is how easy it is to access these jewels on the cheap. Many museums let the public in for free, and many more either have special pay-what-you-wish times or admission prices that are only suggestions. If it all seems a little overwhelming, you can get a professional to guide you through the cultural minefield: New York has a bushel of free tours as well. Just remember to get out there and take advantage—nothing lasts forever.

1 Museum Peace

Museum prices in New York are working their way skyward, with admission inflation running higher than even our outrageous movie tickets. Fifteen bucks seems to be the going price for big institutions, although the Whitney charges $18, and MoMA hits you up for a full $20. It's a good thing that New York's cultural waters run deep. Below you'll find the gamut of (a) places that never charge, (b) places that have select times when the museum is free, and (c) museums that only suggest their admission prices—even the Guggenheim and the MoMA will let you in for next to nothing if you time it right. Go and revel in NYC's embarrassment of cut-rate cultural riches.

ALWAYS FREE

American Folk Art Museum Eva and Morris Feld Gallery `FREE`   The main Folk Art collection moved to 53rd Street to rub shoulders with the MoMA, leaving not much beyond a gift shop in this original location. New acquisitions and a smattering of selections from the permanent collection fill the galleries. `FINE PRINT` A sign at the security desk notes that there's a $3 suggested donation, but nobody hits you up as you go in.

2 Lincoln Sq., Columbus Ave., btw. 65th and 66th sts., across from Lincoln Center. ✆ **212/595-9533.** www.folkartmuseum.org. $3 suggested donation. Tues–Sat noon–7:30pm; Sun noon–6pm. Subway: 1 to 66th St.

Art Students League of New York Gallery `FREE`   This independent art school, founded in 1875, is a New York legend. A host of big names started out here, including Norman Rockwell and Georgia O'Keeffe, who left behind work in the league's permanent collection. The galleries on the second floor exhibit portions of that collection along with art by current students, members, and other contemporaries.

215 W. 57th St., btw. Broadway and Seventh Ave. ✆ **212/247-4510.** www.theart studentsleague.org. Mon–Fri 9am–8:30pm; Sat–Sun 9am–3pm (closed Sun Jan–May). Subway: N/Q/R to 57th St.; B/D/E to Seventh Ave.

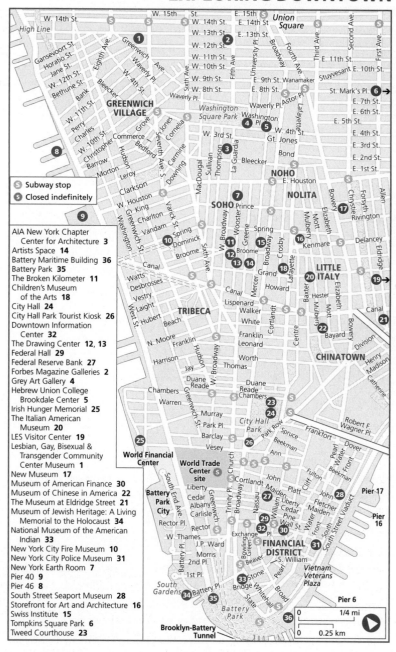

S Subway stop
S Closed indefinitely

AIA New York Chapter
  Center for Architecture **3**
Artists Space **14**
Battery Maritime Building **36**
Battery Park **35**
The Broken Kilometer **11**
Children's Museum
  of the Arts **18**
City Hall **24**
City Hall Park Tourist Kiosk **26**
Downtown Information
  Center **32**
The Drawing Center **12**, **13**
Federal Hall **29**
Federal Reserve Bank **27**
Forbes Magazine Galleries **2**
Grey Art Gallery **4**
Hebrew Union College
  Brookdale Center **5**
Irish Hunger Memorial **25**
The Italian American
  Museum **20**
LES Visitor Center **19**
Lesbian, Gay, Bisexual &
  Transgender Community
  Center Museum **1**
New Museum **17**
Museum of American Finance **30**
Museum of Chinese in America **22**
The Museum at Eldridge Street **21**
Museum of Jewish Heritage: A Living
  Memorial to the Holocaust **34**
National Museum of the American
  Indian **33**
New York City Fire Museum **10**
New York City Police Museum **31**
New York Earth Room **7**
Pier 40 **9**
Pier 46 **8**
South Street Seaport Museum **28**
Storefront for Art and Architecture **16**
Swiss Institute **15**
Tompkins Square Park **6**
Tweed Courthouse **23**

EXPLORING MIDTOWN

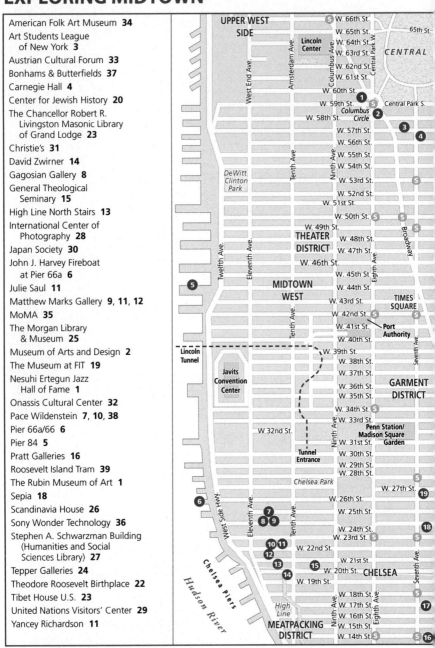

EXPLORING UPTOWN

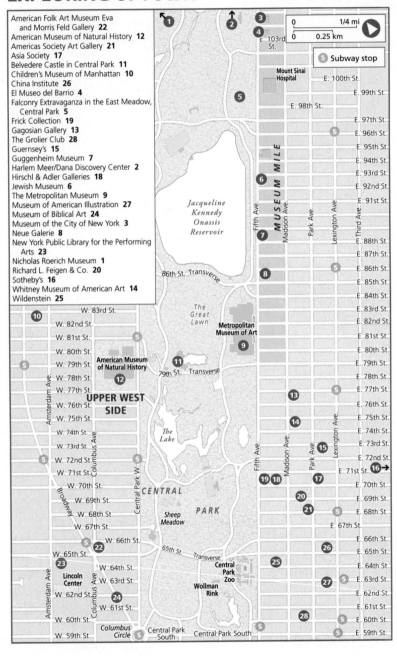

EXPLORING BROOKLYN

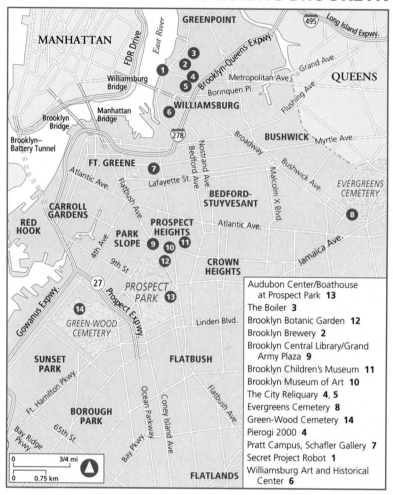

Map legend:
- Audubon Center/Boathouse at Prospect Park **13**
- The Boiler **3**
- Brooklyn Botanic Garden **12**
- Brooklyn Brewery **2**
- Brooklyn Central Library/Grand Army Plaza **9**
- Brooklyn Children's Museum **11**
- Brooklyn Museum of Art **10**
- The City Reliquary **4, 5**
- Evergreens Cemetery **8**
- Green-Wood Cemetery **14**
- Pierogi 2000 **4**
- Pratt Campus, Schafler Gallery **7**
- Secret Project Robot **1**
- Williamsburg Art and Historical Center **6**

Audubon Terrace   Broadway, between 155th and 156th streets, boasts a complex of educational and cultural institutions, housed around a central courtyard with an odd, oversized statue of El Cid. The sedate classical structures are completely unexpected in the middle of a colorful Harlem neighborhood, so unexpected that few people make the trek this far north. As a result, Audubon Terrace has been hemorrhaging institutions at a rapid pace. All but the following two have flown south:

The Hispanic Society of America FREE   Hispanic treasures ranging from Bronze Age tools to Goya portraits, seemingly assembled at

EXPLORING QUEENS

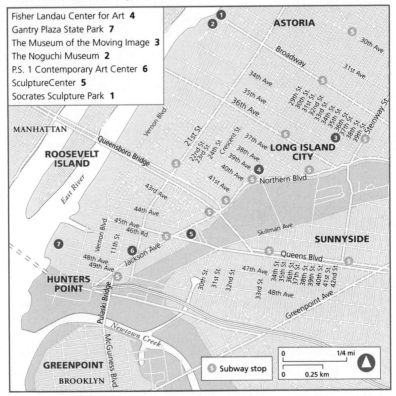

Fisher Landau Center for Art **4**
Gantry Plaza State Park **7**
The Museum of the Moving Image **3**
The Noguchi Museum **2**
P.S. 1 Contemporary Art Center **6**
SculptureCenter **5**
Socrates Sculpture Park **1**

ASTORIA
Broadway
30th Ave.
31st Ave.
34th Ave.
35th Ave.
36th Ave.
29th St.
30th St.
32nd St.
33rd St.
34th St.
35th St.
36th St.
37th St.
38th St.
39th St.
Steinway St.

MANHATTAN

Vernon Blvd.

ROOSEVELT
ISLAND

Queensboro Bridge

East River

21st St.
22nd St.
23rd St.
24th St.
Crescent St.
37th Ave.
38th Ave.
39th Ave.
40th Ave.
41st Ave.

LONG ISLAND
CITY

Northern Blvd.

43rd Ave.

44th Ave.

45th Ave.
46th Rd.

Skillman Ave.

SUNNYSIDE

Queens Blvd.

Vernon Blvd.
11th St.

Jackson Ave.

48th Ave.
49th Ave.

HUNTERS
POINT

Pulaski Bridge

30th St.
31st St.
32nd St.
33rd St.
47th Ave.
48th Ave.
34th St.
35th St.
36th St.
37th St.
38th St.
39th St.
40th St.
41st St.
42nd St.

Greenpoint Ave.

Newtown Creek

McGuiness Blvd.

GREENPOINT

BROOKLYN

Subway stop

0   1/4 mi
0   0.25 km

random, fill this intriguing, newly renovated museum. Free tours are offered every Saturday at 2pm. Don't miss the intricate marble chapel sculptures on the first floor and the gorgeous arabesque tiles upstairs.

Audubon Terrace, Broadway, btw. 155th and 156th sts. ☎ **212/926-2234.** www. hispanicsociety.org. Tues–Sat 10am–4:30pm; Sun 1–4pm. Subway: 1 to 157th St.

American Academy of Arts and Letters FREE   This prestigious century-old organization extends membership to the cream of the nation's writers and artists. Exhibits in March and May highlight the works of these artists, as well as the recipients of Academy prizes.

Audubon Terrace, Broadway, btw. 155th and 156th sts. ☎ **212/368-5900.** www.arts andletters.org. Open when exhibitions are up Thurs–Sun 1–4pm (closed Sat–Sun during holiday weekends). Subway: 1 to 157th St.

Austrian Cultural Forum FREE   The architecture of the Austrian Cultural Forum has garnered more eyebrow raises than critical praise. I find the exterior ominous, like a dagger looming over the street. The interior is more attractive, sleek, if somewhat cold. The multilevel spaces accommodate several galleries. Austrian- and European-themed shows rotate through, and there are regular film and music programs. FINE PRINT Events are free, but many require advance reservations.

11 E. 52nd St., btw. Fifth and Madison aves. © **212/319-5300.** www.acfny.org. Mon–Sat 10am–6pm. Subway: E/M to Fifth Ave./53rd St.

Carnegie Hall FREE   The Rose Museum recounts the practice, practice, practice it takes to get to this storied music hall. A chronology and memorabilia are on view, in addition to temporary exhibits on Carnegie legends like the Gershwins, Maria Callas, and Leonard Bernstein.

154 W. 57th St., 2nd floor, btw. Sixth and Seventh aves. © **212/903-9629.** www.carnegiehall.org. Daily 11am–4:30pm, and to Stern Auditorium and Perelman Stage ticket holders during evening concerts. Closed July 1–Sept 20. Subway: A/B/C/D/1 to 59th St.–Columbus Circle; N/Q/R to 57th St./Seventh Ave.

Center for Jewish History FREE   This multi-floor center hosts several simultaneous exhibitions, from photo shows to manuscripts to paintings, most documenting Jewish contributions to American society. Artifacts are well-lit, and exhibit notes are informative without running on too long. Pass through the metal detector and get a badge at the front desk. Everything is free except for the Yeshiva University Museum galleries, which are $8 (although they're free on Mon, Fri, and Wed nights).

15 W. 16th St., btw. Fifth and Sixth aves. © **212/294-8301.** www.cjh.org. *Reading Room,* Mon 9:30am–7:30pm; Tues–Thurs 9:30am–5:30pm; Fri 9:30am–1:30pm. *Genealogy Institute,* Mon 9:30am–7:30pm; Tues–Thurs, 9:30am–5:30pm; Fri 9:30am–1:30pm. *Yeshiva University Museum,* Mon 3:30–8pm; Sun, Tues, Thurs 11am–5pm; Wed 11am–8pm (free after 5pm); Fri 11am–2:30pm. *All other galleries,* Mon, Wed 9:30am–8pm; Tues, Thurs 9:30am–5pm; Fri 9am–3pm; Sun 11am–5pm. Subway: L/N/Q/R/4/5/6 to 14th St./Union Sq.

The Chancellor Robert R. Livingston Masonic Library of Grand Lodge FREE   The museum front room of the Masons' library is adorned with several display cases. Most artifacts are of limited interest to non-Masons, although there is a grandfather clock that watched over George Washington's visits to a Yorktown, Virginia, lodge. More interesting are the tours of the larger building, which show off colorful, immaculate meeting rooms and the ballroom whose design was lifted for the Titanic. No appointment is necessary; a greeter will meet you by the rear elevators.

71 W. 23rd St. (rear elevators to the 14th floor), btw. Fifth and Sixth aves. ℭ **212/337-6620.** www.nymasoniclibrary.org. Tours Mon–Sat 10:30am–2:15pm. Library Mon, Wed–Fri 8:30am–4:30pm; Tues noon–7:30pm. Subway: F/M or N/R to 23rd St.

Derfner Judaica Museum FREE   The Hebrew Home at Riverdale hosts this newly expanded display of historic Judaica, which ranges from mezuzot to Persian ivory paintings to miniature folk-art arks. More recent treasures are interspersed as well, like an Israeli copper Hanukkah lamp, and a painting by Zygmunt Menkes. A sculpture garden and Hudson views further sweeten the pot for a jaunt to the Bronx.

5901 Palisade Ave., Riverdale, the Bronx. ℭ **718/581-1000.** www.hebrewhome.org/museum. Mon–Fri 10:30am–4:30pm. Subway: 1 to 242nd St.–Van Cortlandt Park.

Federal Hall National Memorial FREE   A former customshouse, this columned Wall Street museum now recounts the long history of the site. The renovated building has recently reopened to the public, with free guided tours offered daily on the hour from 10am to 3pm (no tour at noon). See p. 312 in chapter 8 for a full review.

26 Wall St., at Nassau St. ℭ **212/825-6888.** www.nps.gov/feha. Mon–Fri 9am–5pm. Subway: 2/3/4/5 to Wall St.

Federal Reserve Bank FREE   In addition to the gallery of the American Numismatic Society (p. 316) on the ground floor here, advance sign-up will give you the chance to glimpse a little of the building. It's basically a tour of a bank. A bank with the largest gold cache in the world, but still a bank. Along the way you'll see two short videos, one weirdly defensive about the employees of the currency-processing division, and one weirdly defensive about the employees who work with the gold. Five stories beneath the street you'll get to see the vault itself, which resembles a gym locker room, only with some $200 billion in gold shimmering behind the bars. As a reward for your attention, they'll give you $1,000 in cash. Shredded cash. FINE PRINT Call 1 to 2 weeks in advance to reserve a space.

33 Liberty St., btw. William and Nassau sts. ℭ **212/720-6130.** www.newyorkfed.org. Tours weekdays 9:30, 10:30, 11:30am, 1:30, 2:30, and 3:30pm (they last about an hour). Subway: A/C/J/Z/2/3/4/5 to Fulton St./Broadway Nassau.

Fisher Landau Center for Art FREE   Few New Yorkers know about the 25,000-square-foot exhibition and study center inside this converted Queens industrial space. The pristine galleries display painting, sculpture, and photography from 1960 to the present, including

FREE **Back in the High Line Again**

Tenth Avenue once carried the nickname "Death Avenue" because of the ground-level rail lines that cut a swath of destruction through the residential streets. During the Depression, $150 million was spent to get the trains above ground, only to have the entire system rendered obsolete by the Eisenhower Interstate Highway System. The tracks were abandoned in 1980 and all but 22 blocks through Chelsea and the Meatpacking District were dismantled. In 2009, a spruced-up and exquisitely landscaped version of those tracks was unveiled. Right now you can stroll along 8 blocks (eventually it'll be expanded all the way to 34th St.) of the **High Line,** an elevated park wedged among creaky warehouses and the major glitz of the Standard Hotel. Public art, stargazing, fitness classes (p. 179), lectures, and walking tours are among the park's bonus attractions. I recommend a sunset visit—the Hudson is bathed in color, and up on the tracks you have the feeling of being on a floating island, somehow removed from the city even as you're right in the stylish heart of it. From Gansevoort to 20th streets, near Tenth Ave. ✆ **212/500-6035.** www.thehighline.org. Subway: A/C/E to 14th St.; L to Eighth Ave.

works by the likes of Agnes Martin, Robert Rauschenberg, and Cy Twombly. You'll find three floors of viewing pleasure. You'll also delight in the cultlike glazed eyes of security guards who relay your every move via walkie-talkies.

38–27 30th St., btw. 38th and 39th aves. ✆ **718/937-0727.** www.flcart.org. Thurs–Mon noon–5pm. Subway: N/Q to 39th Ave.

Forbes Magazine Galleries FREE Magazine magnate Malcolm Forbes' galleries here approximate what a 10-year-old boy with unlimited financial means would think to collect. Fortunately, a 10-year-old boy's enthusiasms radiate off the exhibits as well. Every time I visit I find myself infected, caring more than I ever thought I could about model boats, toy soldiers, Monopoly boards, and trophies. For longer attention spans, the collection of presidential papers makes for engrossing reading.

62 Fifth Ave., at 12th St. © **212/206-5548.** www.forbesgalleries.com. Tues–Wed, Fri–Sat 10am–4pm. Subway: L/N/Q/R/4/5/6 to 14th St./Union Sq.

General Grant National Memorial `FREE`   Manhattan is home to the nation's largest mausoleum, the graceful 1897 structure that houses the remains of General Ulysses S. Grant. (For punch-line sticklers, Mrs. Julia Grant is interred here as well.) The hushed interior conveys peaceful repose. There's a small on-site museum where you'll be surprised to discover the huge deal Grant's funeral was in New York. The tomb itself was once a popular attraction, but tourists have found more pressing enticements, and the memorial feels secluded, nearly forgotten. Free guided tours are given on the hour, between 10am and 3pm.

Riverside Dr., at 122nd St. © **212/666-1640.** www.nps.gov/gegr. Daily 9am–5pm. Subway: 1 to 125th St.

Hall of Fame for Great Americans `FREE`   You'd think a gigantic monument designed by Sanford White, with tablets by Tiffany Studios, memorializing American heroes like Mark Twain, Abe Lincoln, and Susan B. Anthony would be a major draw, but this oddball attraction is sadly overlooked. The distant location, on the Bronx Community College campus, might be part of the problem. If you're in the area, don't miss out because the open colonnade with its 102 bronze busts and classical architecture is a wonderful surprise.

Hall of Fame Terrace, 181st St. and University Ave., the Bronx. © **718/289-5161.** www.bcc.cuny.edu/halloffame. Daily 10am–5pm. Subway: 4 to 183rd St.

Hamilton Grange National Memorial `FREE`   Federalist Paper author and first secretary of the treasury Alexander Hamilton started construction on his country home in 1800. Not so country anymore, the National Park Service recently moved the house around the corner to St. Nicholas Park, which better reflects the Federal-style structure's origins nestled among the hills and trees of a vanished Harlem. Fittingly, the current site was within the boundary of Hamilton's original 32-acre estate.

W. 141st St. btw. Convent St. Nicholas aves. © **212/283-5154.** www.nps.gov/hagr. Wed–Sun 9am–5pm. Subway: 1 to 137th St.; A/B/C/D to 145th St.

Hebrew Union College–Jewish Institute of Religion Museum `FREE`   Multiple galleries here display assorted Judaica along with contemporary artwork of a Jewish bent. The historical exhibits are

particularly interesting, like explorations of the Albanian Muslim res-
cuers of the Holocaust, or the internment of Mayor LaGuardia's Jewish sister at Ravensbrück. Shows change regularly, with 8 to 10
moving through each year. FINE PRINT A photo ID is required to enter.

1 W. 4th St., btw. Broadway and Mercer St. ℂ **212/824-2205**. www.huc.edu/
museums/ny. Mon–Thurs 9am–6pm; Fri 9am–3pm; selected Sun 10am–2pm. Subway:
N/Q/R to 8th St.; 6 to Astor Place.

Irish Hunger Memorial FREE This large-scale sculpture on the
downtown Hudson waterfront memorializes the Irish famine of 1845–
52. The center of the installation is a famine-era cottage moved stone
by stone from the old country, resting on a field of blackthorn and
heather. Take the path to the memorial's top and you'll be treated to
sublime views of the Statue of Liberty and Ellis Island.

Vesey St. and North End Ave. ℂ **212/967-9700**. www.bpcparks.org. Daily 6am–1am.
Subway: 1/2/3/A/C to Chambers St.

Lesbian, Gay, Bisexual & Transgender Community Center Museum
FREE This isn't really a museum per se, but a community center
that puts up exhibits in its hallways. There's a lot of erotic art, along
with the occasional historical perspective, like an encapsulation of a
San Francisco public library archive. The real gem in this building is
the Keith Haring Bathroom. Converted to a meeting room on the second floor, this space pulsates with life thanks to a spectacular, sala-
cious mural created by Haring shortly before his death.

208 W. 13th St., btw. Seventh and Greenwich aves. ℂ **212/620-7310**. www.gay
center.org. Lobby Mon–Fri 9am–10pm; Sat 11am–11pm; Sun 11am–9pm. Subway:
1/2/3 or F/M to 14th St.; L to Sixth Ave.

Madame Alexander Heritage Gallery FREE Immigrant daughter
and lifelong New Yorker Madame Beatrice Alexander Behrman pioneered doll making. Her version of *Gone With the Wind*'s Scarlett
was the first doll to be based on a pop culture character. More on the
story can be found in the Harlem headquarters, with its displays of
photos, advertising, and, of course, dolls. Over 600 fill the display
cases. You can catch a free guided tour of the gallery and the showroom every 45 minutes, starting at 9:30am and finishing at 4:15pm.
Pediaphobes should steer clear.

615 W. 131st St., 6th floor, btw. Broadway and Twelfth Ave. ℂ **212/283-5900**, ext.
7128. www.madamealexander.com. Daily 9am–5pm. Subway: 1 to 125th St.

FREE Broadway Stars

Given the city's light pollution, it would seem that whoever came up with the idea of building an observatory in Manhattan wasn't totally clear on the concept. Amazingly, however, some celestial sights do seep through our glowing night skies. On a Columbia University rooftop you can see for yourself. Select nights during the school year, professors and graduate students gloss the stars at the historic Rutherfurd Observatory, starting off with a lecture and slideshow. There are also family nights for kids ages 6 to 10. The price for all this isn't astronomical—it's totally free. **Pupin Physics Laboratory,** 550 W. 120th St., btw. Broadway and Amsterdam Ave. Follow the signs to the lecture hall. ℗ **212/854-1976.** www. astro.columbia.edu. Subway: 1 to 116th St./Columbia University. After sunset and weather permitting, of course (lecture and slideshow go rain or shine).

The Museum at FIT FREE This museum on the campus of the Fashion Institute of Technology is long on historic style, specializing in the 20th century. For contemporary looks, student shows are surprisingly sophisticated. Other rotating exhibits display items from the special collections, like accessories, sketches, or a circa-1870 mourning robe.

The southwest corner of Seventh Ave., at 27th St. ℗ **212/217-5970.** www.fit nyc.edu. Tues–Fri noon–8pm; Sat 10am–5pm. Subway: 1 to 28th St.

Museum of American Illustration FREE Illustrators never seem to get their proper respect as visual artists, constantly upstaged by showoff painters and photographers. The two galleries maintained by the Society of Illustrators strive to remedy that situation. Contest winners and works of Society members can be found on the walls, along with classics from the permanent collection (the Society was formed in 1901, so there's a lot to fall back on). Exhibits change frequently.

28 E. 63rd St., btw. Park and Lexington aves. ℗ **212/838-2560.** www.society illustrators.org. Tues 10am–8pm; Wed–Fri 10am–5pm; Sat noon–4pm. Subway: N/Q/R to Fifth Ave.; F to Lexington Ave.-63rd St.

National Museum of the American Indian FREE Housing Native American treasures in a former arm of the federal government seems a bit of a cruel irony, but the overall effect here is of reverence for endangered arts. This Smithsonian branch augments its exhibits with films and videos; check the schedule at www.nativenetworks.si.edu. There's programming for kids, too, including storybook readings and workshops. Everything is free, though craft workshops can have material fees of up to $25. Some events require reservations. See also p. 316.

1 Bowling Green, btw. State and Whitehall sts. © **212/514-3700.** www.american indian.si.edu. Daily 10am–5pm; Thurs until 8pm. Subway: 4/5 to Bowling Green; 1 to South Ferry.

Nesuhi Ertegun Jazz Hall of Fame FREE   Although this museum is a little redundant—the displays are computer-based and replicate what's on the website—it's housed in a gorgeous space. Touch-activated "virtual plaques" and interactive kiosks tell the stories (and play the sounds) of the music's immortals.

Frederick P. Rose Hall in the Time Warner Center, 60th St. and Broadway, 5th floor. © **212/258-9800.** www.jalc.org. Tues–Sun 10am–4pm and during concert hours. Subway: A/B/C/D/1 to 59th St./Columbus Circle.

Nicholas Roerich Museum FREE   One of New York's least-known museums showcases the Russian scholar and painter Nicholas Roerich. A genteel Riverside Drive town house holds three floors of galleries, cluttered with Roerich's paintings. The images favor Russian icons and Himalayan landscapes, executed with bright colors and stylized lines. Objects gathered in Roerich's Asian explorations are scattered throughout the museum, and a subtle spiritual air pervades. The museum's motto, *Pax Cultura* (Peace through Culture), gets expressed in a full schedule of free concerts and poetry readings. Music generally plays Sundays at 5pm; check online for additional dates and times.

319 W. 107th St., btw. Riverside Dr. and Broadway. © **212/864-7752.** www.roerich. org. Tues–Sun 2–5pm. Subway: 1 to 110th St.

Onassis Cultural Center FREE   Aristotle Onassis—or as most of us know him, Mr. Jackie O.—was the man behind this Midtown institution, which supports Hellenic art and culture. Winding stairs in the middle of the Olympic Tower atrium's south side lead to a warren of galleries with unexpected waterfall views. Samples from Byzantium show off the flat faces of a world before linear perspective was invented. Modern Greek efforts can often be found here as well. On the lobby floor, a long-term display shows off rare casts of Parthenon marbles.

The Olympic Tower atrium, 641 Fifth Ave., entrance just east of Fifth on 51st or 52nd sts. ⓒ **212/486-4448.** www.onassisusa.org. Mon–Sat 10am–6pm. Subway: E/M to Fifth Ave./53rd St.

Pratt Galleries FREE   The fruits of Pratt Institute's prestigious arts and design programs can be found in the galleries the school runs. Current student shows are mixed in with alumni and faculty exhibitions, as well as those of other artistic innovators.

144 W. 14th St., btw. Sixth and Seventh aves. ⓒ **212/647-7778.** www.pratt.edu. Tues–Sat 11am–6pm. Subway: 1/2/3 and F/M to 14th St.; L to Sixth Ave. Other location: *Schafler Gallery, Pratt campus,* 200 Willoughby Ave., Ft. Greene, Brooklyn. ⓒ **718/636-3517.** Mon–Fri 9am–5pm; Sat noon–5pm. Subway: G to Clinton–Washington aves.

Scandinavia House   The Midtown headquarters of the Nordic Center in America is as stylish as the northern nations that spawned it. A third-floor gallery hosts contemporary art from the Norse nations, interspersed with historical looks, like a recent portrait series on Swedish actress Greta Garbo.

58 Park Ave., btw. 37th and 38th sts. ⓒ **212/879-9779.** www.scandinaviahouse.org. Tues–Sat noon–6pm. In summer, call ahead for schedule changes. Subway: 4/5/6/7/S to 42nd St./Grand Central; 6 to 33rd St.

SculptureCenter FREE   Though this institution has been supporting and showcasing modern sculpture since 1928, its new home in a former Queens trolley repair shop can feel like a visit to a start-up. Maya Lin's industrial-chic design is of the moment, but many of the touches are timeless. Ceilings soar 40 feet in the main room, and the basement project spaces are like minimalist catacombs. The rough edges haven't been disguised, but the overall effect is still refined, a perfect backdrop for the contemporary sculptures and installation art exhibited here. I love this place—it's a miniature version of what the Tate Modern in London should have been.

44–19 Purves St., off Jackson Ave., Long Island City, Queens. ⓒ **718/361-1750.** www.sculpture-center.org. Thurs–Mon 11am–6pm. $5 suggested donation, not enforced. Subway: E/M to 23rd St./Ely. G or 7 to 45th Rd./Court House Sq.

Sony Wonder Technology Lab FREE   Sony sucks in new generations of technology addicts with this four-level supermodern demonstration center, which has been recently overhauled. Kids can try their hands at robotics, medical imaging, and video game design, among other expensive toys. Free movies round out the stimuli; see p. 256 in chapter 7. FINE PRINT Call or check online for requirements for reserving in advance, which comes recommended.

550 Madison Ave., at 56th St. ℂ **212/833-8100,** or 212/833-5414 for reservations. www.sonywondertechlab.com. Tues–Sat 10am–5pm; last entrance 30 min. before closing. Subway: E/M to Fifth Ave./53rd St.; 4/5/6/N/R/W to Lexington Ave./59th St.

Storefront for Art and Architecture FREE   Designed with odd panels that expand into the street, this idiosyncratic institution does a lot with its very narrow space. Always intelligent exhibits explore architecture, art, and design.

97 Kenmare St., btw. Mulberry St. and Cleveland Place, near Lafayette St. ℂ **212/431-5795.** www.storefrontnews.org. Tues–Sat 11am–6pm. Subway: 6 to Spring St.; N/Q/R to Prince St.

Theodore Roosevelt Birthplace   An asthmatic son of a prominent New York family, Theodore Roosevelt transformed himself into a symbol of fortitude, becoming a rancher, a soldier, a governor, and eventually the only New York City native elected president. His original birthplace was demolished in 1916, but three years later friends and family built a replica town house on the site. Period pieces, the majority of which belonged to the Roosevelts, fill the stately rooms. Take one of the informative hourly tours and you'll learn Eleanor Roosevelt's maiden name (it was Roosevelt), the origins of the teddy bear, and that T. R. survived the loss of his wife and mother on the same day.

28 E. 20th St., btw. Broadway and Park Ave. S. ℂ **212/260-1616.** www.nps.gov/thrb. Tues–Sat 9am–5pm (tours hourly 10am–4pm). Subway: N/Q/R or 6 to 23rd St.

United Nations Visitors' Center FREE   This is it, the literal capital of the world. After going through the security line, which moves with all the efficiency and enthusiasm of an American airport's, you'll enter the Visitors' Lobby. Built in 1950, it's a little dated but still impressive. Multiple U.N.–related art exhibits fill the space. For $16 you can take a full tour of the building, but for cheaper thrills the Headquarters Park is a worthy diversion. Sculpture is scattered across a grassy expanse built on a scale rarely found in Manhattan.

First Ave. at 46th St. ℂ **212/963-4475.** www.un.org. Daily 9am–5pm; closed weekends Jan–Feb.

SOMETIMES FREE

Several museums that won't give up their goods for free full-time do set aside special hours and days where you can pay what you wish. Beware the last free day before an exhibition ends, though. More than a few procrastinators call New York home, and you'll find them gathered en masse for final free windows of opportunity.

American Folk Art Museum   Although the eclectic, modern design here is fitting for a MoMA neighbor, the high-tech finishes can be something less than harmonious with the rustic works on display. Fortunately, the objects themselves tend to hold up on their own. Rotating exhibitions complement the permanent collection, which boasts some amazing oddball autodidacts, including the world's largest collection of Henry Dargers. Friday evenings, when the museum is free, feature live music.

45 W. 53rd St., btw. Fifth and Sixth aves. ✆ **212/265-1040.** www.folkartmuseum.org. Regular admission $9; free Fri after 5:30pm. Tues–Sun 10:30am–5:30pm; Fri 11am–7:30pm. Subway: E/M to Fifth Ave./53rd St.

Asia Society   John D. Rockefeller III founded the Asia Society in the mid-fifties to encourage cultural exchanges and understanding between Asians and Americans. The newly renovated headquarters building has beautiful galleries, showing off parts of Rockefeller's collection in addition to rotating exhibits. The interior architecture is impressive, especially the sleek staircase that looks like a snake's skeleton wandering up the floors.

725 Park Ave., at 70th St. ✆ **212/288-6400.** www.asiasociety.org. Regular admission $10; free Fri 6–9pm. Tues–Sun 11am–6pm; Fri 11am–9pm, except July 4th–Labor Day, when museum closes 6pm Fri. Subway: 6 to 68th St./Hunter College.

Bronx Museum of the Arts   This hulk of modernity plunked down amid the Art Deco restraint of the Grand Concourse puts on adventurous shows. Most of the artists exhibited here have logged time as Boogie Down residents. If not, they'll represent some aspect of New York's cultural diversity. Entrance is by a suggested admission, though the suggestion gets dropped all day Fridays, which are completely free.

1040 Grand Concourse, at 165th St., the Bronx. ✆ **718/681-6000.** www.bxma.org. Suggested admission $5; free Fri all day. Mon, Thurs, Sat–Sun 11am–6pm; Fri 11am–8pm. Subway: B/D/4 to 161st St./Yankee Stadium.

FREE Date Night: Target First Saturdays at the Brooklyn Museum

One of New York's best cheap date opportunities comes once a month at the Brooklyn Museum. Every first Saturday the museum transforms itself into a house party on a massive scale. The crowd is more diverse than the U.N. General Assembly, with a dizzying range of ages, cultures, and castes represented. The museum keeps most of its galleries open for your perusal. When you run low on witty commentary, distractions like films and lectures beckon. Dance performances can be found, too, or if the date is going particularly well, you might let your feet work the floor yourself. The live music tends to be upbeat and very danceable. There's no charge for any of this, and nobody hits you up for a donation. The night is so festive that your date may not even notice just how cheap it's been. See the Brooklyn Museum review above for address and subway directions. Some attractions require tickets which, although free, may require standing on line.

Brooklyn Museum of Art   The second-largest art museum in the US of A, the Brooklyn Museum is as spruced up and thriving as the borough that hosts it. With a glorious new entryway, remodeled exhibitions, and a building with over half a million square feet, there are several days' worth of exploring to be done here. The Egyptian collection is world-class and beautifully displayed, with informative, well-written notes accompanying each object. The fourth floor's period rooms are definitely worth a peek. Don't miss the Jan Schenck House, a touch of Dutch in old Breuckelen that somehow survived on the edge of Jamaica Bay from 1675 to 1952.

200 Eastern Pkwy., at Washington Ave., Brooklyn. © **718/638-5000.** www.brooklyn museum.org. Suggested admission $10; free 1st Sat of the month 5–11pm. Wed–Fri 10am–5pm; 1st Sat of the month 11am–11pm; each Sat thereafter 11am–6pm; Sun 11am–6pm. Subway: 2/3 to Eastern Pkwy./Brooklyn Museum.

China Institute   A scholarly approach informs the exhibits at this 80-year-old culture and arts center. Two small, square galleries bookend the reception area and display traditional Chinese art, with

Sometimes Free or Pay-What-You-Wish Museums

Monday/ Tuesday	Wednesday	Thursday	Friday	Saturday	Sunday
The Museum at Eldridge Street (Mon 10am–noon)	Brooklyn Children's Museum (Wed 2–5pm)	Children's Museum of the Arts (Thurs 4–6pm)	Bronx Museum of the Arts (Fri 11am–8pm)	Brooklyn Children's Museum (Second Sat 10–11am)	Brooklyn Children's Museum (Second Sun 10–11am)
China Institute (Tues 6–8pm)	Museum of American Finance (Wed 10–11am)	China Institute (Thurs 6–8pm)	Children's Museum of Manhattan (Fri 5–8pm)	Brooklyn Museum of Art (First Sat 5pm–11pm)	Frick Collection (Sun 11am–1pm)
Museum of American Finance (Tues 10–11am)	Museum of Jewish Heritage: A Living Memorial to the Holocaust (Wed 4–8pm)	Museum of American Finance (Thurs 10–11am)	International Center of Photography (Fri 5–8pm)	El Museo del Barrio (Third Sat 11am–6pm)	New York Hall of Science (Sun 10–11am, Sept–June)
		Museum of Arts and Design (Thurs 6–9pm)	Japan Society (Fri 6–9pm)	Guggenheim Museum (Sat 5:45–7:45pm)	The Studio Museum in Harlem (Sun noon–6pm)
		Museum of Chinese in America (Thurs 11am–9pm)	The Morgan Library & Museum (Fri 7–9pm)	The Jewish Museum (Sat 11am–5:45pm)	
		New Museum (Thurs 7–9pm)	Museum of American Finance (Fri 10–11am)	Museum of American Finance (Sat 10–11am)	
			Museum of Modern Art/MoMA (Fri 4–8pm)		
			Neue Galerie (First Fri 6–8pm)		
			The New York Aquarium (Fri 3pm–close)		
			New York Hall of Science (Fri 2–5pm, Sept–June)		
			The Noguchi Museum (First Fri 10am–5pm)		
			The Rubin Museum of Art (Fri 7–10pm)		
			South Street Seaport Museum (Third Fri 6–8:45pm)		
			Whitney Museum of American Art (Fri 6–9pm)		

beautifully crafted examples of calligraphy, painting, architecture, and textile work.

125 E. 65th St., btw. Park and Lexington aves. © **212/744-8181.** www.chinainstitute. org. Regular admission $7; free Tues, Thurs 6–8pm. Daily 10am–5pm (Tues, Thurs to 8pm). Subway: 6 to 68th St./Hunter College.

El Museo del Barrio   A school classroom display was the genesis for this Museum Mile institution, the only U.S. museum dedicated to Puerto Rican, Caribbean, and Latin American art. The artistic history of the region, from pre-Columbian origins to the present, is recounted in a permanent installation. Changing exhibitions cover contemporary subjects and artists.

1230 Fifth Ave., at 104th St. © **212/831-7272.** www.elmuseo.org. Suggested admission $6; free every third Sat. Wed–Sun 11am–6pm. Subway: 6 to 103rd St.

Frick Collection   Coke (the stuff for steel, not the soda or the stimulant) was very, very good to Henry Clay Frick, who was a Gilded Age plutocrat by the age of 30. When it came time to decorate the walls of his Upper East Side palace he looked to the likes of Titian, Vermeer, and Goya. Hank didn't skimp on the furniture or carpeting, either. Though there is a slightly musty quality to this place (it dates to 1914), the collection is undeniably impressive, and special exhibitions have lately garnered plenty of buzz.

1 E. 70th St., at Fifth Ave. © **212/288-0700.** www.frick.org. Regular admission $18; pay what you wish Sun 11am–1pm. Tues–Sat 10am–6pm; Sun 11am–5pm. Subway: 6 to 68th St/Hunter College.

Guggenheim Museum   Artists complained bitterly about the curved walls that spiral up seven stories, but Frank Lloyd Wright knew what he was doing, and flat art mounts on the sides of the Guggie just fine. You'll feel like you're climbing through a nautilus shell as you view the latest installation in the central atrium, recently the host of Cai Guo-Qiang's startling nine-car cascade. A tower alongside the spiral hosts a permanent collection stocked with Chagalls, Matisses, van Goghs, and Picassos. For a whole 120 minutes a week, on Saturday nights in the latest iteration of the program, the Guggenheim lowers itself to letting regular folks poke around for free.

1071 Fifth Ave., at 88th St. © **212/423-3500.** www.guggenheim.org. Regular admission $18; pay what you wish Sat 5:45–7:45pm. Fri, Sun–Wed 10am–5:45pm; Sat 10am–7:45pm. Subway: 4/5/6 to 86th St.

International Center of Photography   The ICP does a good job of balancing photography's past and future, with Daguerreotypes and digital receiving as much wall time as the classic b&w street photographers of the '50s and '60s. Usually three separate exhibitions are up at any given time, except when the museum's two floors are turned over to a larger survey like contemporary African work, or the ICP Triennial, which showcases the best new photography.

1133 Sixth Ave., at 43rd St. ℂ **212/857-0000.** www.icp.org. Regular admission $12; pay what you wish Fri 5–8pm. Tues–Thurs, Sat–Sun 10am–6pm; Fri 10am–8pm. Subway: B/D/F/M to 42nd St.

Japan Society   A waterfall trickling through a bamboo thicket welcomes you to this cultural institution near the U.N. The second floor has several rooms of galleries dedicated to Japanese art, ranging from classical Buddhist sculpture to photography to a spectacular recent exhibit of 19th-century lacquer masterworks.

333 E. 47th St., btw. First and Second aves. ℂ **212/832-1155.** www.japansociety.org. Regular admission $12; free Fri 6–9pm. Tues–Thurs 11am–6pm; Fri 11am–9pm; Sat–Sun 11am–5pm. Subway: 4/5/7/S to Grand Central; 6 to 51st St.

The Jewish Museum   Four thousand years of Jewish history for this? Absolutely. A French Gothic château on the Upper East Side holds this remarkable collection, which chronicles the twists and turns of the Jewish experience, from a foundation stone of the third wall of Jerusalem to prints by Chagall. Lower floors handle temporary exhibits, like the terrific recent William Steig show.

1109 Fifth Ave., at 92nd St. ℂ **212/423-3200.** www.thejewishmuseum.org. Regular admission $12; free Sat. Fri–Tues 11am–5:45pm; Thurs 11am–8pm. Subway: 4/5 to 86th St.; 6 to 96th St.

The Morgan Library & Museum   J.P. Morgan's collection of manuscripts, books, drawings, and prints has been housed in this McKim, Mead & White masterpiece since 1906. The building recently celebrated its centennial by doubling its public exhibition space with a glass and steel Renzo Piano expansion. Lush original rooms are joined by two floors hosting exhibitions dedicated to photography, ancient cylinder seals, Bob Dylan ephemera, and the like.

225 Madison Ave., at 36th St. ℂ **212/685-0008.** www.themorgan.org. Regular admission is $12 adults; free Fri 7–9pm. (McKim rooms are also free Tues 3–5pm and Sun 4–6pm.) Tues–Thurs 10:30am–5pm; Fri 10:30am–9pm; Sat 10am–6pm; Sun 11am–6pm. Subway: 6 to 33rd St.

Museum of American Finance   The elegant 1928 lobby of the former Bank of New York plays host to this concise institution. Exhibits focus on all things fiscal, from wampum to subprime mortgage derivatives. See p. 312 for more information.

48 Wall St., btw. William and Hanover sts. © **212/908-4110.** www.moaf.org. Regular admission is $8; free Tues–Sat 10–11am. Tues–Sat 10am–4pm. Subway: 2/3 to Wall St.

Museum of Arts and Design   Craft design gets its 15 minutes inside the towering new home of this Midtown museum. Exhibits focus on emerging artists and new ideas of form, especially as the latter follows function. Clay, glass, wood, metal, and fiber are among the materials represented. For big spenders, the artisans on display often have their wares available in the shop.

2 Columbus Circle, btw. Broadway and Eighth Ave. © **212/599-7777.** www.mad museum.org. Regular admission $15; pay what you wish Thurs after 6pm. Tues–Sun 11am–6pm; Thurs 11am–9pm. Subway: A/B/C/D/1 to 59th St./Columbus Circle.

Museum of Chinese in America   The Chinese-American population of New York City has more than doubled in just the last 20 years, so it's no surprise MOCA has left its original digs in a crumbling old public school. The new space is six times as large, and bears Maya Lin's peerless touch, with a sensitivity to the structure's industrial history. A core exhibit on the Chinese-American Experience is supplemented by oral history projects, photo shows, and art installations.

215 Centre St., btw. Grand and Howard sts. © **212/619-4785.** www.mocanyc.org. Regular admission is $7; free Thurs. Mon, Fri 11am–5pm; Thurs 11am–9pm; Sat–Sun 10am–5pm. Subway: J/N/Q/R/Z/6 to Canal St.; B/D to Grand St.

The Museum at Eldridge Street   To look at the immaculate stained glass, carved wood, and starry ceilings inside this 1887 synagogue, you would never guess it spent decades on the verge of collapse. Visits here are by guided tour, which will show you the intricate restoration, along with a hidden snuff compartment and a massive central chandelier turned upside down when the building's lighting was converted from gas to electric. Tours are free on Monday mornings, although there is a tzedakah box if you'd like to leave a contribution (the fix-up cost some $20 million, and took 20 years).

12 Eldridge St., btw. Canal and Division sts. © **212/219-0302.** www.eldridgestreet. org. Regular admission $10; free Mon 10am–noon. Sun–Thurs, 10am–5pm, tours on the half-hour. Subway: F to E. Broadway; B/D to Grand St.

Museum of Jewish Heritage: A Living Memorial to the Holocaust
This institution's unwieldy name reflects its dual callings as museum
and memorial. The six-sided original building has a permanent exhibit
that puts a human face on the Holocaust. A recently completed new
wing houses ambitious temporary exhibits. The renovation also brought
an installation by sculptor Andy Goldsworthy. His *Garden of Stones*
juts out towards New York Harbor, creating a contemplative space
enlivened by dwarf oaks growing inside 18 hollow boulders. Though
most of the time there is an admission charge to the museum, access to
the garden is always free.

36 Battery Place, near Little West St. ✆ **646/437-4200**. www.mjhnyc.org. Regular
admission $12; free Wed 4–8pm. Sun–Tues, Thurs 10am–5:45pm; Wed 10am–8pm;
Fri 10am–5pm (closed 3pm during non-daylight saving time and on the eve of Jewish holidays). Subway: 4/5 to Bowling Green, R to Whitehall; 1 to South Ferry.

Museum of Modern Art (MoMA)   MoMA's nothing-left-to-chance
makeover has resulted in a structure with the overall of a Fortune 500
headquarters. Of course, for $650 million, the finishes *should* look
pretty damn nice. The stars of the permanent collection (Cézanne,
Hesse, Mondrian) are joined by high-wattage temporary exhibitions.
You'll pay through the nose for the privilege of wandering these
sepulchral halls, except on Friday nights, which are free courtesy of
corporate sponsorship and feature appallingly long lines. Is it just me,
or could they have spent a little less on top-grade marble, and let the
art be a little more accessible instead?

11 W. 53rd St., btw. Fifth and Sixth aves. ✆ **212/708-9400**. www.moma.org. Regular
admission $20; free Fri 4–8pm. Wed–Thurs, Sat–Mon 10:30am–5:30pm; Fri 10:30am–
8pm. Subway: E/M to Fifth Ave./53rd St.

The Museum of the Moving Image   Adolph Zuckor opened Astoria
Studios in 1920 and the lot soon became the biggest this side of Hollywood. The site still hosts television and film production, two activities that fuel this nearby museum's obsession. Exhibits trace the
moving image's evolution from 19th-century optical toys through film
cameras and television sets. FINE PRINT The Museum is expanding and
renovating and has not set its new admissions policies yet. Even if you
have to pay to get in, though, you'll be able to watch a feature-length
movie or two for your price of admission.

35th Ave., at 36th St., Astoria, Queens. ✆ **718/784-0077**. www.movingimage.us.
Subway: M/R to Steinway St.

Museums with Free Hours for Kids

Brooklyn Children's Museum   The world's first children's museum has kept up with the times, with a newly renovated green building (there's even an indoor stream). The permanent collection isn't kids' play, with some 30,000 artifacts of natural and human history. 145 Brooklyn Ave., at St. Marks Ave. ℭ **718/735-4400.** www.brooklynkids.org. Regular admission $7.50, but free Wed 2–5pm and second weekend of each month 10–11am. Wed–Fri 11am–5pm; Sat–Sun 10am–5pm (also open Tues in summer; check ahead as hours can change to accommodate school schedules). Subway: C to Kingston Ave.; A/C to Nostrand Ave.

Children's Museum of Manhattan   This uptown museum introduces kids to museum patronage before they can even walk. Toddlers can interact with giant talking dragons and play firetrucks, and there's a dedicated soft space for crawlers. Older kids learn through adventures with Dora and Diego, and the hands-on "City Splash" water exploration. 212 W. 83rd St., btw. Amsterdam Ave. and Broadway. ℭ **212/721-1223.** www.cmom.org. Regular admission $10, but free Fri 5–8pm. Tues–Sun 10am–5pm. Subway: 1 to 86th St.

Children's Museum of the Arts   Children 12 and under join their guardians in rolling up their sleeves and getting involved with art. Workshops cover everything from puppet making to computer drawing. On the walls you'll find selections from the museum's permanent collection—some great WPA pieces, and rotating exhibits of kid-friendly artists like Keith Haring. 182 Lafayette St., btw. Broome and Grand sts. ℭ **212/274-0986.** www.cmany.org. Regular admission $10, but pay what you wish Thurs 4–6pm. Wed, Fri–Sun noon–5pm; Thurs noon–6pm. Subway: 6 to Spring St.

Neue Galerie   The Galerie's 1914 brick and limestone mansion is one of the most elegant spots in the city. Ronald Lauder, a billionaire son of Estée Lauder (née Josephine Esther Mentzer of Corona, Queens), spent years adapting the interior to showcase 20th-century German and Austrian art and design. Upstairs in the two floors of galleries you'll find works by the likes of Gustav Klimt, Egon Schiele, Paul Klee, and Max Beckman. Admission is $15, but thanks to a Bloomberg grant, the first Friday of the month is free from 6 to 8pm. (The grant is renewed year to year, so check the website to make sure it's still running.) See also p. 253 for free films.

1048 Fifth Ave., at 86th St. ℂ **212/628-6200**. www.neuegalerie.org. Thurs–Mon, 11am–6pm. Subway: 4/5/6 to 86th St.

New Museum `FREE` "Maximum security" was my first thought when this gray hulk went up on the Bowery, and the caged-in ceiling of the foyer does little to dispel the prison vibe. That said, the free Thursday nights (take a ticket at the entrance and hop upstairs for three galleries of viewing pleasure) are really fun, presenting contemporary artwork that's generally low-fi, playful, and international in scope. Families can take advantage of free programs for kids on the first Saturday of each month (advance registration is required).

235 Bowery, btw. Stanton and Prince sts. ℂ **212/219-1222**. www.newmuseum.org. Regular admission $12; free Thurs 7–9pm. Wed, Sat–Sun noon–6pm; Thurs–Fri noon–9pm. Subway: F to Second Ave.; J/M/Z to Bowery.

The New York Aquarium Origins at Castle Clinton in 1896 make this the oldest aquarium in the U.S., although its Coney Island facility has only been in operation since 1957. Some areas here could definitely stand a spruce-up, but if you come with low expectations (and a passel of impressionable kids), you're sure to enjoy some quality shark, jellyfish, or otter face time. Regular admission is $13, but Fridays after 3pm it's pay what you wish.

Surf Ave. and W. 8th St., Coney Island, Brooklyn. ℂ **718/265-2663**. www.nyaquarium. com. Regular admission $13; pay what you wish Fri after 3pm. Spring and fall hours, Mon–Fri 10am–5pm; until 5:30pm Sat–Sun, holidays; summer, Mon–Fri 10am–6pm; until 7pm Sat–Sun, holidays; winter, daily 10am–4:30pm. Subway: F/Q to W. 8th St./NY Aquarium.

New York Hall of Science Nominally a hall of science, this place is really a big playground. The exhibits are hands on, letting kids get engulfed by a giant soap bubble, float on air in an antigravity mirror, and retrieve astronomical images from the depths of outer space. In summer the huge Outdoor Science Playground provides jungle gyms, slides, seesaws, and spinners to help the physics medicine go down.

47–01 111th St., in Flushing Meadows–Corona Park, Queens. ℂ **718/699-0005**. www. nyhallsci.org. Regular admission $11; free Fri 2–5pm, Sun 10–11am (Sept 1–June 30 only). July–Aug Mon–Fri 9:30am–5pm, Sat–Sun 10am–6pm; Sept 1–June 30 Tues–Thurs 9:30am–2pm, Fri 9:30am–5pm, Sat–Sun 10am–6pm. Subway: 7 to 111th St.

The Noguchi Museum Many New Yorkers have passed the Red Cube sculpture on lower Broadway, the stainless-steel plaque at the AP's headquarters in Rockefeller Center, and the sunken garden at the Chase Manhattan Bank Plaza, without realizing they're all by Japanese-American artist Isamu Noguchi. Noguchi's former home/studio shows off additional creativity in transforming a photo-engraving plant into a graceful oasis in the midst of industrial Queens. Renovated in 2004 and 2008, the museum features galleries of Noguchi's sculptural and architectural forms, and a tranquil birch-shaded sculpture garden.

9–01 33rd Rd., at Vernon Blvd., Long Island City, Queens. ⓒ **718/204-7088.** www.noguchi.org. Regular admission $10; pay what you wish the first Fri of every month. Wed–Fri 10am–5pm; Sat–Sun 11am–6pm. Subway: N/Q to Broadway. Walk 8 blocks along Broadway toward the East River.

The Rubin Museum of Art Occidentals finally got a Himalayan art museum of their own when the Rubin opened up in 2004. A marble and steel spiral staircase, the focal point of the Barneys department store that was the previous tenant, winds through seven floors of painting, sculpture, and textiles. Though bodhisattvas and mandalas may be esoteric to some, wall texts provide helpful background. On Friday nights (p. 251), when entry to the museum is free, you can catch a tour with a contemporary artist and learn even more.

150 W. 17th St., btw. Sixth and Seventh aves. ⓒ **212/620-5000.** www.rmanyc.org. Regular admission $10; free Fri 7–10pm. Mon, Thurs 11am–5pm; Wed 11am–7pm; Fri 11am–10pm; Sat–Sun 11am–6pm. Subway: 1/2/3/F/M to 14th St.; L to Sixth Ave.

South Street Seaport Museum The half-dozen counting houses that make up Schermerhorn Row were built in 1812 and still carry that era's low-rise, red brick charm. Artfully hollowed out and converted to gallery space, they now hold collections of ship portraits, Far East souvenirs, and scrimshaw that illuminate NYC's extensive maritime heritage. Every third Friday of the month, the museum is free; stop in at the main visitor center for a ticket, a calendar of that night's events (most geared toward kids), and directions to other free nearby galleries.

12 Fulton St., btw. Front and South sts. ⓒ **212/748-8600.** southstreetseaportmuseum.org. Regular admission $12; free every 3rd Fri 6–8:45pm. Apr–Dec Tues–Sun 10am–6pm; Jan–Mar Thurs–Sun 10am–5pm. Subway: 2/3/4/5/A/C/J/Z to Fulton St.

The Studio Museum in Harlem Dedicated to the art of African Americans, with a sideline on the African Diaspora, this small museum has gathered together a terrific permanent collection. Exhibits rotate frequently and the calendar is packed with freebies. There are poetry readings, dance, forums, and open studios for the A-I-R program, which shows off the Artists in Residence that the Studio Museum helps support.

144 W. 125th St., btw. Lenox Ave. and Adam Clayton Powell Blvd. ℂ **212/864-4500.** www.studiomuseum.org. Suggested admission $7; free Sun. Sun, Wed–Fri noon–6pm; Sat 10am–6pm. Subway: 2/3 to 125th St.

Whitney Museum of American Art Behind imposing Bauhaus walls on Madison Avenue lies a spectacular collection of 20th-century art. The Whitney is rich in Edward Hoppers, Louise Nevelsons, and Georgia O'Keeffes, and they're good about rotating the permanent collection through their upper galleries. Shows of contemporary artists on other floors tend to be surprisingly cutting edge for a big Uptown institution. The legendary Whitney Biannual—love it or hate it (or both)—is the institution's biggest draw.

945 Madison Ave., at 75th St. ℂ **212/570-3676.** www.whitney.org. Regular admission $18; pay what you wish Fri after 6pm. Wed–Thurs and Sat–Sun 11am–6pm; Fri 1–9pm. Subway: 6 to 77th St.

SUGGESTED ADMISSIONS

Many New York institutions let in visitors on the basis of a "suggested admission." The price you have pay isn't set in stone; it's set by the dictates of your own conscience. Before you decide how much to give, remember that you're already giving if you pay local taxes. We working stiffs support the NYC Department of Cultural Affairs, the largest agency of its kind in the U.S. In 2009, the agency had $152 million set aside for expenses. It also had its largest capital budget yet, with another $1 billion (!) spread over 5 years. Cultural Affairs helps fund dozens of local institutions, many of which are owned by the city (and by extension, you and me). Sometimes $1 seems like the right amount to be spending on one's own museum. That's not to say if you're flush you should be stiffing these institutions, which do spectacular work. If you've got a spare couple of bucks, by all means toss them in the hat.

American Museum of Natural History It's easy to lose yourself within the 4-square-block walls of this legendary museum. Low-profile sections still have the dingy lighting and old-fashioned lettering of a few decades ago, but the big players received radical upgrades. Dinosaurs have been brought into the 21st century and $210 million has spaceaged the Planetarium. With that big an outlay, the museum likes to see its full $15 admission when you come, although technically it's only a suggestion and you can pay what you wish.

Central Park W., btw. 77th and 81st sts. ℂ **212/769-5100** for information, or ℂ 212/769-5200 for tickets (tickets can also be ordered online). www.amnh.org. Suggested admission $16. Space Show and museum admission together are $24, plus additional charges for IMAX movies and some of the special exhibitions. Daily 10am–5:45pm. Subway: B/C to 81st St., 1 to 79th St.

The City Reliquary `FREE` This micro museum is dedicated to the detritus of NYC, with an eye toward quirky collections like vintage thermoses and found snapshots. The permanent collection holds subway tokens and false teeth washed up in Dead Horse Bay. In addition to the small storefront gallery (entry is by a $1 suggested donation), there's a window display on nearby Grand Street, which was the institution's original inspiration.

370 Metropolitan Ave., btw. Havemeyer St. and Rev. Dr. Gardner C. Taylor Blvd., Williamsburg, Brooklyn. Suggested admission $1. ℂ **718/782-4842.** www.cityreliquary. org. Sat–Sun noon–6pm, Thurs 7–10pm. *Window display,* 307 Grand St., at Havemeyer St., Williamsburg, Brooklyn. Subway to both locations: L to Lorimer St.; G to Metropolitan Ave.

The Cloisters Situated on a picturesque Hudson cliff side, this Met subsidiary is a Frankenstein-esque amalgamation of medieval architecture: a Romanesque chapel, a 12th-century Spanish apse, and cloisters from five different monasteries. Tranquil gardens surround the site and enhance the sense that you're not just out of the city, you've dropped out of contemporary time altogether. If you've ever wondered why the Palisades in Jersey aren't more developed, it's because John D. Rockefeller, Jr., bought up that land to preserve this view.

99 Margaret Corbin Dr. (north end of Fort Tryon Park). ℂ **212/923-3700.** www. metmuseum.org. Suggested admission $20. Nov–Feb Tues–Sun 9:30am–4:45pm; Mar–Oct Tues–Sun 9:30am–5:15pm. Subway: A to 190th St., then a 10-min. walk north along Margaret Corbin Dr., or pick up the M4 bus at the station (1 stop to Cloisters). Or take the M4 Madison Ave. to Fort Tryon Park–The Cloisters.

Dyckman Farmhouse Museum   The Dyckman family farmed upper Broadway for two centuries. Three generations called this original Dutch farmhouse home, and their descendents outfitted its museum incarnation with period pieces. In the garden you'll find an original smokehouse and a Revolutionary War–era Hessian hut.

4881 Broadway, at 204th St. ℭ **212/304-9422.** www.dyckmanfarmhouse.org. Admission $1. Wed–Sat 11am–4pm; Sun noon–4pm. Subway: A/1 to 207th St.

Edgar Allan Poe Cottage   Happy-go-lucky Virginian E. A. P. moved to the Bronx in 1846, hoping that the country air would be good for his tubercular wife. She died the next year, and Poe himself checked out only a couple of years later. The cottage is now an anomaly among brick high-rises. The interior has period furnishings and Poe exhibits.

2460 Grand Concourse, at E. Kingsbridge Rd. ℭ **718/881-8900.** www.bronxhistorical society.org. Admission $5. Sat 10am–4pm; Sun 1–5pm. Subway: D/4 to Kingsbridge Rd.

The Historic House Trust of New York City   I find it amazing that anything can survive for long in NYC, especially old houses that don't do anything except clog up prime real estate. The Historic House Trust has information on 23 surviving dwellings, spread across all five boroughs. Admissions are usually under $5, which is not bad for the opportunity to travel back in time a century or two.

830 Fifth Ave. ℭ **212/360-8282.** www.historichousetrust.org.

The Italian American Museum `FREE`   This storefront museum doubles as a time machine: Exhibits are mounted amid the original teller windows of the circa-1885 Banca Stabile (don't miss the ancient vault in back). Although a major expansion is imminent, for now you can enjoy a low-key look at some Italian-American artifacts. The social security card of Luigi Del Bianco (chief carver of Mount Rushmore), the guns of Frank Serpico, and a harrowing letter written by the Black Hand are all on display. `FINE PRINT` Suggested donation is $5.

155 Mulberry St., at Grand St. ℭ **212/965-9000.** www.italianamericanmuseum.org. Wed–Sun 11am–6pm; Fri until 8pm. Subway: J/N/Q/R/Z/6 to Canal St.

The Metropolitan Museum of Art   On the Upper East Side, tucked away just off Central Park, you can find this undiscovered little gem of a collection. Allow yourself a good 10 minutes to see everything they've got. Yeah, well, the Met is the 800-pound gorilla of New York's museum scene, and it's not hiding from anybody. If it's not the greatest museum in the world, it must be damn close, and it's all right there for the price of a suggested admission.

Fifth Ave., at 82nd St. ℂ **212/535-7710.** www.metmuseum.org. Suggested admission $20. Tues–Thurs, Sun 9:30am–5:30pm; Fri–Sat 9:30am–9pm; Mon 9:30am–5:30pm on select holidays only. Subway: 4/5/6 to 86th St.

MoMA PS1   School is out, replaced by art that's in, inside this 19th-century former public school. A gorgeous Renaissance Revival building hosts avant-garde shows rotating through the former classrooms. Formerly the P.S. 1 Contemporary Art Center, this MoMA offshoot does a terrific job of bringing fresh, intriguing art to Queens. Don't miss James Turrell's "Meeting" on the top floor, which frames the dusk sky in an extraordinary way.

22–25 Jackson Ave., Long Island City, Queens. ℂ **718/784-2084.** www.ps1.org. Suggested admission $10. Thurs–Mon noon–6pm. Subway: E/M to 23rd St./Ely Ave.; G to 21st St. and Alst; 7 to 45th Rd./Court House Sq.

The Morris-Jumel Mansion   One of Manhattan's coolest surprises is coming upon the grounds of the Morris-Jumel Mansion in the midst of monolithic Harlem apartment buildings. This genteel Palladian wonder is the oldest house in Manhattan, built in 1765 as a summer getaway. There isn't much land left on the plot, but what remains is pleasant to stroll around. You have to pay to enter the house, which provides a fascinating snapshot of its era (and of history: this was General Washington's headquarters for two months in 1776). *Tip:* Don't miss picturesque Sylvan Terrace across the street (just west of the mansion), one of the city's last blocks of wooden workers' row houses.

65 Jumel Terrace at 160th St., east of St. Nicholas Ave. ℂ **212/923-8008.** www.morris jumel.org. Admission $5. Wed–Sun 10am–4pm. Subway: C to 163rd St.

Museum of Biblical Art `FREE`   With its de rigueur acronym, MOBIA makes a game effort to fit in with its museum brethren in the heart of New Gomorrah. Exhibition subjects have ranged from oil lamps of the Holy Land to engravings by Fauvist Georges Rouault. Pagans and Satanists may tire quickly, as shows are limited to Judeo-Christian expressions. Gallery talks and lectures are also on offer, usually for free. `FINE PRINT` Event seating is limited, so you may want to reserve in advance.

1865 Broadway, at W. 61st St. ℂ **212/408-1500.** www.mobia.org. Suggested admission $7. Wed, Fri–Sun noon–6pm; Thurs noon–8pm. Subway: A/B/C/D/1 to 59th St./Columbus Circle.

Museum of the City of New York   A gracious 1932 neo-Georgian mansion houses exhibits tracing NYC from the windmills of its Dutch colonial days up to its present status as the undisputed capital of the world. Lovely period rooms and a collection of theatrical memorabilia are highlights of the collection. The museum often throws in free music and film programs with the price of your admission.

Fifth Ave., at 103rd St. ℂ **212/534-1672.** www.mcny.org. Suggested admission $10. Free if you work or live in East Harlem (tell the desk you're a neighbor). Tues–Sun 10am–5pm. Subway: 6 to 103rd St.

New York City Fire Museum   FDNY Engine Co. 30's former home holds an impressive collection of fire-service memorabilia. Exhibits range from the 18th century to the present, where the most poignant materials can be found. During the 9/11 attacks, 343 firefighters gave their lives just a few blocks south of the museum.

278 Spring St., btw. Varick and Hudson sts. ℂ **212/691-1303.** www.nycfiremuseum. org. Suggested admission $7. Tues–Sat 10am–5pm; Sun 10am–4pm. Subway: C/E to Spring St.

The New York City Police Museum   The exhibits here border on hagiography, but plenty of good little nuggets can be found, including a 1933 letter from a private citizen suggesting police cars adopt "sirens." See p. 312 for a full review.

100 Old Slip, btw. Water and South sts., 2 blocks south of Wall St. ℂ **212/480-3100.** www.nycpolicemuseum.org. Suggested admission of $7 is not enforced. Mon–Sat 10am–5pm. Subway: 2/3 to Wall St.; J/Z to Broad St.

Queens Museum of Art   This museum has reproductions of Greek marbles and some nice Tiffany glass, but the real draw is The Panorama of the City of New York, the world's largest scale model. Every single building in the five boroughs is represented, in addition to every street and bridge, and even airplanes that take off and land at a tiny LaGuardia. The Museum is located in Corona Park, on the site of the legendary 1964 World's Fair. Don't miss the nearby Unisphere, a highlight of the fair and the largest representation of Earth that we humans have cooked up yet. Twelve gleaming stories high, the Unisphere will give you a good idea of what the planet looks like from 6,000 miles in space.

Next to the Unisphere in Flushing Meadows–Corona Park, Queens. ℂ **718/592-9700.** www.queensmuseum.org. Suggested admission $5. Wed–Sun noon–6pm; Fri in July–Aug noon–8pm. Subway: 7 to Willets Point/Shea Stadium; follow signs through the park.

FREE Governors Island

Native Americans called it *Pagganck* ("Nut Island"), the Dutch called it *Noten Eylant,* and until 1995 3,500 Coast Guard members and their families called it home. Today, the former military base that is Governors Island has been set aside for public use. During the summer, visitors can wander past abandoned mansions, forts, and bucolic parade grounds. It's all free, with a lovely ferry ride across New York Harbor thrown in as well. The breathtaking views make this New York's most ideal picnic spot. The ferry leaves from lower Manhattan every hour on the hour from 10am to 3pm on Fridays and from 10am to 5pm on Saturdays and Sundays in June, July, and August. During these same months, rangers give 90-minute tours (leaving Manhattan at 10am and 1pm) of the northern half of the island, on Wednesdays and Thursdays. Shorter ranger-led tours run Friday through Sunday. Space on the ferries is limited, first-come, first-served. For a beachy scene, complete with volleyball, basketball, food, drink, and live music, check out the 300 tons of trucked-in sand at **Water Taxi Beach Governors Island** (🕿 **877/974-6998;** www.watertaxibeach.com). Service runs from Pier 11 at Wall Street ($5 round-trip) after the free Park Service ferry service has stopped for the evening. The island was only transferred to the public in 2003, so check the website, as policies and programs may be no more permanent than a name. (See also p. 245 for free music.) Battery Maritime Bldg., 10 South St., btw. Broad and Whitehall sts. 🕿 **212/440-2202.** www.nps.gov/gois. Subway: R to Whitehall St.; 1 to South Ferry.

Tibet House U.S. FREE   This blah apartment house seems an unlikely place for inspiring Tibetan art, but the second floor holds a vibrant collection of paintings, sculptures, and artifacts. The art is intricate and the quiet rooms encourage lingering. A large gallery space hosts rotating shows with a Tibetan angle. FINE PRINT There's a suggested admission of $5.

22 W. 15th St., 2nd floor, btw. Fifth and Sixth aves. 🕿 **212/807-0563.** www.tibet house.org. Mon–Fri noon–5pm. Subway: L/N/Q/R/4/5/6 to 14th St./Union Sq.

FREE EXHIBITS AT THE LIBRARIES

Free books are just the beginning with New York's libraries. In addition to free classes (p. 150) and free films (p. 259), Gothamites also get free exhibitions. The libraries really care about their material, which comes through in the impressively well-crafted displays.

Brooklyn Central Library `FREE`   The galleries here present everything from painting to installation art to rare books. The works and the artists often have a local connection.

Grand Army Plaza. ℭ **718/230-2100.** www.brooklynpubliclibrary.org. Tues–Thurs 9am–9pm; Mon, Fri 9am–6pm; Sat 10am–6pm; Sun 1–5pm. Subway: 2/3 to Grand Army Plaza.

New York Public Library for the Performing Arts `FREE`   This library branch is a performance clearinghouse, conveniently located near the arts central that is Lincoln Center. Performing arts exhibitions can be found in the Donald and Mary Oenslager Gallery.

40 Lincoln Center Plaza, btw. 64th and 65th sts. ℭ **212/870-1630.** www.nypl.org. Tues–Wed, Fri 11am–6pm; Mon, Thurs noon–8pm; Sat 10am–6pm. Subway: 1 to 66th St.

Schomburg Center for Research in Black Culture `FREE`   The massive collection of books and art gathered by bibliophile Arturo Alfonso Schomburg is housed at this research branch of the New York Public Library. The Exhibition Hall, the Latimer/Edison Gallery, and the Reading Room all host exhibits related to black culture. Talks and performing arts are also part of the program here. Call or check online for scheduling details.

515 Malcolm X Blvd., at Lenox Ave., btw. 135th and 136th sts. ℭ **212/491-2200.** www.nypl.org. Exhibition hours, Mon–Sat 10am–6pm; Sun 1–5pm. Subway: 2/3 to 135th St.

Stephen A. Schwarzman Building (Humanities and Social Sciences Library) `FREE`   Many local fans of the writer A. A. Milne don't realize that Winnie-the-Pooh has been a fellow Manhattan resident for over half a century. Pooh and friends Piglet, Eeyore, Kanga, and Tigger are all on display here. These are Christopher's actual stuffed animals, instantly recognizable from their portrayals on the page. Though they look a little forlorn for being stuck behind glass, they've held up pretty well for 80-year-olds. The other book- and manuscript-themed exhibits here are lovingly displayed and as well written as you'd expect from a library. See p. 129 for information on free tours.

Moving Views

Straphangers get treated to a few spectacular scenes in exchange for their swipes. I love the 7 line as it approaches Manhattan from Queens. The track twists and turns like a slo-mo roller coaster with the Midtown skyline in the background. The J/M/Z ride across the Williamsburg has great views from windows north and south. The Manhattan Bridge gives B/D/N/Q riders dramatic East River vistas.

The most thrilling public transportation ride is the **Roosevelt Island Tram** (✆ **212/832-4555;** www.rioc.com). As you dangle in the air over the East River you get the East Side skyline, plus the U.N., plus great sightlines of the engineering marvels of the East River bridges. You also get the knowledge that one day in 2006 the tram stalled out for hours, stranding passengers without much of an evacuation plan. Accordingly, in 2010 the tram was shut down for 6 months for a complete overhaul. A frisson of actual danger comes free with the $2.25 one-way price (unlimited-plan Metrocards are accepted as well; you can also return via the F train's Roosevelt Island stop, just a few blocks away). The trip between 60th Street and Second Avenue and Roosevelt Island takes about 4 minutes. The Tram operates daily 6am to 2am; until 3:30am on Fridays and Saturdays.

Fifth Ave., at 42nd St. ✆ **212/869-8089** exhibits and events, or 212/661-7220 for library hours. www.nypl.org. General hours, Mon, Thurs–Sat 10am–6pm; Tues–Wed 10am–9pm; Sun 1–5pm; exhibitions may have shorter hours. Subway: B/D/F to 42nd St.; 7 to Fifth Ave.; 4/5/6/S to Grand Central.

2 Gallery Scene

Art galleries may be Gotham's greatest free cultural resource. Not only do these minimuseums provide us with works of inspiration, they also give us free booze and snacks at their openings. Don't be shy about barging into a show with million-dollar pieces. Gallery owners are almost as happy raising the profiles of their artists as they are closing a sale; both are essential for upping the prices they charge. We should also take a moment to be thankful for the tech stock boom. Not only did we all make a killing on our stock options, the dot.coms made it possible for scruffy people in jeans and sneakers to be stealth millionaires. Gallery owners and employees can no longer easily distinguish between the underemployed and walking gold mines, meaning that our presence in galleries is not merely tolerated, but actively sought and desired.

If you want invitations to openings, you have a couple of options. You can sign in whenever you visit a gallery and they'll keep you informed, or you can check online. Douglas Kelly keeps an amazingly comprehensive list of gallery openings at **http://dks.thing.net**. Typical gallery hours are Tuesday through Saturday from noon to 6pm, but check ahead, as times can vary. Many openings are on Thursday nights. Summers can be pretty dead in the art world, and many galleries keep shorter hours, often closing on Saturdays.

CHELSEA

New York's big-money art scene has put most of its eggs in one basket by clustering galleries between Tenth and Eleventh avenues. For the gallery fan, this means you can visit hundreds of shows without ever leaving **the lower West 20s.** The geography also rewards the serendipitous, allowing for quick pop-ins at randomly selected spaces. Not interested in a bunch of paint splotches on Brillo pads? Pop right back out. My favorite strategy is to write down some interesting-sounding shows from the listings in the *Voice* and then hit a few of their unlisted neighbors. With floor after floor of galleries in the old warehouse buildings here, you're bound to find something of interest.

Subway: C/E to 23rd St.

David Zwirner FREE   One of many SoHo refugees, Zwirner shows a range of interesting, inventive art, usually from emerging artists. His Chelsea holdings now cover three separate units on West 19th St.

519, 525, and 533 W. 19th St., btw. Tenth Ave. and West St. ✆ **212/727-2070.** www. davidzwirner.com.

Gagosian Gallery FREE   Perhaps the heaviest hitter around, this gallery puts on major shows in a space large enough to accommodate sculptures by Richard Serra.

555 W. 24th St. and 522 W. 21st St., btw. Tenth and Eleventh aves. Other location: *Upper East Side* 980 Madison Ave., btw. 76th and 77th sts. ✆ **212/741-1111.** www. gagosian.com.

Matthew Marks Gallery `FREE` Matthew Marks has built a miniempire in west Chelsea. His three galleries show top-tier painting, photography, and sculpture.

523 W. 24th; 522 W. 22nd; 526 W. 22nd, all btw. Tenth and Eleventh aves. ✆ **212/243-0200.** www.matthewmarks.com.

DOWNTOWN

In the early and mid-'80s, the headquarters of New York's avant-garde was the East Village. Tiny galleries dotted the landscape and helped break the era's big names. The stock market crash of '87 put an abrupt end to frivolous spending, and most of the galleries withered away. It's taken more than two decades, but galleries are just now returning. Throughout the **East Village** and **Lower East Side,** and even into **Chinatown,** storefront operations are coming to life. SoHo, conversely, continues to atrophy as an art scene. The galleries can't afford the rents, and every year there are fewer and fewer hanging on. However, a few institutions are firmly embedded in the area, and they put on some of the best shows.

> ### Gallery Sources
>
> The local papers provide rundowns on the higher profile shows. The *Village Voice* has good listings, which can also be perused online (www.village voice.com). The *New York Times, New York* magazine, *Time Out New York,* and the *New Yorker* all provide extensive listing information, both on- and offline.

Subway: *SoHo,* N/Q/R to Prince; C/E to Spring. *Lower East Side/Chinatown,* B/D to Grand St.; F to Delancey St.; J/M/Z to Essex St. *East Village,* F/M to Second Ave.

AIA New York Chapter Center for Architecture `FREE` The exhibits here tend to be esoteric, geared more to the professional architect than the public at large. The space is interesting, however, with a nice layout. Beneath the ground floor is a side room that shows off the building's geothermal heating and cooling system: They drilled down deeper than the Empire State Building is high in order to make it work.

536 LaGuardia Place, btw. Bleecker and W. 3rd sts. ✆ **212/683-0023.** www.aiany.org.

Artists Space `FREE` Young artists get exposure on the walls of this SoHo collective, which has been broadening horizons since 1972.

38 Greene St., 3rd floor, btw. Broome and Grand sts. ✆ **212/226-3970.** www.artists space.org.

FREE Watching the Auction Action

Sure, you know all about New York's auction scene, the way you follow a stranger in, take an inconspicuous seat off to the side, and try to suppress a sneeze just as a gavel comes down to announce you're the proud owner of a $50,000 Ming vase. But there's more to New York auction houses than expensive misunderstandings and antitrust violations. Viewings and sale previews are excellent chances to treat upcoming lots as museum exhibits. The current top house is **Christie's,** at 20 Rockefeller Plaza, 49th Street between Fifth and Sixth avenues (℃ **212/636-2000;** www.christies.com). **Sotheby's** runs a close second on the Upper East Side, 1334 York Ave., at 72nd St. (℃ **212/606-7000;** www.sothebys.com). There are three often-overlooked smaller houses that sell equally intriguing artifacts. **Guernsey's,** 108½ E. 73rd St., between Park and Lexington avenues (℃ **212/794-2280;** www.guernseys.com), focuses on modern collections and memorabilia (note that previews are usually off-site from their corporate offices). The city's oldest privately owned house is **Tepper Galleries** at 110 E. 25th St., between Park and Lexington avenues (℃ **212/677-5300;** www.teppergalleries.com). Fine and decorative arts shows and estate sales are the specialties of the house, with previews usually held on Fridays. **Bonhams & Butterfields** dates back to England and 1793, although its presence in New York is on a recent upswing. American art and natural history rarities have just made their way through the spiffy headquarters at 580 Madison Ave., between 56th and 57th streets (℃ **212/644-9001;** www.bonhams.com).

Full calendars for all houses are available online.

The Drawing Center FREE   This downtown institution supports the often-overlooked discipline of drawing. Two spaces across the street from each other present simultaneous shows. Lectures and screenings, some of which are free, add to the "draw" here.

35 and 40 Wooster St., btw. Broome and Grand sts. ℃ **212/269-2166.** www.drawing center.org.

Grey Art Gallery This small gallery basically doubles as NYU's fine arts museum. There's nothing sophmoric about the visual art displayed here—rotating exhibitions are thoughtful, and usually broadly scoped.

100 Washington Sq. E., btw. Washington Sq. S. and N. ✆ **212/998-6780.** www.nyu. edu/greyart. Suggested admission $3, not enforced.

Swiss Institute `FREE` The artists shown here usually have a Swiss connection. Innovative project ideas include the Institute's "Extension 17 project" featuring free audio art (Sonic Youth's Kim Gordon contributed one)—just call the Institute and dial ext. 17.

495 Broadway, 3rd floor, btw. Broome and Spring sts. ✆ **212/925-2035.** www.swiss institute.net.

MIDTOWN/UPTOWN

With the avant-garde ensconced downtown and in Brooklyn, the galleries that breathe the rarified air of the Upper East Side tend toward the staid side. Art here is of a classic bent, though the definition of classic is pretty elastic these days. Expect to see master works ranging from the Renaissance to the last couple of decades. And if you thought the asking prices were wacky downtown, wait until you see these . . .

Subway: 6 to 68th St.; F to 63rd St.; N/Q/R or 4/5/6 to 59th St.

Americas Society Art Gallery `FREE` The Americas, from Canada all the way down to Patagonia, are the focus of art shows here.

680 Park Ave., at 68th St. ✆ **212/249-8950.** www.americas-society.org.

The Grolier Club `FREE` This society shows off its love of books and graphic arts in galleries on two separate floors. Shows are free, as are some of the club's bibliophilic lectures.

47 E. 60th St., btw. Park and Madison aves. ✆ **212/838-6690.** www.grolierclub.org.

Hirschl & Adler Galleries `FREE` Five floors of galleries display 18th- to 20th-century European and American painting and decorative arts in an exquisite landmark town house.

21 E. 70th St., btw. Fifth and Madison aves. ✆ **212/535-8810.** www.hirschlandadler. com.

Pace Wildenstein `FREE` Modernism is the new classicism, and this gallery specializes in the best of it.

FREE SoHo's Secret Installations

DIA Foundation for the Arts The DIA maintains a pair of hidden galleries with eccentric conceptual works by Walter De Maria. Both galleries are open from Wednesday to Sunday from noon to 6pm (closed 3–3:30pm), and are closed in summer. 141 Wooster St. and 393 West Broadway. ℂ 212/989-5566; www.diacenter.org.

The Broken Kilometer A few blocks away you can find a gallery floor covered with orderly rows of solid brass rods. Placed end to end, the 500 rods would stretch exactly—yup, 1 kilometer. (Its sister piece, a sculpture with identical, unbroken brass rods buried vertically in the ground, is in Germany.) 393 West Broadway, btw. Spring and Broome sts. www.brokenkilometer.org.

New York Earth Room As the name suggests, it's a room full of dirt. Really—140 tons of soil filling up a SoHo loft to a depth of almost 2 feet. It's an oddly compelling sight in the middle of the city, and the rich earthy scent is almost refreshing. 141 Wooster St., btw. Houston and Prince sts. www.earthroom.org.

32 E. 57th St., btw. Fifth and Madison aves. ℂ 212/421-3292. www.pacewildenstein.com. Other locations: *Chelsea,* 534 W. 25th St. and 545 W. 22nd St., btw. Tenth and Eleventh aves. ℂ 212/929-7001.

Richard L. Feigen & Co. FREE Master works of the last few centuries are the focus here.

34 E. 69th St., btw. Park and Madison aves. ℂ 212/628-0700. www.rlfeigen.com.

Wildenstein FREE This gallery has over a century's experience in handling huge-ticket items. Renaissance and Impressionism treasures are a specialty.

19 E. 64th St., btw. Fifth and Madison aves. ℂ 212/879-0500. www.wildenstein.com.

WILLIAMSBURG

Not so long ago, Williamsburg's orthodox Jewish population distributed petitions asking for help from above to stem the "plague of the artists" that encroaches on their community. There's been no immediate response from G-d, but I'd bet that the plague continues to rage for the foreseeable future, as artists flock to Brooklyn and overrun Bedford's hipster boundaries. Though it's still more DIY and low-budget than Manhattan's galleries, the scene here is catching up quickly. The only drawback is that the spaces are spread far apart. To make a full tour here, be prepared to trek some blocks. *Note:* Brooklyn galleries keep different hours from the Manhattan side; many are open from Friday to Monday, or weekends only.

Subway: L to Bedford Ave. or Lorimer St.; J/M/Z to Marcy Ave.; G to Metropolitan Ave.

Pierogi 2000 `FREE`   This small, well-established gallery hangs some of the best painting to be found in Brooklyn. Photo and installation work also go on display, often in the context of intriguing group shows. If you're in need of further visual stimuli, some 750 artists are browsable in the gallery's constantly evolving (and traveling) Flat Files collection.

177 N. 9th St., btw. Bedford and Driggs aves. ✆ **718/599-2144.** www.pierogi2000. com. Tues–Sun 11am–6pm. Other location: *The Boiler*, 191 N. 14th St., btw. Nassau and Wythe aves. Thurs–Sun noon–6pm.

Secret Project Robot `FREE`   This huge warehouse space serves up experimental contemporary art, and works as a launching pad for related live music and art party events.

210 Kent Ave., at Metropolitan Ave. ✆ **917/860-8282.** www.secretprojectrobot.org. Sat–Sun 1–5pm.

Williamsburg Art and Historical Center `FREE`   Housed in an amazing 1867 bank building, this community center is always good for an intriguing art exhibit or two.

135 Broadway, at Bedford St. ✆ **718/486-7372.** www.wahcenter.net. Sat–Sun noon–6pm.

3 Open Studios & Art Fests

Run-down industrial neighborhoods beget artist populations, as the creatively minded come in for cheap, raw studio space. In the old days a few neighbors would open their doors one weekend to show off their work to friends and their floormates' friends. With the explosion of New York's artist population, things have become more organized than the old flier-on-a-lamppost invitation system. Several neighborhoods now offer full-blown arts festivals, with music, installations, theater, and gallery events supplementing open studios.

FREE Mi Casa Es Su Casa: Open House New York

New Yorkers obsess about real estate. As much time as we kill poring over the property blog Curbed (www.curbed.com), however, there's no substitute for actually poking around someone else's space in person. **Open House New York** opens the doors to some of the most mysterious spaces in the city. The first weekend in October brings New Yorkers access to envy-inducing private residences and awe-inspiring public structures. When else are you going to get a peek at the Richard Meier & Partners Model Museum, the Morgan Library's conservation department, or the grounds of the Roosevelt Island Smallpox Hospital? Locales (almost 200!) are scattered across all five boroughs, so you'll have to come up with a schedule or limit your targets to a few spots. Reserve early (© **212/991-6470;** www.ohny.org).

Bushwick Open Studios and Arts Festival (BOS) FREE   Bushwick is starting to feel a little like the old East Village, with a committed core of artistic pioneers and a coalescing sense of community. The studios here are generally in old factories, with semi-legal living quarters set up amid the canvases and installations. Beyond the voyeuristic pleasures of scoping out strangers' homes, there's tons of free music, free beer, and great art. In addition to BOS in June, there's BETA Spaces (group shows in alternative spaces) in November, and the SITE Fest (performance) in March.

Bushwick, Brooklyn. www.bos2010.artsinbushwick.org. Fri night performances; studios Sat–Sun noon–7pm. Subway: L to Morgan Ave., Montrose Ave., Jefferson St., or DeKalb Ave.; J/M/Z to Myrtle Ave., J to Gates Ave. or Flushing Ave.

DAC Art Under the Bridge Festival FREE   The city's preeminent arts fest belongs to DUMBO, where yupster incursions have yet to fully displace the artists whose studios fill these broad-shouldered warehouses. This is probably the best art crop in town, which may or may not be related to the inspiring Manhattan views you'll find through many an artist's window. The festival also features music, dance, video, and gallery extravaganzas, and most of it is free.

DUMBO, Brooklyn. ☏ **718/694-0831.** www.dumboartscenter.org. Usually the last weekend in Sept. Subway: F to York St.; A/C to High St.

Every Last Sunday on the Lower East Side FREE   The "Bargain District" nickname has grown increasingly anachronistic as an influx of tony boutiques and restaurants has upped rents across my beloved LES. Plenty of galleries, studios, and performance spaces remain, however, and on the last Sunday of each month you can tour through them for free. The tours leave at 1pm, April through October.

Tour usually begins from LES Visitor Center at 54 Orchard St., btw. Grand and Hester sts. ☏ **212/226-9010.** www.lowereastsideny.com. Last Sun of the month, Apr–Oct, 1pm. Subway: J/M/Z to Essex St.; F to Delancey St.

Tribeca Open Artist Studio Tour FREE   TriBeCa certainly doesn't qualify as a run-down neighborhood, so the 70 artist studios that open up for T.O.A.S.T. are a bit of a surprise. You'll also find free music and slideshows amid the tony condos. (The Lower Manhattan Cultural Council, in the nearby Financial District, usually opens its studios the following weekend.)

From Canal south to Warren St., and Lafayette west to Greenwich St. ☏ **212/479-7317.** www.toastartwalk.com. Fri 5–9pm; Sat–Mon 1–6pm. Subway: 1 to Franklin St.; A/C/E to Canal St.

Washington Square Outdoor Art Exhibit FREE   This Depression-era idea for helping artists get their work out there is now safely into its eighth decade. Streets near Washington Square Park become a gigantic open-air art gallery, where you can browse through the works of some 200 artists and artisans. The show is juried, so even the crafts have standards to meet. Pick up a free map at the intersection of 8th Street and University.

Show covers University Place btw. 3rd and 10th sts., and spills over to Schwartz Plaza. ☏ **212/982-6255.** www.washingtonsquareoutdoorartexhibit.org. Noon–6pm Sat–Mon on Memorial Day and Labor Day weekends; Sat–Sun the weekends following. Subway: N/Q/R to 8th St.; A/B/C/D/E/M to W. 4th St./Washington Sq.

4 Free Tours

SPONSORED TOURS

New York's Business Improvement Districts (BIDs) started off as coalitions of local merchants who were mostly concerned with picking up trash and herding the homeless into neighborhoods without BIDs.

Now fully established, BIDs have taken on cultural roles in their communities, sponsoring concerts and public art. Always eager to boost their 'hoods, a few now offer free summer tours, with some continuing throughout the year. Though there's always something new to learn about New York, don't expect to hear many critical words about the neighborhood or its friendly, hardworking BID.

The Alliance for Downtown New York `FREE`   Manhattan's non–Native American history began at the island's tip and the area still holds a wealth of history. The Alliance shows it all off with the Wall Street Walking Tour, every Thursday and Saturday at noon. Wander past icons like the New York Stock Exchange, Trinity Church, and Federal Hall. Tours meet on the steps of the National Museum of the American Indian at 1 Bowling Green. Tours last about 1½ hours; reservations not required.

 ℂ **212/606-4064.** www.downtownny.com. Thurs and Sat noon, rain or shine. 4/5 to Bowling Green; 1 to South Ferry.

8th Street Walking Tour `FREE`   Eighth Street, and its East Village equivalent St. Marks Place, are among the city's most colorful commercial strips. Get the inside dirt on the area courtesy of the Village Alliance. Tours meet on the northwest corner of Second Avenue and St. Marks.

 ℂ **212/777-2173.** www.villagealliance.org. Select Sat 11:30am, mid-May to mid-Oct. N/R/W to 8th St.; 6 to Astor Place.

 Grand Central Partnership `FREE`   Grand Central Terminal (not station—train lines end here) is as inspiring as public buildings get. A $175-million restoration has this 1913 Beaux Arts masterpiece looking better than ever. The full story of the building's architecture and history is recounted on a 90-minute tour that leaves from 120 Park Avenue, right across 42nd Street.

 ℂ **212/883-2420.** www.grandcentralpartnership.org. Fri 12:30pm. 4/5/6/7/S to 42nd St./Grand Central.

Orchard Street Bargain District Tour `FREE`   The Lower East Side is a bottomless well of history and lore, a modern-day Byzantium in the words of novelist Richard Price. This tour focuses on the local commercial history. The first NYC district dedicated to discount retail, for decades the Jewish Lower East Side was the only place around where you could shop on Sundays. Fittingly, that's the day this tour runs, meeting at 11am in front of Katz's.

Meet up with the guide in front of Katz's Delicatessen, 205 E. Houston St., at Ludlo
© **866/224-0206** or 212/226-9010. www.lowereastsideny.com. Apr–Dec Sun 11am
rain or shine. Subway: F/M to Second Ave.

Times Square Exposé `FREE`   No one familiar with the seedy Times Square of legend would recognize the lounge chair scene that's there today. No doubt some character has been sacrificed, but at least we've got the tourists concentrated in a single location (and one that lets them feel right at home at that). The local BID shows its pride in its spruced-up streets every Friday at noon, touring past historic theaters and the ultra-modern new additions to this storied nabe.

1560 Seventh Ave., btw. 46th and 47th sts. © **212/768-1560.** www.timessquarenyc. org. Fri noon, rain or shine. Subway: N/Q/R to 49th St.; 1/2/3/7/N/Q/R/S to 42nd St./ Times Sq.

Union Square: Crossroads of New York Walking Tour `FREE`   The park here opened in 1831, about the same time New York's wealthy reached this elevation on their inexorable climb uptown. The elegant neighborhood they created was soon steeped in culture, with an influx of theaters and concert halls. By World War I, though, the moneyed set had moved on and the area was in decline, except for Union Square itself, which remained a popular location for labor rallies and protests. Learn all about the neighborhood's history every Saturday afternoon at 2pm with the help of Big Onion Walking Tours. Meet at the Lincoln statue on the northern end of the park.

16th St. traverse, Union Sq. © **212/517-1826.** www.unionsquarenyc.org. Sat 2pm. Subway: L/N/Q/R/4/5/6 to 14th St./Union Sq.

INDEPENDENT TOURS

Battery Park City `FREE`   Battery Park is justifiably proud of its beautiful landscaped grounds. With the parks restored to pre-9/11 showroom condition, the area is eager to show itself off. On select weekend days in the warmer months, you can catch a public art tour that surveys the mixed bag of installations down here. There are also twilight nature walks and horticultural tours. Check the website for exact times and hours.

© **212/267-9700.** www.bpcparks.org. Subway: 1 to Rector St.; 4/5 to Bowling Green.

Big Apple Greeter `FREE`   These New York boosters roll out the red carpet in an attempt to make their own enthusiasm for the city infectious. Visitors to our city can pick any neighborhood they like, and

find a knowledgeable volunteer to tour them around
. FINE PRINT Reservations should be made 3 or 4 weeks
. www.bigapplegreeter.org.

A Broader View: The African Presence in Early New York FREE   Africans, both free and enslaved, had a big role in the development of
New York City. This Ranger-led tour will tell you all about it, as you
walk from Federal Hall to the African Burial Ground National Monument Memorial. Tours run Tuesdays and Thursdays at 10am; reservations are required. Plan on about 90 minutes (note that tours are
suspended during the winter months).

Federal Hall, 26 Wall St., at Nassau St. ✆ **212/637-2019.** www.nps.gov/afbg. Tues,
Thurs 10am. Subway: 2/3 or 4/5 to Wall St.; J/Z to Broad St.

Brooklyn Brewery FREE   More of a lecture than a tour, this popular
weekend event entails a visit to a room full of silver beer vats followed
by a trip to the company store. Although the complimentary drink
tokens have gone the way of Prohibition, there are tempting discounts
when you buy your pints in bulk ($20 will get you a half dozen). Tours
run Saturdays on the hour between 1 and 5pm, Sundays until 4pm.
Doors open at noon. Friday nights you can enjoy the same beer discounts (pizza delivery is encouraged) starting at 6pm.

79 N. 11th St., btw. Wyeth and Levit sts. ✆ **718/486-7422.** www.brooklynbrewery.
com. Subway: L to Bedford Ave.

Burn Some Dust FREE   These walks are for serious trekkers: Most
cover more than 20 miles. The terrain is diverse, covering scenic
highlights of all five boroughs. Recent trips have covered lesser-
known destinations like the south shore of Staten Island, Morrisania,
Prohibition Park, and Todt Hill.

www.burnsomedust.com.

Central Park Conservancy Walking Tours FREE   Central Park's rich
history and hidden nuggets are explored in these 60- to 90-minute
walks. Themes range from landscaping to Revolutionary War sites to
the rugged Ramble. Check the website because times, dates, and
locations vary. The tours run frequently (some 10 times a week), year
round, in most any weather. Look out for the Conservatory Garden
tours, which take you through Manhattan's most beautiful garden.

✆ **212/360-2726.** www.centralparknyc.org.

City Hall `FREE` When City Hall was finished in 1812, the builders didn't bother with marble and granite in the back, thinking cheaper sandstone would be good enough for a side that would forever face a bunch of hills and trees. Though the city experienced a little bit of subsequent expansion, this small-scale building still houses offices of the mayor and city council. The underpublicized guided tour here takes you through a graceful rotunda and up to the Governor's Room, which has a priceless collection of portraits as well as a desk that was used by George Washington.

Broadway at Murray St. ℂ **212/788-2170.** www.nyc.gov/html/artcom/html/tours/ tours.shtml. Reserve in advance for tours Thurs 10am (group tours are available Mon–Wed and Fri at 10am). Without reservations, Wed at noon, sign in at the tourist kiosk in City Hall Park on the east side of Broadway at Barclay St. (tour limited to 20 people). Subway: R to City Hall; 4/5/6 to Brooklyn Bridge–City Hall; J/Z to Chambers St.; 2/3 to Park Place.

Destination: El Barrio `FREE` East Harlem is always prime for some demystification, at least for most New Yorkers. This tour covers the vibrant streets that surround El Museo del Barrio, which co-sponsors with the local tourism board. The walks are free. Meet at the southeast corner of Fifth Avenue and 104th Street. Walks run from 3 to 5pm on Saturdays between mid-April and October.

1230 Fifth Ave., at 104th St. ℂ **212/831-7272.** www.elmuseo.org. Sat 3pm. Subway: 6 to 103rd St.

Downtown: Where New York Began George Washington took the first presidential oath of office in lower Manhattan, and for more than three years this area was the capital of the fledgling United States. A ton of historic properties remain, and you can get expert insight into them courtesy of the Municipal Art Society. Meet at the Downtown Information Center every Tuesday at 12:30pm (there's a suggested donation of $10). `FINE PRINT` Adults should bring photo ID.

55 Exchange Place, btw. Broad and Williams sts. ℂ **212/935-3960.** www.mas.org. Tues 12:30pm. Subway: J/Z to Broad St.; 2/3 or 4/5 to Wall St.

Evergreens Cemetery Tour `FREE` This boneyard on the Brooklyn/ Queens border seems to stretch forever. As the final resting place for over half a million people, it's a good thing there's ample space (225 acres to be exact). Rolling hills and vegetation galore make a lush contrast to the city. Guided walking tours of this historic site are held on select Saturdays at 11am, covering fascinating stories, like that of the businessman who moved into his late wife's mausoleum and spent the last decade of his life chatting and reading to her. Call or check online for a schedule.

1629 Bushwick Ave., at Conway St., Brooklyn. ℂ **718/455-5300.** www.theevergreens cemetery.com. Tours assemble at the main entrance, Bushwick Ave. and Conway St. Subway: A/C/J/L/Z to Broadway Junction.

Grand Central Terminal   On Wednesdays at half past noon, the Municipal Art Society, which helped save this commuter temple, offers an hour and a half long walking tour. They ask for a $10 donation, but there's no formal fee, just whatever you care to contribute. Meet at the information booth in the middle of the concourse, amid half an acre of gleaming Tennessee marble.

ℂ **212/453-0050.** www.mas.org. Wed 12:30pm. 4/5/6/7/S to 42nd St./Grand Central.

Hudson River Park `FREE`   Friends of Hudson River Park put on these waterfront walking tours, which highlight the area's rich history, from Lenape locals to the landfill construction of the Gansevoort Peninsula to the role the piers played in the *Titanic* tragedy. Tours run once a month from Pier 40. Call ahead for reservations.

Pier 40, Houston St. at the Hudson. ℂ **212/757-0981.** www.fohrp.org. Subway: 1 to Houston St.

Prospect Park Discover Nature Tours `FREE`   My favorite tour here leads into the wilds of Brooklyn, where you can see a newly rehabbed ravine, waterfalls, and Brooklyn's last forest. It's just like the Adirondacks—only with less driving, and better proximity to ethnic food when it's over. Tours run on the weekends and Monday holidays at 3pm, March through November. Meet at the Audubon Center (at the Boathouse), just inside the Lincoln Road/Ocean Avenue entrance. Check the website for other tour destinations, like the Lefferts Historic House and Green-Wood Cemetery.

ℂ **718/287-3400.** www.prospectpark.org. Subway: B/Q/S to Prospect Park.

Shorewalkers   Shorewalkers sure know how to hoof it. This environmental walking group makes some huge treks around the city, usually keeping close to water. `FINE PRINT` Walks are free for members ($20 annual fee); donations are requested from visitors. Dates, times, and locations vary; call or check the website for specifics.

ℂ **212/330-7686.** www.shorewalkers.org.

Stephen A. Schwarzman Building (Humanities and . **Library)** FREE   This 1911 Beaux Arts icon is compe~~~~ from the outside, with its iconic stairs, and twin lion sentrie~~~~ and Patience). The hushed interior is even more impressive~~~~ ~~~~di-tion to free exhibits (p. 114), the library shows itself off with daily guided tours. Tours meet Monday through Saturday at 11am and again at 2pm beside the information desk in Astor Hall; the Sunday tour is at 2pm only. When there's an exhibit mounted at Gottesman Hall, you can get a separate tour. Meet Tuesday through Saturday at 12:30 and 2:30pm, and also on Sunday at 3:30pm, at the entrance to the hall.

Fifth Ave., at 42nd St. *C* **212/869-8089** exhibits and events, or 212/661-7220 for library hours. www.nypl.org. Subway: B/D/F to 42nd St.; 7 to Fifth Ave.; 4/5/6/S to Grand Central.

Take a Walk, New York! FREE   The Listen to your Heart Campaign endeavors to slow the widening of New York waists through a series of guided urban walks. The walks are scheduled for weekends in all five boroughs and last 2 to 3 hours. Go fight the good fight against cardiovascular disease! Check online for current schedules.

C **212/228-3126.** www.walkny.org.

Tweed Courthouse FREE   Boss Tweed used this eponymous struc-ture to fleece the city for millions (Tammany cohort Andrew Garvey, the "prince of plasterers," made a cool $133,187 for just 2 days' work). Recently renovated, the building is a fascinating melding of architectural styles, with elaborate arches and brickwork. An octago-nal skylight lets the sun pour in on the endless conferences conducted by the current tenant, the Board of Ed.

52 Chambers St., btw. Centre St. and Broadway. *C* **212/788-2170.** www.nyc.gov/html/artcom/html/tours/tours.shtml. Reserve in advance for tours Fri noon (group tours Tues at 10am). Subway: R to City Hall; 4/5/6 to Brooklyn Bridge–City Hall; J/Z to Chambers St.; 2/3 to Park Place.

Urban Trail Conference FREE   A diverse selection of sites, from downtown Manhattan to the PepsiCo sculpture gardens in Purchase, New York, are toured by these intrepid trekkers. They ask for a $3 donation from nonmembers (a few events cost a little more), although first-timers get to walk for free. Big spenders can get a year's worth of activity by springing for the club's $10 annual dues.

Phone numbers vary by tour guide. www.urbantrail.org.

5 Green Peace: Gardens

It's just not healthy for humans to go too long without a break from the concrete jungle. New York has some great parks, but the space tends to be pretty cultivated. Our community gardens are nice, too, but they're small and usually don't let the public in for more than a couple of hours a week. Botanical gardens are the best way to inhale fresh country air, and they're closer than you might think. Time your visit right, and they're also completely free.

FREE Clang, Clang, Clang Went the Cultural Trolleys

When it comes to hyping NYC's attractions, the Bronx and Brooklyn can understandably feel shorted by Manhattan. That's why God created **cultural trolleys.**

For a loop around Prospect Park, look no further than **The HOB Connection** (✆ **718/638-7700;** www.heartofbrooklyn.org). On select weekend and holiday afternoons, the Heart of Brooklyn Trolley will get you from the Brooklyn Museum all the way south around Prospect Lake, and back up again. You can also connect First Saturday action at the Brooklyn Museum (p. 99) with local shops, bars, and restaurants via the HOB.

The Bronx has no trolley envy, offering two ways for visitors to get around Jonas Bronck's old stamping grounds. On the first Wednesday night of every month (except Jan and Sept), the **Bronx Culture Trolley** (✆ **718/931-9500,** ext. 33; www.bronxarts.org) whisks visitors around to free art, music, theater, and poetry readings. Free wine and snacks are even offered at the starting point, the Longwood Art Gallery at Hostos Community College, 450 Grand Concourse, at 149th Street. Advance reservations are recommended.

On the first Friday night of every month, City Island shows itself off with its **Bronx Seaside Trolley Program** (✆ **718/885-3090;** www.cityislandchamber.org), which connects the 6 train at Pelham Bay Park with local galleries, shops, and the Bartow-Pell Mansion Museum.

All of these outer borough trolley rides are free—take that, Manhattan.

Brooklyn Botanic Garden Fifty-two acres of cherry trees, roses, formal gardens, and ponds in the heart of Brooklyn is nothing short of a miracle. This is the city's most popular botanic garden and it's spectacular almost year-round. April to early May are particularly worth noting, with the tulips poking out and the blossoms rioting. Don't miss the Fragrance Garden, designed for the blind, and one of the world's largest collections of bonsai. Free tours run on the weekends at 1pm with no reservations necessary, leaving from the Visitor Center. When the cherry blossoms are out, there are also free tours as part of the Hanami celebration. Regular admission is $8, but Tuesdays are free, as are Saturday mornings from 10am to noon. In winter, you can add Tuesday through Friday to the free list (mid-Nov to late Feb).

1000 Washington Ave., at Eastern Pkwy., Brooklyn. ℂ **718/623-7200.** www.bbg. org. Tues–Fri 8am–6pm; Sat–Sun 10am–6pm; closes at 4:30pm Nov to mid-March. Open holiday Mondays, except Labor Day. Subway: 2/3 to Eastern Pkwy./Brooklyn Museum; B/Q to Prospect Park; S to Botanic Garden.

New York Botanical Garden Visions of the Bronx don't conjure up uncut forests, rhododendron valleys, waterfalls, ponds, and wetlands. As unlikely as it may seem, though, for over a century the Bronx has been home to one of America's premier public gardens. With over 250 acres of rolling

---

FREE **Close Encounters**

One of Manhattan's leafiest oases lies in Chelsea, on the campus of the **General Theological Seminary.** The Close, the campus's grounds, are a tranquil patch in the middle of an already-quaint stretch of 1850's row houses. The Seminary's buildings date to the late 19th century, constructed in the English collegiate-Gothic style. Wander the wisteria-choked grounds and you may feel like you've stepped through a wormhole straight onto the campus of a British university. Jack Kerouac and Allen Ginsberg used to stroll here; Kerouac lived across the street in 1951, where he typed his third draft of *On the Road*. Chelsea Square, enter at 440 W. 21st St., btw. Ninth and Tenth aves. (press the buzzer and register to your left, leaving ID). ℂ **212/243-5150.** www.gts.edu. Sept–May, Mon–Sat 10am–3pm; June–Aug, until 5pm; shorter hours when school is out of session; closed for inclement weather and during exam and commencement periods. C/E to 23rd Street.

FREE Parking It

Parks are among the city's best freebies, and we're fortunate to be in an era of expansion. Some 550 acres (!) of new parkland have opened up along the **piers near Chelsea.** The city did a gorgeous job with these urban beaches, including planting some actual slender-leaved vegetation called "grass." Across town, restoration continues on the **East River Park.** When it's finally completed, epic Brooklyn views will complement benches, ball fields, and a wide jogging path. Everyone knows about the great Manhattan views from the **Brooklyn Promenade,** but Queens has an equally impressive skyline vantage that many New Yorkers have never seen. The **Gantry Plaza State Park** in Long Island City is fitted out with piers that jut out over the East River, facing the U.N. and Empire State Building standing tall among Midtown's architectural jumble. My favorite city spot for breathing country air is actually **Green-Wood Cemetery** (© **718/768-7300;** www. green-wood.com), on the south side of Park Slope. On top of landscaped hills, venerable trees, glacial ponds, celebrity graves, and Revolutionary War history, your (free) price of admission also entitles you to the surreal sight of flocks of wild monk parrots, which have infiltrated the intricate Civil War–era front gate and surrounding grounds.

hills and landscaped gardens, if it's flora you can probably find it. Admission to the grounds is $6 ($20 gets you a tram tour and the run of everything), but all day Wednesday and Saturday morning from 10am to noon you can get into the grounds for free.

200th St. and Southern Blvd., the Bronx. © **718/817-8700.** www.nybg.org. Tues–Sun and Mon holidays 10am–6pm. Closes 5pm mid-Jan through Feb. Metro North (© 800/ METRO-INFO [638-7646] or 212/532-4900; www.mta.nyc.ny.us/mnr) runs from Grand Central Terminal to the New York Botanical Garden station; it's a 20-min ride. Subway: B/D/4 to Bedford Park, walk southeast on Bedford Park Blvd. 8 blocks.

Queens Botanical Garden   This little-known park is an oasis in the heart of busy Flushing. Formal gardens are joined by a 21-acre arboretum, plus rose, bee, and Victorian gardens. A gorgeous new visitor center, complete with environmentally friendly technology, opened in

2007. Spring is the natural time to visit—the entire garden is awash with color. Admission is just $4, and that's waived from November through March. During the warmer months, entry is free from 3 to 6pm Wednesdays and 4 to 6pm Sundays.

43–50 Main St., at Dahlia St., Flushing, Queens. ✆ **718/886-3800.** www.queens botanical.org. Nov–Mar Tues–Sun 8am–4:30pm; Apr–Oct Tues–Fri 8am–6pm, Sat–Sun 8am–6pm. Subway: 7 to Main St. Flushing.

Wave Hill   Some of the city's most gorgeous acreage can be found in Riverdale, in the Bronx, where Wave Hill's breathtaking views take in the panorama of the Hudson and the Palisades. Thousands of plant species are spread across the 28 acres here, originally the grounds of a private estate. The plant curious can educate themselves in the carefully labeled herb and flower gardens. Horticultural, environmental, and forestry programs provide further edification. Regular admission is $8, but the grounds are free from 9am to noon on Tuesdays (May–June and Sept–Oct) and Saturdays. In the off-peak months (Nov–Apr, July, and Aug), it's free all day on Tuesday.

675 W. 252nd St., at Independence Ave., the Bronx. ✆ **718/549-3200.** www.wavehill. org. Mid-Apr to mid-Oct Tues–Sun 9am–5:30pm; Mid-Oct to mid-Apr closes at 4:30. Subway: 1 to 242nd St., where you can pick up the free Wave Hill shuttle. Metro North (✆ 212/532-4900) from Grand Central to the Riverdale station; from there, it's a pleasant 5-block walk to Wave Hill, or take the Wave Hill shuttle.

6 Zoo York

New York has plenty of fauna to go with its flora, though it isn't always cheap to check out. The minizoos in the major Brooklyn, Queens, and Manhattan parks charge $7 to $10 and the Bronx Zoo asks for $15. Fortunately, there are alternatives. The Bronx has a pay what you wish policy 1 day a week, and the city's parks are rich with other opportunities for getting close to critters.

Bronx Zoo Wildlife Conservation Park   Yankee Stadium isn't the only place in the Bronx where you can find thousands of animals running wild in their natural habitat. The Bronx Zoo is the largest city zoo in the country, and one of New York's greatest assets. Gibbons, snow leopards, red pandas, Western lowland gorillas, okapi, and red river hogs are just a few of the famous residents. With 265 acres to explore, it's easy to wander away a full day here. For summer visits, try to get

FREE A Midnight Elephant Walk

When the pachyderms visit the big town, they're coming off their Nassau Coliseum stand. Their train only gets them as far as the Long Island City yards. They can't exactly get a lift to the gig from a towncar, so they have to hoof it, through the Queens-Midtown Tunnel and down the streets of Manhattan. Watching the elephants emerge from the tunnel is an amazing spectacle. They walk in a file of trunks holding tails, with clown escorts all around. Often other hoofed beasts like zebras and camels come along for the stroll. The walk goes all the way to the elephants' five-story ramp at Madison Square Garden, but the best scene is at the tunnel entrance around 37th Street between Second and Third aves. The crowd is fun-loving, with the freaks that events in Manhattan invariably bring out well-represented. The procession hits Manhattan around midnight. Whether you come for the spectacle or just to hiss the exploitation of animals, be sure to be on time because the whole thing goes surprisingly quickly. The elephant walk takes place at the beginning of the circus' annual stand (usually late Mar); check the weekly update on the website for the exact date and time. ℂ **212/465-6741.** www.ringling.com. Subway: 6 to 33rd. St.; A/C/E or 1/2/3 to 34th St.

here early or late, as the midday heat often finds the animals sleepy in their enclosures. Admission is $15, but Wednesdays are on a contribution basis (the suggested admission is the full price, but it's pay what you wish). Additional charges ($3 or so) will apply for some exhibits.

185th St. and Southern Blvd. ℂ **718/367-1010.** www.bronxzoo.com. Nov–Mar daily 10am–4:30pm (extended hours for Holiday Lights late Nov to early Jan); Apr–Oct Mon–Fri 10am–5pm, Sat–Sun 10am–5:30pm. Subway: 2/5 to E. Tremont Ave./West Farms Sq., 2 to Pelham Pkwy. Also Metro North to Fordham Rd. (then Bx9 bus) and the BxM11 express bus.

FREE BIRDS

A dearth of rest stops on the Eastern Seaboard makes New York parks essential for avian travelers. For better boning up on our most welcome tourists, you can borrow equipment from three of our most accessible parks.

Battery Park City FREE   Eighty different bird species pass through the lush tip of Manhattan. At the Wagner Park pavilions binoculars and field guides are loaned out for free on select dates. You can learn more with an experienced birder or naturalist on summer Saturdays at 11am.

☎ **212/267-9700.** www.bpcparks.org. Subway: 1 to Rector St.; 4/5 to Bowling Green.

Bryant Park FREE   This green patch in the city's center attracts not only vegetation-craving wage slaves, but a cross-section of Northeast Seaboard birds. Birding tours co-sponsored by the New York City Audubon Society begin at Heiskell Plaza, near the Sixth Avenue and 42nd Street entrance. Mondays from 8 to 9am and Thursdays from 5 to 6pm in April and May. Meet the Birds at Le Carrousel provides a less mundane avian crew. Every Tuesday from April to September between 11:30am and 2pm, you can interact with rescued parakeets, lovebirds, and other exotic fliers from the Arcadia Bird Sanctuary and Education Center.

☎ **212/768-4242.** www.bryantpark.org. Subway: B/D/F to 42nd St.; 7 to Fifth Ave.

Central Park FREE   Birdsong fills the thickets of the Ramble, an unexpectedly rural stretch of the park. You can take a closer

> FREE 🐾 **See Spot Run**
>
> Being trapped in small, dark apartments is just as hard on dogs as it is on us. Fortunately for dogs, they have a release valve in the form of dog runs. The human and canine interactions make great free public theater. The **Tompkins Square** dog run, the city's first, is my favorite. Both the four-legged and two-legged regulars have a ton of character, and their friendships and rivalries are fascinating to observe. Don't miss the creative costumes of the **Dog Run Halloween Parade,** a 20-year tradition held at noon on the Sunday before Halloween. Tompkins Sq. Park, btw. 7th and 10th sts. and aves. A and B. www.dogster.org. Subway: 6 to Astor Place; F/M to Second Ave.

look at the warbling set with a kit (a backpack with binoculars, reference materials, and a map) available from the Belvedere Castle. The kits are available Tuesday to Sunday from 10am to 4:30pm. Two pieces of ID are required. Call ahead for reservations.

Midpark at 79th St. ☎ **212/772-0210.** www.centralparknyc.org. Subway: B/C to 81st St.

Falconry Extravaganza FREE   The falcon has landed: One day a year the birds of prey uncloak in Central Park. All manner of raptors swoop through the air above the East Meadow under the close supervision of the Urban Park Rangers. Meet at the East Meadow on the east side of the park at 97th Street. Leave the Chihuahuas at home.

℃ **212/628-2345.** www.nycgovparks.org. One Sat in Oct 1–3pm. Subway: 6 to 96th St.

Prospect Park FREE   During spring's annual northward migration, hundreds of different bird species pass through here. To get some expert assistance in figuring out what's what, hook up with an introductory bird-watching tour (Sat noon–1:30pm.) To catch the worm-getting birds, you'll have to get up earlier. On the first Sunday of every month, join the Early Bird Walk as it ambles through the park from 8 to 10am. It's free, but you should call in advance to register. All tours leave from the boathouse, just inside the Lincoln Road/Ocean Avenue entrance.

℃ **718/287-3400.** www.prospectpark.org. Subway: B/Q/S to Prospect Park.

GO FISH

It's a fine line between standing along the shore like an idiot with a stick in your hands and going fishing, but kids love baiting up and casting in anyway. The city offers a few spots for gathering fodder for "the one that got away" tales.

Battery Park City FREE   Drop a line in the Hudson and see if you can pull up any three-eyed specimens. (Actually, the river's been mending remarkably in recent years, thanks to antipollution measures.) Bait and equipment are loaned out in Wagner Park. Sessions run from 10am to 2pm on select Saturdays.

℃ **212/267-9700.** www.bpcparks.org. Subway: 1 to Rector St.; 4/5 to Bowling Green.

Central Park FREE   Like the good New Yorkers they are, some 50,000 fish pack uncomplainingly into the confines of the Harlem Meer. You can try your hand at catching a bass, catfish, or bluegill with equipment loaned by the Charles A. Dana Discovery Center. Bait, pole, and instructions are provided. Fish can be fondled, but they're not to be kept: It's catch and release. Open Tuesday to Sunday 10am to 4pm (last pole goes out at 3pm), mid-April to mid-October. Valid photo ID is required.

Inside Central Park at 110th St., btw. Fifth and Lenox aves. ℃ **212/860-1370.** www. centralparknyc.org. Subway: 2/3 to Central Park North.

Hudson River Park FREE   There's no dilemma whether to fish or cut bait here, as the Big City Fishing program takes care of the latter for you. Experienced anglers are on hand to offer advice, and the rods are free to borrow. Reel fun can be found at piers 46 (Greenwich Village), and 84 (Midtown West). Don't get too attached to your oyster toadfishes, flukes, or cunners, however, because everything is catch and release. Available 10:30am to 5pm on summer weekends, weather permitting.

Pier 46, the Hudson just north of Christopher St. © **212/627-2020.** www.hudson riverpark.org. Subway: 1 to Christopher St. *Pier 84*, the Hudson at W. 44th St. Subway: A/C/E/7 to 42nd St./Port Authority.

New Yorkers focus their energy before punching the clock with a free morning tai chi class at Bryant Park. See p. 179 for details.

LOCAL LIVING

Anybody who thinks it's easy to live in New York is sitting on an ungodly mountain of cash. You don't have to look any further than the housing market to find trouble. For the privilege of paying $1,800 a month to live in a noisy veal pen, chances are you'll be hit with a 15% broker's fee. Health care, health insurance, health clubs—just about everything can come with an outrageous price tag. Yet eight million of us stay. The experience of being a New Yorker is too exciting and rich for us to complain long or loudly about the costs of living. We'd much rather talk about which neighborhood our apartment is located. Besides, the city presents plenty of free and cheap opportunities to improve your quality of life, from classes and lectures to grooming and recreation. Leases notwithstanding, it is quite possible to live large on small budgets in NYC.

1 Sense for Cents: Education

LECTURES & SEMINARS

Just walking the streets and riding the subways is all too often a learning experience in New York, but most of us have room for further development along less informal lines. A handful of classes and a nearly endless selection of lectures provide New Yorkers with educational opportunities left and right. Cooper Union looks the other way when it comes to tuition, and although other local institutions aren't quite so generous, most have programs open to the public for little or no charge.

Access Restricted: Law & Representation `FREE` New York's glorious legal bastions are sadly invisible to the civilian class, at least as long as we walk the line. Finding an excuse to open glam council chambers, courts, and law firm conference rooms, the Lower Manhattan Cultural Council sponsors this series of free legal lectures. Not all of it is dry, either—one recent seminar delved into "The Law of Violence in *No Country for Old Men*." The lectures are free but space is limited, so make a reservation first.

Lower Manhattan Cultural Council, various locations. ✆ **212/219-2058.** www.lmcc.net.

Battery Park City `FREE` In addition to giving us gorgeous open space, landscaping, and music aplenty, Battery Park also helps boost our eye-hand coordination. Three separate drawing classes are offered in the summer. Elements of Nature Drawing (Wed 11:30am–1:30pm), Drawing in the Park (Sat, except in Aug, 10am–noon), and Figure al Fresco (Wed 2:30–4:30pm), are all led by a bona fide artist. (Alas, the figure in Figure al Fresco is clothed.) See below for the eye-hand coordination covered by tai chi. Check the website for exact locations.

Battery Park City, along South End Ave., just west of West St. ✆ **212/267-9700.** www.bpcparks.org. Subway: 1/2/3 or A/C to Chambers St.; 1 to Rector St. or South Ferry; 4/5 to Bowling Green.

BMCC Tribeca Performing Arts Center FREE This not-for-profit space brings in an international array of jazz and pop performers. The concerts have standard ticket charges, but you can catch additional edification courtesy of the PAC's free humanities programs, which often run before shows. Documentary film footage and panel discussions (or Q&As) are the primary offerings; check the website for schedules.

199 Chambers St., btw. Greenwich St. and the West Side Hwy. © **212/509-0300.** www.tribecapac.org. Subway: 1/2/3 or A/C to Chambers St.

Columbia University FREE New York City's lone envoy to the Ivy League has an impressive events calendar, with talks and colloquiums supplementing literary readings and musical performances. Topics range from esoteric science ("Vitrification and Depletion Phenomena in Soft Colloidal Systems") to less dry material ("The Place of Ozu within Japanese Film History"). Venues vary, although Lerner Hall is a popular location, 2922 Broadway, at 115th Street. To get smarter in a less academic clime, check out the lectures in the Cafés Columbia series. Four categories of study (arts, humanities, science, and social science) rotate through the PicNic Market & Café (© **212/222-8222;** www.picnicmarket.com) every Monday night from 6 to 7pm. There's a $10 cover, but it includes a drink (you can stick around for a $25 prix fixe dinner).

Main Campus, 2690 Broadway, entrance at 116th St. © **212/854-9724.** www.columbia.edu. Subway: 1 to 116th St.

Cooper Union FREE Self-made entrepreneur and inventor Peter Cooper founded the Cooper Union for the Advancement of Science and Art in 1857 to allow underprivileged talents to receive free educations. The college's mission hasn't changed, and 1,000 students currently attend without tuition. Admission is based solely on merit, and competition is, as you'd expect, fierce. The public can take advantage of the institution in other ways, however. The Saturday Outreach Program (www.saturdayoutreach.org) helps high school students further themselves in the arts with free classes (even the materials fee is waived). Student exhibitions can be seen in free galleries, and free lectures are held in the Great Hall. Check online for an events calendar.

Cooper Sq., 8th St., btw. Bowery and Third Ave. © **212/353-4120.** www.cooper.edu. Subway: 6 to Astor Place; N/Q/R to 8th St.

DOWNTOWN LIVING

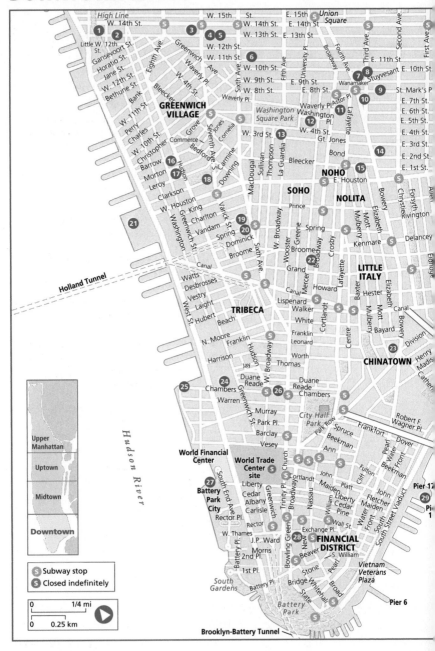

Subway stop

Closed indefinitely

Upper Manhattan

Uptown

Midtown

Downtown

Hudson River

Holland Tunnel

GREENWICH VILLAGE

Washington Square Park

NOHO

SOHO

NOLITA

LITTLE ITALY

TRIBECA

CHINATOWN

World Financial Center

World Trade Center site

Battery Park City

FINANCIAL DISTRICT

Vietnam Veterans Plaza

South Gardens

Battery Park

Brooklyn-Battery Tunnel

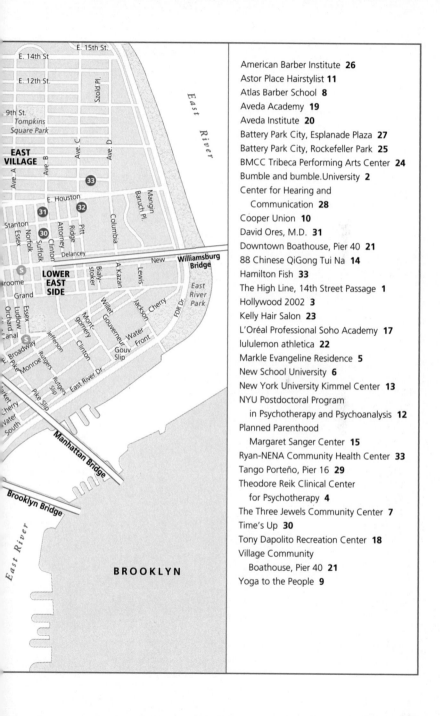

MIDTOWN LIVING

UPTOWN LIVING

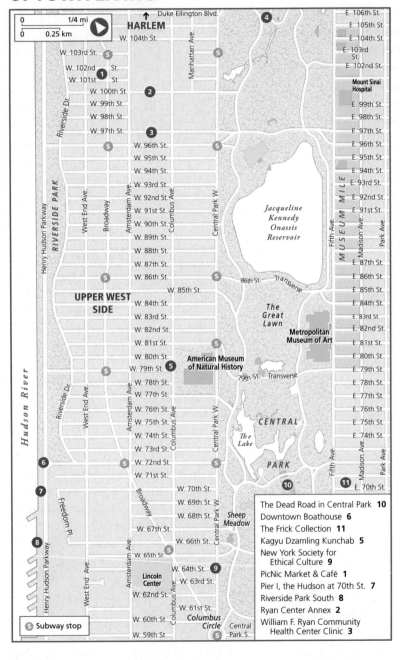

HARLEM

Duke Ellington Blvd.

W. 104th St.

W. 103rd St. Ⓢ

W. 102nd St. ①

W. 101st St.

W. 100th St.

W. 99th St. ②

W. 98th St.

W. 97th St. ③

W. 96th St. Ⓢ

W. 95th St.

W. 94th St.

W. 93rd St.

W. 92nd St.

W. 91st St.

W. 90th St.

W. 89th St.

W. 88th St.

W. 87th St.

W. 86th St. Ⓢ

UPPER WEST SIDE

W. 85th St.

W. 84th St.

W. 83rd St.

W. 82nd St.

W. 81st St. Ⓢ

W. 80th St.

W. 79th St. Ⓢ ⑤

American Museum of Natural History

W. 78th St.

W. 77th St.

W. 76th St.

W. 75th St.

W. 74th St.

W. 73rd St.

W. 72nd St. Ⓢ

W. 71st St.

W. 70th St.

W. 69th St.

W. 68th St.

W. 67th St.

W. 66th St.

W. 65th St. Ⓢ

W. 64th St. ⑨

Lincoln Center

W. 63rd St.

W. 62nd St.

W. 61st St.

Columbus Circle

W. 60th St.

W. 59th St.

Riverside Dr.

West End Ave.

Broadway

Amsterdam Ave.

Columbus Ave.

Central Park W.

Manhattan Ave.

Henry Hudson Parkway

RIVERSIDE PARK

Freedom Pl.

Hudson River

Jacqueline Kennedy Onassis Reservoir

MUSEUM MILE

Fifth Ave.

Madison Ave.

Park Ave.

E. 106th St.
E. 105th St.
E. 104th St.
E. 103rd St.
E. 102nd St.

Mount Sinai Hospital

E. 99th St.
E. 98th St.
E. 97th St.
E. 96th St.
E. 95th St.
E. 94th St.
E. 93rd St.
E. 92nd St.
E. 91st St.

86th St. Transverse

E. 87th St.
E. 86th St.

The Great Lawn

E. 85th St.
E. 84th St.
E. 83rd St.
E. 82nd St.

Metropolitan Museum of Art

E. 81st St.
E. 80th St.
E. 79th St.

79th St. Transverse

E. 78th St.
E. 77th St.
E. 76th St.

CENTRAL

E. 75th St.

The Lake

E. 74th St.

PARK

⑩

⑪ E. 70th St.

Sheep Meadow

Columbus Circle

Central Park S.

Subway stop Ⓢ

①
②
③
④
⑤
⑥
⑦
⑧

0   1/4 mi
0   0.25 km

Downtown Boathouse `FREE` Every Wednesday night in summer, the boathouse offers kayaking classes free to the public. Most classes are held in the waters of Clinton Cove Park. Put your new knowledge to work by coming back to borrow a kayak (free; see "Watersports," on p. 176). Classes start at 6pm, during the warmer months (Apr–Oct).

Pier 96, West Side Hwy. at 56th St. ✆ **646/613-0375.** www.downtownboathouse. org. Subway: A/B/C/D/1 to 59th St./Columbus Circle.

Eglise Français du St-Esprit `FREE` The French Church of St. Esprit, an Episcopal congregation, performs its services in French. Before services, they offer a series of French classes, one for conversation, one for beginners, and a third for intermediate parleyers. The classes are free, at 10am every Sunday. Services start at 11:15am.

100 E. 60th St., btw. Madison and Park aves. ✆ **212/838-5680.** www.stespritnyc.net. Subway: 4/5/6 or N/Q/R to 59th St.; F to Lexington Ave./63rd St.

Etsy Labs `FREE` The virtual DIY marketplace that is Etsy holds down a real-world address in DUMBO. Inside the Etsy Labs you can take advantage of free craft fests every Monday night from 4 to 8pm. Bring your own project and borrow some equipment and supplies, or learn from an expert (teacups, hats, and finger puppets have been items of attention in recent sessions). The Church of Craft (www.churchof craft.org) holds free creativity services the first Sunday of the month from 2 to 6pm.

55 Washington St., Ste. 512, btw. Water and Front sts. ✆ **718/855-7955.** www.etsy. com. Subway: F to York St.

The Frick Collection `FREE` Inside the Gilded Age confines of this elegant art museum, you can catch Wednesday evening lectures. Subjects tend toward painterly subjects like Albrecht Dürer's hands and Goya's black paintings. A series on "Artists, Poets, and Writers" broadens the floor to include in-person luminaries like Frank Stella and analysis of immortals like Henry James. Lectures start at 6pm, with seating at 5:45pm. Don't arrive earlier than that, lest they have time to hit you up for the $18 admission fee.

1 E. 70th St., btw. Madison and Fifth aves. ✆ **212/288-0700.** www.frick.org. Subway: 6 to 68th St./Hunter College.

Gotham Writers' Workshop `FREE` The Microsoft of NYC's writing programs, Gotham churns out some 6,000 writers a year. You can

Where to Get Stuff Fixed (Or Fix Other People's Stuff)

One of the city's more random institutions is **Proteus Gowanus,** a gallery and reading room that also hosts the world's only Gowanus Canal museum. They have some great community programs, like a Wednesday night writing workshop ($5 suggested donation; $2 for a glass of wine), and **The Fixers Collective** (www.fixerscollective.org), which gathers Thursday nights from 6 to 9pm. Pooled intelligence and a smattering of expertise get applied to the likes of busted bikes, fans, clocks, and umbrellas. If it'll fit through the door, it's eligible for some fiddling (although a heads-up via the online Fix Sheet is a help). $5 donations are happily accepted. 543 Union St., down the alley off Nevins St. ✆ **718/234-1572.** www.proteus gowanus.com. Proteus Gowanus gallery open Thurs–Fri, 3–6pm; Sat–Sun, noon–6pm.

sample the goods free at frequent one-hour workshops. The events are held at the major bookstores around town (plus visits to Bryant Park), on topics like dialogue, travel writing, stand-up comedy, and Creative Writing 101.

Various locations. ✆ **212-WRITERS** [974-8377]. www.writingclasses.com.

The Graduate Center at the City University of New York FREE Continuing ed lectures, seminars, and panel discussions can be found here, with more possibilities for finding cheap smarts than any other institution in the city. You want range? Titles run from "Jewish Ethics Under Pressure" to "Unzipping the Monster Dick: Deconstructing Ableist Penile Representations in Two Ethnic Homoerotic Magazines." A program called Science & the Arts has particularly juicy material. Most events are free with seating on a first-come, first-served basis, although some require advance reservations. Also look for the free lunchtime concerts on Thursdays.

365 Fifth Ave., btw. 34th and 35th sts. ✆ **212/817-8215.** www.gc.cuny.edu. Subway: B/D/F/N/Q/R to 34th St./Herald Sq.; 6 to 33rd St.

The Henry George School FREE   Although Henry George is no longer a household name, in the 19th century his economics texts and lectures made him a major political player. His progressive ideas are still taught today, and in keeping with George's antiprivilege stance, the school that bears his name offers all of its programs for free.

Classes are available in English or Spanish, usually in the evenings. Teachings are based on George's championing of shifting tax burdens to landowners. *Note:* Finishing the school's Fundamental Economics course is the prerequisite for most upper-level work. Those interested in samples of the material can attend the Friday Evening Forum, a free lecture series held Fridays at 6:30pm. Film fans can do their learning via regular Saturday movie screenings, at 3pm.

121 E. 30th St., btw. Park and Lexington aves. © **212/889-8020.** www.henrygeorge school.org. Subway: 6 to 28th St.

The New School FREE   Though no longer so new (a 90th birthday celebration has recently passed), the New School stays pretty up-to-date, and there's still a progressive edge to its programs. The calendar of free events is cluttered with readings, lectures, panel discussions, student films, and even investing seminars. Events are open to the public, with some requiring advance reservation; check online for a full calendar.

66 W. 12th St., btw. Fifth and Sixth aves. © **212/229-5600.** www.newschool.edu. Subway: F/M to 14th St.; L/N/Q/R/4/5/6 to 14th St./Union Sq.

FREE Learning English As a Second Language

If you've read this far, you probably don't need English lessons. Should there be newly minted Americans in your circle of acquaintance, however, you can steer them to a couple of great city resources.

The **Riverside Language Program** assimilates people quickly through their intensive 6-week program. Open to permanent residents, classes run from 9:30am to 3:30pm, for levels from beginner to high intermediate. Riverside Church, 490 Riverside Dr., at 120th St. and Riverside (enter at 91 Claremont Ave.). © **212/662-3200.** www.river sidelanguage.org. Subway: 1 to 116th St.

For evening-only classes (and for people without permanent resident status), the **New York Public Library** has an extensive English program. Classes are conducted at some 20 different branch libraries, and also include civics lessons for prospective citizens. Check www. nypl.org for schedules, or call © **212/340-0918.**

New York Public Library `FREE`   It would be easier to list the classes not available for free at New York's public libraries than to mention all of the possibilities. Practical courses predominate, covering topics like writing, crafts, résumé updating, job searches, using the Internet, and the ins and outs of genealogical research. For a meta experience, you can also attend a self-directed class on how to take maximum advantage of library resources. The best way to get started is to get online and check out the options at your local branch.

For the Bronx, Manhattan, and Staten Island branches, log on to **www.nypl.org/branch**, or call ℂ **212/930-0800.** For the Queens Borough Public Library, check **www.queenslibrary.org**, or call ℂ **718/990-0700.** In Brooklyn, log on to **www.brooklynpubliclibrary.org**, or you can call ℂ **718/230-2100.**

Every branch of the New York Public Library offers computers with free Internet, access to electronic databases, and Microsoft Office applications. Many branches also have computers loaded with multimedia CD-ROMs. You can focus on SimCity or ResumeMaker, depending on your level of job market optimism.

New York Society for Ethical Culture `FREE`   For over a century and a quarter now, this organization has been providing New Yorkers with humanist alternatives to organized religion. A liberal outlook is usually presented in the free lectures that are held here, as well as at the regular talks on Sunday mornings. Log on to the website for exact schedules.

2 W. 64th St., at Central Park W. ℂ **212/874-5210.** www.nysec.org. Subway: 1/A/B/C/D/E to 59th St./Columbus Circle.

New York University `FREE`   The streets around Washington Square Park are dominated by NYU architecture and NYU students, but the community is invited to take advantage of this private university's immense resources. Lecture programs (the history of the Village, say), talks, and symposia can be found for free here. Other events carry nominal admission charges, in the $2 to $5 range. The new Kimmel Center is a good place to start for tracking down free culture.

Kimmel Center, 60 Washington Sq. S., btw. LaGuardia Place and Thompson St. ℂ **212/998-4900.** www.nyu.edu. Subway: A/B/C/D/E/F/M to W. 4th St./Washington Sq.

Park Slope Food Co-op `FREE`   This Brooklyn cooperative keeps its community informed with lectures, demonstrations, and even a few film screenings. Topics here are left-leaning, concerning food, the environment, and timely advice about how not to be killed by eating beef. Don't expect to see Karl Rove on the roster anytime soon. Everything is free, even to non-co-op members, although sometimes a small materials fee is added to food classes. Check online for the latest schedule. Classes and lectures are held on the second floor meeting room (which also hosts a periodic free clothes swap) unless otherwise noted.

782 Union St., btw. Sixth and Seventh aves., Park Slope, Brooklyn. ℭ **718/622-0560.** www.foodcoop.com. Subway: R to Union St.; 2/3 to Grand Army Plaza; B/Q to Seventh Ave.

Teachers and Writers Collaborative Literary readings and lectures fill the calendar at this long-running nonprofit. For high school students, there's also an excellent after-school program dedicated to the spoken word (www.urbanwordnyc.org). Check the website for upcoming events.

The Center for Imaginative Writing, 520 Eighth Ave., btw. 36th and 37th sts. ℭ **212/691-6590.** www.twc.org. Subway: A/C/E to 34th St./Penn Station.

FREE Getting Down to Business

The **Brooklyn Business Library** fosters the local small business scene with classes and workshops of an entrepreneurial bent. Everything from start-ups to small investing is covered by talks, and backed up with an excellent book collection. On Wednesday mornings from 10:15 to 11am you can get a free tour of the resources available. 280 Cadman Plaza W., btw. Tech Place and Tillary St. ℭ **718/623-7000.** www.biz.brooklynpublic library.org. Mon, Wed, Fri 10am–6pm; Tues 1–8pm; Thurs 1–6pm; Sat 10am–5pm. Subway: 2/3/4/5 to Borough Hall; R to Court St.; A/C/F to Jay St./Borough Hall.

TANGO & NO CASH

Central Park Tango FREE Under the Bard of Avon's watchful gaze, couples spin away Saturday nights here. Meet up at the south end of The Mall, right next to the Shakespeare statue. Tyros can take advantage of free classes, usually offered at 7:30pm. In inclement weather, dancers seek the shelter of the nearby Dairy. Otherwise it's alfresco under dusk skies, as they dance their ringlets to the whistling wind.

`FREE` Dancing Days

If you're getting married, or have some other compelling reason to be interested in learning to dance, look into **Dance Manhattan.** The Hustle and Carolina Shag are among the offerings. To get your feet wet for free, check out their monthly open houses. At 8pm, there's a lesson, half in ballroom and half in Latin. Lessons are followed by a party, and a performance after that. If you get hooked then and there, you'll be eligible for a discount on regular registration. 39 W. 19th St., 5th Floor, btw. Fifth and Sixth aves. © **212/807-0802.** www.dancemanhattan. com. Subway: N/Q/R or F/M to 23rd St.

If the wedding has already taken place and nature has run its course, you may have children that need entertaining. Battery Park City hosts a series of **Family Dances** on Fridays and Saturdays during the summer. This being New York, expect an international array of steps. West African, Swedish, and swing dancing are usually on the bill. Neither children nor experience with West African, Swedish, or swing dance moves is required. Battery Park City, along South End Ave., just west of West St. © **212/267-9700.** www.bpcparks.org. Subway: 1/2/3 or A/C to Chambers St.; 1 to Rector St. or South Ferry; 4/5 to Bowling Green.

If Battery Park's locale isn't idyllic enough for you, fox trot on up to **Riverside Park South** for sunset lessons. Summer Sundays provide the backdrop for a series of salsa, cha-cha, and bachata lessons taught by the **Piel Canela Dance & Music School.** There's some group steps, too, if you need a couple of bodies to hide behind—6 to 9pm. Pier 1, the Hudson at 70th St. © **212/408-0219.** www.nycgovparks.org. Subway: 1/2/3 to 72nd St.

Central Park, enter around 65th St. © **212/726-1111.** www.newyorktango.com. June–Sept, Sat 6pm–9pm. Subway: F to Lexington Ave./63rd St.; 6 to 68th St./Hunter College; 1 to 66th St./Lincoln Center.

Tango Porteño   Sultry summer nights are made for tangoing. On the Seaport piers, Tango Porteño hosts a Sunday night dance party with a great atmosphere. The East River rushes gently by, and the lights of downtown glitter overhead as couples make their angular dips and spins. Instead of a band there's a somewhat tinny sound system, but no one seems to mind. To cover pier rental costs, a $5 donation is requested. It takes two, but if you arrive alone, just watching can be entertainment enough. Free lessons are conducted at 8:30pm.

Pier 16 at the South St. Seaport, btw. the Ambrose and the Peking. In case of rain go to Pacific Grill restaurant, just to the north at Pier 17. ☎ **212/726-1111.** www.spiceevents.net/tango_cp_sssp.html. May–Oct, Sun 7:30pm–midnight (or later). Subway: A/C/J/Z/2/3/4/5 to Fulton St./Broadway Nassau, walk east to the river.

TriANGuIO FREE   As a reflection of their confidence in tango's ability to hook new dancers, this studio throws in free beginner's workshops (one Fri evening a month). They also run specials for newbies, like $70 for a month's worth of classes. Check the website for dates and details.

135 W. 20th St., btw. Sixth and Seventh aves. ☎ **212/633-6445.** www.tangonyc.com. Subway: 1 to 18th St.; F/M to 23rd St.

2 Health Sans Wealth

Sadly, far too many New Yorkers get by on a "just don't get sick" health plan. As many as one-fourth of us are uninsured, and medical fees aren't getting any cheaper. New health care legislation may soon change the insurance landscape, but in the short term folks of minimal means can be thankful for the sliding scale. Several good-hearted community-minded organizations provide care at rates commensurate with an individual's income. If your income is low enough, you may also be eligible for subsidized insurance with an HMO. A good website to check out is that of the **Actors' Fund of America** (www.actorsfund.org). The fund has comprehensive listings for actors and artists who don't have the kinds of day jobs that throw in insurance and health care. If you're a documented entertainer, you can take advantage of the Al Hirschfeld Free Health Clinic. Civilians on small budgets can also look into the **Rock Dove Collective** (www.rockdovecollective.org), which matches up health practitioners with folks of a mutual aid mind. Dentists, shrinks, and acupuncturists can also be tracked down for bodies on budgets.

HEALTH INSURANCE
Folks with cushy jobs can expect to see insurance on their laundry list of benefits. With more and more arts and media freelancers in the

marketplace, however, it's easy to find oneself on the wrong side of the feudal walls. The **Freelancers Union** and **Working Today** (✆ **718/ 222-1099;** www.freelancersunion.org) have combined to garner some of the bulk-rate buying power of a corporation. Even with a high deductible (like $10K high), the lowest you can go is $196 per month, and that's just for an individual. For $285 a month you can get a better deductible and co-pay arrangement, although it's still no bargain. The program is for artists and media types, leaving out our chef and waitress friends. **Healthy New York** is New York State's program for lower-income residents who earn too much for Medicaid. If you work and make less than $27,000 a year (individual) or $36,432 (couple), you may be able to take advantage of this plan. The premiums in Manhattan range from $253 to $341, without drug coverage, depending on which HMO you sign up with. Log on to www. healthyny.com or call ✆ **866/HEALTHY-NY** [432-5849] for more info. Hopefully the new legislation signed by President Obama will bring costs down. In the meantime, just to keep things simple, stay healthy.

HEALTH CLINICS
New York's clinics tend to target specific constituencies. Though they may specialize in helping the indigent, or the HIV-positive, the clinics make it a policy not to discriminate against anyone. Even if you're uninsured, you can get some attention in places other than the city's emergency rooms. The **U.S. Department of Health and Human Resources** has a useful website (www.findahealthcenter.hrsa.gov) that lists HRSA-sponsored health centers that provide sliding-scale care.

Callen-Lorde Community Health Center   This primary care center caters to the LGBT (lesbian, gay, bisexual, transgender) community, but makes a point to be open to all. The general medicine and health and wellness programs are charged on a sliding scale.

356 W. 18th St., btw. Eighth and Ninth aves. ✆ **212/271-7200.** www.callen-lorde. org. Subway: A/C/E to 14th St.; L to Eighth Ave.; 1 to 18th St.

David Ores, M.D.   Many a Lower East Sider, including your humble correspondent, is grateful to general practitioner Dr. Dave for his attentive care and humane prices. Dr. Dave's tiny clinic serves the neighborhood with a nod to the uninsured. Prices have crept up a little in recent years, but the scale still slides, and Dr. Dave always treats his patients fairly. Call first for an appointment.

15 Clinton St., btw. E. Houston and Stanton sts. ✆ **212/353-3020.** www.david joresmd.org. Subway: F/M to Second Ave.; J/M/Z to Essex St.

Gay Men's Health Crisis Dedicated to slowing the spread of HIV and to helping out those already affected, this organization offers a host of services for the HIV-positive community. Health care is provided on a sliding scale basis, and there are also workshops, seminars, and even free legal services offered. The well-known GMHC Hot Line is open for calls Monday through Friday from 10am to 9pm, and Saturdays from noon until 3pm.

The Tisch Building, 119 W. 24th St., btw. Sixth and Seventh aves. ✆ **800/AIDS-NYC** [243-7692]. www.gmhc.org. For other information, the main office line is ✆ 212/367-1000.

New York City Department of Health and Mental Hygiene `FREE` The city operates 11 clinics in all five boroughs that offer free testing and treatment for STDs and HIV. They also follow up with no-cost counseling. Wait times can be on the long side, so show up before the clinic opens or bring a good book, and make sure you've eaten. (The same city department provides free condoms, at locations across the city; they also connect smokers with cessation programs, most of which are free—check the website.)

303 Ninth Ave., at 28th St. ✆ **311** for hot line, or 212/427-5120. www.nyc.gov/html/doh. Mon–Fri 8:30am–4pm; Sat 8:30am–noon; HIV testing only, Tues–Thurs 5–7pm. Subway: C/E to 23rd St. Check the website for other locations throughout the city.

New York City Free Clinic `FREE` NYU med students work with a professional at this Saturday morning clinic, where the homeless and the uninsured can get consultations, physicals, and other medical help. Advance appointments are required. If your chromosomes run XX, a new Women's Health Free Clinic may be suited to you, operating out of the same building. The Free Clinic website serves as an excellent clearinghouse for sliding scale and no-cost healthcare, too.

Inside the Sidney Hillman Clinic, 16 E. 16th St., btw. Union Sq. West and Fifth Ave. ✆ **212/206-5200.** www.med.nyu.edu/nycfreeclinic. Sat 9am–1pm. Subway: L/N/Q/R/4/5/6 to 14th St./Union Sq.

Planned Parenthood `FREE` Free pregnancy tests are among the many reproductive-oriented services handled by this organization.

FREE Frugal Legal Advice

As a freelance writer, when I snap my fingers clients come running, tardy backpay in hand. Not everybody has the juice to ensure justice is always served, though, and for that we should be thankful for **Legal Services NYC** (☎ **646/442-3600;** www.legalservicesnyc.org), which keeps neighborhood offices in all five boroughs. The group provides free counsel on a huge range of issues, from employment, education, housing, family, and domestic violence to income tax and beyond. Families, children, seniors, people living under the poverty line, and folks with disabilities or HIV are the main constituancy, although consumers and people protecting their communities are also supported.

Artists have their own advocates in **Volunteer Lawyers for the Arts** (☎ **212/319-2787;** www.vlany.org), which makes *pro bono* placements for low-income creatives and nonprofits. During business hours you can get help via the Art Law Line (ext. 1 at the number above), which is staffed by lawyers and law students Monday through Friday from 10am to 6pm. An online browse through the current VLA case list will convince you your troubles ain't so bad.

Brooklyn, the Bronx, and Manhattan each have a clinic that can help out. Other services, including HIV counseling and assistance with STDs, have reasonable fees. Call the main number, ☎ **212/965-7000,** to schedule an appointment in any one of the clinics. FINE PRINT Hours are sometimes shorter than those listed below, call in advance to be sure.

Margaret Sanger Center, 26 Bleecker St., at Mott St. www.ppnyc.org. Mon–Tues 8am–4:30pm; Wed–Fri 8am–6:30pm; Sat 7:30am–4pm. Subway: 6 to Bleecker St.; B/D/F/M to Broadway/Lafayette. *Borough Hall Center,* 44 Court St., btw. Remsen and Joralemon sts. Mon–Wed 8am–4:30pm; Thurs 8am–6:30pm; Fri 8am–5:30pm; Sat 8am–4pm. Subway: 2/3/4/5 to Borough Hall; R to Court St.; A/C/F to Jay St./Borough Hall. *Bronx Center,* 349 E. 149th St., at Courtland Ave. Tues, Wed, and Fri 8am–5pm; Thurs 8am–7pm; Sat 8:30am–4:30pm. Subway: 4 to 149th Ave.; 2/5 to Third Ave./149th St.

Ryan Center   The three associated Ryan clinics (on the Upper West Side, the Lower East Side, and in Midtown) provide a huge range of services, from HIV counseling to general medicine to mental health.

Prices are set on a sliding scale. There is also a new Harlem satellite, and a mobile clinic that serves people from age 13 to 24.

William F. Ryan Community Health Network, Clinic at 110 W. 97th St., btw. Columbus and Amsterdam aves. ✆ **212/749-1820.** www.ryancenter.org. Subway: 1/2/3 or B/C to 96th St. *Ryan Center Annex,* 160 W. 100th St., btw. Columbus and Amsterdam aves. ✆ **212/769-7200.** Subway: 1/2/3 or B/C to 96th St. *Ryan-NENA Community Health Center,* 279 E. 3rd St. btw. aves. C and D. ✆ **212/477-8500.** Subway: F/M to Second Ave. All three clinics above open Mon and Thurs 8:30am–7pm; Tues–Wed and Fri 8:30am–4:30pm; Sat 9:30am–1pm (except July–Aug). *Ryan Chelsea-Clinton Community Health Center,* 645 Tenth Ave., btw. 45th and 46th sts. ✆ **212/265-4500.** Mon–Tues and Thurs 8:30am–7pm; Wed and Fri 8:30am–4:30pm. Subway: C/E to 50th St. *Thelma C. Davidson Adair/William F. Ryan Community Health Center,* 565 Manhattan Ave., btw. 123rd and 124th sts. ✆ **212/222-5221.** Mon–Fri, 9am–5pm. Subway: A/B/C/D to 125th St. *SHOUT mobile clinic,* ✆ **212/316-7912.** Locations vary, calendar online.

DIRT CHEAP SHRINKS

National Psychological Association for Psychoanalysis   In an attempt to lessen the barriers to psychological treatment, this organization runs a referral service for affordable psychoanalysis and psychotherapy. Potential analysands whose income levels qualify can take advantage of sliding-scale fees that start at $35 per session.

Theodore Reik Clinical Center for Psychotherapy, 150 W. 13th St., btw. Sixth and Seventh aves. ✆ **212/262-5978.** www.npap.org. Subway: F/M or 1/2/3 to 14th St.; L to Sixth Ave.

NYU Postdoctoral Program in Psychotherapy and Psychoanalysis As the largest psychoanalytic training program in the country, the range of techniques and treatments here is wide. You can help yourself while giving a postdoc the opportunity to practice on a real, live psyche (the training is excellent, and trainees are supervised by professors). There's a sliding scale, which gets very low for people with limited incomes—call for more information.

240 Greene St., 3rd floor, at Washington Place. ✆ **212/998-7890.** www.nyu.edu. Subway: N/Q/R to 8th St.; 6 to Astor Place; A/B/C/D/E/F/M to W. 4th St./Washington Sq.

Training Institute for Mental Health   This institute, run by the University of the State of New York, trains psychiatric nurses, psychologists, and social workers. Get yourself sorted out while helping someone learn the field. Sliding scale fees go as low as $35 per session. They also offer couples therapy, again on a sliding scale, with fees averaging $50 per session.

115 W. 27th St., btw. Sixth and Seventh aves. ℭ **212/627-8181.** www.timh.org. Subway: 1 or N/Q/R to 28th St.

ACUPUNCTURE

Pacific College of Oriental Medicine Clinic and Acupuncture Center
More and more people are seeking out Chinese herbs and medicine as an alternative to the escalating costs of Western medicine. This teaching clinic provides relatively inexpensive services, though the best bargains are for going under an intern's needles. Each session costs $45, with the eighth one free.

915 Broadway, 3rd floor, btw. 20th and 21st sts. ℭ **212/982-4600.** www.pacific college.edu. Mon–Thurs 9am–9pm; Fri–Sat 9am–5pm. Subway: N/Q/R to 23rd St.

Swedish Institute College of Health Sciences It's been over 10 years since this learning center added acupuncture to its roster, putting it somewhat ahead of the curve in New York. The Yu Wen Acupuncture Clinic lets students gain experience with patients under the watchful eye of licensed instructors. Thirteen sessions are $360, but the program is popular so don't expect to get in immediately. You can download an application from the website or have it mailed to you by calling ℭ **212/924-5900,** ext. 130, and leaving your name and address.

226 W. 26th St., btw. Seventh and Eighth aves. ℭ **212/924-5900.** www.swedish institute.edu. Patient hours are seasonal, check the website. Subway: 1 to 28th St.

Touro College Acupuncture Clinic Touro has an extensive Oriental Medicine graduate program, with an herbal pharmacy and training in acupuncture. Services to the public are performed by students, making for some deep discounts: $10 for an initial visit and then $25 for each follow-up. The clinic is brand-new, located on Touro's main campus in the Flatiron.

33 W. 23rd St., btw. Fifth and Sixth aves. ℭ **212/463-0400,** ext. 313. www.touro.edu. Subway: N/Q/R or F/M to 23rd St.

DENTAL

Columbia University College of Dental Medicine You can get Ivy Leaguers to poke around your mouth for cheap. The students and residents at this popular teaching clinic are well-trained and fully supervised. With several eyes on your teeth, the visit will take longer than a trip to a private clinic, but you'll pay a lot less. A first visit, which includes an oral health screening and X-rays, is $85.

Columbia Presbyterian Medical Center, Vanderbilt Clinic, 622 W. 168th St., 7th floor, btw. Broadway and Fort Washington Ave. ☎ 212/342-4160. www.dental.columbia. edu. Registration desk Mon–Fri 8:30am–2pm. Subway: 1/A/C to 168th St./Washington Heights.

New York College of Technology   Student work makes for a seriously deep discount at the Dental Hygiene Clinic here. It will take a while—professors supervise the work and have to check it over before you're let out on your way—but the students here are working for a grade and tend to be thorough about cleaning your teeth. IG you've got the time, the prices are amazing: a cleaning is only $10, and X-rays are only $15.

300 Jay St., btw. Tech Place and Tillary St. ☎ 718/260-5074. www.citytech.cuny.edu. Subway: 2/3/4/5 to Borough Hall; R to Court St./Borough Hall; A/C/F to Jay St./Borough Hall.

New York University College of Dentistry   NYU runs the largest dental college in the country and offers deep discounts on dental care. An initial appointment (which may require two visits) is $90 and covers a checkup, X-rays, and oral cancer screenings. For further work, the costs here are half of what they would be in a professional office (a cleaning is $60), and for most folks the location is more convenient than Columbia's.

345 E. 24th St., at First Ave., Clinic 1A. ☎ 212/998-9872. www.nyu.edu/dental. Mon–Thurs 8:30am–8pm; Fri 8:30am–4pm. Subway: 6 to 23rd St.

HEARING

Center for Hearing and Communication FREE   Auditory problems aren't just for rock stars, airline mechanics, and people who live beneath NYU students. Most of us haven't followed up on the tests we had in elementary school, but after years of headphone abuse and live-band karaoke, it may be past time for a checkup. This nonprofit offers free hearing screenings on Wednesdays from noon to 2pm and Thursdays from 4 to 6pm (call ahead to confirm the times and reserve a space). If it turns out you do need services, this group has never turned away anyone due to an inability to pay.

50 Broadway, 6th floor, btw. Morris St. and Exchange Alley. ☎ 917/305-7700. www. chchearing.org. Subway: 4/5 to Bowling Green; R or 1 to Rector St.; J/Z to Broad St.

ALEXANDER TECHNIQUE

The American Center for the Alexander Technique FREE Tasmania-born thespian F. Matthias Alexander pioneered this enigmatic science, which seeks to retrain the body out of a lifetime of bad habits. To learn more, check out the free monthly demonstrations at this 40-year-old institution. They're held the first Monday of the month from 7 to 8:30pm. Seating is limited; call in advance to reserve a spot. Should you wish to follow up afterwards, third-year students at the center need volunteers to receive free work. E-mail volunteer@acat nyc.org to get involved.

39 W. 14th St., Room 507, btw. Fifth and Sixth aves. ✆ **212/633-2229.** www.acatnyc. org. Subway: F/M to 14th St.; L to Sixth Ave.; N/Q/R/4/5/6 to 14th St./Union Sq.

3 In the Housing

What would New Yorkers have to talk about if we weren't complaining about our living arrangements? Or, for a lucky few of us, bragging about them? I, for example, pay $264 a month for my rent-stabilized four-bedroom with stunning views of the East River, Paris, and Cairo. The sad fact is, even as the economy only jogs along, NYC rental rates and housing prices remain firmly in the realm of the absurd. One concept we learn all too well in New York is that of the "relative bargain." For those not easily discouraged, however, a couple of resources can help a home-seeker get ahead.

For hotels, hostels, and other short-term digs, see Chapter 2, "Cheap Sleeps."

NO-FEE RENTALS

Broker's fees, the 10% to 15% surcharge slapped on by the realtor who tours you around a series of spaces that are way too small and more than you can afford anyway, are the painful cost of renting in NYC. You can beat the system by contacting real estate firms directly, through their classifieds in the *Voice* and *Times,* and through their websites. It takes some legwork, but if your need for housing isn't urgent, it's the way to go. If you know a specific building you're interested in, try to talk to the super. They'll know what units might be available soon. Another option is **www.apartmentsource.com.** This website is a clearinghouse that lists low- and no-fee apartments, although the listings tend toward big buildings with high prices.

Patient trolling of Craigslist may be the best bet of all.

MIXED INCOME DIGS

In an effort to keep neighborhoods from becoming entirely monolithic, the city offers tax breaks to developers who are willing to set aside a certain number of units for middle- and low-income residents. As with everything else in life, the key is persistence. Waiting lists can be long and your lottery odds can be slim, but every time you make the effort to apply you tilt the playing field in your favor.

Department of Housing Preservation & Development This city agency connects buyers and sellers. The website lists lotteries for subsidized housing purchases, which will give you the keys at a substantially reduced cost. You'll have to meet income eligibility thresholds, and the property will have to be your primary residence. Most housing is in lower-income neighborhoods, often in outer reaches of the outer boroughs. Right now the pickings are pretty slim, but check the website for future apartment availability. There's also a lottery list for rental apartments, which are available way below market rates if you're lucky enough to have your application pulled from the hopper. ⓒ **311.** For purchases, www.nyc.gov/html/hpd/html/buyers/lotteries.shtml; rentals www.nyc.gov/html/hpd/html/apartment/lotteries.shtml.

Mitchell-Lama Housing Companies This program has been around since 1955, offering housing to New Yorkers with lower-end incomes. You can choose from 132 city-sponsored buildings and 82 co-sponsored by the federal government. Rents are highly subsidized, but the application process is cumbersome and not every building has an

FREE Manhattan Kansas

If New York real estate really has you down, look no further than depressed Midwestern towns for the ultimate giveaway: free land. All across the heartland, places with limited access to drag burlesque nights, human beat box subway train parties, and a decent bagel are giving up their soil for anyone who wants it. There are a couple of little strings attached—you have to build a house or business on the site and then you have to stay there—but the price cannot be beat. Especially in New York. Visit www.kansasfreeland.com for county-specific details on claiming your free slice of the continent.

FREE Renters' Assurance

Despite the incursions of the open market in recent years, there remain some 850,000 regulated apartments in NYC. The **Metropolitan Council on Housing** (www.metcouncil.net) has spent the last 50 years fighting for the rights of renters, and the preservation of affordable housing. It's an uphill battle against the big-money powers that be, but individuals can arm themselves with knowledge. The Met Council Hot Line provides information on tenant rights and dispenses advice. Call ✆ **212/979-0611** on Monday, Wednesday, and Friday afternoons between 1:30 and 5pm for help. Check the website for neighborhood-specific assistance (they list a dozen-plus groups).

---

open waiting list. To get a PDF file (viewable with Adobe Reader) listing buildings with open lists, log on to http://www.nyc.gov/html/hpd/downloads/pdFl_open.pdf. Each building has to be applied for individually. There are also state-administered units, which can be found at http://www.dhcr.state.ny.us/Apps/hsgdevls/hsgdevls.asp. For general information, call ✆ **212/863-6500** for city units, or ✆ **866/275-3427** for state units.

New York City Housing Development Corporation The city promotes several mixed-income new developments in the five boroughs. The **80/20** program is fairly common. Twenty percent of a building is rented at discount rates to people who earn significantly less than the neighborhood's median income. You have to apply directly to the developer and the process takes a while, but if you get in you'll score a great deal. In many cases, you can move up in income brackets without jeopardizing your cheap rent (or cheap purchase). Note that the buildings involved are usually in developing neighborhoods, not in the city's trendiest zip codes. Log on to www.nychdc.com for a full list of HDC-financed sites, or call ✆ **212/227-5500.**

WOMEN'S RESIDENCES

Members of the fairer sex can also take advantage of the cheap accommodations offered by women's residences. These throwbacks to a more genteel era generally don't allow gentleman callers above the parlor levels, nor do they permit boozing (some residences even have curfews). However, rates are lower than New York's multigender hotels, and for newcomers to the city it's a great way to make friends.

Markle Evangeline Residence   Built by the Salvation Army, the Markle has been providing women with a viable alternative to the New York housing mire for 80 years. The rules are predictably strict—no alcohol, no smoking, no men under 55 inside—and the rooms will never be described as spacious, but a resident gets her own fully furnished bedroom with private bathroom and two squares a day. A great location on top of access to a TV room, computer labs, a rooftop garden, and organized social activities help justify the somewhat high rates. *Note:* More communal souls can save cash by opting for shared doubles or quads, which charge lower rates. Summer student residents under 16 must have a female parent or guardian reside with them. Non-student residents must be between 18 and 35. Two references, an application, and a security deposit of $1,600 are required for long-term stays.

123 W. 13th St., btw. Sixth and Seventh aves. ℂ **212/242-2400.** www.themarkle.org. Long-term monthly (minimum 90 days): $1,335–$1,465 single; $1,240–$1,360 double; $980–$1,010 quad. Facilities: Private bathroom; in-room phone; 24-hr. security; maid service (once a week); roof garden; computer lab; TV lounge; laundry. Subway: 1 to Christopher St.

Sacred Heart Residence   In a historic brownstone right across from the General Theological Seminary, this Chelsea boarding house holds down a prime location (Jack Kerouac wrote the third draft of *On the Road* just up the block). The Congregation of San Jose de la Montana administers the building, providing temporary lodging for women 18 to 30 years old. You'll need to apply in advance and put down a $50 reservation, and there's a curfew (11pm on weeknights, midnight on the weekends). Rent is due in advance, $240 a week. Bathrooms are shared.

432 W. 20th St., btw. Ninth and Tenth aves. ℂ **212/929-5790.** www.sacredheart residence.com. 28 rooms. Single or share of double, $240 weekly. Two meals a day on weekdays. Subway: C/E to 23rd St.

The Webster Apartments   One of Macy's major shareholders gave a little back to working women by endowing this midtown residence. Interns and working students pay only $265 a week, and employed women are charged by a sliding scale that tops out at $295 a week. If you're here on business (and female), it's just $85 a night, with a three-night minimum. Bathrooms are in the hallway, but sharing has its advantages when it comes to enjoying the large walled garden and rooftop plot. You need to fill out an application to get in (the average stay is about three months).

419 W. 34th St., btw. Ninth and Tenth aves. ℭ **212-967-9000.** www.webster apartments.org. 373 rooms. Single rooms: $265–$295 weekly, shared bathrooms, breakfast and dinner included. Facilities: Roof garden; TV lounge; maid service (once a week); laundry. Subway: A/C/E to 34th St.

4 Beauty & Massage

HAIR TODAY

NYC's hirsute astute take advantage of salon training sessions. Both students and pros need live heads to demonstrate on, and in exchange for your modeling they'll provide all kinds of services for little or no money. Though there's no guarantee you'll get an expert cut, a lot of salon students in New York have the scissor skills to eclipse the masters. In addition to cuts, coloring services are sometimes available. Some salons want to look you over first (it helps if you've got a sympathetic face and a surplus of hair begging for a snipping), but generally it's pretty easy to get your grooming on the house. *Note:* Many salons need models, but not all like to advertise it. If you've got your eye on a prohibitively expensive spot, give them a call and see if they can use you. For a great online source, check out www.salonapprentice.com, which lists dozens of volunteer hair model opportunities every week.

SALON STYLINGS

Aveda Institute New York   The popular environmentally conscious spa Aveda offers up its many services at deep discounts if you go through the students at the institute. Haircuts, coloring, blowouts, perms, facials, and waxing are all available. The prices aren't dirt cheap ($20 for a cut and simple style), but they're relative bargains compared to the rest of the neighborhood. If you want to model for a student, you can find free cuts and deeply discounted coloring at both the institute and at Aveda Academy classes.

Institute, 233 Spring St., btw. Sixth Ave. and Varick St. ℭ **212/807-1492.** www.aveda instituteny.com. Subway: C/E to Spring St. *Academy,* 20 Vandam St., btw. Sixth Ave. and Varick St. ℭ **212/524-2424.** Subway: C/E to Spring St.; 1 to Houston St.

Bumble and bumble.University FREE 🏷 The old-school butchers would never have believed it, but the Meatpacking District is now style central in Manhattan. Bumble and bumble's salon is right in the thick of it, but you can partake of the services for no money down. Their stylist training program puts on model calls for heads of hair deemed worthy in pre-evaluation (fill out the form online to wangle your invitation). If you make it through, they'll fuss over you for 2 hours or so, leaving you with a new cut and style. Once you're in the program, you can stay tapped into the gravy train with a follow-up every 3 or 4 months. (If you make the cut for cuts, you'll also be eligible for free color work.) You must be willing to get more than a trim, though they'll consult with you first to figure out what works. Tips aren't even necessary.

415 W. 13th St., 6th floor, btw. Ninth Ave. and Washington St. ℂ **866/7-BUMBLE** [728-6253]. www.bbmodelproject.com. Subway: A/C/E or L to Eighth Ave./14th St.

Christine Valmy International School of Esthetics, Makeup and Nail Artistry What you give up in experience, you gain in price here. Facials are a great deal. Instructors do the supervising while students do the work. A full hour and a half facial ($38 on Sat) is only $27 if you come in between 9:30am and 3:30pm on a weekday. Call a week ahead for an appointment.

437 Fifth Ave., btw. 38th and 39th sts. ℂ **212/779-7800.** www.christinevalmy.com. Subway: 7 to Fifth Ave.; 6 to 33rd St.

L'Oréal FREE If you want first dibs on the latest L'Oréal products, sign up with their Consumer Expressions Research Center. Participants get free gift bags of products at the end of their home trials, although the test products themselves have to be returned lest they fall into enemy hands. You'll also score a guest pass to shop at the L'Oréal company store, where beauty products (including the ever-popular Kiehl's) are offered at a big discount. L'Oréal also runs a free testing facility at the L'Oréal Professionnel Soho Academy. Hair models can receive hair coloring, styling, cutting, and relaxer services. Check online for the next model call. If you're selected, you'll get breakfast, lunch, and a free gift bag, on top of revamped tresses.

Consumer Expressions Research Center, 575 Fifth Ave., 3rd floor, at 47th St. ℂ **212/984-4164.** www.cercny.com. Subway: B/D/F/M to 47th–50th sts.–Rockefeller Center. *L'Oréal Professional Soho Academy,* 435 Hudson St., btw. Morton and Leroy sts. ℂ **212/866/SOHONYC** [764-6692]. Subway: 1 to Houston St.

The Dealin' Barbers of Cheap Street

Barber colleges offer cut-rate cuts. The level of experience varies, however, from student to student, so I don't recommend going for anything too tricky. In fact, you might limit these visits to summertime—when hair grows back its quickest.

American Barber Institute   Haircuts are only $4.99 here, though you'll have to sign a waiver before going under the shears. Manicures are just a penny more, at $5. 252 W. 29th St., btw. Seventh and Eighth aves. ✆ **212/290-2289.** www.americanbarberinstitute.com. Subway: 1 to 28th St. *Other location,* 113 Chambers St., btw. Church St. and W. Broadway. ✆ **212/227-6353.** Subway: A/C or 1/2/3 to Chambers St. N/Q/R.

Atlas Barber School   Both men's and women's stylings are only $5. Feeling lucky? Try out a student shave for just $2. 34 Third Ave., btw. 9th and 10th sts. ✆ **212/475-1360.** www.atlasbarbersch.com. Subway: 6 to Astor Place; N/Q/R to 8th St.

   You can get cheap cuts from pros, too. The cuts will run you a bit more, but you can rest easier knowing the scissors are in experienced hands.

Astor Place Hairstylist   This family-run basement hides a vast array of barbers and hairstylists. Cuts are professional, and a lot more stylish than you might expect for $14. (Astor Place has had charge of my locks for years, and of course I look like a million bucks.) 2 Astor Place, btw. Broadway and Lafayette St. ✆ **212/475-9854.** www.astorplacehair nyc.com. Subway: N/Q/R to 8th St.; 6 to Astor Place.

Hollywood 2002   Prime West Village real estate doesn't prevent this amiable shop from delivering a host of affordable crops. A men's cut will cost $12, and the barbers here take their time to make sure it's right. 204 W. 14th St., btw. Seventh and Eighth aves. ✆ **212/741-9680.** Subway: 1/2/3 or A/C/E to 14th St.; L to Eighth Ave.

Kelly Hair Salon   Pell Street has turned into a Chinatown beauty row, with cheap nail and hair work available up and down the block. This salon does big-volume business without losing a personal touch; cuts start at $7 for men and $12 for women. 19 Pell St., btw. Doyers and Mott sts. ✆ **212/732-7688.** Subway: J/N/R/Q/Z/6 to Canal St.

New York International Beauty School The salon here will swap service for experience, as trainees learn best on live bodies. Simple haircuts are just a few bucks, with a full-on blow-out averaging $10. Highlighting, braiding, and facials are among the other services on offer. Walk-ins only, weekdays from 9am to 2pm and 6 to 7pm.

500 Eighth Ave., btw. 35th and 36th sts. ✆ **212/868-7171.** www.nyibs.com. Subway: A/C/E to 34th St./Penn Station.

Salon Ziba FREE Every Monday morning, this upscale-ish salon puts on a cutting class, led by a senior stylist. Send them a picture of your hair and if you're suitable they'll give you a free salon cut. Both male and female models are used.

200 W. 57th St., at Seventh Ave. ✆ **212/767-0577.** www.salonziba.com. Subway: N/Q/R to 57th St.

TIGI Hairdressing Academy FREE Complementary and complimentary cuts and colors are on offer at this international school. The model call goes out every Friday night at 6pm. If they like your locks, you'll be invited back for a class the next week (classes are held Sun–Wed).

673 Madison Ave., 2nd floor, at 61st St. ✆ **212/702-9771.** www.tigihaircare.com. Subway: N/Q/R to Fifth Ave.

Qigong Show

The methods offered by Chinatown's massage joints are as varied as the neighborhood itself. Everything from shiatsu to reflexology to my personal favorite, qigong, is available (and you don't even need to get all the way to Chinatown to enjoy them). Qigong, one of the world's oldest methods of healing, is the root of many popular forms of massage therapy. At **88 Chinese QiGong Tui Na,** trained therapists with startlingly strong hands will expertly knead your knotted muscles until you're ready to weep with relief. The space is bare bones but clean, with curtains and shoulder-height walls for privacy, and soothing Zen-like music tinkling in the background. The cost is $42 an hour, which leaves some room for much-appreciated tipping. 329 Bowery, btw. 2nd and 3rd sts., basement level. ✆ **212/260-7829.** Subway: 6 to Bleecker St.; B/D/F to Broadway/Lafayette. Daily, 11am–10pm.

—*Stephanie Kramer*

INSTANT MASSAGING

Swedish Institute College of Health Sciences   Swedish massage has been around for a couple of centuries now, but you don't need to travel all the way to Stockholm to improve your circulation. Since its founding by a Swede in 1916, this institution has dedicated itself to natural approaches to health, which it makes available to the public at reduced rates. You'll be worked on by a student, but they're very well trained. Two clinical programs are offered, stress-reduction (for the healthy) and therapeutic massage (for people with medical conditions). The former program provides six 1-hour sessions for $210, and the latter is 12 hours in 12 weeks for $360. Both programs are very popular, so registration is by mail only. Call the P. H. Ling Clinic at ✆ **212/924-5900** (ext. 6208) and leave your name and address, or download the form from the website.

226 W. 26th St., btw. Seventh and Eighth aves. ✆ **212/924-5900.** www.swedish institute.edu. Subway: 1 to 28th St.

5 Recreation in the City

BIKE GANGS

Biking makes a virtue of New York's hard paved surfaces, turning our miles of roadway into recreational opportunities. One of the best ways to take advantage is by banding up with fellow riders. If you're not yet of the wheeled class, consider checking out **Recycle-A-Bicycle.** This nonprofit sells refurbished rides at low prices from two retail locations (p. 207). For a free bike loan, look into the "Bike Around Downtown" program (✆ **212/566-6700;** www.downtownny.com.) Leave a credit card for a deposit and you'll be on your way. Some 30 bikes are available from May through September, picked up from Bike and Roll's kiosk in the South Street Seaport. Bike and Roll offers a similar program on Governors Island Fridays from mid-June through early October. (Check in advance to confirm the programs are still running—communalism has a poor track record with these kinds of things.)

Fast and Fab   Whether you're a fast rider or a fabulous rider, or both, this LGBT biking group will welcome you. Annual membership is $30 ($20 if you join after May 1, and only $10 after Sept 1), but it'll get you invites to a series of rides around the city and out of town (say, a day trip to DIA Beacon). Intermediate cyclists are the target group. Meals and socializing often follow the rides.

(212/567-7160. www.fastnfab.org.

Five Borough Bicycle Club FREE
This friendly club hosts a slew of day trips in and around the city. Beaches, the Bronx greenways, and Woodlawn Cemetery are among the attractions. The club runs some great tune-ups (as long as 90 miles) leading up to the 100 miles of the annual Montauk Century ride in May. Registration for day rides isn't necessary; just show up with water and wheels (the trip is free except for lunch money). A year's dues to join the club aren't particularly onerous at $20.

(212/932-2300, ext. 115. www.5bbc. org.

FREE **Outdoor Gaming**

"Geek Olympics" is probably an unfair way of summarizing the **Come Out & Play** street game festival. Technology does lend a major hand, with laptops and cellphones performing various tracking functions, but the event is more about playful use of public space than Internet addicts blinking their eyes against the harsh imposition of daylight. Urban mini golf, human Pong, and citywide scavenger hunts are among the draws, which fill a long weekend, usually in June. Check www.comeoutandplay. org for a schedule of games, or to volunteer one of your own.
(**646/280-8311;** various locations.

TIME'S UP! FREE 🗡 This environmental group sponsors several well-organized rides. The most well known is **Critical Mass,** held on the last Friday of every month and taking place simultaneously in over 300 cities worldwide. The ride is designed to raise consciousness about environmental alternatives and biker rights. It's fun for sidewalk spectators, too, who can watch every kind of bike and bike-rider pedal past to a chorus of perversely gratifying taxi horns. The route varies, usually starting from the north side of Union Square (the Brooklyn version goes off the second Fri of the month from Grand Army Plaza and Staten Island leaves the first Fri from Borough Hall, across from the ferry). TIME'S UP! also hosts rides on tri-state rural routes, but the best trip to the country comes on the first Friday of the month. The **Central Park Moonlight Ride** shows off the water and trees and general tranquillity of the park at night. With guides riding point and taking up the rear, it's a safe and leisurely pedal. Rollerbladers with at least intermediate skills are welcome, too. The ride meets at 10pm at the southwest corner of Central Park, across from Columbus Circle. The trip is around 10 miles, and runs all 12 months of the year. A Prospect Park Moonlight Ride has also been recently added. TIME'S UP! is on the hunt for permanent headquarters, but you can take advantage of bike repair workshops and classes at their temporary spaces in Williamsburg and on the Lower East Side. All events are free, although as a volunteer-run organization, donations are cheerfully accepted.

156 Rivington St., btw. Suffolk and Clinton sts. ✆ **212/802-8222.** www.times-up.org. Subway: F to Delancey St.; J/M/Z to Essex St. *Other location,* 99 S. 6th St., btw. Bedford Ave. and Berry St. Subway: J/M/Z to Marcy Ave.; L to Bedford Ave.

GYM NEIGHBORS

When hauling groceries and laundry up to your sixth-floor walk-up is no longer exercise regimen enough, it's time to hit a gym. The cheapest choice by far is signing up with the department of parks and recreation, though other options that don't much exceed $1 a day are available. If you want to shop around first, the website **www.gym search.net** has free coupons and guest passes for gyms around the region. It's free, but you have to register your contact info. If you want an even larger sampling of what's available around NYC, look into the PassBooks put together by the **American Health & Fitness Alliance** (✆ **212/808-0765;** www.health-fitness.org). It costs $79 to sign up, but free passes for health clubs (up to one month in some instances), classes, and training sessions technically tally up to $3,500. There are also similar versions for yoga and Pilates.

Department of Parks and Recreation　On top of playing fields and courts, the city also runs 51 recreation centers spread across all five boroughs. The amenity list is long and varied, including indoor and outdoor tracks, weight rooms, dance studios, and boxing rings. All of this can be yours for only $50 a year. If you want to join a center with a pool, it's an additional $25. (For seniors age 55 and over, it's only $10 a year with or without pools, and for under-18s, it's all free.) Many centers also offer classes in Pilates, aerobics, karate, kickboxing, wrestling, swimming, and the like. Some centers even have personal trainers. Usually an extra fee applies for classes, say $5 for an hour of yoga instruction. If you want to sample the goods, check out

BeFitNYC Free First Mondays, which provides classes and equipment at no charge (a few classes may carry a nominal fee). Other days of the week, catch the **Shape Up NYC** program, which offers free fitness classes around the city. Although scenes vary from rec center to rec center, generally city-run facilities are family-friendly and community oriented—look elsewhere if you're in the market for a meat market.

© **311.** www.nycgovparks.org.

OTOM Gym Physical Culture   In addition to the Y below, Greenpoint residents have this large, affordable gym. A year's membership is $449, and you can buy a 3-month summer trial for just $119.95.

169 Calyer St., btw. Lorimer St. and Manhattan Ave., Greenpoint, Brooklyn. © **718/ 383-2800.** www.otomgymny.com. Subway: G to Greenpoint Ave.

YMCA of Greater New York   The Y (© **212/630-9600;** www.ymca nyc.org) runs 23 health and wellness centers in the five boroughs. The facilities vary from site to site, but the general roster includes gyms, pools, racquetball and handball courts, aerobics studios, exercise machines, steam rooms, and saunas. (There's also cheap lodging at some locations, see p. 37). Fees vary. The state-of-the-art facility is the new McBurney location (125 W. 14th St., btw. Sixth and Seventh aves.; F/M or L to Sixth Ave./14th St., or 1/2/3 to 14th St.; © **212/741-9210**). A 1-year membership is $1,068, plus the $125 initiation fee. To get fit at a less central location is a much better deal—the Greenpoint YMCA (99 Meserole Ave., btw. Leonard St. and Manhattan Ave.; G to Nassau Ave. or Greenpoint Ave.; © **718/389-3700**) is only $612 for a year, with a $75 initiation fee. For a citywide YMCA pass, which allows access to every center, it's $125 to join and $93 a month after that.

CHEAP SKATES

The Pond at Bryant Park FREE   Frank J. Zamboni's brainchild smoothes the ice on this ingenious use of Bryant Park's center. Surrounded by the boutique stalls of the Holiday Shops, the ice-skating rink has a European small-town feel. Thanks to the bottomless pockets of Citi, skating is free, though folks whose skates are hanging by their laces in their parents' garages will have to plunk down $12 per session for rentals. The rink is open from November through mid-January.

Bryant Park, btw. W. 40th and 42nd sts., along Sixth Ave. © **866/221-5157.** www. thepondatbryantpark.com. Daily 8am–10pm, until midnight Fri–Sat. Subway: B/D/ F/M to 42nd St.; 7 to Fifth Ave.

FREE NYC's All Skate

The Dead Road in Central Park is one of my favorite spots in the city for a workout (well, an eyeball workout to be completely accurate). Watching dozens of expert roller skaters and bladers dancing and spinning to a jamming disco beat is a hypnotic sight. Some of the regulars have been rolling together for more than 2 decades and the skill level is very high, but if you're halfway competent you shouldn't feel intimidated. The scene is friendly and inclusive, so strap on some wheels and jump in. Even for nonskaters, this event is a highlight of the park. The DJs are great, especially now that the city has relented on its antibeat campaign. (In 1995, music was temporarily banned from the park so skaters wore Walkmen all tuned to the same radio channel, creating a surreal silent choreography.) The outdoor roller disco is in session from 2:30 to 6:30pm most Saturdays, Sundays, and national holidays between mid-April and October. For specifics about dates and DJs, check the **Central Park Dance Skater's Association**'s website (www.cpdsa.org). The Dead Road is in the middle of the park, between 66th and 69th streets, just a little southwest of the Bethesda Fountain.

If skating in a boogielicious roller inferno is a little daunting to you, find safety in numbers with **Wednesday Night Skate** (www.we skateny.org). New York's biggest skating event wheels away from Union Square Park every Wednesday night. The routes vary from week to week, but generally you'll get to see a few miles' worth of NYC, say up Park Avenue, into Central Park, and back on over to Times Square. The event usually lasts 2 hours. The flock meets at the south end of Union Square Park at 7:45pm, from April to October. Helmets and wrist guards are required before you turn yourself into a vehicle.

Riverbank State Park   One of only two state parks in the city, Riverbank is skating on thin ice thanks to major budget mismanagement in Albany. Hopefully the rink will survive. An arching roof provides some protection from the elements and crowds are blissfully moderate. Standard admission is $5 and it's $6 to rent skates. In summer, the rink turns to unbladed skating, with admission just $1.50, and roller skate rentals going for $6.

679 Riverside Dr., at 145th St. ℂ **212/694-3642.** www.nysparks.state.ny.us. Ice skating Fri 6–9pm; Sat–Sun 1–4pm, 5–8pm. Subway: 1 to 145th St.

Wollman Rink   Central Park's Trump Wollman Rink runs about twice the price of Brooklyn's Wollman, on the southeast side of Prospect Park. Adults can cut figure eights for just $5, with rental skates tossed in for $6.50. Look for specials like a free session with the cost of a rental, and half-price Friday admissions.

Prospect Park, near the Parkside and Ocean aves. entrance. ℂ **718/287-6431.** www.prospectpark.org. Daily 8am–10pm, until midnight Fri–Sat. Subway: B/Q/S to Prospect Park.

POOLING RESOURCES

It costs $75 a year to use the city's indoor pools (see "Gym Neighbors," above), but if you're a frequent crawler, the price turns out to be pretty reasonable. There are 54 outdoor pools scattered across the city, and they're free and open to the public. The indoor pools stay open year-round (unless they're superseded by an on-site outdoor pool), but the tubs under the sun sync up with the school year. Late June to Labor Day is the usual season, and you will find many, many kids taking advantage. General hours of operation are 11am to 3pm, and 4 to 7pm; call individual pools for more information. In addition to the city pools (**www.nycgovparks.org**), the state runs an Olympic-size natatorium in Manhattan. Local favorites include:

Asser Levy   An indoor and outdoor pool make this a great year-round swimming destination.

E. 23rd St. and Asser Levy Place, near the FDR Dr. ℂ **212/447-2020.** Subway: 6 to 23rd St.

Astoria Park Pool   This is one of largest (designed to hold some 2,000 swimmers) and most famous pools in the country. Built in 1936 through the WPA, it features stunning skyline and bridge views.

Astoria Park, 19th St. at 23rd Dr., Astoria, Queens. ℂ **718/626-8620.** Subway: N/Q to Astoria–Ditmars Blvd.

Floating Pool   A decommissioned river barge in Morgan City, Louisiana provided the raw material for this popular city freebie. Some 50,000 swim fans visited during 2007's inaugural year, when the pool was parked in the shadow of the Brooklyn Bridge. Barretto Point Park in the Bronx currently holds the facility, although a floating pool can always change its coordinates. Check online to confirm the current season's whereabouts.

www.floatingpool.org.

Hamilton Fish   Despite its enormous size, this Lower East Side outdoor pool fills up quickly. Kids from the neighborhood splash while parents relax in the spacious adjoining plaza.

128 Pitt St., btw. E. Houston and Stanton sts. ℂ **212/387-7687.** Subway: F to Second Ave.; J/M/Z to Essex St.

Metropolitan Pool   Williamsburg is kept buoyant at the indoor Met Pool, which still gleams from a recent multimillion-dollar renovation. (Outdoor swimming is coming soon, too, when concert venue McCarren Park Pool is restored to its pre-rock purposes.)

261 Bedford Ave., at Metropolitan Ave. ℂ **718/599-5707.** Subway: L to Bedford Ave.

Riverbank State Park   This 28-acre park on the Hudson ably disguises its foundation, which is a wastewater treatment plant. The indoor pool here is run by the state, which charges $2 per visit, or $30 for a one-month lap swimming pass.

679 Riverside Dr., at 145th St. ℂ **212/694-3600.** www.nysparks.state.ny.us. Pool general hours (adult swimming is limited; check in advance) Mon–Fri 6:30am–8:15pm; Sat–Sun 6:30am–6pm. Subway: 1 to 145th St.

Tony Dapolito Recreation Center   Another pool with both indoor and outdoor bases covered, this rec center is a long-time West Village fave.

1 Clarkson St., btw. Seventh Ave. S. and Hudson St. ℂ **212/242-5228.** Outdoor pool July–Aug, indoor pool Sept–June. Subway: A/B/C/D/E/F/M to W. 4th St./Washington Sq.

OM MY GOODNESS: MEDITATION

In a town so loud it can be hard to hear one's own thoughts, the contrast of a quiet meditation space can be startling. Though just about any house of worship in the city will suffice, sometimes it's nice to get a little guidance for inner journeying.

Kagyu Dzamling Kunchab   This Tibetan organization brings the east to the west (side), with a traditional Dharma practice led by an ordained lama. Wednesday nights are open to the public for meditation, followed by a Buddhist teaching and Chenrezi practice. The evenings run from 6:30 to 9pm, but you can stay for as much of it as you'd like. The suggested donation is $10, which is tax deductible.

410 Columbus Ave., btw. 79th and 80th sts. ✆ **212/989-5989.** www.kdk-nyc.org. Subway: B/C to 81st St.; 1 to 79th St.

Shambhala FREE   Two lovely meditation rooms host the open meditations offered by this Tibetan Buddhist group. Beginners can learn more at weekly lessons, Wednesdays at 6pm and Sundays at noon. When you've got some seasoning, come back for public sittings and evening chants on weeknights from 5:30 to 7pm and Sundays from 9am to noon. Every Tuesday night at 7pm is the weekly dharma gathering, which is a half-hour of group meditation followed by a talk, a discussion, and a reception. Suggested donation for Tuesday evenings is $5, $10 for meditation lessons. Public sittings are free.

118 W. 22nd St., 6th floor, btw. Sixth and Seventh aves. ✆ **212/675-6544.** www. ny.shambhala.org. Subway: 1 or F/M to 23rd St.

The Three Jewels Community Center FREE   To further the teachings of the Buddha, this impressive organization offers much of its programming for free. In conjunction with the Asian Classics Institute, you can find a wide range of classes, many of which are suited to beginners. There are also meditation sessions, with on-hand instructors to help conduct them. The main loft near Astor Place houses a combination dharma, yoga, meditation, and outreach center. Check the calendar for the latest schedule (some offerings do come with a charge, like the $12 suggested donation for yoga).

61 Fourth Ave., 3rd floor, btw. 9th and 10th sts. ✆ **212/475-6650.** www.threejewels. org. Subway: 6 to Astor Place; N/Q/R to 8th St.

Zen Center of New York City   Discover what one hand clapping sounds like at this Zen center in Brooklyn. Contributions are requested to participate in the meditation sessions (generally $3–$5), which are held almost every day. If you're new to zazen, you can attend an introductory session on a Sunday morning. Sessions start at 9:15am and last around 3 hours. Admission is by a suggested contribution of $5.

500 State St., btw. Nevins St. and Third Ave., Boerum Hill, Brooklyn. ✆ **718/875-8229.** www.mro.org/firelotus. Subway: B/D/N/Q/R/2/3/4/5 to Atlantic Ave./Pacific St.; 4/5 to Nevins St.; A/C/G to Hoyt-Schermerhorn.

WATERSPORTS

New York's waterways were once great recreational resources, but years of environmental laxity made much of the local liquid too toxic to touch. A handful of burgeoning groups are trying to speed along the rivers' rebounds with giveaways along the shore. The East River, Hudson, and Gowanus are all available for seaworthy (or at least sea-curious) New Yorkers. If you can swim, you're eligible to take advantage.

Brooklyn Bridge Park `FREE` The cove between the Manhattan and Brooklyn bridges has about as spectacular a view as can be found in NYC. To enjoy the skyline rippling across the water, take advantage of this new boating program, which runs on select weekends from mid-July through early September. The voyages are first-come, first-served, aboard 20 recently purchased kayaks. Sessions are held in two locations, check the website for details.

Brooklyn Bridge Park, at Pier 1 and Main St., DUMBO, Brooklyn. ℂ **718/802-0603.** www.bbpboathouse.org. Subway: F to York St.; A/C to High St.

Downtown Boathouse `FREE` If you know how to swim, you're eligible for free Hudson paddling. Out of the goodness of their hearts (and a desire to promote the Hudson as a recreational outlet), this group loans out kayaks and equipment all summer long. Some 50,000 people get out on the river between mid-May and mid-October. The trips are limited to 20 minutes in protected areas near three west-side piers, but if you show up a few times and get into shape, you'll be eligible for a long paddle from Pier 96 into New York Harbor. This spectacular field trip lasts 3 hours, with unbelievable views all the way. Potential paddlers gather before 8am and wait to have names picked from a hat. On a nice day you've got about a 50/50 chance of going, though you can increase your odds by arriving on a day with cloud cover. The long-trip season runs mid-June to mid-September (call ℂ **646/613-0740** to check the daily status; in really lousy weather the kayaks stay docked). The Hudson is cleaner than it's been for decades, so getting splashed here and there no longer requires immediate hospitalization. Yay.

Pier 96, Clinton Cove Park, West Side Hwy., at 56th St. ℂ **646/613-0375.** www. downtownboathouse.org. Subway: A/B/C/D/1 to 59th St./Columbus Circle. 9am–6pm weekends and holidays; weekday evenings July–Aug, 5–7pm. *Pier 40,* at Houston St. and the Hudson. 9am–6pm weekends and holidays, select weeknights 5–7pm. Subway: 1 to Houston St.; A/C/E to Canal St. *Riverside Park,* 72nd St., at the Hudson. 10am–5pm weekends and holidays. Subway: 1/2/3 to 72nd St.

The Gowanus Dredgers Canoe Club FREE   The Gowanus Canal is in a transitional phase between being the butt of jokes and serving as a genteel Brooklyn natural resource. A canoe trip here still leans toward the former, providing a surreal float through what is mostly a forgotten industrial wasteland. Guided tours that run down to the Gowanus Bay are available by appointment. The season lasts from late March through the end of October. Pick up is near 2nd Street and Bond Street in Brooklyn, but check the calendar for availability details first. For landlubbers, the Dredgers also offer free bike tours. There's no charge for any of these programs, but as this is a grassroots organization, every little bit of generosity helps.

Carroll Gardens, Brooklyn. ✆ **718/243-0849.** www.gowanuscanal.org. Every other Wed, 6–8pm; every other Sun, 1–5pm. Subway: F/G to Smith/9th St.

L.I.C. Community Boathouse FREE   The East River (it's not really a river; it's a tidal strait) is also open to experienced and newbie paddlers alike. Select Sunday afternoons from 1 to 5pm or so (depending on the tides), you can get out on the Queens waterfront from Hallets Cove. Besides that walk-up program, the boathouse also offers more elaborate kayak tours. Spaces are awarded in an online lottery; you can choose from weekday, weekend, and Socrates Sculpture Park cinema (p. 258) trips. The shore here may be industrial, but as a tidal strait the possibilities of porpoise and whale sightings are significantly greater than they are on the Hudson. The walk-up season runs mid-May to mid-October, weather permitting.

Kayak tours, L.I.C Community Boathouse at Anable Cove, Hunters Point, Queens. 44th Dr. and the East River. ✆ **718/228-9214.** www.licboathouse.org. Check the calendar for trip schedules. Subway: 7 to Vernon-Jackson; E/M to 23rd St./Ely Ave.; G to 45th Rd./Court Square. *Walk-up kayaks,* L.I.C Community Boathouse at Hallets Cove, Astoria, Queens. 31st Ave. and the East River. Sun 1–5pm. Subway: N/Q to Broadway.

Red Hook Boaters FREE   Native red clay (*Roode Hoek* in Dutch) is the origin of the name of this Brooklyn outlier, which is rapidly gentrifying thanks to the new IKEA and a host of restaurants and bars. One great way to explore the area is via the Red Hook Boaters, a group dedicated to maintaining local waterfront access and raising general aquatic awareness. Their free programs offer canoes and kayaks for 15- to 20-minute runs into the protected area near Louis Valentino, Jr. Park and Pier. In return, they ask that you pitch in with beach cleanup before or after (gloves, trash bags, and life jackets are all provided, in addition to boats). When you've logged some time as a volunteer, you can make an appointment to join in on an open-water tour of Governors Island, Brooklyn Bridge Park, or the Buttermilk Channel. Walk-up kayaking runs Sunday afternoons from late May to early October, and Thursday evenings from mid-June until mid-August.

The beach at Louis Valentino, Jr. Park and Pier, Red Hook, Brooklyn, near Coffey and Ferris sts. ℂ **917/676-6458.** www.redhookboaters.org. Sun 1–5pm; Thurs 6–8pm. Subway: F/G to Smith/9th St.

Village Community Boathouse FREE The rowboats known as Whitehall gigs used to flourish on New York Harbor, but human-powered boat travel has mostly gone the way of the U.S. shipping industry. To get a glimpse of what waterfront life was like (and to take advantage of fresh air and nice views), join up with the free rides this community organization hosts. You'll be captained by an experienced coxswain as you ply the waters near Pier 40, which is not so far from Whitehall Street, where the boats were once manufactured. (For the boathouse's DUMBO program, see Brooklyn Bridges Park above.)

Pier 40, at Houston St. and the Hudson. ℂ **917/929-3670.** www.villagecommunity boathouse.org. Tues, Thurs 5:30pm–dusk; Sun noon–3pm. Subway: 1 to Houston St.; A/C/E to Canal St.

YOGA, TAI CHI & MORE

New York offers several free and dirt cheap classes in tai chi and yoga. Tai chi has been slow to gather momentum as a trend, but yoga is well entrenched as the aerobics of the new millennium. Similar forms of fitness also pay visits to our parks. It's a good idea to wear comfortable clothing for these classes, and bring a mat or towel for yoga in the parks.

Battery Park City FREE From 8:30 to 9:30am on most Fridays in summer (and into fall) you can get a master's guidance in tai chi at Battery Park's Esplanade Plaza (at the end of Liberty St.). No experience necessary.

Battery Park City, along South End Ave., just west of West St. ℂ **212/267-9700.** www. bpcparks.org. Subway: 1/2/3 or A/C to Chambers St.; 1 to Rector St. or South Ferry; 4/5 to Bowling Green.

Brooklyn Bridge Park FREE Torso stabilization is the goal here, in classes led by a fitness guru and guress. The technique is Pilates mat work, and all skill levels are welcome. Registration begins at 6:30pm, the class starts at 7pm, and space is limited. Class is held on brand-spanking-new Pier 1, moving to a tent in the Tobacco Warehouse in case of rain.

Pier 1, the East River, at Old Fulton St. ✆ **718/802-0603.** www.brooklynbridgepark. org. Subway: A/C to High St.; F to York St.

Bryant Park `FREE`   Bryant Park loans its central location to a host of activities, most notably Tuesday and Thursday morning tai chi classes. The class is taught from 7:30 to 8:30am, May through September, so you can focus your energy before punching the clock. If you're new to the practice, World Tai Chi Day might be the thing for you. On the last Saturday in April, Bryant Park is the site of a day of classes and demonstrations. Thursday evenings (6–7pm) here are dedicated to yoga. From June until late August, on the southwest corner of the lawn, you can salute the setting sun and improve your flexibility. Morning people can catch the Tuesday yoga class from 10 to 11am. As an added bonus, you can take a knitting class (✆ **212/989-3030**) on Tuesday afternoons between 1:30 and 3pm in summer; yarn and needles are provided. Been on the fence about taking up fencing? Let the Manhattan Fencing Center tip the scales in favor of passés with their free beginner lessons from 1 to 2pm, April through June.

Bryant Park, btw. 41st and 42nd sts., and Fifth and Sixth aves. ✆ **212/768-4242.** www.bryantpark.org. Subway: B/D/F/M to 42nd St.; 7 to Fifth Ave.

Dharma Yoga Brooklyn   Receiving through giving is the economic plan for this Park Slope newcomer. A tranquil second-floor studio hosts meditation, chanting, and workshops, on top of the classical yoga. The cost? That's up to you and your conscience—sessions are by donation.

82 Sixth Ave., 2nd fl., at St. Marks Ave., Park Slope, Brooklyn. ✆ **718/395-7632.** www. dharmayogabrooklyn.com. Subway: 2/3 to Bergen St.; B/Q to Seventh Ave.

The High Line `FREE`   The Shape Up NYC program pays a visit to the far west side Tuesday mornings in summer to teach a 45-minute class in the Feldenkrais Method. "Awareness Through Movement" is the M.O., with breath and vision employed to bump up your flexibility and coordination. Stick around afterwards for the Pilates fusion class, which will increase your strength and flexibility. No reservations are necessary, but do bring a yoga mat.

High Line, 14th Street Passage, btw. 13th and 14th sts. ✆ **212/500-6035.** www.the highline.org. Tues 9am for Feldenkrais; 10am for Pilates. Subway: A/C/E to 14th St.; L to Eighth Ave.

lululemon athletica `FREE`   This Vancouver-born apparel store puts the free back in free-spirited with complimentary Sunday morning classes. Stop by any of the four locations for an hour of prime posture edjimication—usually yoga, but also branching out into Pilates and CrossFit training. They'll even let you borrow a mat (although if you choose to gear up you won't have far to go). There are also free Wednesday night Central Park jogging sessions ("the Run Club"), and yoga in Bryant Park (p. 179). Sunday morning class times vary, check online for the latest.

1928 Broadway, at 64th St. ✆ **212/712-1767.** www.lululemon.com. Subway: 1 to 66th St./Lincoln Center. Other locations: *Upper East Side*, 1127 Third Ave., at 66th St. ✆ **212/755-5019.** Subway: F to 63rd St./Lexington Ave.; 6 to 68th St./Hunter College. *Union Square*, 15 Union Square W., btw. 14th and 15th sts. ✆ **212/675-5286.** Subway: L/N/Q/R/4/5/6 to Union Sq. *Soho*, 481 Broadway btw. Broome and Grand sts. ✆ **212/334-8276.** Subway: 6 to Spring St.; N/Q/R to Canal St.

Riverside Park South `FREE`   Unwind after work in Riverside Park, where hatha yoga for beginners is taught every Wednesday from 6:30 to 7:30pm. The "Evening Salute to the Sun" class meets from early June to late September. Show up on a Tuesday and you'll be able to tone your muscles with a Pilates mat class. Hey, the art of contrology just might be the new yoga. Classes are from 6:30 to 7:30pm between mid-June and mid-August; bring your own mat.

Riverside Park, the Plaza at 66th St., at the Hudson. ✆ **212/408-0219.** www.riverside parkfund.org. Subway: 1 to 66th St.

Sivananda Yoga Vedanta Center `FREE`   Once a month this yoga center introduces the community to their practice via an open house. The day begins at 10:30am with a lecture and demonstration, followed by a trial class, a vegetarian meal, and finally an introduction to meditation. If you don't have your own mat, bring a towel to place over one of their mats. The first or second Saturday of the month.

243 W. 24th St., btw. Seventh and Eighth aves. ✆ **212/255-4560.** www.sivananda. org/ny. Subway: C/E or 1 to 23rd St.

Socrates Sculpture Park `FREE`   Waterfront fields and killer Manhattan views make for a lovely setting for classes. Kilipalu yoga is taught in two sessions on Saturdays, from 9:30 to 10:30am and 11am to noon, open to all levels. The course runs from May to late September, rain or shine. During those same months from 11am to noon on Sundays you can get a free tai chi class, also suitable for all levels. More? How about Brazilian martial art Capoeira on Saturdays from noon to

1:30pm, or Pilates on Sundays from 10 to 11am? Plus bike decorating, workshops, and movies (p. 258). Oh yeah, and sculpture.

32–01 Vernon Blvd., at Broadway, Long Island City, Queens. ✆ 718/956-1819. www.socratessculpturepark.org. Daily 10am–sunset. Subway: N/Q to Broadway. Walk 8 blocks along Broadway toward the East River.

Union Square FREE   The Union Square area has a spate of yoga spots, which take turns providing these free weekly classes. From March through the fall you'll find practitioners leading warrior forward bends and downward-facing dogs. Classes are open to all ages and abilities. Check the website for exact times; in recent years the classes have been held on weekend mornings, and Thursday mornings from June through August.

Union Square. ✆ 212/460-1200. www.unionsquarenyc.org. Subway: L/N/Q/R/4/5/6 to 14th St./Union Sq.

Yoga at the Commons   Inside a massive community space known for sustainability lectures and third-Thursday sharing sessions comes a new yoga series. Classes are taught along Vinyasa and Sivananda lines, with gentle and pre-natal yoga offered as well. Several nights a week in temperate weather catch a rooftop sunset class. All classes are pay what you can (suggested donation is $10).

388 Atlantic Ave., btw. Hoyt and Bond sts., Boerum Hill, Brooklyn. www.yogaatthecommons.wordpress.com. Subway: A/C/G to Hoyt-Schermerhorn; F/G to Bergen St.

Yoga to the People   As the name suggests, this organization seeks to return yoga to its grassroots origins, away from the pricey boutique practices. Power Vinyasa Flow classes are taught in the St. Marks studio for a suggested donation of $10, but nobody tracks it—the people pay what they can. Classes run seven days a week, with a special candlelit session on Sunday nights. You can also find traditional hot yoga classes (90 min., $8) at the 27th Street studio, and hot Vinyasa at 38th Street (60 min., $5).

12 St. Marks Place, btw. Second and Third aves. ✆ 917/573-YOGA [9642]. www.yogatothepeople.com. Subway: 6 to Astor Place; N/Q/R to 8th St. *Chelsea*, 115 W. 27th St., 3rd fl., btw. Sixth and Seventh aves. Subway: 1 or N/Q/R to 28th St. *Midtown*, 1017 Sixth Ave., at 38th St. Subway: B/D/F to 42nd St.

On Sundays, Orchard Street closes to car traffic and cheap clothes deals fill the pavement of the Lower East Side's "Bargain District." See p. 185 for more information.

SHOPPING

The last time my country friend came to visit, I noticed him limping around the avenues of New York with a broken shoelace. I immediately tried to steer him into the nearest drugstore, but he resisted, telling me he didn't want to be slammed with those "big-city shoelace prices."

I still chuckle at this story when I'm scoring some crazy deal in the heart of the city. The volume advantage that eight million citizens provide can't be touched out in the sticks. Clothes, electronics, furniture, food, and, yes, even shoelaces, are available here for a fraction of their price in the hinterland. Plus Gotham's refined taste is great news for the cost-conscious when it comes time for gowns and coffee tables to begin their second and third lives. New York thrift stores, flea markets, and curbside trash piles are all treasure-troves for the patient and sharp-eyed, meaning savvy New Yorkers can finish off their cheap shopping lists better than anybody else in the U.S. of A. Which is helpful when your rent bill ensures you're living on a shoestring.

1 Dirt Cheap Shopping Zones

Maybe I was dozing through my Capitalism 101 classes, but I don't understand why New York stores of similar stripe all jam themselves into the exact same neighborhood. The Bowery is dotted with restaurant supply shops, and then suddenly every storefront is dedicated to lighting. Lampshade shops gather on nearby side streets. Whatever the initial cause, the effect of the single-product density is bargaining power galore for the consumer. Don't like the price? Walk next door and see if you can do a little better.

DOWNTOWN

THE FINANCIAL DISTRICT

Come lunchtime downtown, the streets fill with office workers scurrying around the cheap shopping outlets. **Fulton, Nassau,** and **Chambers** streets are big destinations, although there isn't anything here that can't be found in other places in the city. The two exceptions to that rule are the city's best electronics and best clothes stores, both near City Hall (see "Department Stores for Cheapskates" and "Electronics," later in this chapter).

Subway: A/C/J/Z/2/3/4/5 to Fulton St./Broadway Nassau; R to City Hall; 6 to Brooklyn Bridge/City Hall.

CHINATOWN

A trip to Chinatown can feel like a visit to a foreign country. Even better is the way it feels like a visit to a foreign economy, with prices that are only a fraction of what's charged across the border. Although the days of easy access to knockoff Oakley sunglasses and Kate Spade bags are gone (the city has cracked down on counterfeiting, although the hucksters can still be found **around Canal Street**), this is still the city's premier bargain destination. **Division Street and East Broadway** don't attract many tourists, but locals take advantage of the abundance of cheap apartment-ware shops, where good prices on appliances, furniture, knickknacks, and hardware can be found.

Subway: A/C/E/J/N/R/Q/Z/6 to Canal St.

THE BOWERY

Chinatown inflections can be found on nearby **Bowery.** The street is rapidly transforming from a district of missions to a nightlife destination, but its primary character in daylight still derives from a profusion of restaurant- and kitchen-supply stores. Many are wholesalers, oriented toward the industry. Those that sell to the public often also have great deals on chairs, small tables, and stools. When you cross **Delancey Street** heading south, you'll be in the cheap-lighting district. Having so many dealers in one place gives the buyer leverage when it comes time to barter on the price.

Subway: J/Z to Bowery; F/M to Second Ave.; 6 to Spring St.

NOLITA & THE EAST VILLAGE

NoLita and the East Village are stylish boutique playgrounds. As such, bargains can be hard to find. The good news is that low—if not dirt cheap—prices on haute couture can still be tracked down, if you put in the legwork. NoLita's **Elizabeth, Mott, and Mulberry streets** (btw. Houston and Prince) are dotted with an ever-increasing number of fashionable stops, including one of the city's best consignment stores (see "Designer Consignment Stores," later in this chapter). In the Village, **East 9th Street,** between Second Avenue and Avenue A, is home to a slew of up-and-coming local fashion designers—great for window shopping, if nothing else—and loads of small gift shops.

Subway: N/Q/R to Prince St.; 6 to Spring St.; F/M to Second Ave.; J/Z to Bowery.

THE LOWER EAST SIDE

Holdover street signs designate the chunk of Manhattan south of Houston and east of the Bowery as the "Bargain District." You can still find fabric, bedding, and some clothing, but expensive boutiques and trendy restaurants are crowding the bargains out. The state of flux makes it fun to visit, especially on Sundays. **Orchard Street** closes to traffic **between Delancey and Houston streets,** and vendors lay out cheap goods on tabletops, in the spirit of the pushcarts that were once ubiquitous here. In the warmer months you may also get a free band, fashion show, or pickle festival. On the weekdays, you're more likely

SHOPPING DOWNTOWN

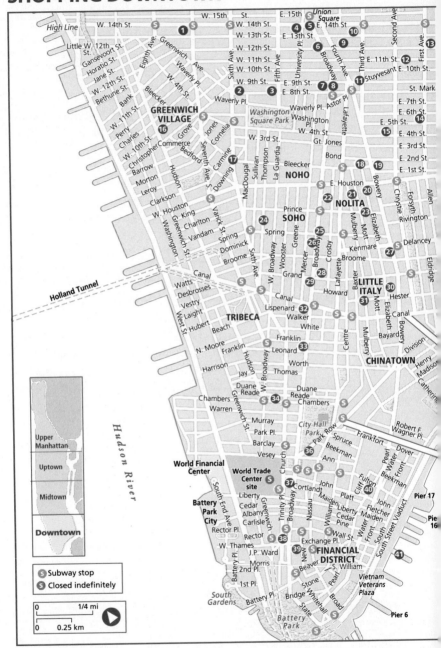

Subway stop
Closed indefinitely

| 0 | 1/4 mi |
| 0 | 0.25 km |

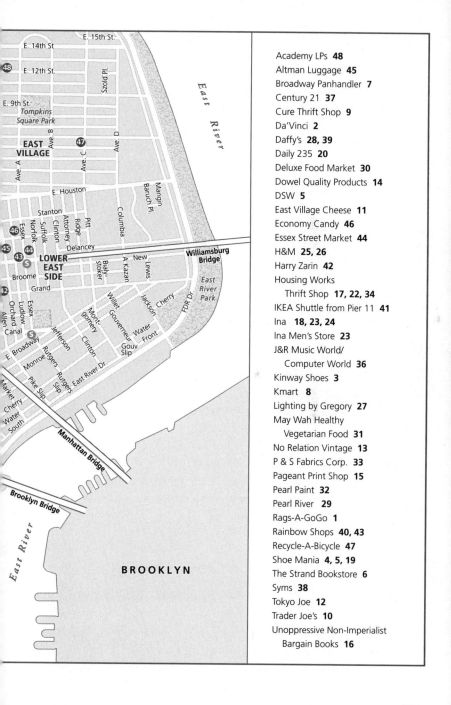

to hear the atavistic hard sell of a barker. Many of the shopkeepers will bargain, if that's in your skill set. Little hipster shops have infiltrated Orchard and can also be found scattered around **Ludlow and Stanton** and other nearby streets. Much cheaper goods are available off **Delancey and Clinton streets,** which have a few holdout 99¢ stores and bargain-bin housewares.

Subway: F to Delancey St.; J/M/Z to Essex St.

On Broadway

The stretches of **Broadway between Bleecker and Canal streets** are a fashion runway for New York youth. With cheap stores abounding, the streets stay packed until nightfall. Though it's sometimes semi-derisively referred to as the "Cheap Sneaker District," lower Broadway has a great selection of hip and affordable jeans, sweats, jackets, and, yes, sneakers. The area's traffic flow has only increased with the opening of a Bloomingdale's satellite in the dearly departed Canal Jeans' space. The high-profile addition has yet to price out its cut-rate neighbors.

Subway: B/D/F/M to Broadway/Lafayette; 6 to Spring St.; N/Q/R to Prince St.

Chelsea

Proximity to Fifth Avenue's deep purses helped propel Chelsea's stretches of **Sixth Avenue and Broadway** to the top of Manhattan's shopping heap in the late 19th century. The fancy folk eventually moved uptown and the department stores followed, but not before leaving behind some lovely cast-iron architecture. Big discount chains have moved in, including a popular Old Navy, and a couple of good thrift stops on **17th Street between Fifth and Sixth avenues.**

Subway: L to Sixth Ave.; F/M to 23rd St.

Gramercy

The residential enclave of Gramercy, sandwiched between hectic Midtown and East Village streets, is often overlooked as a shopping destination. That's great news for thrift aficionados, who can take advantage of less competition. Gramercy's almost total lack of hipster cred makes the cool clothing, furniture, and collectibles somewhat easier to come by than in picked-over East Village and NoLita stores. The shops along **23rd street between Second and Third avenues** are well stocked, and the goods are priced low enough that they're continually flowing. For my money, this is the best place in the city to bargain hunt for thrift threads.

Subway: 6 to 23rd St.

MIDTOWN
THE GARMENT DISTRICT

The huge old buildings in **the 30s between Madison and Eighth avenues** still bear faded advertisements for the furriers and milliners whose shops and factories filled the lofts here. Although much of the manufacturing has moved to cheaper zip codes, the garment trade is still active in ground-floor showrooms. Most are wholesale only, particularly the stretch on **Broadway that runs into the 20s.** A few places are open to the retail public, but the majority of plastic gewgaws they sell are on the express track for a landfill eternity. Toward the west, Penn Station is a hub for light rail and subway trains, and the streets nearby are a natural mecca for shoppers. Several big discounters are stationed here, as is the largest store in the world, Macy's. For garment shopping, however, downtown is a better bet.

Subway: B/D/F/N/Q/R/ to 34th St./Herald Sq.; 1/2/3 or A/C/E to 34th St./Penn Station.

UPTOWN

Clustered on the Upper West and Upper East sides are some of the highest per capita incomes in the world. The big chains and department stores that cater to those lofty budgets dominate the local retail trade, though a few exceptions exist for discerning shoppers. For high-end fashions at low-end prices, the consignment shops on **Madison and Amsterdam avenues** are some of the best in the city.

Subway: 1/2/3 to 72nd St.; B/C to 72nd St.; 4/5/6 to 86th St.

2 Dirt Cheap Threads & More

DIRT CHIC

Used clothing falls into two categories in New York, "thrift" and "vintage." In a thrift shop you'll have to sort through racks of junk to find that one perfect shirt, but it won't set you back more than a few bucks. A good vintage proprietor will do the editing for you, but you'll pay for access to her good taste. For the trendiest items—like a '70s rock concert T-shirt—a couple of holes in the sleeve may not lower the

SHOPPING IN MIDTOWN

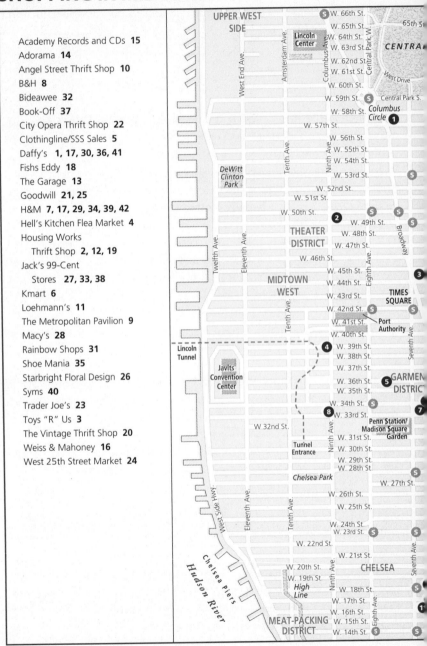

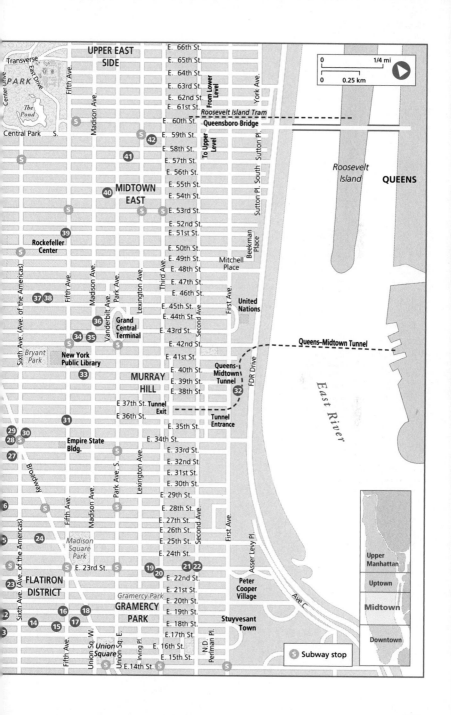

SHOPPING UPTOWN

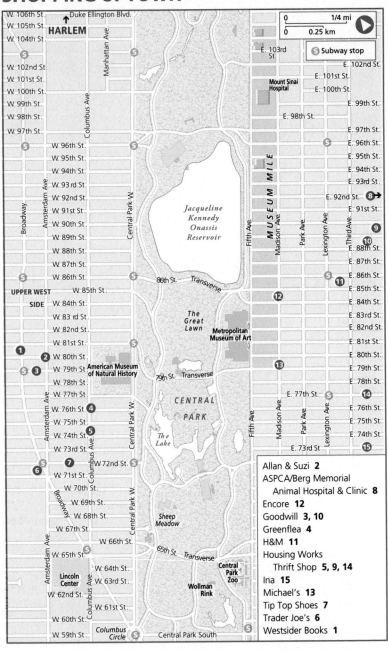

Allan & Suzi **2**
ASPCA/Berg Memorial
  Animal Hospital & Clinic **8**
Encore **12**
Goodwill **3, 10**
Greenflea **4**
H&M **11**
Housing Works
  Thrift Shop **5, 9, 14**
Ina **15**
Michael's **13**
Tip Top Shoes **7**
Trader Joe's **6**
Westsider Books **1**

$90 price tag. Uptown consignment shops will sell you a Chanel suit at a fraction of the original cost, but that's still going to be a several-hundred-dollar commitment. My favorites are shops that split the difference between thrift and vintage, selling used stuff that's still got some life left in it, but not at budget-busting prices. Many of the city's thrift shops are charitable nonprofits, so not only will you be getting a bargain, you'll also be helping out a worthy cause.

Note: Clothing isn't the only reason we tightwads love thrift stores. Most of the shops listed below also stock an impressive variety of used furniture, jewelry, electronics, books, records, and even art.

LORD HAVE GRAMERCY: CHEAP SHOPPING ON 23RD STREET

My favorite shopping cluster is 23rd Street, near Third Avenue. Gramercy is prosperous enough to ensure high quality levels for hand-me-down goods, and a lack of hipster competition in these parts makes the racks less pawed-through.

City Opera Thrift Shop   Locals sing the praises of this lovely shop, with its balconies full of deals on art, books, and bric-a-brac. Prices for furniture are excellent. Costumey looks dominate the clothing selection, including some pieces that appear to have just left the stage. 222 E. 23rd St., btw. Second and Third aves. © **212/684-5344.** www.nyc opera.com. Subway: 6 to 23rd St.

Goodwill   The style quota in these stores tends to be pretty low, with racks full of the fashion miscues of the last couple of decades. However, there's tons to look at here, and it's in a lot better shape than the next-door Salvation Army. Plus, when you do find your diamond in the rough you won't pay much for it. (If it were easy all the time, the big scores wouldn't be nearly as thrilling, right?) 220 E. 23rd St., btw. Second and Third aves. © **212/447-7270.** www.goodwillny.org. Subway: 6 to 23rd St. Other Manhattan locations: *Harlem,* 2196 Fifth Ave., at 135th St. © **212/862-0020.** Subway: 2/3 to Lenox Ave. *East Harlem,* 2231 Third Ave., btw. 121st and 122nd sts. © **212/410-0973.** Subway: 4/5/6 to 125th St. *Upper West Side,* 217 W. 79th St., btw. Broadway and Amsterdam Ave. © **212/874-5050.** Subway: 1 to 79th St. *Washington Heights,* 512 W. 181st St., at Audubon St. © **212/923-7910.** Subway: 1 to 181st St. *Upper East Side,* 1704 Second Ave., btw. 88th and 89th sts. © **212/831-1830.** Subway: 4/5/6 to 86th St. *Chelsea,* 103 W. 25th St., near Sixth Ave. © **646/638-1725.** Subway: 1 or F to 23rd St.

Housing Works Thrift Shop   Housing Works has the city's best thrift shops, with a constant stream of quality donations coming and going. Designer names pop up often on the clothes racks, and the jewelry shelves are filled with intriguing items. The real draw, however, is the furniture. Although the premium pieces end up in those gorgeously arrayed store windows (they're up for grabs in silent auctions), many a well-preserved table or chair finds its way to the sales floor. 157 E. 23rd St., btw. Third and Lexington aves. ✆ **212/529-5955.** www.housingworks.org. Subway: 6 to 23rd St. Other locations: *Chelsea,* 143 W. 17th St., btw. Sixth and Seventh aves. ✆ **212/366-0820.** Subway: 1 to 18th St.; F to 14th St.; L to Sixth Ave. *Upper East Side,* 202 E. 77th St., btw. Second and Third aves. ✆ **212/772-8461.** Subway: 6 to 77th St. *Upper East Side,* 1730 Second Ave., at 90th St. ✆ **212/722-8306.** Subway: 4/5/6 to 86th St. *Upper West Side,* 306 Columbus Ave., btw. 74th and 75th sts. ✆ **212/579-7566.** Subway: B/C to 72nd St. *West Village,* 245 W. 10th St., btw. Hudson and Bleecker sts. ✆ **212/352-1618.** Subway: 1 to Christopher St. *Brooklyn Heights,* 122 Montague St., at Henry St., Brooklyn. ✆ **718/237-0521.** Subway: R/2/3/4/5 to Borough Hall. *Hell's Kitchen,* 732 Ninth Ave., btw. 49th and 50th sts. ✆ **646/963-2665.** Subway: C/E to 50th St. *SoHo,* 130 Crosby St., at Jersey St. ✆ **646/786-1200. Subway:** B/D/F to Broadway/Lafayette , N/Q/R to Prince St., 6 to Spring St. *TriBeCa,* 119 Chambers St., btw. W. Broadway and Church St. ✆ **212/732-0584.** Subway: 1/2/3 or A/C to Chambers St.

The Vintage Thrift Shop   Most items here are in good enough shape to make this feel more like a boutique than a thrift shop. Vintage glasses, glassware, prints, clothes, and more can be found, with a certain amount of self-awareness evident in the pricing. There isn't room for much furniture, but what's here is priced to sell. 286 Third Ave., btw. 22nd and 23rd sts. ✆ **212/871-0777.** www.vintagethriftshop.org. Subway: 6 to 23rd St.

Cheap Shopping Outside of Gramercy

Angel Street Thrift Shop   Angel Street does an impressive job of keeping its recycled goods au courant. The clothes are in good shape and most don't scream, "just bought at a thrift shop." Some unused ringers like sealed sheets and electronics sneak into the bric-a-brac and bedding sections. 118 W. 17th St., btw. Sixth and Seventh aves. ✆ **212/229-0546.** www.angelthriftshop.org. Subway: 1 to 18th St.; F to 14th St.; L to Sixth Ave.

Beacon's Closet   Hipsters delight in the well-stocked palaces of the two Beacon's Closets. As a clothing exchange, this store actively buys clothes off its customers, with no appointment necessary. Clean out your closet and turn it into cash. Pick up 20% more by getting paid off in store credit and putting all those newly empty hangers to immediate use. The stores can be picky about what they'll take, but that just makes for better selection for shoppers. Both locations have extensive collections of stylish clothes and shoes. Park Slope, 92 Fifth Ave., at Warren St. ☏ **718/230-1630.** www.beaconscloset. com. Subway: R to Union St./Fourth Ave. Other location: Williamsburg, 88 N. 11th St., btw. Berry and Wythe sts. ☏ **718/ 486-0816.** Subway: L to Bedford Ave.

Cure Thrift Shop The cure in the name is for diabetes, which afflicts the founder, along with some 24 million other Americans. While you're helping a worthy cause, help yourself to great deals on furniture and high fashion. Designer dresses start at little more than $10, and skirts and scarves can be found for $5 or less. Students, seniors, diabetics, and readers of the shop's Tumblr can lower their tabs by a further 15% on select days. See the website for details. 111 E. 12th St., btw. Third and Fourth aves. ☏ **212/ 505-7467.** www.curethriftshop.com. Subway: L/N/Q/R/4/5/6 to 14th St./ Union Sq.; L to Third Ave.

Rags-A-GoGo It's a rare thrift-vintage shop that hits the trifecta of good selection, good condition,

Finds & Relations

Just don't call it a thrift store: The East Village's **No Relation Vintage** prides itself on well-preserved *vintage* picks spread out amid row upon row of $10 duds. NYU kids and tourists ransack the rapidly changing stock for armfuls of soft horsehide jackets, glittery '60s party looks, '70s prairie dresses, buttondowns, jerseys, and screen-printed tees. As a bonus, they'll let you reach even further back with low-priced furs from the '50s. Women plunder purses and round-toe heels while guys who fondly remember America's awkward years score Air Jordans and Levis E jean jackets. (To the dismay of the staff, this is also the official source for hideous Christmas sweaters.) The near-limitless stock makes squeezing into the shoe-box-sized dressing room and the smell of formaldehyde worth it. I crave high-quality vintage dresses, but with their explosive popularity, most surrounding boutiques mark their buys up too much. Here I can dress myself head to toe for $30 and avoid being a walking fresh-from-the-East-Village-boutique cliché. 204 First Ave., btw. 12th and 13th sts. ☏ **212/228-5201.** www.norelationvintage. com. Subway: L to First Ave.

—*Ashley Hoffman*

and good prices the way R.A.G.G. does. This Chelsea charmer succeeds with rack after rack of cool pants, T's, sweatshirts, and buttondowns. Dusty stuffed animals survey the scene, increasing the atmosphere of quirkiness essential to a good thrifting trip. 218 W. 14th St., btw. Seventh and Eighth aves. ✆ **646/486-4011.** www.rags-a-gogo.com. Subway: 1/2/3 or A/C/E to 14th St.; L to Eighth Ave.

Shop the Ops   Ample warehouse space was the fertilizer for Bushwick's recent rise. OfficeOps puts their 6,000-square-foot ground floor to good use with rack after rack of cheap hipster boots, belts, shoes, jackets, plaid pants, and T's. 57 Thames St., enter at Knickerbocker Ave. ✆ **718/418-2509.** www.officeops.org. Subway: L to Morgan Ave.

The Urban Jungle Vintage/Thrift Warehouse   A love of vintage that approaches the level of fetish imbues this massive Bushwick space. You can find accessories and art on top of the usual sneaker, T, housedress, and leather jacket suspects. Prices are good and the selection is extensive. 118 Knickerbocker Ave., btw. Thames St. and Flushing Ave. www.urban junglevintage.wordpress.com. ✆ **718/497-1331.** Subway: L to Morgan Ave.

DESIGNER CONSIGNMENT STORES

It's not that hard to look like a million bucks in NYC, even if your clothes budget tops out at a substantially smaller number. New York's best consignment shops carry loads of pre-owned, vintage, and overstock garments in near-showroom condition. The duds are by no means dirt cheap, but for the high end of design, the prices are as low as they come.

Allan & Suzi   From the window this looks like a shop targeting transvestites, but there's consignment for all tastes inside. Heavy hitters like Halston and Versace mix with one-off numbers and the rest of the best of 20th-century design. 416 Amsterdam Ave., at 80th St. ✆ **212/724-7445.** www.allanandsuzi.net. Subway: 1 to 79th St.; B/C to 81st St.

Encore   For resale women's wear, the Upper East Side is the place to be. Encore is the best of the best, chock-full of big, big names on two floors. A lot of it costs a fortune the first time around and it's still not cheap, but periodic sales can bring luxury into reach. Some of Jackie O's wardrobe made its curtain call here (which says a lot about the store's demographic). 1132 Madison Ave., btw. 84th and 85th sts., 2nd floor. ✆ **212/879-2850.** www.encoreresale.com. Subway: 4/5/6 to 86th St.

Ina When *Sex and the City*'s wardrobe department sold off its leftovers, of course it turned to Ina. This designer consignment shop carries the height of style, including the likes of Halston, Prada, and Daryl K. The racks are filled with both vintage and current items, and they're always in excellent shape. Shoes and accessories are here as well, and everything is marked way, way down (though outside of the sales, it's still not cheap). A men's store on Mott Street caters to the burgeoning metrosexual class. *NoLita,* 21 Prince St., btw. Mott and Elizabeth sts. © **212/334-9048.** www.inanyc.com. Subway: 6 to Spring St.; N/Q/R to Prince St. *NoHo,* 15 Bleecker St., btw. Lafayette St. and Bowery. © **212/228-8511.** Subway: 6 to Bleecker St.; B/D/F/M to Broadway/Lafayette. *SoHo,* 101 Thompson St., btw. Prince and Spring sts. © **212/941-4757.** Subway: C/E to Spring St. *Men's store,* 19 Prince St., btw. Mott and Elizabeth sts. © **212/334-2210.** Subway: 6 to Spring St.; N/Q/R to Prince St. *Uptown,* 208 E. 73rd St., btw. Second and Third aves. © **212/249-0014.** Subway: 6 to 77th St.

Michael's Designer wear for women is the focus of this much-loved two-story consignment boutique. The names are familiar—Chanel, YSL, Prada, and Gucci—but the prices are barely recognizable. As pickers, they're very careful, making sure no rips or stains make it onto the floor. 1041 Madison Ave., 2nd floor, btw. 79th and 80th sts. © **212/737-7273.** www.michaelsconsignment.com. Subway: 6 to 77th St.

Tokyo Joe When hipsters need the good stuff, they turn straight to this designer consignment shop. Cramped quarters can make for tough browsing, but the clothes themselves are in excellent shape. Don't miss the big section of lightly used and new shoes, going for a fraction of their cost Uptown. 334 E. 11th St., btw. First and Second aves. © **212/473-0724.** Subway: L to First Ave.

OTHER TRES CHEAP FASHIONS

H&M Swedish discounter Hennes & Mauritz knocks off the latest styles at low, low prices. They specialize in hip looks for adults, and as such they're a big hit with the teens. Durability is not the greatest, though it is about what you'd expect for these prices. 1328 Broadway, at 34th St. © **646/473-1165.** www.hm.com. Subway: 1/2/3/B/D/F/N/Q/R/ to 34th St./ Herald Sq. Other locations: *Midtown,* 640 Fifth Ave., at 51st St. © **212/656-9305.** Subway: E/M to Fifth Ave. *Times Square,* 505 Fifth Ave., at 42nd St. © **212/661-7012.** Subway: 1/2/3/7/N/Q/R/S to 42nd St. *Flatiron,* 111 Fifth Ave., at 18th St. © **212/539-1741.** Subway: L/N/Q/R/4/5/6 to 14th St./Union Sq. *SoHo,* 558 Broadway, btw. Prince and Spring sts. 🕿 **212/343-2722.** Subway: N/Q/R to Prince St.; 6 to Spring St. *SoHo,* 515 Broadway, btw. Spring and Broome sts. 🕿 **212/965-8975.** Subway: 6 to Spring St.; N/Q/R to Prince St. *Midtown,* 731 Lexington Ave., at 59th St. 🕿 **212/935-6781.** Subway: 4/5/6 or N/Q/R to 59th St./Lexington Ave. *Herald Square,* 435 Seventh Ave., btw. 33rd and 34th sts. 🕿 **212/643-6955.** Subway: 1/2/3/A/B/C/D/E/F/N/Q/R to 34th St./Herald Sq. *Upper East Side,* 150 E. 86th St., at Lexington Ave. 🕿 **212/289-1724.** Subway: 4/5/6 to 86th St. *Harlem,* 125 W. 125th St., at Lenox Ave. 🕿 **212/665-8300.** Subway: 2/3 to 125th St.

Loehmann's   When the original Barneys faltered, longtime discount fave Loehmann's was quick to fill much of the square footage. Casual wear comes in at one-third to two-thirds off the department-store prices, and you can reel in even deeper discounts on the likes of Donna Karan and Versace inside the "Back Room." Great prices for women's shoes, too, and there's an underpublicized men's floor. 101 Seventh Ave., btw. 16th and 17th sts. 🕿 **212/352-0856.** www.loehmanns.com. Subway: 1 to 18th St. Other location: 2101 Broadway, at 73rd St. 🕿 **212/882-9990.** Subway: 1/2/3 to 72nd St.

Rainbow Shops   When the new women's and girl's clothes lines come out, Rainbow wastes no time in coming up with affordable copies. Urban styles predominate, with the target audience well under 25. They have shoes and accessories, lots of plus sizes, and you won't have to part with a pot of gold. 110–114 Delancey St., btw. Essex and Ludlow sts. 🕿 **212/254-7058.** www.rainbowshops.com. Subway: F to Delancey St.; J/M/Z to Essex St. Other locations: *Harlem,* 308 W. 125th St., btw. Manhattan Ave. and Frederick Douglass Blvd. 🕿 **212/864-5707.** Subway: A/B/C/D to 125th St. *Herald Square,* 380 Fifth Ave., btw. 35th and 36th sts. 🕿 **212/947-0837.** Subway: B/D/F/N/Q/R/ to 34th St./Herald Sq. *Financial District,* 40 Fulton St., at Pearl St. 🕿 **212/346-0865.** Subway: 2/3/J/Z to Fulton St. Many locations in Brooklyn, too.

Weiss & Mahoney   Camo patterns seem to have finally fallen out of fashion (green-shaded organics are about the worst ways to camouflage oneself in NYC—if it's stealth you seek, a series of large gray and black squares would better do the trick). Military lite looks are in, though, and Weiss & Mahoney is loaded with peacoats, parkas, and field jackets. Work clothes are just at normal prices, but surplus and camping goods are way below retail. 142 Fifth Ave., at 19th St. 🕿 **212/675-1915.** www.weissmahoney.com. Subway: N/Q/R or 6 to 23rd St.

SHOE INS & OUTS

All the miles New Yorkers log as pedestrians help explain the occasional obsessive bent applied to our shoe shopping. My favorite footwear cluster can be found downtown. **Lower Broadway from East 4th Street down to Canal** has some great options. **West 8th Street between Fifth and Sixth avenues** is another nearby minidistrict, with the stylish and all-too-stylish intermixed. NYU undergrads haunt both areas, and prices often accommodate student budgets.

ON BROADWAY

DSW This chain came all the way from Ohio to liberate New Yorkers from high shoe prices. Their warehouse-style mega-stores are packed with recent releases. Special sale areas have the best buys, with markdowns exceeding 75%. Ladies in particular will have to exhibit patience, as the selection goes on forever. 40 E. 14th St., 3rd Floor, btw. University Place and Broadway. ✆ **212/674-2146.** www.dswshoe.com. Subway: L/N/Q/R/W/4/5/6 to 14th St./Union Sq.

Shoe Mania This popular discount store has a wide-ranging selection, putting Kenneth Coles sole to sole with Doc Martens, Birkenstocks, and Mephistos. Whether you go for style or comfort, you'll find a good price on it here. 853 Broadway, at 14th St. ✆ **212/253-8744.** Subway: 4/5/6/L/N/Q/R to 14th St./Union Sq. www.shoemania.com. Other locations: *Midtown,* 331 Madison Ave., btw. 42nd and 43rd sts. ✆ **212/557-6627.** Subway: 4/5/6/7/S to 42nd St./Grand Central. *Union Square,* 30 E. 14th St., btw. University Place and Fifth Ave. ✆ **212/627-0420.** Subway: 4/5/6/L/N/Q/R to 14th St./Union Sq. *SoHo,* 654 Broadway, at Bond St. ✆ **212/673-0904.** Subway: 6 to Bleecker St.; B/D/F to Broadway/Lafayette.

Tip Top Shoes This Uptown shop is tops for walking shoes, which are essential equipment in New York. Rockport, Mephisto, and Ecco are among the brands represented here, sold at reasonable prices. They also carry shoes of a less practical nature for those who prefer form to function. Staff is knowledgeable, if a little harried by the frenetic pace of business here. 155 W. 72nd St., btw. Broadway and Columbus Ave. ✆ **800/WALKING** [925-5464] or 212/787-4960. www.tiptopshoes.com. Subway: 1/2/3 to 72nd St.

ON 8TH STREET

Da'Vinci On-the-spot discounts are part of the code here. With a little bargaining savvy, you can get great prices on styles fresh off the boat from Italy. 37 W. 8th St., btw. Fifth and Sixth aves. © **212/982-9879.** www. davincishoesvillage.com. Subway: A/B/C/D/E/F/M to W. 4th St./Washington Sq.

Kinway Shoes   A family-run friendliness permeates this ramshackle shop. Selection is surprisingly broad given the close quarters. 5 W. 8th St., btw. Fifth and Sixth aves. © **212/777-3848.** www.villageshoes.com. Subway: A/B/C/D/E/F/M to W. 4th St./Washington Sq.

3 Flea New York

New Yorkers seeking free stimuli can certainly do worse than whiling away a few hours at a flea market. The rows of tables function as touchable museums, and the sheer width and breadth of available stuff is stunning. Prices for goods are generally not as cheap as they should be given the low-overhead locales, but there are ways to tip the scales in your favor. Sunday, as closing time approaches, the last thing a dealer wants to do is reload that half-ton armoire back into the truck. Likewise, a sudden rain can make parting with a wooden antique or a suede jacket more sweetness than sorrow. Use the elements to your advantage when it's time to haggle.

Brooklyn Flea   This upbeat Fort Greene market has scored one of the nicest slices of real estate in the borough: the Deco wonderland inside the Williamsburgh Savings Bank. More than 100 vendors lay out affordable clothing, crafts, vinyl, vintage jewelry, and architectural salvage. An even bigger draw here is the food—Korean hot dogs and Salvadorian papusas are just two of the cheap eat possibilities. April through November, the market runs outdoors from 10am to 5pm at Bishop Loughlin Memorial High on Saturdays, and inside the bank on Sundays. The rest of the year it's at the bank both weekend days, at least until a deeper-pursed tenant inevitably steps in. 1 Hanson Place, at Flatbush Ave. www. brooklynflea.com. Subway: B/D/N/Q/R/2/3/4/5 to Atlantic Ave./Pacific St. Outdoor location: 176 Lafayette Ave., btw. Clermont and Vanderbilt Aves. Subway: G to Clinton/Washington aves, A/C to Layafette Ave.

The Garage   Imagine a series of yard sales jammed up right on top of each other and you'll have an idea of the scene at the Garage. They've got lots of art, loose photos, and other oddball junk, and the prices are in the same stratosphere as you'd find on a suburban lawn. Two floors, open Saturdays and Sundays from 9am to 5pm. 112 W. 25th St., btw. Sixth and Seventh aves. © **212/243-5343.** www.hellskitchenfleamarket.com. Subway: F/M or 1 to 23rd St.

Come Sale Away

When out-of-towners marvel that anyone would pay what's printed on a New York price tag, they aren't taking into account that most locals never touch full retail prices. The key to dirt cheap shopping in the Big Apple is timing the sales. Seasons' ends, like just before back-to-school and just after Christmas, are routinely great for bargain hunters. Buy your sundresses and air conditioners in August, and wait until February to pick up that new winter coat. If your tastes run to vintage or barely used, try looking around in January, when a fresh crop of nonreturnable items get consigned. My favorite Web sources for sale info are: www.nymag.com/sales, www.ny.racked.com, www.thechoosybeggar.com, and www.topbutton.com. The newsletters from www.dailycandy.com are also great for keeping up to date.

Another great New York feature is the sample sale. Fashion designers can't sell just everything they lay their scissors to. Sample outfits made specially for store buyers end up sitting on a rack, along with canceled orders, overstock, and items whose day in the fashion sun has come and gone. In addition to the Internet sources above, check in at www.clothingline.com. **Clothingline/SSS Sales** (© **212/947-8748**) has 20 years' experience running sample sales for a host of huge names like rag & bone, J. Crew, and Calypso. Days of the week and hours vary; usually opens 10am. 261 W. 36th St., 2nd floor, btw. Seventh and Eighth aves. Subway: 1/2/3 or A/C/E to 34th St./Penn Station.

Greenflea   This bustling indoor/outdoor Upper West Side fair is a favorite way to spend a Sunday afternoon. The antiques tend to be priced fairly, marginalized as they are by dealers offering less-inspired contemporary imports, crafts, and clothes. The latter also line the nearby strip of Columbus Avenue. Open 10am to 5:30pm, until 6pm April to October. W. 76th St., at Columbus Ave. © 212/239-3025. www.greenfleamarkets.com. Subway: B/C to 72nd St.; 1 to 79th St.

Hell's Kitchen Flea Market   Though it hasn't quite caught up with its dearly departed predecessor in Chelsea, this is still the flea scene to beat in the city. Over 150 vendors bring vibrancy to a dingy strip behind the Port Authority. Open weekends, 9am to 6pm. 39th St., btw. Ninth and Tenth aves. ☎ **212/243-5343.** www.hellskitchenfleamarket.com. Subway: A/C/E to 42nd St./Port Authority.

West 25th Street Market   This churchyard fair is conveniently close to The Garage. Some 125 vendors pack the space with good retro/ antique picks, including clothes and art. Open weekends, 9am to 6pm. 29-37 W. 25th St., btw. Broadway and Sixth Ave. ☎ **212/243-5343.** www.hells kitchenfleamarket.com. Subway: F/M or N/Q/R to 23rd St.

4 Shekels & Chains: Department Stores

New York traditionally makes it hard for big franchises and chains to survive. The city is competitive to an extreme and there just isn't enough profit margin to pay a bunch of middle management salaries. Though there are a few chains sprinkled through these pages, for the most part I avoid the national retailers. They don't give enough bang for your buck.

Century 21   Nearly destroyed on 9/11, Century 21 has risen from the ashes to reclaim its place as the top clothes-shopping destination in the city. Fancy labels are fully represented here, sans the fancy prices. Expect designer goods at less than half the prices they carry in other department stores. There are great deals on sunglasses, linens, and housewares, too. Euro-fueled shopping euphoria has made this place mobbed even beyond peak lunch and weekend times, but recently extended hours (9pm or later Thurs–Sat) have helped some. Don't be too intimidated by long lines for the women's dressing room; the queue moves quickly. 22 Cortlandt St., btw. Broadway and Church St. ☎ 212/227-9092. www.c21stores.com. Subway: E to World Trade Center; A/C/ J/Z/2/3/4/5 to Fulton St./Broadway Nassau; R to Cortlandt St.; 1 to Rector St. Other locations: *Bay Ridge,* Brooklyn, 472 86th St., btw. Fourth and Fifth aves. ☎ **718/748-3266.** Subway: R to 86th St. *Rego Park, Queens,* 61–01 Junction Blvd., at 62nd Dr. ☎ **718/699-2121.** Subway: M/R to 63rd Dr./Rego Park.

Daffy's   Daffy's never seems as crowded as it should be, given how inexpensive the clothes are. The merchandise usually isn't big names, and you have to sort through some cheesy-looking Italian designs, but patient shopping always reveals some diamonds in the striped-shirt rough. Excellent for staples for men, and New Yorkers are just starting to discover the great kids' selection. The Herald Square location is

FREE Take an Unböring Trip to IKEA

Escape from Manhattan Island, courtesy of **IKEA,** the Swedish-born affordable style haven. There's an in-store cafeteria should you need a break from the action, with inexpensive food (including Swedish meatballs, of course).

The Red Hook location is IKEA's first foray into New York City proper, and it's spectacular. In addition to the goods indoors, there's a sprawling six-acre esplanade with amazing Harbor views. It costs $5 to ride the New York Water Taxi (© **212/742-1969;** www.nywatertaxi.com), leaving weekdays from Pier 11 on the East River end of Wall Street every 40 minutes between 2 and 7:40pm. If you spend $10 or more at IKEA, you'll get a $5 credit for the trip home. 1 Beard St., at Otsego Street, Red Hook, Brooklyn. © **718/246-IKEA.** See www.ikea.com for the full shuttle bus route via Park Slope.

For the Elizabeth, New Jersey, mothership, there's a bus from Port Authority. Unfortunately the bus only runs on weekends, and weekends at IKEA are *insane.* Take Academy Bus, Gate #5, lower concourse, Port Authority, Eighth Avenue at 42nd Street. Buses (round-trip only) leave every half-hour between 10am and 2:30pm and return from Jersey every half-hour between noon and 6pm. The trip takes about 30 minutes each way (© **800/BUS-IKEA** [287-4532]; www.ikea-usa.com). *Note:* The bus can accommodate your new possessions on the ride back, as long as they're not too big to carry.

comprehensive. 1311 Broadway, at 34th St. © **212/736-4477.** www.daffys.com. Subway: B/D/F/N/Q/R/W to 34th St./Herald Sq., 1/2/3 to 34th St./Penn Station. Other locations: *SoHo,* 462 Broadway, at Grand St. © **212/334-7444.** Subway: N/Q/R to Canal St. *Flatiron,* 3 E. 18th St., at Fifth Ave. © **212/529-4477.** Subway: 4/5/6/L/N/Q/R to 14th St./Union Sq. *Midtown,* 335 Madison Ave., at 44th St. © **212/557-4422.** Subway: 4/5/6/7/S to 42nd St./Grand Central. *Midtown,* 125 E. 57th St., btw. Park and Lexington aves. © **212/376-4477.** Subway: 4/5/6 or N/Q/R to 59th St./Lexington Ave. *Financial District,* 50 Broadway, btw. Exchange Alley and Morris St. © **212/422-4477.** Subway: R/W or 1 to Rector St.; 4/5 to Wall St.; J/Z to Broad St. *Midtown,* 1775 Broadway, btw. 57th and 58th sts. © **212/294-4477.** Subway: 1/A/B/C/D to 59th St./Columbus Circle.

Or *Don't* Go to IKEA: Shop Brooklyn Sidewalks

Take a tour of Brownstone Brooklyn and along with the tree-lined streets and historic architecture, you can also enjoy a favorite local tradition: stoop giveaways and weekend sales. The egalitarian spirit of Brooklyn is nowhere more alive than along the borough's sidewalks and iron railings, where cramped living spaces get unburdened. Books are the most common find. Brooklyn reads, and when it's done, it enjoys nothing more than setting that book out on the stoop for the next person to enjoy. If it has a still-cold glass of iced tea next to it, maybe assume they just stepped inside, but otherwise, the tome is yours.

Furniture is another easy acquisition, especially the night before trash pick-ups. It's a mystery to me why anyone shops at the Red Hook IKEA when you can regularly find almost-new Björkuddens and easily repaired Liatorps. (With the bedbug issues plaguing New York, it might be best to pass over upholstered pieces, though.) If you're willing to part with a buck or two, you can also find fine pickings at weekend stoop sales. Treat it as an experiment in sociology and economics, trying to fathom why a Cobble Hill corporate lawyer whose hourly rate is $450 would choose to spend an entire beautiful Saturday outside on the stoop for a total take of $86 from unopened wedding gifts and last year's scuba equipment. Actually, who cares, as long as you can make off with the Tiffany keychain still in the box for $3, or the kids' massive LEGO hoard for just a couple of bucks more. Most of what doesn't sell will end up curbside or draped over the railing, joining the virtuous cycle of Brooklyn's recycling tradition. If a more curated approach is your style, stop by my shop, Fork + Pencil (p. 206) for all your railroad piston mold, 19th-century Japanese erotica, and royal Coldstream Guards coat needs.

—*Alex Grabcheski*

Jack's 99-Cent Stores   If you think a dollar doesn't get you far in the big city, you don't know Jack. With central locations and a loyal/rabid clientele, these stores bustle at all hours with bargain-hunters stocking up on housewares, gifts, appliances, and chocolate bars.

They even have groceries, at unbeatable prices. Daily specials, unadvertised to appease suppliers, reward frequent visits. 16 E. 40th St., btw. Madison and Fifth aves. ☎ **212/696-5767.** Subway: B/D/F/M to 42nd St.; 7 to Fifth Ave. Other locations: *Midtown,* 45 W. 45th St., btw. Fifth and Sixth aves. ☎ **212/354-6888.** Subway: B/D/F/M to 47th–50th sts.–Rockefeller Center; 7 to Fifth Ave. *Herald Square,* 110 W. 32nd St., btw. Sixth and Seventh aves. ☎ **212/268-9962.** Subway: B/D/F/N/Q/R to 34th St./Herald Sq.; 1/2/3 to 34th St./Penn Station.

Kmart The words Kmart and inspiring are rarely found in the same sentence, but for me every trip to Astor Place's K is a thrilling reminder of NYC's cultural diversity. Students, yuppies, outer-borough homemakers, and Japanese hipsters all rub shoulders as they prowl the long aisles for cheap clothing, housewares, furniture, and even food. The hardware and paint departments have great deals, and there's an excellent plant section. Direct access to the subway makes it easy to drag your haul home. 770 Broadway, btw. 8th and 9th sts. ☎ **212/673-1540.** www.kmart.com. Subway: 6 to Astor Place; N/Q/R to 8th St. Other location: 250 W. 34th St., btw. Sixth and Seventh aves. ☎ **212/760-1188.** Subway: B/D/F/N/Q/R to 34th St./Herald Sq; 1/2/3 to 34th St./Penn Station.

Macy's (One-Day Sales) Covering 10 stories and an entire city block, this megalith has just about everything, including at any given time a large chunk of the metropolitan shopping population. The key is to buy during the frequent sales. The famous One-Days are the best, usually held on Wednesdays, with the occasional Saturday thrown in. Check the *New York Times* for Macy's full-page advertisements, which sometimes include clip-out coupons for additional 10% to 15% discounts. Herald Sq., W. 34th St. and Broadway. ☎ **212/695-4400.** www.macys.com. Subway: B/D/F/N/Q/R to 34th St./Herald Sq.; 1/2/3 to 34th St./Penn Station.

FREE 🏵 **Macy's Flower Show**

Outside of sales (which can be great for bargain-hunters), the big department stores aren't much help for the budget-minded. For free entertainment, though, they hold their own. Window displays make great theater, and floor after floor of regal goods make for fun browsing. The first 2 weeks of April bring some serious spectacle when Macy's goes nuts for flowers. The store is transformed by over a million blossoms in 10 gardens. Free 20-minute tours run every half-hour from 11am to 4pm. www.macys.com. Flower hot line ☎ **212/494-4495.**

Peachfrog This housewares-slash-clothing store is like a hipster version of Daffy's. When you step in you're greeted by complimentary coffee and goods priced so low you wonder why they bothered with a price tag. Upstairs are racks full of designer leftovers and samples. Leather handbags start at $59, sneakers at $21, and sunglasses at $6. 136 N. 10th St., btw. Berry St. and Bedford Ave. ℂ**718/387-3224.** www. peachfrog. com. Subway: L to Bedford Ave.

Pearl River This minidepartment store couples Chinatown prices with SoHo ambience. The inventory favors Asian classics like paper lanterns, silk pajamas, and sequined slippers. Glazed bowls and other housewares make for inexpensive kitchen outfitting. This is a great spot for cheap gift hunting, too. 477 Broadway, btw. Broome and Grand sts. ℂ **212/431-4770.** www.pearlriver.com. Subway: N/Q/R to Canal St.; 6 to Spring St.

Syms Don't let the hoary slogan ("An educated consumer is our best customer") scare you off. This long-running discount shop keeps the styles plenty fresh, and selection is excellent, with five floors of fashion goodness to peruse. Cater-waiters and symphony conductors can slash their rental bills with tux purchases: My own penguin suit set me back just $139 here. 400 Park Ave., at 54th St. ℂ **212/317-8200.** www. syms.com. Subway: E/M to 53rd St.; 6 to 51st St. Other location: 42 Trinity Place, btw. Rector and Edgar sts. ℂ **212/797-1199.** Subway: R/W or 1 to Rector St.

5 Dirt Cheap Shopping: A to Z

ANTIQUES
See also "Flea New York," earlier in this chapter.

Fork & Pencil The twist here is that the proceeds go to charity: A big part of this shop's mandate is to raise awareness about nonprofits and community awareness. While you're doing some good, you can also fill in the gaps in your home decoration and gift lists. Cool vintage dishes, silverware, lamps, and art fill the petite space. For furniture and larger items, ask about the annex around the corner on Bergen Street. 221A Court St., at Warren St. www.forkandpencil.com. ℂ **718/488-8855.** Subway: F/G to Bergen St.

Green Village Used Furniture & Clothing The epic junk collection here requires some rifling, but the low prices reflect the need for elbow grease. For clothes, find quality on the racks and quantity in the bins—purchase 50 pounds or more and it's just $1.50 per pound.

Props, costumes, books, dishes, chairs, and miscellaneous antiques round out the 10,000 square feet of possibilities. 276 Starr St., btw. St. Nicholas and Wyckoff aves. www.gogreenvillage.com. ℂ **718/456-8844.** Subway: L to Jefferson St.

Junk   The name here isn't exactly self-deprecating: Wares tend to the low-end and you'll have to do some digging. Your reward, however, is solid kitsch at cheap prices. New stock comes in twice a week and turnover is high, so come back often to fill your comic book, needle-point, and taxidermy needs. 197 N. 9th St., btw. Bedford and Driggs aves. ℂ **718/640-6299.** www.myspace.com/brooklynjunk. Subway: L to Bedford Ave.

RePOP   All manner of stylish vintage furnishings here seek second (and third and fourth) lives in the big city. Chairs, tables, desks, and cabinets can be picked up in pop iterations for prices that are a fraction of those at Manhattan vendors. Pratt proximity brings in artisan crafts, and the events calendar serves up the occasional artist's reception. 68 Washington Ave., btw. Flushing and Park aves. ℂ **718/260-8032.** www.repopny.com. Subway: G to Clinton/Washington aves.

BIKES

Recycle-A-Bicycle   The organization that runs these shops promotes biking in the city by selling rehabbed bikes at reasonable prices. A top-of-the-line bike could set you back $500 or more, but that's a fraction of its cost new, and your purchase is helping out a worthy cause. 75 Ave. C, btw. 5th and 6th sts. ℂ **212/475-1655.** www.recycleabicycle.org. Subway: L to First Ave.; F/M to Second Ave. Other location: DUMBO, Brooklyn, 35 Pearl St., at Plymouth St. ℂ **718/858-2972.** Subway: F to York St.; A/C to High St.

BOOKS

See the "Word Up: Readings," section on p. 284 for other great sites for literary browsing.

Book-Off   A huge, clean, insanely cheap book store in the heart of Midtown may seem like a mirage, but brother, this thing's all real. A Japanese chain, Book-Off retails *manga, anime,* and Tokyo pop bands, along with English-language music, movies, books, and video-games. Acres of shelf space are dedicated to $1 and $2 book specials, with plenty of first edition hardcovers represented. More recently arrived books average $5, which is also the median price for CDs. Games and DVDs are generally $7 propositions. FINE PRINT They buy books, too, if you're looking to turn over a home library. 49 W. 45th St., btw. Fifth and Sixth aves. ✆ **212/685-1410.** www.bookoffusa.com. Subway: B/D/F to 47th–50th sts.–Rockefeller Center.

The Strand The Strand is as legendary for its 18 miles of books as it is for its 5 inches of aisle space to maneuver in. The big crowds are a testament to the great prices. Review copies of recent books share space with art books at 85% off list and used fiction hardbacks that go for under $5. Bibliophiles with small apartments beware—it's hard to leave empty-handed. 828 Broadway, at 12th St. ✆ **212/473-1452.** www.strand books.com. Subway: L/N/Q/R/4/5/6 to 14th St./Union Sq.

Unoppressive Non-Imperialist Bargain Books Positioning itself as the anti-B&N, this friendly family-owned shop won't blow you away with the breadth of its selection of Donald Trump autobiographies. It will, however, impress you with its well-chosen bargains in musician biographies, political philosophy, and Eastern religion. Prices start around $2, and great gift ideas abound. 34 Carmine St., btw. Bleecker and Bedford sts. ✆ **212/229-0079.** www.unoppressivebooks.blogspot.com. Subway: A/B/C/D/E/F/M to W. 4th St./Washington Sq.

Westsider Books This tiny, charming shop has the best used books Uptown. There's a broad selection of literary and historical works, and the occasional reviewer's copy can also be found, at discounted prices. It's also great for CD and record shoppers. 2246 Broadway, btw. 80th and 81st sts. ✆ **212/362-0706.** www.westsiderbooks.com. Subway: 1 to 79th St.

EDIBLES

Cooking at home is an obvious way of cutting costs, but a trip to the corner deli for necessities can feel like a shakedown by the time you step away from the cash register. Most NYC grocery stores aren't much better, but a few specialty shops offer accessible comestibles.

Deluxe Food Market, Inc. This market is a mishmash of a bakery, buffet, and grocery store. It's menacingly crowded, but the high-volume turnover keeps things fresh, and the price is right. The steam table in front has fluffy, jumbo-sized dumplings (four for $1.50), along with hot dishes that are priced at two for $3.25, three for $3.75, or four for $4.50 (if you don't speak Chinese, just point). The bakery keeps pastry prices below $1, a pre-made ham sandwich is $2, and a packaged chef's chicken platter is $3.50. Past the small eat-in section, you'll find a scrum forming around the regular grocery store goods.

Fish, meats, and greens are all at rock-bottom prices. You can also load up on frozen specialties, like big packs of dumplings (the no re-selling signs posted all over the shop are an indicator that you're get-ting a good deal). 79 Elizabeth St., btw. Hester and Grand sts. ℂ **212/925-5766.** Subway: B/D to Grand St.; J/Z to Bowery.

Dowel Quality Products   Many shoppers only know this store for its unrivalled beer selection, conveniently located near the BYOB res-taurants of Curry Row. There's a lot more to like here, however, including health and beauty items, incense, teas, and fruits and veg-etables. The best savings come on Dowel's own packaged goods, with bulk rice, chutneys, lentils, and curries of every hue among the highlights. 91 First Ave., btw. 5th and 6th sts. ℂ **212/979-6045.** Subway: F/M to Second Ave.

East Village Cheese Store   This discount dairy destination is the per-fect starting point for your next cocktail party. You can get bread, crackers, pâtés, pickles, and other side items, although the jaw-drop-ping prices are on the cheeses. In the front refrigerators, goat cheese tubes, double-cream brie wedges, and Boursin packages are all under $2. Behind the counter you'll find a long list of specials on fancy gou-das and cheddars for $2.99 a pound. The giveaway prices aren't indicative of quality, either. These aren't second-rate goods, just items picked up when some importer added a mistaken zero to an order. Their mistake is your gain. 40 Third Ave., btw. Ninth and Tenth sts. ℂ **212/477-2601.** Subway: 6 to Astor Place; N/Q/R to 8th St.

Essex Street Market   When the city squeezed the pushcarts off the Lower East Side 50 years ago, it built a garagelike city market as a replacement. The market evolved into a low-rent grocery store and shopping mall, frequented by Spanish and Chinese locals, who love the prices. (As this is the L.E.S. 2.0, gourmet cheeses, pasta, and choc-olate can now be found as well—though not all of them qualify as dirt cheap). **Essex Farm** (ℂ **212/533-5609**), a huge Korean deli, has taken over the north end of the market. They sell just about everything, but the best deals are on fresh fruit and vegetables. A huge container with a blend of gourmet lettuces is just $2.99, fruit salads are around $3, and when the mangos are ripe they're two for $1. The middle of the market has butchers, fishmongers, and a botanica. In the back you'll find **Batista Grocery** (ℂ **212/254-0796**), with great prices on Goya and other dry goods. Cafe tables are available if you want to make a picnic (on nice days you can take your meal down to the East River). Eat-in diners can also take advantage of the legendary **Shopsin's** (✆ **212/924-5160;** www.shopsins.com), relocated here after decades in the West Village. Kenny Shopsin, who curses like a sailor as he cooks up "Blisters on my Sisters" (a rice/beans/eggs/tortillas combo for $9) along with some 500-plus additional items. Kenny and his kids are classic New York characters, and if you've ever seen their documentary *I Like Killing Flies,* a visit here will be a definite brush with celebrity. Since this is downtown, there's even an art gallery tucked away in the very back (**Cuchifritos;** ✆ 212/598-4124; www.aai-nyc. org/cuchifritos; Mon–Sat noon–6pm). 120 Essex St., btw. Rivington and Delancey sts. ✆ **212/312-3603.** www.essexstreetmarket.com. Subway: F to Delancey St.; J/M/Z to Essex St.

May Wah Healthy Vegetarian Food, Inc.   Sometimes a vegetarian needs a break from the bean sprout and tofu regimen. The Chinese are fake meat experts, and this little Chinatown shop has a massive selection. A big package of frozen unchicken nuggets is only $3.15, and my personal favorite, citrus spare ribs, are only $3.30. 213 Hester St., btw. Centre St. and Centre Market Place. ✆ **212/334-4428.** www.vegieworld. com. Subway: J/N/Q/R/Z/6 to Canal St.

Sahadi's   This brightly lit and perennially mobbed Brooklyn grocery store is a great source for Middle Eastern cooking staples. Dozens of varieties of olive oil are available, as are nuts, dried fruits, olives, lentils, chickpeas, and of course top quality *maleb* (the Lebanese seasoning made from the insides of cherry pits). 187–189 Atlantic Ave., btw. Court and Clinton sts., Boerum Hill, Brooklyn. ✆ **718/624-4550.** www.sahadis.com. Subway: R to Court St.; 2/3/4/5 to Borough Hall.

Trader Joe's   Few new arrivals in the city have been awaited as breathlessly, by Californians and non-Californians alike, as Trader's. This legendary grocery store sells its own brands, eliminating the middle man and his attendant price premiums. Beyond the great prices are great products, with fresh, often organic ingredients. Somehow the Hawaiian-shirt-wearing staff stays California-friendly, despite the hordes of hardcore New York shoppers. The wine shop next door carries legendary and quite drinkable "Two-Buck Chuck" (though in New York, Charles Shaw's finest runs us three bucks). 142 E. 14th St., btw. Third Ave. and Irving Place (wine shop is next door at #138). ✆ **212/529-4612.** www.traderjoes.com. Subway: L to Third Ave.; N/Q/R/4/5/6 to 14th St./Union Sq.

Other locations: *Chelsea*, 675 Sixth Ave., btw. 21st and 22nd sts. Subway: F to 23rd St. *Upper West Side*, 200 W. 72nd St., at Broadway. Subway: 1/2/3 to 72nd St. *Cobble Hill, Brooklyn*, 130 Court St., at Atlantic Ave. ℂ **718/246-8460.** Subway: R to Court St.; 2/3/4/5 to Borough Hall. *Forest Hills, Queens*, 90–30 Metropolitan Ave., at 73rd Ave. ℂ **718/275-1791.** Subway: E/F/R to 71st Ave./Forest Hills.

ELECTRONICS

J&R Music World/Computer World   I'm constantly surprised how often an online search for discounted electronics brings up J&R as the cheapest supplier out there. Save the shipping cost by coming in to the bustling block-long series of stores. The staff is well-informed and not too brusque (at least by New York standards). The prices on cameras, stereos, computers, and software are excellent, and there's good music, film, and houseware shopping as well. Check the paper or the website for dates on the frequent sales.

Along Park Row, at Ann St., opposite City Hall Park. ℂ **800/426-6027** or 212/238-9000. www.jandr.com. Subway: 2/3 to Park Place; 4/5/6 to Brooklyn Bridge/City Hall.

FABRICS

Gray Line Linen   Savvy seamsters know their way around linen, which has more than double the strength of cotton. Those in-the-know go to this place, which offers rack after colorful rack at crazy-low prices. Linens that high-end stores sell for $30 a yard or more hover in the $8 range here. Considering that Restoration Hardware sells linen curtains for over $100, this is DIY bargain central.

260 W. 39th St., btw. Seventh and Eighth aves. ℂ **212/391-4130.** www.graylinelinen. com. Subway: 1/2/3/7/N/Q/R/S to Times Sq./42nd St.; A/C/E to 42nd St./Port Authority.

Harry Zarin Company   The fabric selection in this old-timer upstairs warehouse goes the whole nine yards, with an overwhelming selection of textures and styles. Deep discounts get even deeper for overruns and closeouts. Downstairs you'll find a recently remodeled conventional furniture store.

318 Grand St., btw. Ludlow and Orchard sts. ℂ **212/925-6112.** www.zarinfabrics. com. Subway: B/D to Grand St.; F to Delancey St.; J/M/Z to Essex St.

P & S Fabrics Corp.   Beyond the extensive collection of fabrics, you'll find patterns, trimmings, yarn, and notions at this cluttered downtown shop. Retail accessibility at wholesale prices makes this a great place for fashion DIYers to stock up. Don't miss the clearance rack.

358 Broadway, btw. Franklin and Leonard sts. © **212/226-1534.** Subway: J/M/N/Q/R/W/Z/6 to Canal St.

GIFTS & OTHER CURIOSITIES

Daily 235 For gift shopping, this tiny, creative shop has tiny, creative gifts for under $10. In one convenient stop, fill all your Japanese lamp, John Paul II paper doll, wind-up lederhosen, Bond-Aid brand bondage tape, and evil unicorn figurine needs.

235 Elizabeth St., btw. Prince and Houston sts. © **212/334-9728.** www.daily235.com. Subway: F/M to Second Ave.; J/Z to Bowery.

Pageant Print Shop Some 10,000 antique prints and maps are packed into this tiny storefront. You can find great New York City ephemera, as well as images of everything else humans have been interested in during the last century. The owners, who've been in the business their whole lives, pride themselves on having the lowest prices in the city. Don't miss the poster file, with plenty of under-$5 images for combating apartment wall white space.

69 E. 4th St., btw. Second Ave. and Bowery. © **212/674-5296.** www.pageantbooks.com. Subway: F/M to Second Ave.; 6 to Bleecker St.

SKSK Steve Keene is somewhere between the Henry Ford and the McDonald's of indie art. With his one-man assembly line, he's made over 200,000 paintings. If you're looking to decorate

Toys "R" Them

Among the hideous chains that characterize the new Times Square, **Toys "R" Us** stands out for its free entertainment. The central Ferris wheel, which rises 60 feet in the center of the store, is beloved by the kiddies, who don't begrudge the sometimes long waits. A 5-ton animatronic T-Rex is another crowd pleaser, as is the pink-overload zone of Barbie's envy-inducing duplex dollhouse. Prices here are good and made better by frequent in-store specials. Demonstrations are fun to watch and usually come with discounts on the product at hand. Even if you don't have a buying agenda, this is an easy place to fill time on a rainy day. 1514 Broadway, at 44th St. © **646/366-8858.** www.toysrus.com. Subway: 1/2/3/7/N/Q/R/S to Times Sq./42nd St.

on the cheap, you could do worse than S.K.'s factory outlet in Brooklyn (a part of his studio). There's an array of plywood cutouts, silk-screens, and paintings. A $20 investment will bring you enough to decorate two or three rooms, with change left over. Open Sundays 2 to 6pm, or by appointment.

93 Guernsey St., btw. Norman and Nassau aves. No phone. www.stevekeene.com. Subway: G to Nassau Ave.

HOUSEWARES

Broadway Panhandler Pan reviews consistently put this place at the top. For restaurant-quality cookware and kitchen tools, you can't find a better combo of selection, price, and service.

65 E. 8th St., at Mercer St. ✆ **212/966-3434.** www.broadwaypanhandler.com. Subway: N/Q/R to 8th St.

Fishs Eddy You can reel in remainders of custom china here. Prices are relatively low, certainly the best you'll do on a plate marked "Blue Plate Special." You can also find retro designs, including soda fountain glasses and vintage-looking flatware.

FREE Get On the Yarn Bus

Knitters and their ilk can widen their shopping options by trekking up to Westchester on the Yarn Bus. The bus connects New Yorkers with the Flying Fingers Yarn Shop, which carries those tofu and bamboo yarns you have so much trouble tracking down in Manhattan. The ride to charming Irvington, on the Hudson, takes about a half-hour, and it's totally free. The bus runs twice a day on the weekends, leaving from various spots around Mid- and Uptown. If those times and places aren't convenient, they'll make a custom arrangement for you. Call or e-mail in advance to reserve your place. Look for the blue van with the lamppost-sized needles piercing three jumbo yarn balls on the roof. 19 Main St., Irvington, New York. ✆ **877/359-4648.** www.flyingfingers.com.

889 Broadway, at 19th St. ✆ **212/420-9020.** www.fishseddy.com. Subway: 4/5/6/L/N/Q/R to 14th St./Union Sq.

Lighting by Gregory Great selection and good prices on lighting, plus a big collection of ceiling fans. The latest lighting trends can always be found.

158 Bowery, btw. Delancey and Broome sts. ✆ **888/811-FANS** [3267] or 212/226-1276. www.lightingbygregory.com. Subway: J/Z to Bowery; F/M to Second Ave.

The Flower District

Two green thumbs go up for the selection of plant and flower stores on **28th Street between Sixth and Seventh avenues,** and overflowing onto Sixth Avenue. (For those with brown thumbs, a great selection of plastic plants awaits as well.) The stores are a mix of wholesale and retail, with the best prices going to bulk buyers. Small purchasers can also reel in good buys, especially at **Starbright Floral Design** (150 W. 28th St., btw. Sixth and Seventh aves.; ℂ **800/ 520-8999;** www.starflor.com; subway: 1 or N/Q/R to 28th St.).

Pearl Paint   Pearl Paint has the city's best art supply prices and selection, in a sprawling compound tinted by an air of genial disarray. Specialty stores on the rear block (Lispenard) back up five floors of supplies in front (Canal). Frames, papers, canvas, and incidentals like day-planners and portfolios all carry the lowest prices in the city.

308 Canal St., btw. Broadway and Mercer St. ℂ 212/431-7932. www.pearlpaint. com. Subway: A/C/E or 1 to Canal St.

LUGGAGE

Altman Luggage   This old-time LES classic has wheeled luggage galore, in addition to business-person sundries like pens, wallets, and watches. Already deep discounts get even deeper for closeouts and items that have been too long on the showroom floor.

135 Orchard St., btw. Rivington and Delancey sts. ℂ 212/254-7275. www.altman luggage.com. Subway: F to Delancey St.; J/M/Z to Essex St.

MUSIC

Between burning, shredding, and downloading, brick and mortar music stores are increasingly imperiled. If you still take your music in tangible form, you can join fellow music junkies at **Academy Records and CDs.** The second-hand CD shelves are packed with classical, jazz, opera, and rock. Prices are excellent, and the selection is forever in motion as Academy aggressively acquires collections. For vinyl, try **Academy LPs** in the East Village and the Academy Annex in Williamsburg.

12 W. 18th St., btw. Fifth and Sixth aves. ℂ 212/242-3000. www.academy-records. com. Subway: 4/5/6/L/N/Q/R to 14th St./Union Sq.; F to 14th St. *Academy LPs,* 415 E. 12th St., btw. First Ave. and Ave. A. ℂ 212/780-9166. Subway: L to First Ave. Academy Annex, 96 N. 6th St., btw. Berry St. and Wythe Ave. ℂ 718/218-8200. Subway: L to Bedford Ave.

📻 Vinyl Haven: The WFMU Record Fair

If you've got an issue with piracy, or album art is a must, old-fashioned vinyl is the way to go. Thrift stores top out at $2 per disk, though DJs assure there are slim pickings outside of classical. For record fanatics, the paramount weekend is in late October, when the **WFMU Record Fair** comes to town. WFMU's free-form radio is one of New York's greatest cultural assets, and the record fair brings an incredible array of dealers. The show costs $6 to enter, but that fee includes free live bands, screenings in an AV room, and table after table of cheap CDs and vinyl. I ignore the $70 collector disks and head straight for the boxes under the table, where the two for $1 disks are most likely to be found. The fair is held at the **Metropolitan Pavilion** (125 W. 18th St., btw. Sixth and Seventh aves.; subway: 1 to 18th St.). For more information, call ✆ **201/521-1416,** ext. 225, or log on to www.wfmu.org/recfair. *Tip:* Sunday afternoon is the best bargain-hunter's time. Buyers are burned out and dealers are doing everything they can to keep from hauling all that obsolete technology back home.

PHOTO

Adorama   Photo pros flock to Adorama, which has unbelievably low prices on digital accessories, photo prints, and sundry items like blank cassettes. There's also film and second-hand lenses and SLR bodies in the back, although most of that is headed the way of the 8-track tape. FINE PRINT Closed Friday afternoons, all day Saturday, and Jewish holidays.

42 W. 18th St., btw. Fifth and Sixth aves. ✆ **212/741-0466.** www.adorama.com. Subway: 1 to 18th St.; F/M to 14th St.; L to Sixth Ave.

B&H   A bustling 35,000-square-foot space holds B&H's massive inventory of digital equipment, lighting, DVD players, home theater systems, and a host of photo-related products. Prices are very competitive, especially for used cameras and accessories. If you don't know exactly what you want, the pros here provide expert advice. FINE PRINT Closed Friday afternoons, all day Saturday, and Jewish holidays.

420 Ninth Ave., btw. 33rd and 34th sts. ℭ **800/606-6969** or 212/444-6615. www. bhphotovideo.com. Subway: A/C/E to 34th St.

SALVAGE

Build It Green! NYC   As a side-effect of working to save the planet, this non-profit offers up deeply discounted building materials, which it diverts from landfill languishment. The warehouse holds 75 tons of doors, floors, sinks, and trim. For even cheaper stock, come by during a Stop 'N Swap block party and trade up for another man's treasure (every Jan they host a re-gifting exchange in a local bar, too.) If you're remodeling, Build it Green! will do your kitchen demolition work for free.

3–17 26th Ave., at 3rd St., Astoria, Queens. ℭ **718/777-0132.** www.bignyc.org. Subway: N/Q to Astoria Blvd.

SWEETS

Economy Candy   The Lower East Side of the '30s was littered with small specialty shops like this one, which remains a family business 70 years later. With the other shops now defunct, Economy Candy has taken on their responsibilities, selling everything from coffee to nuts to dried fruit. Oh yeah, they also sell a little candy. From floors to rafters, the store is packed with lollipops, gum drops, halvah, gourmet candy bars, bulk chocolate, and pretty much anything else sweet you can think of. Prices are very reasonable, especially when you buy by the pound.

108 Rivington St., btw. Essex and Ludlow sts. ℭ **212/254-1531.** www.economy candy.com. Subway: F to Delancey St.; J/M/Z to Essex St.

6 Free from New York

My apartment would be an exercise in minimalism if it weren't for the generosity of the sidewalks of New York. Lamps, chairs, prints, and even the lovely beveled mirror in the kitchen have all been harvested from the bounty of the curbs. The key is to strike without hesitation because good stuff doesn't lay around the streets for long.

A good place to start is the Department of Sanitation's website (www.nyc.gov/html/dsny), where you can find out the current collection schedule for any address in any of the boroughs. Unless you're a van owner, you'll probably want to target places that are within close

MANHATTAN SIDEWALK GIVE-AWAY/
TRASH PICKUP DAYS

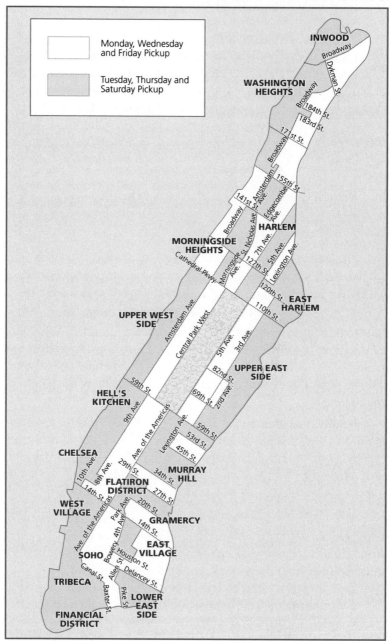

Monday, Wednesday and Friday Pickup

Tuesday, Thursday and Saturday Pickup

INWOOD

Broadway

WASHINGTON
HEIGHTS

Dykman St.

Broadway

184th St.

183rd St.

171st St.

Broadway

155th St.

141st St.

Amsterdam
Ave.

Edgecombe
Ave.

HARLEM

Broadway

St. Nicholas Ave.

7th Ave.

5th Ave.

Lexington Ave.

MORNINGSIDE
HEIGHTS

Cathedral Pkwy.

Morningside
Ave.

127th St.

120th St.

EAST
HARLEM

110th St.

UPPER WEST
SIDE

Amsterdam Ave.

Central Park West

5th Ave.

3rd Ave.

82nd St.

UPPER EAST
SIDE

HELL'S
KITCHEN

59th St.

69th St.

2nd Ave.

9th Ave.

Ave. of the Americas

Lexington Ave.

59th St.

53rd St.

45th St.

CHELSEA

10th Ave.

8th Ave.

29th St.

34th St.

MURRAY
HILL

FLATIRON
DISTRICT

27th St.

WEST
VILLAGE

14th St.

Park Ave.

20th St.

GRAMERCY

Ave. of the Americas

4th Ave.

14th St.

SOHO

Bowery

Houston St.

EAST
VILLAGE

Canal St.

Allen St.

Delancey St.

TRIBECA

Baxter St.

Pike St.

LOWER
EAST
SIDE

FINANCIAL
DISTRICT

Getting Free & Dirt Cheap Furniture Online

Many of New York's eight million residents live in tiny spaces, and **eBay** (www.ebay.com) is loaded with our local treasures. But dressers, desks, and other pieces with heft can cost several hundred dollars to ship, doubling or tripling the cost of an eBay purchase. When you're doing your bidding keep an eye out for New York zip codes—you may be the only person who can get a Man with a Van to take it home for a reasonable price. **Craigslist** (www.craigslist.org) is another good option, coupled with the Man with a Van. A whole section of postings is reserved for free items. Ugly furniture, moving boxes, pit bulls, boa constrictors, and computers are easy to come by, as well as less essential items like box turtles, hermit crab shelters, and 12-packs of nonalcoholic beer purchased in error. Look for "Curb Alerts," which tip off the public to salvagable items about to be dumped unceremoniously on the street. If you're paying: Search for high-end brands (like "ABC Home," "Room & Board," "West Elm," or "Thomas O'Brien"), and you'll occasionally get lucky price-wise.

hauling distance. (Trash-picking pros invest in small, wheeled hand trucks.)

Generally, just after the first of the month is the best time to be on the prowl. People have just moved in or out, and they're more likely to have been of a disposing bent. Late May, at the end of the school year, is another excellent time. The streets around NYU and Columbia overflow with abandoned student goods. Though much of what you'll see is better suited to a dorm than your swanky digs, with careful culling you can always find gems.

Freecycle NYC `FREE` This grassroots organization has grown into a serious waste-fighter, with over 7 million members worldwide. To connect in NYC, check out their Yahoo Group (www.groups.yahoo.com/group/freecyclenewyorkcity), which generates over 2,000 leads on free goods every month. There's no cost to join; the main stipulation is that everything offered must be free—not even trading is allowed.

Greencycle Swaps   Greenpoint and Williamsburg represent the cutting edge of New York culture, so it's no surprise to find a local community group there embracing the free market movement. Town Square hosts swaps between 1 and 4pm on the second Saturday of each month, spread around churches and schools in the two neighborhoods. They ask for a $5 donation and whatever clothes, shoes, bikes, books, and electronics you wish to divest yourself of. Check in at **www.townsquareinc.com** for site addresses and more information.

Score! **Pop-up Swap**   With the likes of Bust, Flavorpill, and Mean-Red hosting, these swaps are surefire spots for hipster goodies. Curators cull the junk from collections of music, books, housewares, clothing, shoes, and accessories. The result is like shopping a flea market, except instead of haggling for your price, just take what you want for free! A small donation (around $3) may be requested for entry, and of course they'd love you to bring some of your own discards to sweeten the pot. Cheap cocktails will help keep you going through a full afternoon of riffling. Check **www.scoredatscore.com** for times and locations.

Swap-O-Rama-Rama   Sort through 4,000 pounds of clothes, for free! That's the come-on to this community event, where you dump off some of your own fashion don'ts and then replenish your closet with whatever you find. A $10 donation is requested, which entitles you to both duds and DIY workshops. "Shoppers" can get help with on-the-spot iron-ons, silk-screening, and tailoring. Successful projects are oohed and aahed over at the end-of-the-day fashion show. Check the website for dates and location, **www.swaporamarama.org**.

Thrift Collective   Trading parties are the M.O. of this swap scene, which meets once a month or so to rotate closet fodder. Events sometimes have entrance fees (say, $10 in advance or $15 at the door), but that entitles you to browse through gently worn stocks of dresses, pants, T's, scarves, purses, shoes, and more. You're asked to bring some discarded duds of your own (in good condition, without rips, stains, or broken zippers, thank you). Discounted drinks help lower inhibitions about taking home strappy black-leather pumps. To keep up with the swaps, which vary between women-only and co-ed, follow along on Facebook or check in at the website, **www.thriftcollective.com**.

The Art of the Trade

If you're too ashamed of those Spice Girls and Limp Bizkit CDs to bring them to a live swap meet, you could always go the virtual route. **Swaptree** (www.swaptree.com) has over 100,000 items itching to ride the consumer carousel. Join for free and then put up some of your less-essential books, CDs, DVDs, and games for adoption. The site's software will connect you with more desirable products and shipping labels to help you get your surplus on its merry way. For even larger selections, check out **www.paperbackswap.com**, **www.swapacd.com**, and **www.swapadvd.com**. These sites work similarly to Swaptree, but with more options—4.5 million titles are available on Paper-Back Swap. There's no cost to you besides postage, although there are some risks involved (this ain't Amazon, you're relying on the trust system). Scammers do lurk out there, and there's no way to know for sure the condition of the item you're trading for. Checking the ratings of a potential trade partner can give you a decent idea of who you're dealing with.

7 Pet Project

Sure, your loyal, vicious Yorkie saves you thousands of dollars a month in bodyguards and private security services, but you don't want to turn around and sink all that cash into an expensive pet-care proposition. Fortunately, New York has a couple of places that provide veterinary support at pint-sized prices. Don't yet have that mouse-killing tabby in the house? NYC also has pets available at low, low costs.

American Society for the Prevention of Cruelty to Animals Subsidized pet care is available at the Bergh Memorial Animal Hospital & Clinic, run by this legendary group. An appointment for an exam with a vet costs $90, and an emergency visit is $130. They also provide shots, around $25 for rabies or distemper on top of the regular exam fee. If you need to get a pet before you can start worrying about pet care, the ASPCA also has adoption services. Cats and dogs start at around $75 and puppies, kittens, and purebreds go up from there.

The cost covers several necessities, including "pet Lojack"—a micro-chip should your new best friend make a break for freedom. If you want to microchip your current pet, the cost is $35 with an exam, and $55 for walk-ins. 424 E. 92nd St., btw. First and York aves. ℭ **212/876-7700.** www.aspca.org. Subway: 4/5/6 to 86th St.

Bideawee   The name of this century-old charitable organization derives from the Scottish for "stay awhile," though they'd just as well put cats and dogs through the revolving door as quickly as possible. Adoptions here can be had for a processing fee of around $125, which covers a host of services (spaying, neutering, microchipping, and more). When it's time for follow-up, Bideawee's veterinary clinic is subsidized and among the most reasonable in the city. 410 E. 38th St., 2nd floor, btw. First Ave. and the FDR. ℭ **212/532-5884.** www.bideawee.org. Subway: 4/5/6/7/S to 42nd St./Grand Central.

The Brooklyn Animal Resource Coalition   Love dogs, but not ready for the full-out commitment of daily walking and feeding? Billyburg's BARC will let you test-drive a pooch during morning or evening hours. You'll be helping the shelter out by giving one of their minions some exercise, you'll have a handy conversation-starter, and who knows? Maybe you'll form a bond. Allow a couple of hours if you want to walk or adopt. 253 Wythe Ave., at N. 1st St., Williamsburg, Brooklyn. ℭ **718/486-7489.** www.barcshelter.org. Subway: L to Bedford Ave.

Mayor's Alliance for NYC's Animals   Mayor Mike has ambitious plans to make us a no-kill city (we're on track for a 2015 happy ending to that story). To that end, his alliance connects low-income residents with low-cost spaying and neutering services. If you're in the pet market, the alliance puts on a series of adoption festivals, including the annual Adoptapalooza blowout. In addition to spontaneously falling for an unclaimed cur there, you can hook up your current pets with micro-chips at a special $25 rate. Mobile microchipping clinics also pay visits to all five boroughs with that same $25 deal. For citywide pet services, the alliance's website is a very helpful clearinghouse. ℭ **212/252-3250.** www.animalalliancenyc.org.

Savvy Web surfers avoid long lines for Shakespeare in the Park tickets by logging onto www. shakespeareinthepark.org and nabbing free passes online. See p. 263 for a full review.

ENTERTAINMENT & NIGHTLIFE

For a little while there in the boom years, it looked like i-bankers and heirs would be the only folks able to afford New York entertainment. Taverns upped cover charges, cigar and champagne bars came into fashion, and Broadway ticket prices went through the roof. But that was a whole different city. With youth pouring into the area and the economy still on shaky ground, entertainment for the people has made a major comeback. It's easy to find top-tier dance, drama, film, and comedy for no more than the price of showing up in NYC. Shakespeare in the Park, the Metropolitan Opera, and the Upright Citizens Brigade are among the New York legends that give it away free. Big-time wits can be found at TV-show tapings, and big-name scribes make themselves accessible at complimentary literary readings. Meanwhile, music seeps up from the subway platforms and fills our parks and bars. Everything from jazz to classical to country to rock can be heard in NYC, and a surprising amount of it comes without cost. For those attractions that do charge, discerning patrons can easily keep the cost down in the $5 range. New York is a magnet for talent, and even the performances on the cheap end of the entertainment spectrum can be spectacular. In short, money should be no barrier to experiencing great New York entertainment. It's more an issue of time management.

1 Music Uncovered

New York is in the midst of yet another great rock-'n'-roll scare. A slew of young musicians have rediscovered the jittery energy of New York's '70s and '80s heyday, and they're threatening to become a movement. Phosphorescent, The Hold Steady, and The National are among the parade of hot new bands putting down Brooklyn roots. It's not just rock, either. Classical, acoustic, salsa, jazz, and even alt-country make a stand in Yankee confines. The only fly in this ointment is capitalism; the bars where groups play have to pay rent. Most places try to keep the booze flowing, although with a few exceptions New York is not super uptight about enforcing its drink minimums. The musicians certainly don't care—most of the time they're just happy you're there to listen. You'll find free music waiting 7 nights a week. You might as well embrace the cacophony, because Lord knows it's hard to find a quiet hour in New York City.

FREE Free & E-Zeens

With a city in endless flux and so much stuff going on, it's hard to stay abreast of the best in free and cheap events. My favorite means of keeping up is via electronic newsletters, conveniently e-mailed right to my inbox. Of the e-lists, **Nonsensenyc**'s (www.nonsensenyc.com) is my favorite, specializing in the cheap and offbeat, and providing a comprehensive rundown of the city's many hipster events. Other newsletters worth reading can be found at **www.dailycandy.com**, **www.flavorpill.net**, and **www.manhattanusersguide.com**.

FOR THOSE ABOUT TO ROCK

Banjo Jim's `FREE`   This inheritor to 9C's mantle hasn't changed the space or sound much. Solid live alt-country, folk, and rock still fill most bills, with a little Loisaida Latin flavor thrown in as well. Music runs 7 nights a week, with multiple acts on offer, and weekend afternoons feature jam sessions. Outside of the occasional festival there's no cover (although the hat is passed), and the one-drink-per-set minimum is loosely enforced. 700 E. 9th St., at Ave. B. © **212/777-0869.** www.banjojims.com. Subway: L to First Ave.

The Lakeside Lounge `FREE` The Lakeside may lack in lake views, but it has no shortage of great music. Steve Earle, Amy Allison, and Freedy Johnston have all played the intimate back room here. If you arrive late, it'll be hard to score a seat, although there's extra standing room off to the side. Never a cover or a minimum, and during set breaks you can purchase yourself a souvenir from the notorious black-and-white photo booth. 162 Ave. B, btw. 10th and 11th sts. © **212/529-8463.** www.lakesidelounge.com. Subway: L to First Ave.

`FREE` **Chelsea Pickin'**

The Chelsea Market Music Hallway splits the difference between a venue and a subway platform, allowing buskers the opportunity to play for a sampling of the ten thousand pairs of ears that pass through daily. The music on offer is as diverse as the city itself, rolling from blues to bluegrass to jazz to Latin. (Despite the high cringe potential, dixieland, a capella, and vaudeville also make the cut.) All shows are free on the ground floor; check online for scheduling. 75 Ninth Ave., btw. 15th and 16th sts. www.chelseamarket.com. Subway: A/C/E to 14th St.; L to Eighth Ave.

The Living Room   A mellow music mecca, the Living Room hosts a slate of live performances every night, biased toward acoustic and otherwise low-key up-and-comers. Shows here are increasingly high profile, with the occasional national act storming through. Usually no cover, though they do pass the hat and suggest a $5 contribution, and there's a one-drink minimum per set. 154 Ludlow St., btw. Stanton and Rivington sts. © **212/533-7235.** www.livingroomny.com. Subway: F/M to Second Ave.; J/M/Z to Essex St.

ENTERTAINMENT & NIGHTLIFE DOWNTOWN

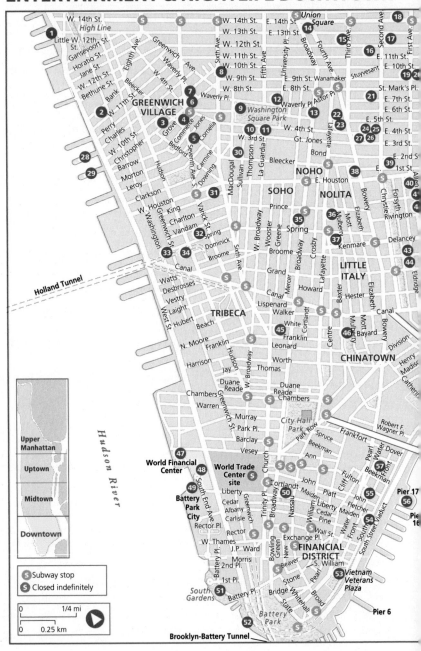

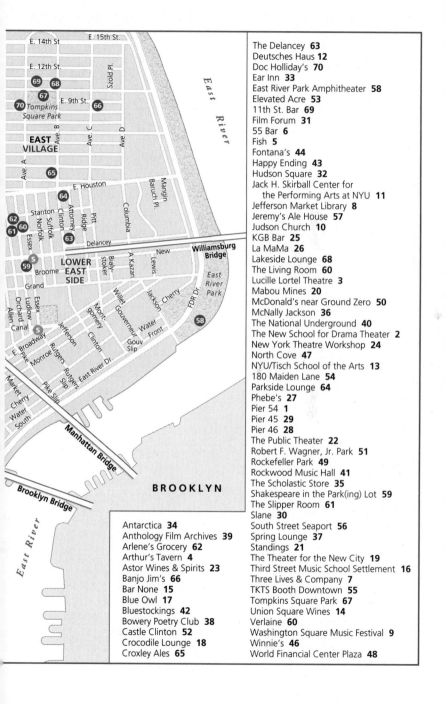

The Delancey **63**
Deutsches Haus **12**
Doc Holliday's **70**
Ear Inn **33**
East River Park Amphitheater **58**
Elevated Acre **53**
11th St. Bar **69**
Film Forum **31**
55 Bar **6**
Fish **5**
Fontana's **44**
Happy Ending **43**
Hudson Square **32**
Jack H. Skirball Center for
    the Performing Arts at NYU **11**
Jefferson Market Library **8**
Jeremy's Ale House **57**
Judson Church **10**
KGB Bar **25**
La MaMa **26**
Lakeside Lounge **68**
The Living Room **60**
Lucille Lortel Theatre **3**
Mabou Mines **20**
McDonald's near Ground Zero **50**
McNally Jackson **36**
The National Underground **40**
The New School for Drama Theater **2**
New York Theatre Workshop **24**
North Cove **47**
NYU/Tisch School of the Arts **13**
180 Maiden Lane **54**
Parkside Lounge **64**
Phebe's **27**
Pier 54 **1**
Pier 45 **29**
Pier 46 **28**
The Public Theater **22**
Robert F. Wagner, Jr. Park **51**
Rockefeller Park **49**
Rockwood Music Hall **41**
The Scholastic Store **35**
Shakespeare in the Park(ing) Lot **59**
The Slipper Room **61**
Slane **30**
South Street Seaport **56**
Spring Lounge **37**
Standings **21**
The Theater for the New City **19**
Third Street Music School Settlement **16**
Three Lives & Company **7**
TKTS Booth Downtown **55**
Tompkins Square Park **67**
Union Square Wines **14**
Verlaine **60**
Washington Square Music Festival **9**
Winnie's **46**
World Financial Center Plaza **48**

Antarctica **34**
Anthology Film Archives **39**
Arlene's Grocery **62**
Arthur's Tavern **4**
Astor Wines & Spirits **23**
Banjo Jim's **66**
Bar None **15**
Blue Owl **17**
Bluestockings **42**
Bowery Poetry Club **38**
Castle Clinton **52**
Crocodile Lounge **18**
Croxley Ales **65**

ENTERTAINMENT & NIGHTLIFE IN MIDTOWN

ENTERTAINMENT & NIGHTLIFE UPTOWN

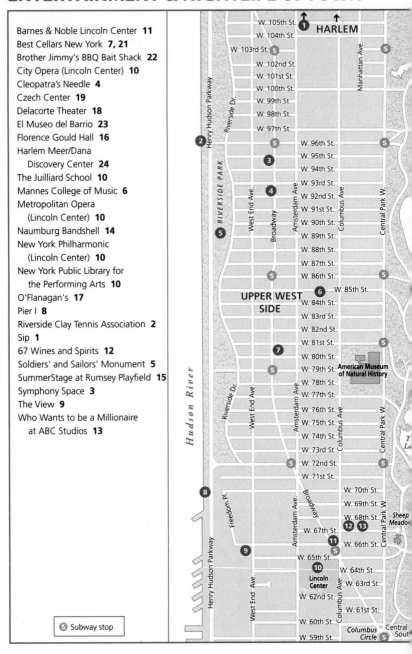

Barnes & Noble Lincoln Center **11**
Best Cellars New York **7, 21**
Brother Jimmy's BBQ Bait Shack **22**
City Opera (Lincoln Center) **10**
Cleopatra's Needle **4**
Czech Center **19**
Delacorte Theater **18**
El Museo del Barrio **23**
Florence Gould Hall **16**
Harlem Meer/Dana
    Discovery Center **24**
The Juilliard School **10**
Mannes College of Music **6**
Metropolitan Opera
    (Lincoln Center) **10**
Naumburg Bandshell **14**
New York Philharmonic
    (Lincoln Center) **10**
New York Public Library for
    the Performing Arts **10**
O'Flanagan's **17**
Pier I **8**
Riverside Clay Tennis Association **2**
Sip **1**
67 Wines and Spirits **12**
Soldiers' and Sailors' Monument **5**
SummerStage at Rumsey Playfield **15**
Symphony Space **3**
The View **9**
Who Wants to be a Millionaire
    at ABC Studios **13**

Ⓢ Subway stop

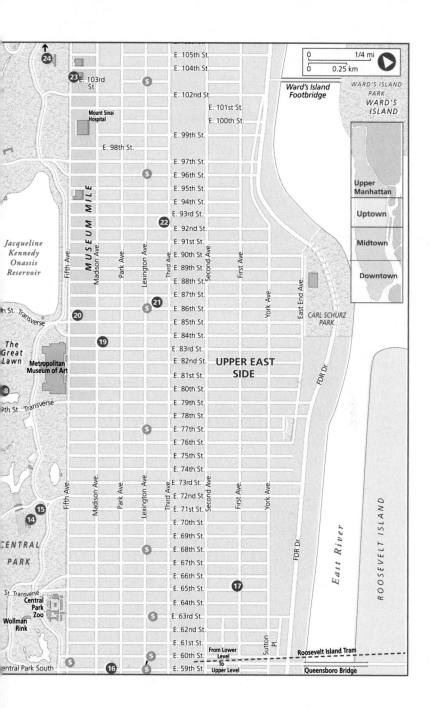

E. 105th St.
E. 104th St.
23 E. 103rd St.
Mount Sinai Hospital
E. 98th St.
E. 102nd St.
E. 101st St.
E. 100th St.
E. 99th St.
E. 97th St.
E. 96th St.
E. 95th St.
E. 94th St.
E. 93rd St.
22 E. 92nd St.
E. 91st St.
E. 90th St.
E. 89th St.
E. 88th St.
E. 87th St.
21 E. 86th St.
E. 85th St.
E. 84th St.
19 E. 83rd St.
E. 82nd St.
E. 81st St.
E. 80th St.
E. 79th St.
E. 78th St.
E. 77th St.
E. 76th St.
E. 75th St.
E. 74th St.
E. 73rd St.
E. 72nd St.
E. 71st St.
E. 70th St.
E. 69th St.
E. 68th St.
E. 67th St.
E. 66th St.
17 E. 65th St.
E. 64th St.
E. 63rd St.
E. 62nd St.
E. 61st St.
E. 60th St.
E. 59th St.

Ward's Island Footbridge

WARD'S ISLAND PARK
WARD'S ISLAND

Upper Manhattan

Uptown

Midtown

Downtown

0   1/4 mi
0   0.25 km

Jacqueline Kennedy Onassis Reservoir

MUSEUM MILE

Fifth Ave.
Madison Ave.
Park Ave.
Lexington Ave.
Third Ave.
Second Ave.
First Ave.
York Ave.
East End Ave.

th St. Transverse

The Great Lawn

Metropolitan Museum of Art

th St. Transverse

20
8

UPPER EAST SIDE

CARL SCHURZ PARK

FDR Dr.

East River

ROOSEVELT ISLAND

St. Transverse

Central Park Zoo

15
14

Wollman Rink

CENTRAL PARK

entral Park South

16

Sutton Pl.

From Lower Level
To
Upper Level

Roosevelt Island Tram

Queensboro Bridge

24

ENTERTAINMENT & NIGHTLIFE IN BROOKLYN

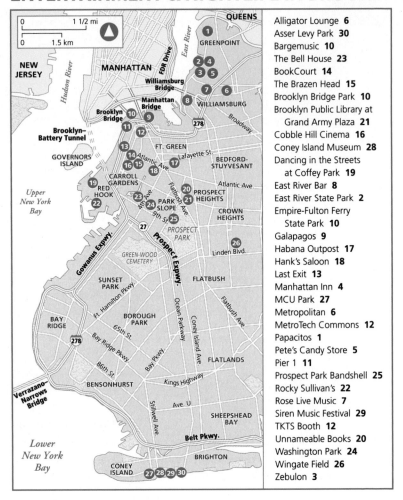

Alligator Lounge **6**
Asser Levy Park **30**
Bargemusic **10**
The Bell House **23**
BookCourt **14**
The Brazen Head **15**
Brooklyn Bridge Park **10**
Brooklyn Public Library at
    Grand Army Plaza **21**
Cobble Hill Cinema **16**
Coney Island Museum **28**
Dancing in the Streets
    at Coffey Park **19**
East River Bar **8**
East River State Park **2**
Empire-Fulton Ferry
    State Park **10**
Galapagos **9**
Habana Outpost **17**
Hank's Saloon **18**
Last Exit **13**
Manhattan Inn **4**
MCU Park **27**
Metropolitan **6**
MetroTech Commons **12**
Papacitos **1**
Pete's Candy Store **5**
Pier 1 **11**
Prospect Park Bandshell **25**
Rocky Sullivan's **22**
Rose Live Music **7**
Siren Music Festival **29**
TKTS Booth **12**
Unnameable Books **20**
Washington Park **24**
Wingate Field **26**
Zebulon **3**

The National Underground   A much-needed low-pretense zone is provided by this little pocket of Americana on East Houston. PBR in cans and
roots rock soundtracks are the key ingredients for laid-back nights. There are
two stages, with as many as eight different bands a night. Although most of
the performers aren't name acts, you won't be dropping money on a cover
either. FINE PRINT If you're in the 'hood at lunchtime, don't miss the $5 burg-
ers. 159 E. Houston St., btw. Allen and Eldridge sts. ☎ **212/475-0611.** www.thenational
underground.com. Subway: F to Second Ave.

ENTERTAINMENT & NIGHTLIFE IN QUEENS

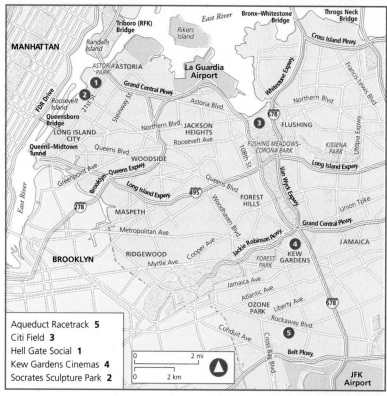

Aqueduct Racetrack **5**
Citi Field **3**
Hell Gate Social **1**
Kew Gardens Cinemas **4**
Socrates Sculpture Park **2**

arkside Lounge   Nestled between projects and East Village tenements, is former brothel brings in an eclectic crowd. Being too far east for most ndroids helps, too. The back room puts on rock shows and electric Friday-ght salsa. Comedy and improv also appear on the calendar. [FINE PRINT] If ere's a cover, it'll be $5 or so for the band and often a two-drink mini-um applies, although it's loosely enforced. 317 E. Houston St., at Attorney St. **212/673-6270.** www.parksidelounge.net. Subway: F/M to Second Ave.

ete's Candy Store [FREE]   So much good music comes through here that u'll feel like a kid in a great music venue. Housed in a friendly former untain shop on a quiet Williamsburg block, the small stage area in back ings in surprisingly big acts. There's also a rotating selection of nonmusi-l entertainment, from readings to Scrabble to quiz night (check out "Word p: Readings" and "Game Night," on p. 284 and 279, respectively). o cover or drink minimum, but the staff encourages contributions to the

Todd P. & the Brooklyn Renaissance

With so many bands calling Brooklyn home, it's no surprise to find a thriving live music scene east of the East River. The DIY movement skews young for both fans and performers, and as such the prices are rock bottom. Shows go off without covers (or for $3–$5 a head), and there's cheap booze to go with them. Venues are improvised: an old Masonic lodge, a cheap Mexican restaurant, and above an auto parts store (logically enough it carries the name **"Above The Auto Parts Store"**). Impresario Todd P. (www.toddpnyc.com) is a major mover, putting on dozens of shows every month at his **Monster Island Basement, Silent Barn,** and **Market Hotel** venues. Check in at his website for details. As long as you're in the Williamsburg/Bushwick nabe, you might also check out the cheap shows at **Shea Stadium** (http://www.myspace. com/sheastadiumbk), **Death by Audio** (http://www.myspace.com/ deathbyaudioshows), and **GlassLands Gallery** (www. glasslands.com).

musicians' tip jar. 709 Lorimer St., btw. Frost and Richardson sts., Williamsburg, Brooklyn. ℂ **718/302-3770.** www.petescandystore.com. Subway: L to Lorimer St.; G to Metropolitan Ave.

Rockwood Music Hall   It took some vision—and a well-developed sense of irony—to conceive of these two postage stamp–size spaces as a "music hall." The close quarters don't seem to scare off the crowds, though, and the intimacy makes for great sound. Local singer-songwriters are interspersed with the occasional touring band, usually six acts or so per night. The sidewalk outside hosts a hopping overflow scene. Usually no cover, but the tip jar is passed and there's a one-drink minimum. 196 Allen St., btw. Houston and Stanton sts. ℂ **212/477-4155.** www.rockwoodmusichall.com. Subway: F/M to Second Ave.

Rodeo Bar   This is as country as Manhattan gets, which admittedly isn't saying much. Rodeo's sprawling space doesn't have the feel of an intimate honky-tonk, but the stage area is segregated and more or less self-contained. The cream of the local crop rounds up here, as do a handful of national acts. Mostly Americana and alt-country (whatever that is). There's no cover, usually a one-drink minimum. 375 Third Ave., at 27th St. ℂ **212/683-6500.** www.rodeobar.com. Subway: 6 to 28th St.

Sidewalk Café Having outlived the other live-music spots on Avenue A, the Café serves as a home base for East Village singer-songwriters. A little comedy and open mics get thrown in as well. Each night sees a big bunch of acts. FINE PRINT No cover, but a two-drink minimum during performances. 94 Ave. A, at 6th St. (℡) **212/473-7373.** www.sidewalkmusic.net. Subway: F/M to Second Ave.

JAZZ IT UP

Arthur's Tavern A West Village relic, Arthur's would be eligible for social security if it were a person and not an amiable, low-rent jazz joint. The music runs the Dixieland-to-trio gamut, and the quality can be spotty, but something's on stage 7 nights a week. FINE PRINT No cover, but a one-drink per set minimum. 57 Grove St., btw. Bleecker and W. 4th sts. (℡) **212/675-6879.** www.arthurstavernnyc.com. Subway: 1 to Christopher St.

Cleopatra's Needle Organ trios and quartets highlight the calendar at this Upper West Side neighborhood club. On Wednesday evenings and Sunday afternoons things get even more neighborhoody with open mics. In the wee hours, the floor belongs to jam sessions. Never a cover, though there is a $10 minimum per set. A decent Mediterranean menu provides an alternative to boozing the night away. Shows start at 7 or 8pm. 2485 Broadway, btw. 92nd and 93rd sts. (℡) **212/769-6969.** www. cleopatrasneedleny.com. Subway: 1/2/3 to 96th St.

Ear Inn FREE This laid-back old-timer was once a waterfront tavern, although in the course of a couple of centuries, the Hudson has slipped a block or two. There's solid dinner fare and pints aplenty here, and Monday and Wednesday nights you can enjoy midnight music. Jazz and blues are the usual Ear candy, although country and folk sneak in as well. Sunday evenings at 8pm the Ear Regulars perform jazz variations on trumpet, reed, guitar, and bass. 326 Spring St., btw. Greenwich and Washington sts. (℡) **212/226-9060.** www.earinn.com. Subway: C/E to Spring St.; 1 to Canal St.

55 Bar Still not entirely recovered from its Prohibition days, 55 Bar has been entertaining the Village on the sly since 1919. The cluttered room brings in top-shelf acts. The cover charges reflect it on some nights, but generally you can slip in for $10, which is a pretty good deal for this level of quality. Tuesday and Sunday nights are your best bets for inexpensive jazz. FINE PRINT Officially, there's a two-drink minimum, but the laid-back staff enforces it loosely. 55 Christopher St., btw. Seventh Ave. and Waverly Place. (℡) **212/929-9883.** www.55bar.com. Subway: 1 to Christopher St.

FREE The Underground Scene

In this modern world it's hard to find a spontaneous public expression that can't be codified and regulated. Even street performers in New York get caught up in bureaucracy's net, but the result is (mostly) high-quality music providing the soundtrack to our transfers and eye-contact avoidance. The New York Metropolitan Transit Authority's program is called "Music Under New York" (www.mta.info/mta/aft/muny), and it allows preselected performers to legally play at preselected stations. Times Square, Penn Station, Union Square, and Columbus Circle are the most heavily trafficked in the system, and it takes very little to draw an audience. In addition to the ubiquitous pan-flute Andean bands and tumbling demonstrations, you can hear amplified funk bands, jazz quartets, weird Chinese bow work, Brazilian drumming, blues, gospel, Calypso, and rock. The quality often competes with the music played aboveground on gel-lit stages. Not bad for the price of a swipe.

Zebulon FREE   The French owners here manage to blend European sophistication with the low-pretense quotient of greater Brooklyn. Afrobeat, funk, and improv jazz lead the charge. A tin ceiling and jazz posters and album covers add to the charm. There's never a cover (although the hat is passed), and drinks are inexpensive, at least by contemporary standards. 258 Wythe Ave., btw. Metropolitan Ave. and N. 3rd St., Williamsburg, Brooklyn. ✆ **718/218-6934.** www.zebuloncafeconcert.com. Subway: L to Bedford Ave.

CLASSICAL ACTS

Gotham's classical pedigree is hard to knock, as we boast the nation's oldest orchestra (the New York Philharmonic), on top of a couple of venues whose renown just might extend beyond New York Harbor (Carnegie Hall and Lincoln Center leap to mind). The future of music can also be found here, with the nation's most prominent conservatories (think Juilliard) settled on Manhattan schist. Although high prices can accompany the high notes, you aren't obligated to pay through the nose. Schools present a bevy of free shows, big-name venues offer

obstructed-view cheap seats, and the Philharmonic and the Metro-
politan Opera both gig for free in the summer (see "High Culture for
Free," in the Outdoor Summer Concerts section, later in this chapter).
So weigh your musical options carefully before settling for that Quiet
Riot tribute band on Bleecker Street.

Bargemusic `FREE` Of all the world's barges dedicated to chamber
music, this one is my favorite. Docked just off the Fulton Ferry landing in Brooklyn Heights, the recital room here hosts over a hundred
concerts a year. Tickets are generally $35, but at least once a month
one concert is given away (usually Sat at 1pm). It's "pot-luck," so you
won't know the program until showtime, but it'll be classical, and the
performance will be intimate. (There are only 130 seats.) No reservations are taken, so show up before the doors open, which is an hour
before showtime. 26 New Dock St., at Water St., at the East River. ✆ **718/624-
2083.** www.bargemusic.org. Subway: 2/3 to Clark St.; A/C to High St.

The Bronx Symphony Orchestra With over 6 decades of music
making, this entirely democratic group has plenty of experience in
bringing Tchaikovsky, Mendelssohn, and Mozart to the masses. All
the concerts were once free, but funding constraints have made them
a mix of ticketed (still inexpensive, in the $7–$12 range) and complimentary. Check the website for the calendar and locations, which hit
all corners of the borough. Various locations around the Bronx. ✆ **718/601-
9151.** www.bronxsymphony.org.

Carnegie Hall A mere Hamilton is all it takes to waltz into Carnegie
Hall. Concerts held in the Stern Auditorium or the Perelman Stage are
accessible by same-day $10 RUSH tickets. The number of available
tickets is pretty limited, so you'll want to get there well before the box
office opens (11am Mon through Sat, noon on Sun). If you don't mind
seeing only half the show, you can also get into Carnegie for half price.
Partial-view seats (hey, you're here for the sound anyway) are made
available for Stern Auditorium and Perelman Stage shows (Gala and
Weill Music Institute events excepted). Carnegie Hall Family Concerts
are also excepted, but then they're already a bargain in their own
right—targeted to the wee ones, tickets are only $9. Carnegie Hall also
takes its show on the road. The Neighborhood Concert Series fans out
across all five boroughs, bringing everything from classical to jazz to
folk. Some 80 shows a year are performed for free—check the website

for details. 154 W. 57th St., at Seventh Ave. ℂ **212/247-7800.** www.carnegiehall. org. Subway: A/B/C/D/1 to 59th St./Columbus Circle; N/Q/R to 57th St./Seventh Ave.

City Opera   Since its 1943 inception, City Opera has strived to be an accessible alternative to the Met. With innovative programming, at times the upstart can even eclipse its rival. Though premium tickets top out over $130, the "Opera For All" program ensures democratic representation at all performances. One-fourth of all tickets go for less than $25. For the good seats, there are Orchestra Rush Tickets—without the rush, even, as you can buy them starting at Monday 10am for any performance in the week. You don't even need to hoof it to the box office: They're also available online and via phone sales. For nosebleed seats that won't bleed you dry, look to the fourth and fifth rings, which go for $20 and as low as $12. Or save that $12 by attending the VOX: Showcasing American Composers program, which comes around every spring. Some dozen young composers get a chance to air their work, and the public gets to preview the future of opera. Free tickets can be reserved online for the performances at NYU's Skirball Center downtown (565 LaGuardia Place at Washington Sq. S.; www.nycopera. com). City Opera, David H. Koch Theater, 20 Lincoln Center. ℂ **212/870-5570.** www. nycopera.com. Subway: 1 to 66th St./Lincoln Center.

Free for All at Town Hall `FREE`   One of the city's newer classical programs, the 2010 Free for All put on two free performances at gracious Town Hall. From solo piano to string quartets, the shows bring serious music to knowledgeable fans. Tickets are distributed at the box office, two per person, at noon on the day of the show (usually there are still tickets available right up until showtime). Sunday afternoons in late spring. 123 W. 43rd St., btw. Sixth Ave. and Broadway. ℂ **212/707-8787.** www.freeforalltownhall.org. Subway: B/D/F/M to 42nd St.; 1/2/3/7/N/Q/R/S to 42nd St./Times Sq.

The Juilliard School `FREE`   Juilliard's reputation couldn't be much more burnished, with luminaries like Philip Glass, Yo-Yo Ma, and Itzhak Perlman among its alums. Since its current students are nominally amateurs, the Lincoln Center school presents most of its concerts for free. Soloists play Morse and Paul Hall, and you can catch the entire orchestra at Alice Tully Hall. Though there is no charge, tickets are required for some shows, available from the box office up to 2 weeks prior to the show. Regular lunchtime concerts keep NYC's morale up; Tuesdays at 12:30pm, an office building atrium at 180

FREE Quarter Pounding the K

McDonald's and classical music go together li[...]
Er, maybe not. Sunday afternoons see a bizarre [...]
McDonald's nearest Ground Zero. Classical p[...]
and his occasional guests, layer lovely new-agey music ove[...]
of seared meat. Tourists wander in with only an occasional perplexed
glance at the grand piano in the window of the second-floor balcony.
For erudite music fans, this is probably the calmest it's possible to feel
inside a McDonald's. 160 Broadway, btw. Liberty and Cortlandt sts.
℃ 212/385-2063. www.andrewshapiro.com. Subway: R to Cortlandt
St.; A/C/J/Z/2/3/4/5 to Fulton St./Broadway Nassau. Sundays, sets beginning at noon, 1, 2, and 3pm, season usually runs November through
June.

Maiden Lane hosts student performances (see p. 314 in "Free & Dirt
Cheap Days"); and "Wednesdays at One" programs can be found at
Alice Tully Hall. Tuesdays run most of the year, but Wednesdays are
limited to the school year. Both are free with no tickets required. 60
Lincoln Center Plaza. ℃ 212/769-7406. www.juilliard.edu. Subway: 1 to 66th St./Lin-
coln Center.

Manhattan School of Music FREE With an Art Deco auditorium and
six other venues, there's no shortage of places to listen here. Classical
music performances are joined by jazz, which snuck into the curricu-
lum after MSM's founding 90 years ago. Many shows are free to the
public (no ticket required, although reservations are requested for
some), as are a series of master classes. Nearby Riverside Park hosts
even more performances, at the 116th Street Overlook on mild-weather
Sunday afternoons. Most events take place during the school year;
check online for a full schedule. 601 W. 122nd St., at Broadway. ℃ 917/493-
4428. www.msmnyc.edu. Subway: 1 to 125th St.

Mannes College of Music FREE During the school year, this 90-year-
old institution presents some 400 free concerts. Student groups include
baroque chamber, guitar, brass, and opera ensembles. Two concert
halls at the college's headquarters host the free shows. There are also
remote performances at places like The New School (Mannes merged

Divine Inspiration: Concerts at the Churches

Even heathens can find entertainment under the city's steeples. Choirs are only the beginning, as recitals and operas also take the altars, often for free. Worker bees downtown love the **"Concerts at One"** series at St. Paul's Chapel and Trinity Church (p. 316). Midtowners can enjoy the spring lunchtime concerts at **The Church of the Transfiguration** (better known as The Little Church Around the Corner; ℂ **212/684-4174;** www.littlechurch.org; $5 suggested donation.) Uptown, **The Interchurch Center** (ℂ **212/870-2200;** www.interchurch-center.org) hosts Wednesday Noonday Concerts. For an evening of polished classical performances, check out the **New York Repertory Orchestra.** Though this all-volunteer group has many amateurs in its ranks, the renditions of Brahms, Mahler, and Stravinsky are all professional. Programming is adventurous, and the shows are free. Usually Saturday nights at 8pm. Church of St. Mary the Virgin, 145 W. 46th St., btw. Sixth and Seventh aves. ℂ **212/662-8383.** www.nyro.org. Subway: B/D/F to 47th–50th sts.–Rockefeller Center.

with it in 1989), where lunchtime performances are followed by receptions. Check the website's calendar for the full listings. 150 W. 85th St., btw. Amsterdam and Columbus aves. ℂ **212/580-0210,** ext. 4817. www.mannes.edu. Subway: B/C to 86th St.

Metropolitan Opera　When it comes to opera, the Met is the biggest (240 shows a year, each with seating for 4,000) and the best, with elaborate productions and unrivalled star power. Seats start around $26 and soar from there to over $375. In addition to the free summer shows (see below), standing-room-only tickets can be found. Prices tend to be $20 for orchestra and $15 for family circle, available online with a $7.50 surcharge, plus a $2.50 facilities fee. "Day of" standing room is also availble for $15 from the box office, cash only, limit two tickets per person, and the line gets long quickly. If you can't weather a 4-hour show on your feet, you can vie for Varis Rush Tickets. You'll get a seat in the orchestra for just $20 for a Monday through Thursday show. Distribution starts at the box office two hours before curtain. Metropolitan Opera at Lincoln Center, btw. W. 62nd and 65th sts. and Columbus and Amsterdam aves. © **212/362-6000.** www.metoperafamily.org. Subway: 1 to 66th St./Lincoln Center.

New York Grand Opera FREE Conductor Vincent La Selva has spent the last 30 years performing the quixotic—or Sisyphean—task of mounting fully staged grand operas for no charge. He's pulled it off, too, with compelling performances that shine despite the occasional lack of polish. Shows are held over three nights in summer at Central Park's Naumburg Bandshell, weather permitting. Naumburg Bandshell, Central Park, midpark, just below 72nd St. © **212/245-8837.** www.newyorkgrand opera.org. Subway: B/C to 72nd St.; 6 to 68th St./Hunter College.

New York Philharmonic The Philharmonic has been satisfying New Yorkers since 1842. The symphony's international fame translates into pricey tickets (usually it's over $100 to sit in the orchestra), but pikers needn't despair. In addition to free summer shindigs in the parks (see below), there are low-priced kid-friendly shows, $12 student rush tickets, and the Open Rehearsal program. Watching a piece take shape under a conductor's molding is a fascinating process, and it's only $16 (plus a $2 handling fee) to sit in. Avery Fisher Hall, 10 Lincoln Center Plaza. © **212/875-5900.** www.nyphil.org. Subway: 1 to 66th St./Lincoln Center.

Peoples' Symphony Concerts A good bet on I.B.M. stock in 1923 is the basis for the endowment of these popular populist concerts. Three separate groupings, the Festival, Mann, and Arens Series, give the people the world-class ensembles they demand. Festival shows are held at Town Hall, and the two others are at Washington Irving High School (with a 1,500-seat capacity and good acoustics, this is not your high school's auditorium). Most single tickets are $10 to $12, but if you invest in a series subscription, the per-show price dips to the $6 to $9 range. Washington Irving High School, 16th St., at Irving Place. © **212/586-4680.** www.pscny.org. Subway: L/N/Q/R/4/5/6 to 14th St./Union Sq. Other location: *Town Hall,* 123 W. 43rd St., btw. Sixth Ave. and Broadway. Subway: B/D/F/M to 42nd St.; 1/2/3/7/N/Q/R/S to 42nd St./Times Sq.

Third Street Music School Settlement FREE The oldest community music school in the country, this institution helps reach thousands of students with musical instruction. The talented faculty shows off their own chops at weekly free concerts. Classical pieces predominate, although there is the occasional jazz ringer thrown in. The Anna-Maria

Kellen Auditorium does the hosting, Friday nights at 7:30pm, October through May, no reservations or tickets necessary. Thursday afternoons in June and July also look for "Music in Abe Lebewohl Park," a series of free concerts held at 12:30pm in front of St. Mark's Church-in-the-Bowery (Second Ave. and 10th St.). 235 E. 11 St., btw. Second and Third aves. ℂ 212/777-3240. www.thirdstreetmusicschool.org. Subway: L to Third Ave.

Wall to Wall at Symphony Space `FREE` This long-running giveaway is a long runner, filling the Symphony Space stage with some 12 hours of music. The focus changes from year to year, with one source singled out for comprehensive exploration. The range is extensive, Bach to Beethoven to Joni Mitchell to Kurt Weill. Performances start at 11am, but folks will line up hours before that. Openings in the general admission seating come in waves, every 3 hours or so. The event usually coincides with the Upper West Fest; check the website for exact dates. Symphony Space, 2537 Broadway, at 95th St. ℂ 212/864-5400. www.symphony space.org. Subway: 1/2/3 to 96th St.

OUTDOOR SUMMER CONCERTS

The high season for free music is summer, when cool sounds seem to be coming from every corner of the city. You would think that with so many events the crowds would spread thin, but concerts tend to be consistently well attended. If you're going primarily to see the band, better allow at least an hour to carve out some space. For particularly big names you'll have to get there even earlier. If the scene is more interesting than the sound, however, New York concerts are laid-back enough that you can just wander in and out as the mood strikes you. With concerts at so many spectacular sites, a sunset on the Hudson or late afternoon light on the Brooklyn skyline often come with your (metaphorical) price of admission.

BAM Rhythm & Blues Festival at MetroTech `FREE` MetroTech Commons is as close to a municipal center as Brooklyn gets, and in the summer it's the site of a free lunchtime concert series. As the name suggests, R&B is the focus, though the definition stretches to include blues, reggae, and funk as well. Surprisingly big names like the Neville Brothers and Ohio Players come through. Ten shows are held in all, Thursdays from noon to 2pm, mid-June to mid-August. MetroTech Commons, at Flatbush and Myrtle aves. ℂ 718/636-4100. www.bam. org. Subway: 2/3 to Hoyt St.; R to Lawrence St.; A/C/F to Jay St./Borough Hall.

Free Outdoor Summer Concerts

Monday	Tuesday	Wednesday	Thursday	Fri
Martin Luther King Jr. Concert Series, 7:30pm	Naumburg Orchestral Concerts, 7:30pm	Madison Square Park, 7pm	BAM Rhythm & Blues Festival at MetroTech, noon	
	Washington Square Music Festival, 8pm	Rockefeller Park, 7pm	Castle Clinton, 7pm	Garden the MoMA, 8pm
	World Financial Center, 7pm		Seaside Summer Concert Series, Coney Island, 7pm	
			Summer Soul Nights, Battery Park, 7pm	

Battery Park FREE Battery Park has the city's most spectacular gardens and shoreline, but its corner-pocket location causes it to be overlooked. Come quitting time, much of the working crowd rushes off to subway cars and ferries, leaving the rest of us more space to enjoy the cultural resources. The River to River Festival cosponsors several summer concerts down here, many of which are underattended by New York standards. There's no better way to watch dusk settle over the island. My favorite spot is **Robert F. Wagner, Jr. Park,** at the south end of the park. Boat traffic in New York Harbor and the Statue of Liberty provide the backdrop. A little ways north is the **World Financial Center Plaza,** which brings in music as well as theater. Wednesday nights the place to be is **Rockefeller Park,** on the northernmost end of Battery Park, for another series of 7 o'clock concerts. Indie rock and alt-country are favored here, with biggish names like Beth Orton making the scene. Check www.rivertorivernyc.com for full schedules. Robert F. Wagner, Jr. Park, btw. Battery Place and New York Harbor. © 212/267-9700. www.bpcparks.org. Subway: 1 to Rector St. or South Ferry; 4/5 to Bowling Green. *World Financial Center Plaza,* due east of the North Cove Yacht Harbor. © **212/528-2733.** www.worldfinancialcenter.com. Subway: E to World Trade Center; R to Cortlandt St. *Rockefeller Park,* at the west end of Chambers and Warren sts. © **212/528-2733.** www.batteryparkcity.org. Subway: 1/2/3 or A/C to Chambers St.

...rk `FREE` Every year, Bryant Park seems to pack its live ...chedule a little tighter. There's a big range of genres, and ...ark's central location makes it a convenient place to catch some ...nds. Broadway's brightest croon for your lunchtime pleasure on ...elect summer Thursdays (p. 265), and you can hear pianists weekdays from May through October. The songs are old-timey, popularized by the likes of Fats Waller, Scott Joplin, and the Gershwins. Piano in the Park can be heard Mondays through Fridays from 12:30 to 2:30pm (or some days 2 to 4pm). Bryant Park, btw. W. 40th and 42nd sts., along Sixth Ave. ℂ 212/768-4242. www.bryantpark.org. Subway: B/D/F/M to 42nd St.; 7 to Fifth Ave.

Castle Clinton `FREE` This old defensive battery took a turn as a fashionable concert hall in the first half of the 1800s, and it recalls those former duties on Thursday nights in July. Indie favorites like The Magnetic Fields, Calexico, and Del McCoury have done the honors in the past. Distribution begins at Castle Clinton at 5pm on the day of the show, although people start lining up a good couple of hours before. Battery Park, on the west side, at New York Harbor. ℂ 212/566-6700. www.downtownny.com. Subway: 1 to South Ferry; 4/5 to Bowling Green.

Celebrate Brooklyn! The Prospect Park Bandshell is a perfect place for a concert, with a festive and friendly crowd. The audio selections are as eclectic as Brooklyn, with acts like Rufus Wainwright, the Spanish Harlem Orchestra, and the Brooklyn Philharmonic. Shows are generally well attended, so show up early if you want a decent view. Check the website for schedules. A $3 donation is suggested, with a couple of pricey benefit shows thrown in. The Prospect Park Bandshell, Park Slope, Brooklyn. ℂ 718/855-7882. www.bricartsmedia.org. Subway: F or B/Q to Seventh Ave.; 2/3 to Grand Army Plaza. Enter at Prospect Park W. and 9th St.

City Parks Foundation `FREE` This group is a major player in New York's free music scene, putting on some 1,100 performances every year. Shows take place in parks across the boroughs; check online to see what's playing and when. One event to keep an eye out for is late August's **Charlie Parker Jazz Festival.** Bird gets honored with shows in two of his home neighborhoods, Harlem and the East Village. The Harlem show is Saturday afternoon in Marcus Garvey Park. Tompkins Square Park takes over on Sunday. Marcus Garvey Park, 18 Mount Morris Park West, at Fifth Ave. ℂ 212/860-1373. www.cityparksfoundation.org. Subway: 2/3 or 4/5/6 to 125th St. Tompkins Sq., btw. 7th and 10th sts. and aves. A and B. Subway: 6 to Astor Place; F/M to Second Ave.

Citysol `FREE` There's a little bit of a bait and switch here: Solar One puts on a big weekend of free music, comedy, and installation art in an attempt to capture your attention for some hard facts about renewable energy. With the perils facing our planet, it's a highly benign Trojan Horse, and the lineup of entertainment is impressive. Oh, plus free beer—write a letter for the I Heart PV campaign and a brew's on them. Mid-July. Stuyvesant Cove Park, 23rd St. and the FDR. © **212/505-6050.** www.citysol.org. Subway 6 to 23rd St.; L to First Ave.

Crotona Park Jams `FREE` Revisiting epic Boogie Down park jams of the '70s, this series celebrates hip-hop culture. A surfeit of spinning DJs, often legends like GrandWizzard Theodore and Kool DJ AJ Scratch, set the tempo. The party is hosted by Tools of War and runs from 5 to 9pm on Thursday nights in July. Check their MySpace for free Harlem grassroots hip-hop events, too. Crotona Park E. and Charlotte St. © **718/378-2061.** www.myspace.com/toolsofwar. Subway: 2/5 to 174th St. Walk south on Boston Rd. to Suburban Place, take a right on Crotona Park E. and then a left onto Charlotte St., where you'll see Indian Lake and the jam.

East River Park Amphitheater `FREE` This renovated spot on the East River, with beautiful Brooklyn and bridge views, hosts free music programs in summer. Ted Leo and Cat Power have played here in the past, but recent years have seen smaller-profile performers. The amphitheater's capacity is around 1,000 and these shows aren't particularly well publicized, so most times you'll be able to wander in late and still snag a seat. 600 Grand St., at the East River. Subway: F to Delancey St.; J/M/Z to Essex St. Walk along the south side of the Williamsburg Bridge and take the pedestrian bridge over the FDR. Turn left and follow the river down to the amphitheater.

Governors Island `FREE` Our over-technical age seems to be breeding some analogue craving, which might account for folk music's resurgence. The Folks on the Island series has brought surprisingly big names out to Governors Island, with Richie Havens and Slaid Cleaves putting on memorable recent shows. The concert site, on a verdant lawn, is perfect for blanket-spreading and picnicking. The island also hosts a massive punk rock day, world music shows, and some pricey ticketed concerts. The newest venue at Governors is "The Beach," a sandy oasis served by the New York Water Taxi, in addition to the regular free ferry. Several shows are free under the "Gone to Governors" heading, check www.thebeachconcerts.com for details. Governors Island, ferries depart from

High Culture for Free

Met in the Parks `FREE` Critics may sniff that the Metropolitan Opera rests on its laurels, but this institution maintains extremely high standards. Tickets can soar to near $400 for shows at the Opera House, but for 2 weeks every summer the fat lady sings for free. Shows are held in parks in all five boroughs. Usually 6 performances in all. Check the website for exact locations and times; no tickets are required. ℂ **212/362-6000.** www.metoperafamily.org.

New York Philharmonic Concerts in the Parks `FREE` The New York Philharmonic, one of the world's premier symphonies, gives away some 4 shows every summer. Composers range from Sibelius to Strauss to Ives. While the atmosphere is more hackey sack than Harnancourt— background for a group picnic rather than an event for the serious music lover—the performances by guest conductors and musicians are often inspired. If the classical music doesn't lure you in, you might stop by just for the free fireworks show afterwards. Performance locations vary, but generally there's a visit to Central Park and a stop in Queens and Brooklyn. Check www.newyorkphil.org for exact locations. Shows start at 8pm, no tickets required. ℂ **212/875-5709.**

Battery Maritime Bldg., 10 South St., btw. Broad and Whitehall sts., see p. 113 for more info. ℂ **212/253-2727.** www.governorsislandalliance.org. Subway: R to Whitehall St.; 1 to South Ferry.

Harlem Meer Performance Festival `FREE` Latino and African sounds predominate at this meer-front festival. The scene is as upbeat as the music, which is usually very danceable. Blankets and picnics are encouraged. Concerts are Sunday afternoons from 4 to 6pm, Memorial Day weekend through late August, near the Charles A. Dana Discovery Center. Central Park, at 110th St., btw. Fifth and Lenox aves. ℂ **212/860-1370.** www.centralparknyc.org. Subway: 2/3 to Central Park N.

Hudson Square Music & Wine Festival `FREE` Impresario Michael Dorf has followed the arc of maturity from a grungy music spot (The Knitting Factory) to a refined restaurant and wine bar (City Winery). This festival in the winery's backyard combines Greenmarket goods with fresh grooves, served up by the likes of C.J. Chenier, Popa Chubby, and Naomi Shelton. The event drops Tuesday evenings 5 to 7pm, from late June through mid-August. FINE PRINT Yes, they serve wine. Hudson Sq., enter on north side of Spring St., btw. Varick and Hudson sts. © 212/608-0555. www.citywinery.com. Subway: C/E to Spring St.; 1 to Houston St.

Lincoln Center Out of Doors FREE   Lincoln Center is a veritable city of performing arts, and every summer for over 30 years now, the great public square has been home to a diverse series of shows. The breadth is breathtaking, from Chinese opera to Greek dance to cutting-edge jazz to children's story time. Incredibly, it's all free. Check online for exact schedules, covering 2½ weeks from late July to mid-August. *Note:* Several shows take place in the nearby Damrosch Park Bandshell, at West 62nd Street and Amsterdam Avenue. 70 Lincoln Center Plaza, at Broadway and 64th St. © 212/546-2656. www.lincolncenter.org. Subway: 1 to 66th St./Lincoln Center.

Madison Square Music FREE   Madison Square's refurbished park has joined the summer music scrum, with the Oval Lawn Series on Wednesday nights. (A second "Studio Series" runs on Sat afternoons in the fall.) Radio thrift shop proprietress Laura Cantrell and jazz axeman Charlie Hunter have been heard here, although the performers are generally not household names. Taste buds more than cochleae are what make this concert special, however. The legendary Shake Shack (© 212/889-6600; www.shakeshacknyc.com), with its $3.75 burgers, makes for the perfect accompanying picnic. (*Note:* If you're planning on eating from the Shake Shack, allow an extra day or so to get through the line, which in nice weather stretches to Brooklyn.) Madison Square Park, Fifth Ave. at 23rd St. © 212/538-4071. www.madison squarepark.org. June–Aug Wed 7pm. Subway: N/Q/R or 6 to 23rd St.

Martin Luther King, Jr. Concert Series FREE   Jazz, soul, gospel, and old school (MC Hammer!) are some of the genres that can be heard on the Monday night program here. Seating is limited, so you might want to bring your own chair. In case of rain, concerts are postponed to Tuesday. Shows start at 7:30pm. Wingate Field, Winthrop St., btw. Brooklyn and Kingston aves., Brooklyn. © 718/469-1912. www.brooklynconcerts.com. Subway: 2/5 to Winthrop St.

Music in the Square FREE   Union Square invites you to stop by with a blanket and a picnic to enjoy live after-work music. Shows are Thursday evenings at 6pm from mid-June through mid-August, in the

South Plaza. Jazz, indie bands, and world music nights provide a diversity of beats. Union Sq. © **212/460-1200.** www.unionsquarenyc.org. June–Aug Thurs 6pm. Subway: L/N/Q/R/4/5/6 to 14th St./Union Sq.

Music on the Oval `FREE` The massive housing development that is Stuy Town (some 80 acres hold 25,000 residents) hosts summer music parties on its central green. From mid-June to mid-July, half a dozen Wednesday nights are dedicated to the likes of Afro-Beat, Latin folk-pop, and soul performances. Reggae/dub legends Easy Star All-Stars have been on the bill the last four years—if they come around again make sure to catch 'em. Shows start with DJs at 6pm, bands at 7. Stuyvesant Town Oval, btw. aves. A and B at 17th St. © **212/598-5296.** www. stuytown.com. Mid-June to mid-July Wed 6pm. Subway: L to First Ave.

Naumburg Orchestral Concerts `FREE` The Naumburg Bandshell in Central Park hosts this short concert series, which varies from classical orchestral presentations to brass to flamenco. The series is one of the oldest in the country, with over a century's worth of experience in entertaining New Yorkers. Shows are on four Tuesday nights at 7:30pm, with no rain dates. Midpark, Central Park, just below 72nd St. © **718/340-3018.** www.naumburgconcerts.org. Subway: B/C to 72nd St.; 6 to 68th St./Hunter College.

Riverside Clay Tennis Association Sunset Concert Series `FREE` Perhaps the least wait ever to get on a tennis court in New York City. Blankets and picnic baskets are encouraged at this Riverside Park shindig, as accompaniment for live jazz, classical, samba, and blue-grass. The setting is lovely, and you can hang around afterwards to enjoy the summer night air. Shows are Saturdays from 7 to 9pm, with rain dates set for the same time on Sunday. Riverside Park, the Hudson at 97th St. © **212/978-0277.** www.rcta.info. Subway: 1/2/3 to 96th St.

RiverRocks `FREE` I love the festive atmosphere of this concert series. The crowd is friendly, and sunset over the Hudson and the Jersey skyline is inspiring. Roomy Pier 54 does the hosting. If you show up late you won't get very close to the band, but you will find plenty of space for hanging out, or even dancing. Recent performers have been first-rate indie groups like The Antlers and Phosphorescent. Check the website for times and dates, and also check for Tuesday and Friday night shows on nearby Pier 45. Pier 54 on the Hudson, at 14th St. © **212/533-PARK** [7275]. www.hudsonriverpark.org. Subway: A/C/E to 14th St.; L to Eighth Ave.

Seaport Music Festival FREE   The South Street Seaport isn't much more than a glorified mall, which is cause enough for most locals to give it a wide berth. In the summer, however, Pier 17 is loaded with great free music. Booking is excellent and selections are diverse, from salsa to zydeco, with memorable recent visits from Animal Collective, Dave Alvin, and Jay Farrar. Events are usually held on Friday nights. The festival runs late June through August. FINE PRINT For a low-key lunchtime scene, check out the Fulton Stall Market, which puts on periodic live shows nearby at the former site of the Fulton Fish Market. Pier 17, btw. Beekman and Fulton sts., just east of South St. ℂ **212/SEAPORT** [732-7678]. www.seaportmusicfestival.com. Subway: A/C/J/Z/2/3/4/5 to Fulton St./ Broadway Nassau.

Seaside Summer Concert Series FREE   This free series attracts Coney Island locals, who settle into Asser Levy Park for convivial evenings. The booking for this event is borderline scary, with Michael Bolton, Liza Minnelli, and Air Supply playing in recent years. (The B-52's in '07 helped balance things out.) Concerts begin at 7:30pm on Thursday nights from mid-July to late August. W. 5th St. and Surf Ave., Coney Island, across from the aquarium. ℂ **718/222-0600.** www.brooklynconcerts. com. Subway: F/Q to W. 8th St./NY Aquarium.

Siren Music Festival FREE   The best in below-the-radar rock can be found at the *Village Voice*'s annual Siren Music Festival. Over a hundred thousand fans assemble near the Coney Island boardwalk for music on two stages. The bands tend to be high-quality performers, on the cusp of breakthroughs, or not too far removed from indie-rock triumphs. See p. 306 for more information. Main stage, 10th St., at the boardwalk. Second stage, Stillwell Ave., at the boardwalk. ℂ **212/475-3333.** www.villagevoice.com/siren. Sat in mid-July noon–9pm. Subway: D/F/Q to Stillwell Ave./Coney Island.

SummerGarden FREE   For almost 40 years, MoMA has been throwing these jazz-inflected summer concerts. The Abby Aldrich Rockefeller Sculpture Garden plays host, so if your mind wanders from the music you have Philip Johnson's elegant layout to enjoy. Juilliard students and groups vetted by Jazz at Lincoln Center do the performing. The garden gates on 54th between Fifth and Sixth avenues open at 7pm, but seating is limited, so show up earlier if you don't want to stand. In case of rain, the concerts move indoors to The Agnes Gund Garden Lobby. 11 W. 53rd St., btw. Fifth and Sixth aves. ℂ **212/708-9400.** www. moma.org. July–Aug Sun 8pm. Subway: E/M to Fifth Ave.

SummerStage `FREE` Words like summer and music and free conjure an idyllic picture, especially in the context of Central Park. SummerStage is a crack outfit that brings big-name performers to a stage just off the Rumsey Playfield. To get a seat in the bleachers, better show up a couple of hours before start time. If you're not that patient, you can just wander in at any time, and you should be able to find a spot to stand and/or dance. Since no tickets are required, it's easy to come and go freely unless it's a super popular show. Acts as varied as James Brown, Sonic Youth, and Hugh Masekela have taken the stage, and recent years have seen film, readings, and comedy added to the mix. A few of the shows are pricey benefits, with tickets going for $40 to $60, but they're there to keep the free part going. Further supporting the series, donations are solicited as you enter, but no contribution is required. Central Park, at the Rumsey Playfield, near E. 72nd St. ✆ **212/360-2777.** www.summerstage.org. Subway: 6 to 68th or 77th sts.; B/C to 72nd St.

Washington Square Music Festival `FREE` One of the city's oldest festivals brings classical music (and a little jazz and folk) to the heart of the Village. Three or four pieces, connected by an overall theme, are played Tuesday nights in July and early August from 8 to 10pm. The last Tuesday of the month is often set aside for jazz, salsa, or swing. The festival is held in the northwest corner of Washington Square Park, in front of the Alexander Lyman Holley Monument. Limited seating is available. In case of rain, concerts move to the Church of St. Joseph (371 Sixth Ave., btw. Washington and Waverly places). Near Washington Sq. N., btw. Fifth Ave. and Washington Sq. W. ✆ **212/252-3621.** www.washingtonsquaremusicfestival.org. Subway: A/B/C/D/E/F/M to W. 4th St./ Washington Sq.

Williamsburg Waterfront `FREE` This music series evolved out of the epic rock shows hosted by Jelly at McCarren Park Pool. A venue switch, to East River State Park along the Williamsburg/Greenpoint waterfront, hasn't diminished the energy any. Thousands of hipster music fans descend for some eight afternoon-into-evening concerts, featuring major names in indie rock. Check the website for details (and to make sure Albany's budget axe hasn't killed the concerts). 90 Kent Ave., btw. N. 7th and N. 9th sts., Williamsburg, Brooklyn. ✆ **718/782-2731.** www.jellynyc.com. Subway: L to Bedford Ave.

2 The Reel Cheap World

The movies love New York. Blithely ignoring our existing congestion, productions flock to the city to steal our parking spaces and tie up our sidewalks. Gotham-themed films line the video store shelves. Is it because we're a convenient symbol of urban glamour? Or is it simply because New York is the greatest city in the history of the world? Either way, NYC has a lot of cinematic pride, which allows New Yorkers to be extorted with $12 movie tickets, a dearth of cheap afternoon matinees, and new releases sold out by 4pm even on gorgeous sunny days. Fortunately in New York there are always alternatives. Our libraries are stocked with videos, our bars screen in their backrooms, and in the summer we get spectacular film alfresco. Most events are on the house, and those that aren't won't break the bank.

INDIES, CULT CLASSICS & MORE

African Diaspora Ciné-Club FREE   The "global Black experience" is the focus of this monthly screening. Films from as far afield as Rwanda, Haiti, and Chad make the cut, and help viewers expand their perspective beyond the paltry range of mainstream African and African-American fare. The actual directors often make the post-flick Q&As, and refreshments are served. Screening locations at Teachers College vary, usually Room 263 Macy; films are shown the last Friday of every month at 6pm. Teachers College, Columbia University, 525 W. 120th St., btw. Broadway and Amsterdam Ave. ✆ 212/864-1760. www.nyadff.org. Subway: 1 to 116th St.; A/B/C/D to 125th St.

Cabaret Cinema   Beneath the Rubin Museum of Art's sparkling galleries is an intimate candlelit screening room. Friday evenings see projections of a terrific lineup of films. When the *Holy Madness* exhibit was up, the museum screened related reels that ranged from *Siddhartha* to *Monty Python's Life of Brian*. Shows come with related commentary from a big-time introducer, like Wallace Shawn answering questions about *My Dinner with Andre*. The movies roll at 9:30pm. There's a $7 bar minimum (purchase a drink or snack upstairs and ask the bartender for a chit, which you'll trade for a free ticket at an adjacent table.) 150 W. 17th St., btw. Sixth and Seventh aves. ✆ 212/620-5000. www. rmanyc.org. Subway: 1/2/3/F/M to 14th St.; L to Sixth Ave.

Film Clubs That Actually Save You Money

Film Forum   Does Hollywood still make movies that aren't just flimsy remakes of second-rate television shows? Just when we're ready to give up forever on the medium, the marquee of the **Film Forum** draws us in with some irresistible nugget and we're hooked again. Three screens rotate between revivals, retrospectives, and indies that can't be found elsewhere. The crowd is just as interesting, with big-shot actors and directors often in the house, upping their avant-garde cinematic cred. A 1-year membership to Film Forum is one of the city's best steals. Seventy-five bucks buys you close to half-price movie tickets for all three screens 365¼ days a year. That's $6 instead of $12. The next membership level up is an even sweeter deal: $110 entitles you to *two* half-price tickets for every show. Imagine: cheap date opportunities every single day. Membership is good for 1 year from the date of purchase. But wait, there's more. It's also 100% tax deductible (as are the memberships listed below). Now if only they could make the seats a little more comfortable. 209 W. Houston St., btw. Sixth Ave. and Varick sts. ✆ **212/727-8110.** www.filmforum.com. Subway: 1 to Houston St.

MoMA   As frustrating as the new MoMA can be, a membership there carries too many perks for me to resist. On top of complimentary museum admission and sneak previews to new exhibitions, members also get a year's worth of free film. MoMA's programming is excellent

Chelsea Classics   Clearview 9 Cinema keeps the natives from getting too restless by breaking the regimen of mainstream Hollywood fare for a weekly night of camp classics. Drag darling Hedda Lettuce warms up the room before the early showing. Joan Crawford and Bette Davis do not go overlooked. Thursdays at 7 and 9:30pm; only $7.50. After the movie, your ticket stub morphs into a free drink if you take it to the nearby XES Lounge (www.xesnyc.com). 260 W. 23rd St., btw. Seventh and Eighth aves. ✆ **212/777-FILM** [3456]. www.clearviewcinemas. com. Subway: 1 or C/E to 23rd St.

Coney Island Museum   On Saturday nights in summer, the museum screens movies made in the spirit of Coney Island's sideshow past.

and with movies showing in 3 separate theaters daily, it's hard to run out of cinematic possibilities. Members can also buy half-price tickets for up to 5 friends (just $5 per ticket). At $75 per year, membership will pay for itself after eight flicks. 11 W. 53rd St., btw. Fifth and Sixth aves. ℂ 212/708-9400. www.moma.org. Subway: E/M to Fifth Ave./53rd St.

The Maysles Cinema Documentaries like Gimme Shelter and Grey Gardens forged the legend of brothers Albert and David Maysles. Although David has passed on, Albert continues to be an active force in the film world, making documentary film and video accessible to underserved populations from his new Harlem HQ. A $50 membership here will get you a year's worth of free screenings. 343 Malcolm X Blvd. (Lenox Blvd.), btw. 127th and 128th sts. ℂ 212/582-6050. www.mayslesfilms.com. Subway: 2/3 to 125th St.

Anthology Film Archives For over 40 years now, the cinephiles at this totally indie spot have been programming the best of the avant-garde along with cheeky mainstream combos (a recent series called "For the Birds" covered everything from documentaries to Hitchcock). Your $60 membership entitles you to free admission for the classic films of the Essential Cinema program, and $6 for all regular shows. 32 Second Ave., at 2nd St. ℂ 212/505-5181. www.anthologyfilmarchives.org. Subway: F to Second Ave.

Expect uplifting cinematic triumphs with the words "bikini" and/or "bandit" in the title. Low-budget productions beget budget prices: just $5. And the popcorn's free! Saturdays at 8:30pm. In late September, look out for the Coney Island Film Festival. Most programs are only $6 and run through a full weekend of shorts and features. 1208 Surf Ave., 2nd floor, near 12th St. ℂ 718/372-5159. www.indiefilmpage.com. Subway: D/F/N/Q to Coney Island/Stillwell Ave.

Neue Galerie FREE This elegant museum tailors its film program to dovetail with the 20th-century German and Austrian masterpieces in the galleries above. A recent Otto Dix exhibit was matched with a series of battlefield-themed films that spanned from 1930 to 2001. Movies are

Current Releases for Little Currency

"That $3 theater" became "that $4 theater" and then closed altogether. The uptown bargain-matinee place got torn down to make way for million-dollar condos. It's becoming harder and harder to find a current release for anything less than the usurious $12 charged for prime-time viewing. If you're in the right neighborhood, though, there are still options left.

Cobble Hill Cinemas Monday through Friday all shows before 5pm are only $6.50, as are the first shows of the day on the weekend (as long as they start before 2pm). If matinees don't do it for you, there are also two bargain days, Tuesdays and Thursdays, when all seats for all shows all day and all night are a humble $6.50. The only exceptions are special engagements and holidays. 265 Court St., at Butler St., Boerum Hill, Brooklyn. ✆ **718/596-9113.** www.cobblehilltheatre.com. Subway: F/G to Bergen St.

Kew Gardens Cinemas First-run films play here, usually more interesting indie fare, with several bargain showtimes. Tuesdays and Thursdays are $6.50 for all seats all day. Monday, Wednesday, and Friday, all seats are $6.50 until 5pm, as are seats for the first show before 2pm on Saturdays and Sundays. Holidays and special engagements are excepted for the cheap seats. ✆ **718/441-9835.** www.kewgardens theatre.com. 81–05 Lefferts Blvd., at Austin St., Kew Gardens, Queens. Subway: E/F to Kew Gardens/Union Turnpike.

Cheap A.M.s at AMC Although it's a little ridiculous settling into a theater seat when most folks are still finishing up their first cup of coffee, we should be thankful to American Multi-Cinema all the same. Just $6 gets you into some pre-noon shows at their theaters all across the city (weekends and holidays at some theaters, daily at others). See www.amcentertainment.com.

free Monday afternoons at 4pm in Café Fledermaus. 1048 Fifth Ave., at 86th St. ✆ **212/628-6200.** www.neuegalerie.org. Subway: 4/5/6 to 86th St.

Nuevo Cine: Recent Films from Latin America FREE Wednesday night movie night in Latin America is the inspiration for this film series, which screens the first Hump Day of every month. Features and documentaries are interspersed, usually starting at 6:30pm. 1230 Fifth Ave., at 104th St. ℭ **212/831-7272.** www.elmuseo.org. Subway: 6 to 103rd St.

Rooftop Films What began as a lark atop a downtown tenement has now expanded to lawns, parks, and rooftops across Manhattan, Brooklyn, and Queens. On summer nights, God dims the overheads, and indie shorts and features play. Despite screening low-budget productions, Rooftop Films does an incredible filtering job, and quality is impressively high. Film themes run along the lines of "Home Movies" or "Scenes from Texas." Screenings cost $10, but that's a bargain if you value films made by actual human beings and not Hollywood-studio automatons. Check the website for exact locations and times. Movies start after sunset (9pm usually), with live music beforehand. ℭ **718/417-7362.** www.rooftopfilms.com.

Sony Wonder Technology Lab `FREE` Sony goes to bat for high-def technology by hosting free films in its 73-seat theater. The flicks tend to be well-known Hollywood products of recent vintage. Sprinkled throughout the year are additional screenings for the kiddies. Adults get select Saturdays at 2pm, the kids get select Thursdays at 2pm and Saturdays at noon. Reservations recommended, call on Monday morning when a screening is scheduled for later in the week. 550 Madison Ave., at 56th St. ℭ **212/833-7858.** www.sonywondertechlab.com. Subway: 4/5/6 to 59th St.; N/Q/R to Lexington Ave./59th St.

NYC'S DRIVE-IN: OUTDOOR SUMMER SCREENINGS

We may be too cheap for insurance, garages, tickets, tolls, and all the other joys of car ownership, but New Yorkers do know how to enjoy their very own brand of drive-in movie. Come summer, the parks roll out the big screens and the locals trundle in with blankets and picnic dinners. Each festival has its own identity, with movies ranging across the decades and the genres, assuring something for every cineaste's taste. As dusk settles over the city, around 8:30pm or so, the crowd hushes and the reels spin. Lie back and be transported by the magic of the movies under the starry skies. Well, skies.

Central Park Film Festival `FREE` Central Park has been lending atmosphere to films since 1908 (a silent version of *Romeo and Juliet* was the first movie shot here). The Park celebrates its long starring career with this late-summer fest, which screens several of the more

Free Outdoor Summer Movies

Monday	Tuesday	Wednesday	Thursday	Friday	Saturday	Sunday
HBO Bryant Park Summer Film Festival		Crotona Park Hip Hop Film Festival	Brooklyn Bridge Movies With a View	RiverFlicks– Pier 25		RiverFlicks– Pier 54
		Outdoor Cinema Program at Socrates Sculpture Park				
		Summer on the Hudson: Movies Under the Stars				

than 200 movies that have had major scenes here. *Breakfast at Tiffany's* and *Tootsie* are among past players. Admission is free, at the Rumsey Playfield, usually over five nights (Tues–Sat) at the end of August. Gates open at 6pm, screenings at 8. Central Park, at the Rumsey Playfield, near E. 72nd St. ✆ **212/310-6600.** www.centralparknyc.org. Subway: 6 to 68th or 77th sts.; B/C to 72nd St.

Films on the Green `FREE` The Cultural Services department of the French Embassy tries to cut through our reflexive disdain for all things Gallic by giving away these summer flicks. "The green" in the title refers to a rotating selection of parkland (Central, Tompkins, and Washington Sq. are the usual suspects). The film series are themed, like '10's run through French musicals. Projectors whirl Friday evenings in June and July at sunset (around 8:30pm). `FINE PRINT` Wear your reading glasses, as movies are in French with English subtitles. Various locations. ✆ **212/439-1400.** www.frenchculture.org.

Habana Outpost `FREE` This Fort Greene restaurant is the city's first "eco-eatery," a restaurant dedicated to Earth-friendly practices (you can save a buck on your brunch margarita by powering the bike blender yourself). The converted–parking lot location couldn't be more laid-back, with a menu of moderately priced Cuban and Mexican food. On Sunday nights between May and October, free movies like camp classics *The Last Dragon*, *Saturday Night Fever*, and *Shaft* are projected on a big back wall. There's no charge or minimum, but it's cheap here ($2 for corn or a hot dog, $2.50 for a draft beer). Films start at 8pm. 757 Fulton St., at S. Portland St., Fort Greene, Brooklyn. ✆ **718/858-9500.** www.ecoeatery.com. Subway: C to Lafayette St.; G to Fulton St.

That's the Ticket: Giveaways

To fan the flames of early buzz, some films and plays give seats away early in their runs. If your inbox can handle more junkmail, you can sign on with **New York Show Tickets Inc.** (www.nytix.com) and hope to win big in their daily Broadway ticket lottery. You can also find the occasional giveaway on Craigslist, and there's more on offer at the *Village Voice* and *Time Out New York* websites. Both latter sources have dedicated sections (www.villagevoice.com/promotions/freestuff and the "Free Flix" button at www.timeoutny.com) where you can vie for a movie premiere or two. It's a lottery and the odds are on the long side, but hey, the price is right. A sharp eye can also reward a person with preview seats. Check *Time Out* and the *Village Voice* for advertisements of newly opening productions. In addition to specials on tickets for the first few weeks, sometimes you'll spot an offering for a preview. You'll get something halfway between a dress rehearsal and the final polished show, but it won't cost a cent.

Hell Gate Social   This arty spot behind an unmarked door ladles on the incentives to get folks to an obscure stretch of Astoria Boulevard. Sunday nights in warmer weather feature BBQ afternoons capped off with free flicks. The grilled meat is all you can eat from 3 to 8pm ($10), and there are two-for-one drinks at happy hour (7 to 9pm, an offer that's good seven days a week). 1221 Astoria Blvd., btw. 12th and 14th sts., Astoria, Queens. (C) 718/204-8313. www.hellgatesocial.com. Subway: N/Q to Astoria Blvd.

HBO Bryant Park Summer Film Festival FREE   Bryant Park is the most famous and most popular of New York's outdoor talkies. A huge screen goes up along Sixth Avenue across from the library's back porch, and the lawn fills with friendly movie fanatics. Film selections run from kitsch like *Jailhouse Rock* to classics like *The Philadelphia Story* to tripped-out wonders like *2001: A Space Odyssey*. Watching the latter from the grass brings a creepy resonance, given Bryant Park was once a potter's field. The gates open for blanket spreading at 5pm, and if you want a decent view you should be on-site by then. Bring a crossword puzzle and a picnic dinner and pretend you're just sitting in the park and not waiting for a show. Latecomers have to watch from way back or the wings. It's not untenable; it's just not as much fun as dancing through the HBO trailer from the heart of the crowd. If you time things right, and the director's done his work, this event is totally worth its logistical impositions. Monday nights June through August. W. 40th to 41st, on the Sixth Ave. side of Bryant Park. ℂ **212/512-5700.** www.bryant park.org. No rain dates. Subway: B/D/F/M to 42nd St.; 7 to Fifth Ave.

Movie Nights on the Elevated Acre `FREE` Despite a glowing beacon, a huge swath of open space, and gorgeous harbor views, this downtown park flies well under the radar. Introduce yourself to the spot during free Thursday movie nights in late July and August. Programming focuses on NY classic films (Woody Allen is well represented), paired with indie shorts. The crowd is capped by a ticketing system: Pick up your passes at the ground-level Water Street entrance (two per person) starting at 6pm the evening of the screening. Films begin around 8pm. 55 Water St., at Old Slip. ℂ **212/566-6700.** www.downtown ny.org. Subway: R or 1 to South Ferry.

Movies With a View `FREE` What could be better than the spectacular sight of downtown lights shimmering behind the Gothic span of the Brooklyn Bridge? A free movie flickering in front, that's what. Every summer, the Brooklyn riverfront turns into a giant alfresco cinema. This series was once the anti–Bryant Park, with limited attendance, but like its hosting borough it has blown up in recent years and you should arrive early if you want a decent spot. Special bonuses include free valet bike parking, DJs at 6pm, and shorts projected before each feature. Thursday nights at dusk, in July and August. Check the website for location (in 2010 the films were at the newly opened Pier 1). Empire–Fulton Ferry Park, just west of Water St. ℂ **718/802-0603.** www.brooklynbridgepark. org. Subway: F to York St.; A/C to High St.; Water Taxi to Fulton Ferry Landing.

Outdoor Cinema Program at Socrates Sculpture Park `FREE` Queens is the most culturally diverse spot on the planet, so it makes sense that a Queens film festival would show off movies from around the world. You'll also find culture-appropriate food vendors, so you can nosh on Italian during *The Bicycle Thief* or Indian while *Monsoon Wedding* plays. The movies flicker at Socrates Sculpture Park in Long Island City, a former dump site resuscitated as an artistic oasis along the East River. There are great skyline sightlines, and they throw in free music and dancing as well, beginning at 7pm. Wednesday nights in July and August; movies start at dusk. 32–01 Vernon Blvd., at Broadway,

Astoria, Queens. ✆ **718/784-4520.** www. socratessculpturepark.org. Subway: N/Q to Broadway. Walk 8 blocks along Broadway toward the East River.

RiverFlicks FREE   The waters of the Hudson and the Jersey skyline provide the backdrop for RiverFlicks. This is a viewer-friendly scene, with chairs laid out on the pier, free popcorn, and themed films that tend toward crowd-pleasing recent hits. *Legally Blonde, 8 Mile,* and *Gladiator* have all made the cut. This is not actually one of my favorites, as the spot is loud, and over-bright lighting makes the screen hard to scan. On the plus side, as a result there are usually seats left over (if not, there's blanket-spreading space in back and on the wings). Pier 54 hosts Wednesday nights for adults, and Pier 46 takes Fridays for kids, in July and August. Pier 46, at Charles St. and the Hudson. ✆ **212/533-7275.** www.hudsonriverpark.org. Subway: 1 to Christopher St. Walk toward the river. Pier 54, at 14th St. and the Hudson. Subway: A/C/E to 14th St.; L to Eighth Ave. Walk toward the river.

Solar-Powered Film Series FREE Solar One is New York's first free-standing building to get all of its power not from recycled dinosaurs, but from Helios himself. To celebrate this achievement (and to raise awareness

FREE **Watching Between the Lions**

New York's book repositories bear no hard feelings for the many indignities the movies have imposed over the years. Our libraries are so forgiving, in fact, they lend out extensive video collections. It's like Blockbuster, only with less censorship and you don't have to pay for anything. The **New York Public Library for the Performing Arts** (p. 114) holds the massive Reserve Film and Video Collection, with more than 6,000 16mm films, 5,000 VHS tapes, and 1,000 DVDs. Most films circulate for 7 days. You can also make an appointment to watch a film on-site. For documentary and world cinema video, head over to the **Mid-Manhattan Library,** 455 Fifth Ave., at 40th St. (✆ **212/340-0863;** www.nypl.org). Subway: 7 to Fifth Ave.; 4/5/6/S to 42nd St./ Grand Central; B/D/F/M to 42nd St. You can also find screenings at select libraries. The New York Public Library for the Performing Arts is a good place to look, as is the Jefferson Market Library (✆ **212/243-4334**), and the main branch of the Brooklyn Public Library (✆ **718/230-2100;** www.brooklynpubliclibrary.org).

about the inevitable need to live greener in NYC), the building hosts an annual film festival. Over two September weekends, projectors running on sun power alone show six well-chosen films, often documentaries that highlight some aspect of our environmental plight. See also p. 275 for the dance series. Stuyvesant Cove Park, 23rd St. and the FDR. 📞 **212/505-6050**. www.solar1.org. Subway 6 to 23rd St.; L to First Ave.

Summer Movie Series at the Intrepid Sea, Air & Space Museum FREE How 40,000 tons can float is beyond my limited engineering comprehension, but I'm all over any chance to check out a battleship flight deck for free. On the third Friday of each summer month, the *Intrepid* screens a flick related to the sea, air, or space on its up-top runway. Doors open at 7:30pm and films start about an hour later; picnics, blankets, and lawn chairs are encouraged (although no booze, to fend off drunken jet-plane joyriding). Pier 86, 46th St. at Twelfth Ave. 📞 **212/245-0072**. www.intrepidmuseum.org. Subway: A/C/E/7 to 42nd St./Port Authority.

Summer on the Hudson: Movies Under the Stars FREE With Trump residential structures rising seemingly overnight, lower Riverside Park is filling out, providing green space for a few thousand newly minted West Siders. For their—and our—entertainment, the park's acreage opens itself up to culture in summer. In addition to acoustic music Sundays and other concerts, there's an underrated movie series at 8:30pm on Wednesdays. Curating is usually thematic, with titles like "On the Hudson River Waterfront" and "The Great Outdoors." Picnics encouraged, at the end of Pier I. Pier I, the Hudson at 70th St. 📞 **212/408-0219**. www.nycgovparks.org. Subway: 1/2/3 to 72nd St.

Tribeca Drive-In FREE The North Cove plaza of the World Financial Center shows off the big-budget capabilities of the Tribeca Film Festival. A huge screen and sweet sound make the most of crowd pleasers like *Saturday Night Fever* and *Dirty Dancing,* with an accompanying party atmosphere. Late April, over three nights. Check the website for details; gates open at 6:30pm, screenings at around 8:15. Plaza, North Cove, btw. Vesey and Liberty sts. 📞 **212/941-2400**. www.tribecafilmfestival.org. Subway: 1/R to Rector St.; E to World Trade Center, 4/5 to Fulton St.; 2/3 to Park Place.

3 The Theatah

Just as models make their way to California for its surfeit of Beach Girl #4 roles, dramatic actors are drawn to New York City. They're not just waiting on our tables, either. In NYC you can find great performances on every level of theater, from big-time Broadway (with its $100-plus orchestra seats) to $10 Off-Broadway to raw productions in the basements of bars, performed for whatever can be garnered by passing the hat. Cost is not necessarily a barometer of quality. You can drop a few Jacksons to discover the cast of a Broadway blockbuster is just phoning it in, while across town some hungry young talent is drawing tears at a free production of Shakespeare. Other giveaways are offered up by schools, institutions, and work-in-progress programs. If you need something more polished than that, try downtown, where dirt-cheap theaters will get you the dramatic goods for $10 or less.

FREE THEATER

Free Willie: Shakespeare Alfresco

Troupes love to try their hand at the Bard, and free Shakespeare abounds in the Big Apple. Join your fellow mortals and enjoy the midsummer night dreams.

Boomerang Theatre FREE This Off-Off-Broadway stalwart comes back each year with performances of Shakespeare's plays in parks around New York City. Riverside, Central, and Prospect have all served as stages, usually two weekends' worth (Fri nights followed by Sat and Sun matinees). There's also a Rotating Repertory program, and "First Flight," a series of new play readings, which carries a $5 suggested donation. © 212/501-4069. www.boomerangtheatre.org.

Gorilla Rep FREE Artistic Director Christopher Carter Sanderson has been pioneering free classical theater for some two decades now. His troupe is known for its outdoor performances of *A Midsummer Night's Dream*, most recently seen shifting around the landmarks of Central Park. For 2012, they've set their sites extremely high: a Guinness World Record attempt to stage all 42 Shakespeare plays in a single year. Free. © 212/252-5258. www.gorillarep.org.

FREE Rise of the House Ushers

If you have the ability to pass out Playbills, point to seats, and enunciate the phrase "enjoy the show," then you're qualified to see free plays. Many smaller theater companies save money on the cost of ushers by trading your sweat equity for a complimentary seat. Each house has a different set of rules, and the number of volunteers needed varies from one to eight per night. Popular productions can have a backlog of a few weeks. The best plan of attack is to find a play you want to see and call the front office to see what their deal is. It may take some tenacious dialing, but it'll be easily worth it when you settle back in your seat without a penny spent. The two venues listed below are just a starting point; dozens of stages in the city will let you usher your way to free entertainment.

New York Theatre Workshop   This small downtown theater doesn't shy away from experimentation, including occasional hip-hop fare. Five ushers are used per show. Call ☎ **212/780-9037** during regular business hours to sync your schedule with theirs. FINE PRINT Beyond ushering, Sunday night tickets are discounted to $20. 79 E. 4th St., btw. Second Ave. and the Bowery. www.nytw.org. Subway: 6 to Astor Place.

Second Stage Theatre   This organization specializes in giving contemporary playwrights second chances to find audiences. Their new 296-seat theater is nicely designed and a comfortable place to usher. Call to see when your available dates match their needs. 307 W. 43rd St., at Eighth Ave. ☎ **212/246-4422.** www.2st.com. Subway: A/C/E/7 to 42nd St./Port Authority.

Hudson Warehouse FREE   The neoclassical marble and granite Soldiers' and Sailors' Monument puts a dignified cap on a Riverside Park knoll. For several summers now, it's also served as the backdrop for a rival free-summer-Shakespeare troupe (in a rival park). The players of Hudson Warehouse put on shows in June, July, and August at 6:30pm, Thursday through Sunday, with a work or two of the Bard, plus tangential material like *The Trojan Women* or *Cyrano*. The setting is informal, but the actors work hard to be heard over the ambient sound of park and parkway. [FINE PRINT] Also look for Hudson Warehouse's "Shakespeare in the Bar" series, with ale-friendly staged readings. Soldiers' and Sailors' Monument, Riverside Park, 89th St. at Riverside Dr. ℂ **917/775-9837.** www.hudsonwarehouse.net. Subway: 1 to 86th St., 1/2/3 to 96th St.

Inwood Shakespeare Festival FREE   Inwood Hill Park, with its Bald Eagles and huge natural forest, is as un-Manhattan as Manhattan gets. The verdant hills here are the backdrop for the Moose Hall Theatre Company's annual takes on Shakespeare. They also branch out to other classic material, like *The Three Musketeers* or *The Hunchback of Notre Dame,* and throw in a children's concert or two. Shows are casual, with a tailgating feel, as local families kick back on blankets. The plays run a dozen times each, Wednesdays through Saturdays at 7:30pm. Inwood Hill Park Peninsula, Isham St. at Seaman Ave. ℂ **212/567-5255.** www.moosehallisf.org. Subway: A to 207th St.; 1 to 215th St.

New York Classical Theatre FREE   NYCT takes advantage of the natural contours of Central Park to stage its summer Shakespeare productions. Plays begin around 103rd Street and Central Park West, but NYCT's innovation is Panoramic Theatre, which is careful not to cast performers' feet in cement. As scenes shift, the location does as well, furthering the sense of an unfolding story. A second Shakespearean series runs downtown, with Castle Clinton and the World Financial Center as backdrops. Central Park, ℂ **212/252-4531.** www.newyorkclassical. org. Usually 3 plays per summer; no tickets or reservations required. Check website for showtimes. June–Aug Thurs–Sun 7pm. Subway: B/C to 103rd St. Battery Park, Subway: 4/5 to Bowling Green; R to Whitehall; 1 to South Ferry. World Financial Center, Subway: E to World Trade Center; R/W to Cortlandt St.

Shakespeare in the Park FREE   Shh! Top secret! No one else knows about this amazing cultural giveaway. Every summer a William Shakespeare play is performed in a gorgeous open-air theater in the center of enchanted Central Park. Just show up a couple of minutes before showtime and whisper the password "Birnam Wood." Oh, were it that easy. Some 90,000 people attend the Public Theater/Delacorte Theater's productions every summer, and it's the worst-kept free secret in the city. It takes a lot to justify an hours-long Soviet-style wait for a lousy two-ticket ration, but Joseph Papp's Public Theater rarely comes up short. Design, direction, and acting (often featuring A-list stars) are all world-class. The productions vary from faithful classical interpretations to avant-garde re-imaginings. In summer, 1,800-some seats are given out at the Delacorte in Central Park. You'll need some determination for your free Will, as people start lining up 2 or 3 hours early for the 1pm giveaways. For a hot show, you'll find bodies outside the Delacorte before 8am (in some cases, folks will wait overnight). Just treat the ticket queue, with its natural camaraderie, as part of the experience. If you like your luck, you can vie for tickets from the convenience of a computer. The Virtual Ticketing system (www.shakespeareinthepark.org) is a lottery, but with a little persistence you can nab a pair of free seats—I've managed to score the last two years. Iffy weather or a panned production will up your odds. The Public's ticket distribution also goes on the road to Harlem and the four outer boroughs, usually one visit per location per play. Check the Shakespeare in the Park website for the dates.

The season runs June through August and features one or two Shakespeare plays (many years the second play is completely unrelated to the Bard). *Delacorte Theater,* Belvedere Castle, near 79th St. and West Dr. ✆ **212/539-8750.** www.publictheater.org. Subway: B/C to 81st St.

Shakespeare in the Park(ing) Lot `FREE` Central Park is classy and well groomed, with lush grass and trees softening the hard edges of the city. The municipal parking lot on Ludlow Street has none of these charms, but the graffiti-slathered asphalt patch can compete in the realm of Tudor drama. The troupe Drilling CompaNY puts on Shakespeare every summer, with a wealth of energy and wit to make up for the lack of big-name casts and big-budget backdrops. It's a wonderfully surreal scene, with sword fights and intrigue in the foreground while befuddled neighbors cut through the parking spaces in back. Seating is first-come, first-served, or bring your own (padding is a must, as that pavement gets hard when you've been parked for a while). Two plays per summer over six weekends, 8pm. `FINE PRINT` Parking is available, and it's very convenient. Ludlow St., btw. Broome and Delancey sts. ✆ **212/877-0099.** www.drillingcompany.org. July–Aug Thurs–Sat 8pm. Subway: F to Delancey St.; J/M/Z to Essex St.

MORE ALFRESCO THEATER

Circus Amok `FREE` Amok rakes muck as it entertains, combining activist sentiments with traditional circus arts. Acrobats, jugglers, and a bearded woman are among the draws. The Circus Amok band often trolls through neighborhoods, gathering an audience for shows

FREE Tune In to Broadway Revues

Give our regards to theatrical greatest-hits packages. The casts of the Great White Way leave the confines of their stages to flog their shows in Midtown, usually in musical form. Huge stars wander down from nearby dressing rooms, making these very popular events. And you thought Times Square was crowded already.

Broadway in Bryant Park Every summer Broadway teases fans with a quick sampler on the Bryant Park stage. *In The Heights, Billy Elliot,* and *Jersey Boys* are among the headliners that perform excerpts for a crowded lawn. Shows are held during Thursday lunch hours (12:30–1:30pm) in July and early August. Behind the Public Library, btw. 40th and 42nd sts. and Fifth and Sixth aves. © **212/768-4242.** www.bryant park.org. Subway: B/D/F/M to 42nd St.; 7 to Fifth Ave.

Broadway on Broadway A special stage in Times Square hosts this massive concert on a Sunday in mid-September. At least a baker's dozen of shows make an appearance, including heavy hitters like *The Lion King, Avenue Q,* and *Mamma Mia!* For the finale, enough confetti rains down to give onlookers flashbacks to New Year's Eve. Times Square. © **212/768-1560.** www.broadwayonbroadway.com. Usually around 11:30am. Subway: N/Q/R/S/1/2/3/7 to Times Sq./42nd St.

Broadway's Stars in the Alley On the Wednesday before the Tonys, Shubert Alley brings out representatives from some two dozen shows to prance about for your amusement. Though appearances are brief, wattage is high, with the likes of Leslie Uggams and Harvey Fierstein. Shubert Alley, access from 45th St., just west of Seventh Ave. © **212/764-1122.** www.starsinthealley.com. Usually 11am, early June. Subway: N/Q/R/S/1/2/3/7 to Times Sq./42nd St.

performed in local parks. Look for some two dozen shows spread out across the month of September. © **718/486-7432,** ext. 1. www.circusamok.org.

The Classical Theatre of Harlem FREE This decade-old troupe brings the classics to audiences that aren't exactly inundated with *The Cherry Orchard* or *Waiting for Godot.* They also stretch the definition of classic, as in '08's production of Melvin Van Peebles's musical

Ain't Supposed to Die a Natural Death. In late July and early August, there are free outdoor performances. No tickets or reservations necessary; shows mostly Friday and Saturday nights, check the website for details. FINE PRINT Also look for their "Future Classics" reading program, which is free at the Schomburg Center (p. 114). ✆ **212/564-9983.** www.classicaltheatreofharlem.org. Locations vary; check the website.

Piper Theatre Productions FREE This grassroots troupe uses the Old Stone House of Gowanus as a backdrop for its alfresco frolics. An original focus on adventurous Shakespeare (their *A Midsummer Night's Dream* was set in 19th-c. Coney Island) has shifted to modern, lesser-known dramas. Shows are free (a $10 donation per family is suggested), mid to late July in Park Slope's Washington Park (formerly J.J. Byrne Park). Washington Park, 3rd St. btw. Fourth and Fifth aves., Park Slope, Brooklyn. ✆ **718/768-3195.** www. pipertheatre.org. Subway: F/G/R to 9th St./Fourth Ave.; R to Union St.

Theatreworks USA FREE Every summer, this organization puts up a production aimed at rug-rat edification (or at least amusement). The group concentrates on one play per season, usually a modern musical. Tickets are distributed on the day of the performance, with four per person available 1 hour before curtain time. Shows run between one and three times a day, every day but Saturday. Summer camps usually reserve the bulk of weekday afternoon seats, so your best bet is an evening or Sunday show. Lucille Lortel Theatre, 121 Christopher St., btw. Bleecker and Hudson sts. ✆ **212/647-1100.** www.theatreworksusa.org. Subway: 1 to Christopher St.

THEATER WITH CLASS

In the working and reworking of new plays, feedback devices are essential. An audience of warm bodies makes a great barometer for figuring out which scenes are killing and which lines are bombing. With so much untested drama in NYC, it's easy to find showcases, workshops, and readings that are eager for your presence. You'll often be sharing the room with a parcel of pros: agents, producers, and casting directors on the prowl for the next big things. If you don't mind putting up with some unsanded edges, it's a great way to catch a night of free theater.

Cap21 FREE The Collaborative Arts Project dedicates itself to fostering innovative productions. Part of the process involves developing new audiences, which are invited in for free programs on Monday nights. The focus is usually on emerging artists. The seats do fill up, so make sure to get a reservation. 18 W. 18th St., 6th floor, btw. Fifth and Sixth aves. ℭ 212/352-3101. www.cap21.org. Select Mon 7:30pm (check the website). Subway: L/N/Q/R/4/5/6 to 14th St./Union Sq.

The Juilliard School FREE The fourth-year students of Juilliard's Drama Division mount full-scale productions to catch the eyes of agents, casting directors, and the press. The general public is invited in as well. Third-years also put on free shows, usually as high-minded as a Shakespearean production. FINE PRINT The free tickets go fast. You'll have to wait at the box office the first day they become available, although there's also a same-day standby line. The Janet and Leonard Kramer Box Office (Juilliard Box Office), 155 W. 65th St., btw. Broadway and Amsterdam Ave. ℭ 212/769-7406. www.juilliard.edu. Subway: 1 to 66th St./Lincoln Center.

Mabou Mines/Suite FREE Somehow this avant-garde troupe has managed to stay on the cutting edge for over 40 years. A commitment to taking chances and providing opportunities for new voices probably hasn't hurt. Mabou's Resident Artist Program presents works in evolution during March and April. Some 9 shows play multiple times, all for free. Call ahead for reservations. 150 First Ave., btw. 9th and 10th sts. ℭ 212/473-1991. www.maboumines.org. Subway: 6 to Astor Place, L to First Ave.

The Martin E. Segal Theatre Center FREE This center is run by CUNY's PhD program in theater, home to a talented crop of scholars, students, actors, and playwrights. The schedule is laden with freebies, including visits from international theatrical heavy-hitters, lecture series, and excerpted plays. In September, check out the Prelude festival (www.preludenyc.org), with nearly two dozen performances, readings, and open rehearsals of works in progress. No tickets or reservations are required. 365 Fifth Ave., btw. 34th and 35th sts. ℭ 212/917-1860. http://web. gc.cuny.edu/mestc. Subway: B/D/F/N/Q/R to 34th St./Herald Sq.; 6 to 33rd St.

The New School for Drama FREE The New School integrates the arts of acting, directing, and playwriting. The fruits of these synergies can be found during "New Voices," an annual playwrights' festival. Seven original plays are presented in repertory, showing three times each. The performances are free, but it's best to reserve a seat in advance.The New School for Drama Theater at the Westbeth, 151 Bank St., 3rd floor, btw. Washington St. and the West Side Hwy. ℭ 212/279-4200. www.new school.edu/academic/drama. Subway: A/C/E to 14th St.; L to Eighth Ave.

NYU Graduate Acting Program NYU's Tisch School of the Arts is justly famous for the high-profile directors, actors, and dramatic writers it has produced. You can get a glimpse of burgeoning talents at periodic free shows. Most are put on by second years (by third year they can get away with charging), in various theaters on and around the NYU campus. The tickets for charged shows tend to be reasonable, in the $6 to $20 range. Tisch Main Bldg., 721 Broadway, btw. Waverly and Washington places (just south of 8th St.). ℂ **212/998-1921.** www.gradacting.tisch. nyu.edu. Subway: 6 to Astor Place; N/Q/R to 8th St.; A/B/C/D/E/M to W. 4th St./Washington Sq.

The York Theatre Company FREE Inside the tasteful modern confines of St. Peter's Church, the York Theatre trots out unsung new musicals for free performances. The **Developmental Reading Series** has warbled its way through Depression-era Chicago, *fin-de-siècle* Paris, and the present-day Smoky Mountains in recent years. FINE PRINT The shows are free but do sometimes "sell out," so reserve early. 619 Lexington Ave., at 54th St. ℂ **212/935-5824,** ext. 524. www.yorktheatre.org. Subway: E/M to Lexington Ave.; 6 to 51st St.

DIRT CHEAP THEATER

ALL ABOUT LA MAMA: BIG DRAMA IN SMALL SPACES

Small theater groups are notorious for their shoestring budgets, which means most don't have the luxury of permanent stages. All it takes to make a theater is some matte-black paint, a few gelled lights, and a bunch of folding chairs. Walk-up lofts in Midtown are constantly taking form as Off-Off-Broadway bastions. Downtown, especially the area around East 4th Street, is a locus with more staying power. Several companies work out of the area and most shows have East Village–friendly prices of $15 or less.

chashama FREE The innovative use of multiple spaces is a reinforcement of this arts group's name (it's Farsi for "to have vision"). Storefront windows in scattered locales host art exhibits, live music, and theatrical productions. There're also more permanent spaces, where the annual October chashama Film Festival can be found. The storefront entertainment is free; films are only $7. Various locales. ℂ **212/391-8151.** www.chashama.org.

Emerging Artists Theatre For over a dozen years, EAT has been nurturing new playwrights. New York debuts are frequent here, part of a collaborative process that involves company actors and associ-ated directors. Although prices can approach Broadway levels, there are labs, and festivals like the EAT Developmental Series, which is often just $10. 15 W. 28th St., btw. Fifth Ave. and Broadway. ℰ 212/247-2429. www.eatheatre.org. Subway: N/Q/R to 28th St.

Galapagos Art Space   This Brooklyn bar began with a mini–Temple of Dendur moat in an old Williamsburg mayonnaise factory. In their new DUMBO space, they've built an even bigger lake, which helps cool the structure in summer and warm it in winter. Compelling com-edy, theater, music, and film fill the calendar. Most events are in the $10–$15 range, but plenty of free shows are peppered through the schedule. 16 Main St., btw. Water and Plymouth sts., DUMBO, Brooklyn. ℰ 718/222-8500. www.galapagosartspace.com. Subway: F to York St.; A/C to High St.

La MaMa   This venerable avatar of the avant-garde is fully established in the East Village, where it remains dedicated to artistic experimenta-tion. Productions are high quality, and the ticket prices reflect it—shows can run from $5 to $30. One notable exception is the free **Experiments** readings series, performed in La MaMa's first-floor theater space. The series features in-progress plays read with the writers in attendance, to provide instant-gratification feedback. Look also for the **Coffeehouse Chronicles,** a homecoming of sorts, which recalls the ori-gins of the Off-Off-Broadway world with the original instigators. Those shows are free, although nostalgia is preserved with a passed hat. Check the website for exact days and times. 74 E. 4th St., btw. Second Ave. and the Bowery. ℰ 212/475-7710. www.lamama.org. Subway: F/M to Second Ave.; 6 to Bleecker St.

The Public Theater   Shakespeare in the Park is only the beginning for the Public Theater, which churns out amazing drama all year long. The New Work Now! series presents readings of fresh material by both established dramaturges and up and comers. From December to March, you can catch PUBLIC LAB, which puts on bare-bones productions at a price friendly to threadbare budgets. Just $10 gets you into these still-evolving shows, presented by the LAByrinth Theater Company (www.labtheater.org). Also keep an eye out for LAByrinth's 29 Hour Develop-ment Workshop, with readings. Come July, look for the Summer Play Festival (www.spfnyc.com), with some eight different shows each for a very accessible $10. 425 Lafayette St., just below Astor Place. ℰ 212/539-8500. www.publictheater.org. Subway: 6 to Astor Place; N/Q/R to 8th St.

NYC's Best Theater Discount Strategies

Academic Advantages   If you've got an in with a library or a school, you may have an in for discount coupons through the **School Theater Ticket Program.** Musicals, Broadway on and off, and opera and ballet at Lincoln Center are among the offerings. Tickets are purchased directly from sponsoring theaters via the coupons. Check out the website, www.schooltix.com, for all the details. ℂ **212/354-4722.**

Evening Rush   For those of the serendipitous bent, there are always last-minute rush ticket specials. Broadway, Off-Broadway, and even a few mega-hits set aside seats for students (sometimes seniors and regular folks are included, too). The seats are made available between 30 minutes and an hour before curtain (although for a hot show, you'd better be in the queue at least 2 hours ahead). Make sure to bring plenty of ID. Another option is SRO seats. The seats for either program are usually $25 and up, which on the surface is no great bargain, but is actually pretty respectable when you consider what a full-price ticket would cost. A good place for the rundown is www.talkinbroadway. com/boards. For an even quicker survey, check out www.nytix.com/ Links/Broadway/listofcurrentshows.html.

For Teens: High 5 Tickets to the Arts   High 5 doesn't shy away from the controversial notion that the children are our future. To uplift the level of cultural literacy of today's teens, High 5 makes a bushel of $5 theater and museum programs available. Mentors, parents, and friends also have the opportunity to cash in. Check the website for ticket details; Broadway tickets rarely appear here, but there's plenty of others, plus a listing of free and nearly free events. On the museum side, it's even cheaper—$5 covers two admissions to a short list of New York's finest institutions. ℂ **212/750-0555.** www.highfivetix.org.

TDF Vouchers   The Theatre Development Fund also brings us an Off-Off-Broadway equivalent to the TKTS booth. For $36 you get four vouchers that can be used for a host of shows. At $9 a pop, it's an affordable way to get into the cutting edge. ℂ **212/221-0885.** www.tdf.org.

TKTS   TKTS has been dispensing same-day up-to-half-price seats for some 3 decades now. At any given time, you can probably select from

25 different Broadway shows, and another 30 or so from Off-Broadway. The main Duffy Square TKTS booth, in the heart of Times Square, is open from 3 to 8pm Monday through Saturday for evening performances (opens at 2pm on Tues), 10am to 2pm for Wednesday and Saturday matinees, and from 11am until 3pm for Sunday matinees. Sunday night shows go on sale at 3pm, until a half-hour before the last curtain time. Between Broadway and Seventh Avenue on 47th Street. Subway: N/Q/R to 49th St.; 1 to 50th St.; B/D/F to 47th–50th sts.–Rockefeller Center. Show availability is posted on a digital bulletin board that's updated as ticket supplies dwindle. Discounts are generally 50%, with a few shows at 20%, 30%, or 40% reductions. © **212/221-0885.** www.tdf.org.

The second TKTS location is at the corner of John and Front streets, near 199 Water Street in the South Street Seaport area. The lines are much shorter here and matinee tickets are sold for the following day only, if you're the type that plans ahead (11am–6pm Mon–Sat; 11am–4pm Sun for Sun night performances only). Subway: A/C/J/Z/2/3/4/5 to Fulton St./Broadway Nassau.

Brooklynites are the latest constituency to have TKTS convenience, with a booth at 1 MetroTech Center, at the corner of Jay Street and the Myrtle Avenue Promenade. As with the Seaport, matinees are sold 1 day ahead. The booth closes for lunch between 3 and 3:30pm, otherwise it's open Tues–Sat 11am–6pm. Subway: R to Lawrence St.; A/C/F to Jay St./Borough Hall; 2/3 to Borough Hall.

Other Discounts   Several online sites will hook you up with discount codes for half-price tickets. Some require you to join to play, but the only tax they levy is the occasional piece of spam; otherwise, they're free. **Playbill Online** (www.playbill.com) has the best range of Broadway and Off-Broadway shows. **Best of Broadway** (© **212/398-8383;** www.bestofbroadway.com) has coupons and puts together group discount packages. The **Hit Show Club** (© **212/581-4211;** www.hitshowclub.com) is good for tourists. They have several packages that combine restaurants and attractions with well-known Broadway hits.

The Slipper Room This Lower East Side bar hosts all manner of risqué business. Comedy and drama make the scene, but the best night is Saturday, when New York's longest-running burlesque holds court. **Mr. Choad's Upstairs/Downstairs** allows vaudeville acts and go-go girls to split time under the lights. A recent renovation has finally fixed the poor sightlines, and doubled the ceiling height for the convenience of the fire jugglers. Covers vary, starting at around $5. 167 Orchard St., at Stanton. ℂ **212/253-7246.** www.slipperroom.com. Subway: F/M to Second Ave.

The Tank This up-and-coming theater group lost its first space to the wrecking ball and its replacement to bad plumbing. Perhaps three times is the charm for their latest location inside Hell's Kitchen's 45th Street Theatre. Public affairs are the latest addition to an already strong lineup of comedy, film, music, and theater. Shows can run as high as $15, but much of the calendar stays at a mere $5. 354 W. 45th St., btw. Eighth and Ninth aves. ℂ **212/563-6269.** www.thetanknyc.org. Subway: A/C/E to 42nd St./Port Authority.

The Theater for the New City This alternative theater is known for giving breaks to unknown playwrights. Productions are consistently high quality, though ticket prices are usually only $15, with some shows as low as $5. The "New City, New Blood" reading series gives playwrights the opportunity to

---

Theater at the Edge: Fringe NYC

In late August a chunk of the city goes on vacation and the **Fringe Festival** comes rushing in to maintain Gotham's equilibrium. This annual theatrical explosion brings over a thousand performances to downtown spaces. The troupes hail from around the world and range from the baldly amateurish to the highly polished. Tickets aren't super-cheap, but at $15 they're less than a trip to the Guggenheim or the MoMA. Since it's summer in New York City, free outdoor events are all but obligatory. The FringeAL FRESCO series offers up free plays, dance, and even the odd bit of Parkour in locations scattered around downtown. Some events are just teaser versions of longer Fringe shows, but others are the full affair, given away across multiple performances. Check the website for times and venues. ℂ **212/279-4488.** www.fringenyc.org.

absorb audience feedback (readings carry a $5 suggested donation, but there's wine and cheese). Over Memorial Day you can sample dramatics for free during the Lower East Side Festival of the Arts. Theater is only the beginning, as spoken word, cabaret, film, video, and dance performances take over East 10th Street, between First and Second avenues. Events run until after midnight, and everything is free. Also free is the Annual Summer Street Theater, which puts on operettas in a baker's dozen locations spread across five boroughs. 155 First Ave., btw. 9th and 10th sts. ✆ 212/254-1109. www.theaterforthenewcity.net. Subway: 6 to Astor Place, L to First Ave.

4 Let's Dance

The modern enforcement of cabaret regulations hit most New Yorkers by surprise. Laws regulating public dance had been on the books forever, but it had been many years since anyone had thought to enforce them. Innocuous tremors and inadvertent hip shakes were suddenly categorized as unlicensed dance expressions. Fortunately, dance in New York has never been limited to clubs and bars. In the parks, on stages, and even in sanctuaries of the city, dance of all levels can be found, and often for free.

Baryshnikov Arts Center FREE   Even people who can't tell the difference between a plié and a piqué know Mikhail Baryshnikov's name. His eponymous dance foundation advances collaboration among performers, choreographers, directors, and writers. The BAC welcomes the public with free workshops, open lessons, and concerts. The Movado Hour, a monthly series of intimate chamber music performances that last exactly 60 minutes, is especially worth a listen. Most events require reservations; call 1 week ahead of the concert date for the Movado series. 450 W. 37th St., at Dyer Ave. ✆ 646/731-3200, or 212/868-4444 for reservations. www.baryshnikovdancefoundation.org. Subway: A/C/E to 34th St./Penn Station.

Dance Conversations @ The Flea FREE   Choreographers present works in progress at this monthly program. Each evening presents four different choreographers. It's a discussion series as well, so expect jawing to following the dancing. Usually on the first Tuesday of the month at 7pm. Flea Theater, 41 White St., btw. Broadway and Church St. ✆ 212/226-0051. www.theflea.org. Subway: 1 to Franklin St.

Dance Gotham: A Festival Usually running three nights in January at NYU's Skirball Center, this weekend revel presents a huge range of dance. Performances run from the polished to the rustic, with folk dance, classical theatrics, and postmodern experiments all filling out the multi-performer bills. Tickets are only $10, and there's usually an adjunct performance or two thrown in for free. Jack H. Skirball Center for the Performing Arts at NYU, 565 LaGuardia Place at Washington Sq. S. ✆ **212/928-6517.** www.gothamarts.org. Subway: A/B/C/D/E/F to W. 4th St./Washington Sq.

Dance Theater Workshop `FREE` The Judson Memorial Church has been an anchor of the West Village since 1890. The aging church has recently been renovated (a lovely new dance floor has been installed), and is again hosting the Dance Theater Workshop's popular Movement Research dance program. Dancers and choreographers vary from week to week, but the emphasis on pushing boundaries remains consistent. No reservations are taken. Mondays at 8pm, doors open at 7:45pm, performances are seasonal (spring and fall). There are also free Studies Project performances, dance festivals, and the Open Performance program at DTW's HQ. The latter shows are non-curated and open to all (sign up in advance), with a moderated discussion afterwards. Wednesdays at 8pm, suggested donation of $3. Judson Church, 55 Washington Sq. S., btw. Thompson and Sullivan sts. ✆ **212/539-2611.** www.movementresearch.org. Subway: A/B/C/D/E/F/M to W. 4th St./Washington Sq. Open Performance, 219 W. 19th St., btw. Seventh and Eighth aves. Subway: 1 to 18th St.

Dancing in the Streets `FREE` This arts organization brings site-specific performances to spots across the city. The integration of cityscape and moving bodies is a great way of seeing familiar spaces in a new way. Their signature shows are **Hip Hop Generation Next** and **Breaking Ground—A Dance Charrette.** Check the website for complete performance details; Hip Hop Generation Next can be found in Red Hook as part of a block party, among other locations. Coffey Park, btw. Richards and Dwight sts., near Visitation Place, Red Hook, Brooklyn. ✆ **212/625-3505.** www.dancinginthestreets.org. Subway: F/G to Smith/9th St., then B77 bus to Dwight St. Other sites vary.

Downtown Dance Festival `FREE` **Battery Dance Company** showcases both professional and emerging dancers at these outdoor shows. Originality is prized here, as is range—major companies from around the world have joined famed choreographers like Lê Minh Tâm, Paul Taylor, and Mary Anthony. The alfresco setting suggests informality, but the artists take their steps seriously. Look for a reprisal of the Everybody Dance Now! program, which invites audience members up on stage for demonstrations. Locations vary, but as the name suggests, sites are usually downtown, one week in mid to late August. Locations vary. ✆ **212/219-3910.** www.batterydance.org.

Evening Stars FREE The **Joyce Theater** has been at the forefront of NYC's modern dance since 1982. Every September they help sponsor the best of American dance with free performances as part of downtown's River to River Festival. Programs pivot from the music of Sinatra to the Sugar Hill Gang to the Grateful Dead. Generally there are evening shows at 7 or 7:30pm (Thurs–Sun) in a couple of spots around Battery Park. There's a large main stage, but if you want to be up close you can spread your blanket up to 2 hours earlier, when the park opens. (That blanket is all but obligatory, as no seating is provided, unless there's rain and the event is moved to the Stuyvesant High School Auditorium at Chambers and West sts.) Co-sponsored by the Lower Manhattan Cultural Council and the Joyce Theater, at Battery Park, on State St. at Pearl St. ✆ **212/219-9401,** ext. 304. www.lmcc.net. Subway: 4/5 to Bowling Green; R to Whitehall; 1 to South Ferry.

MoonDance FREE July and August bring marvelous nights for this dance on Pier 54. Sunday evenings begin with a lesson at 6:30pm and cede to dancing a half-hour later, when you're a full-fledged expert. Dance varieties run from swing to salsa to R&B. Live music from crack bands enhances the lovely riverside setting. Pier 54 on the Hudson, at 14th St. ✆ **212/533-PARK** [7275]. www.hudsonriverpark.org. Subway: A/C/E to 14th St.; L to Eighth Ave.

Sitelines FREE This annual series puts creative steps into site-specific settings. Venues have been as varied as a laundromat, a church courtyard, and the outdoor bar tables of the South Street Seaport. The performances, some five each summer, are held across downtown (with the occasional foray to Governors Island). The series runs from May to August; dances usually have multiple performances. Locations vary. ✆ **212/219-9401.** www.lmcc.net.

Solar-Powered Dance Series FREE An "eco stage" made of recycled materials and a solar-powered sound system support the fancy footwork at this annual series. The environmental advocacy group Solar One does the hosting, with six days of performances spread across two weekends in late July. Stuyvesant Cove Park, 23rd St. and the FDR. ✆ **212/505-6050.** www.solar1.org. Subway 6 to 23rd St.; L to First Ave.

5 Sing, Sing: Karaoke

Maybe it's a side-effect of our new blog culture, but it seems the old gate-keeping editorial controls have fallen by the wayside. Local music is no exception, with a profusion of live-band karaoke nights allowing amateur lungs to step up to the mic and perform frontsperson duties. Join the caterwauling carousel and do your part to reaffirm the inherent dignity of the human race by drinking way too much tequila and then letting loose on a heartfelt version of "Feel Like Making Love." More traditional canned-music-and-bouncing-ball karaoke can also be found citywide, often for little more than the price of your boozing. The venues below don't enforce drink minimums, and often karaoke nights are too crowded for anyone to notice if you're not tippling. Then again, doesn't sobriety kind of go against the very spirit of karaoke?

Arlene's Grocery FREE   If you've ever wondered where the tri-state has been hiding its best Ozzy and David Lee imitators, you've been missing out on the live music karaoke at Arlene's Grocery. Legendary Monday night shows fill 3 hours with the soul-uplifting sounds of '70s classic rock and '80s hair metal. If you sign up and ascend the stage, you'll find the crowd enthusiastic, and nothing beats the thrill of belting out "Black Dog" or "Paradise City" over an ass-kicking band. It's worth a visit just to check out the regulars. Many of them have come all the way from Jersey to show off how well they can work a club full of rabid fans with fingers spread in devil's horns. Best of all: There's no cover for these covers. 95 Stanton St., btw. Ludlow and Orchard sts. ✆ **212/358-1633.** www.arlenesgrocery.net. Karaoke Mon 10pm–1am. Subway: F/M to Second Ave.; J/M/Z to Essex St.

Hill Country FREE   The legendary Kreuz Market was the inspiration for this slice of Texas in the big city. The low-ceilinged basement here is a rollicking spot to catch some twang-tinged tunage. On Tuesday nights at 8:30pm, you can add your voice by singing lead with the Wicked Messengers. David Allen Coe makes the set list, but you can also find plenty of hard rock staples. Unfortunately the BBQ don't come free. 30 W. 26th St., btw. Broadway and Sixth Ave. ✆ **212/255-4544.** www.myspace.com/wickedmessengers. Subway: F to 23rd St.; N/R to 28th St.

Hip Hop Karaoke   We all know the extraordinary levels of talent required to make it in the rap world (just look at Kid Rock), but that doesn't mean the unpolished among us can't entertain. "Hip Hop

Karaoke" is quickly becoming a phenomenon, with packed shows letting little Biggies rhyme away for a forgiving crowd. (No one will think less of you if you're reading off a crib sheet.) Venues vary, with recent appearances at Mercury Lounge on the Lower East Side. Cover is only $5 with flyer. www.hiphopkaraokenyc.com. Locations vary.

Keyboard Karaoke `FREE` Loser's Lounge keyboardist (and ex-Psychedelic Fur) Joe McGinty tickles the keys for the pleasure of your pipes. His song list hops from Boz Skaggs to Bette Midler, with special guests often joining in. Hosting venues change periodically, although the white grand piano at the Manhattan Inn, where Joe is currently ensconced, will be hard to outdo. First Friday of the month at 11pm. Manhattan Inn, 632 Manhattan Ave., at Nassau Ave. © **718/383-0885.** www.joe mcginty.com. Subway: G to Nassau Ave.

O'Flanagan's `FREE` The Human Karaoke Experience boasts a play-list of over 500 songs, so it shouldn't be hard to find something in your range. Daughter of Brooklyn Pat Benatar (née Patricia Andrzejewski) has five songs represented, and there's a full complement of Beatles, Stones, and Elvii (both Presley and Costello). The hosting pub, O'Flanagan's on the Upper East Side, is congenial, if a little cookie-cutter. 1215 First Ave., btw. 65th and 66th sts. © **212/439-0660.** www. human karaoke.com. Two Thurs a month, 9pm–1:30am. Subway: F to 63rd St./Lexington Ave.; 6 to 68th St.

Punk Rock Heavy Metal Karaoke For over a decade, this quartet has been getting heads banging with high-energy rock and the borrowed talents of a revolving door of guest singers. Fifth wheels can choose from almost 300 songs, with arena rock classics heavily represented. Fontana's, on the fringe of Chinatown, is the scene's current home. Gigs are once a month, with a $5 cover. 105 Eldridge St., btw. Broome and Grand sts. © **212/334-6740.** www.punkmetalkaraoke.com. Subway: B/D to Grand St.; F to Delancey St.; J/M/Z to Essex St.

Rock Star Karaoke `FREE` This hard-working band doesn't let the moss settle, rolling through four gigs a week, sometimes twice a night! The playlist is diverse, covering AC/DC to Britney Spears, with stop-offs at Weezer and Roxette along the way. Look for Wednesday night appearances at the honky-tonks Johnny Utah's and Hank's Saloon (9:30pm), and Thursday and Saturday nights at Brother Jimmy's BBQ Bait Shack (10pm). *Rock Star Karaoke,* © **917/446-0098.** www.rockstarkaraoke nyc.com. *Johnny Utah's,* 25 W. 51st St., btw. Fifth and Sixth aves. © **212/265-8824.**

www.johnnyutahs.com. Subway: E/M to Fifth Ave./53rd St.; B/D/F to 47th–50th sts.–
Rockefeller Center. *Hank's Saloon*, 46 Third Ave., at Atlantic Ave., Brooklyn. ✆ **718/
625-8003.** www.exitfive.com/hankssaloon. Subway: B/D/N/Q/R/2/3/4/5 to Atlantic
Ave./Pacific St. *Brother Jimmy's BBQ Bait Shack*, 1644 Third Ave. at 92nd St. ✆ **212/
426-2020.** www.brotherjimmys.com. Subway: 6 to 96th St.

Winnie's   Hipsters and Chinatown locals just never have enough
opportunity to chill together, which is where Winnie's comes in
handy. The place is an ungentrifiable dive, but the savings get passed
on to the crooning customer: It's only a buck a song to play along
with the hit machine (they're still using laser disks, so don't expect to
sing anything more recent than Huey Lewis). 104 Bayard St. ✆ **212/732-
2384.** Karaoke daily 8pm–4am. Subway: J/N/Q/R/Z/6 to Canal St.

6 Humor Us: Comedy

There's no shortage of frustrating and surreal experiences in New York,
ensuring plenty of fodder for the comedians in our midst. The city is
stacked with young comic talent, which means amateur nights are more
common than headliner-thick extravaganzas. Alas, amateur nights can
also be express trips to the nether regions of stand-up hell. Somehow
bad comedy is infinitely more painful than bad tragedy. I advise step-
ping carefully through the city's improv, open mic, and stand-up minefield. Fortunately, plenty of quick wits can be found in this town. Small
investments can lead to big laughs if you hit the right nights. For all the
side-splitting and beer-nose-spewing details, see below.

SHOWCASES, IMPROV & OTHER COMEDY ANTICS

Magnet Theater   This third entry into the "Improv Comedy District"
of north Chelsea learned its comedic lessons in Chicago and at the
UCB. Emphasizing a more theatrical feel than its neighbors, the shows
here attract student, resident, and pro players, generating laughs 7
nights a week. Most shows are $5, some are free, there's no drink
minimum, and you can enjoy $1 PBRs during select performances.
254 W. 29th St., btw. Seventh and Eighth aves. ✆ **212/244-8824.** www.magnet
theater.com. Subway: 1 to 28th St.

New York Comedy Club **FREE**   Monday night's open mic night is
the only affordable slot on the schedule here. It's the longest-running
open mic in New York, there's no drink minimum, and although it's
statistically unlikely, it is possible to see an overlooked talent just

breaking in. Open mic on Mondays, 5 to 7:30pm. For aspiring comedians (most everyone in the audience), it's $5 for 5 minutes on stage. 241 E. 24th St., btw. Second and Third aves. ☏ **212/696-LAFF** [5233]. www.new yorkcomedyclub.com. Subway: N/Q/R or 6 to 23rd St.

The Pit This upstart has yet to reach the UCB's level of improv evolution, but they're headed in the right direction. The Peoples Improv Theater's primary mission is as a school, with an ex-SNL writer and Second City alum among the faculty. Many shows involve student performers and are priced accordingly (Mon–Fri there's at least 1 free show per night, with Fri evening's happy hour performance also boasting $3 drinks). Regular tickets run between $5 and $8. Wednesday night is the night not to miss. The Faculty and Big Black Car are among the five free sets that bring out the heights of the Pit. 154 W. 29th St., btw. Sixth and Seventh aves. ☏ **212/563-7488.** www.thepit-nyc.com. Subway: 1 or N/Q/R to 28th St.

The Upright Citizens Brigade The UCB brings Chicago-style longform improv comedy to the Big Apple. With founders that can be found on SNL and in the movies, the talent level is high, which is crucial in the hit-or-miss medium of improvisation. Plus, the complete lack of scripts saves you money. Sunday night sees two performances of ASSSSCAT 3000. The extra S's? For savings: The 7:30pm show is $10, but the 9:30pm version is absolutely free. Tickets for the latter are distributed at 8:15, but it's popular so try to get there at least 45 minutes early. Shows on Monday and Wednesday at 11pm are also free. The rest of the schedule runs between $5 and $10 (mostly $5), which is still a steal. The Harold Night's two $5 shows (Tues at 6:30 and 8pm) are especially noteworthy, with some rapier wits putting the old Harold technique through its paces. [FINE PRINT] A new location is in the works, under Two Boots in the East Village, but the opening date hasn't been set yet. Upright Citizens Brigade Theatre, 307 W. 26th St., btw. Eighth and Ninth aves. ☏ **212/366-9176.** www.ucbtheatre.com. Subway: C/E to 23rd St.

7 Game Night

Too damn smart? Bars (and other public spaces) across the city offer trivia nights, an excuse to meet new people and show off the fruits of all those wasted hours learning to differentiate between Arnold Snarb and Arnold Strong. New York will also let you flash your skills at

Scrabble, spelling, and song recognition. Gather up some compatriots, or join a team of fellow-stragglers, and convert that synaptic alacrity into bragging rights and bar tabs.

Fontana's `FREE` Rock is the focus of the weekly Smartass quiz night here. Your host, Todd S., augments questions with musical cues. Winners can gloat over prize bar tabs. Whether or not Van Halen is Yacht Rock won't be definitively answered, although the color of the M&M's banished from the band's backstage spreads will be. Thursdays from 7 to 9pm, includes the last hour of happy hour and free pizza. Yes, free pizza! 105 Eldridge St., btw. Broome and Grand sts. ✆ **212/334-6740.** www. smartasstrivia.blogspot.com. Subway: B/D to Grand St.; F to Delancey St.; J/M/Z to Essex St.

Last Exit Pop Quiz @ Last Exit isn't free, but the $5 cover can be considered an investment. The cash goes into a pot for the eventual winner. Groups of four compete, and if you show up short-handed, they'll make a team for you. ***Warm up:*** Who wrote *Last Exit to Brooklyn?* First and third Mondays of the month, from 9 to 11pm. Register around 8:30pm and bring a pen or pencil. (***Answer:*** The late Hubert Selby, Jr.) 136 Atlantic Ave., btw. Clinton and Henry sts., Brooklyn Heights, Brooklyn. ✆ **718/222-9198.** www.lastexitbar.com. Subway: R/2/3/4/5 to Borough Hall; F/G to Bergen St.

Pete's Candy Store At Pete's Wednesday Quizz-Off, categories range from general knowledge to music to top 10s, with prizes for the top three finishers. The action starts at 7:30pm. Alternatively, wordsmiths hammer at their tile forges during Scrabble Saturdays. Bring a partner and try your luck at doubles on Saturdays from 5 to 8pm. Tuesday nights from 7:30 to 9pm, Pete's feels even more small-town than usual when bingo scorecards fill the bar. Old and young show off their number/letter cognitive prowess for gag prizes. Not all gamed-out yet? How about revisiting ancient humiliations with a spelling bee? Every other Monday trip over words like "roriferous" and "keratic." Or is it kerratic? That's why the Williamsburg Spelling Bee operates on a gentle three-strike basis. Every other Monday during the spelling season from 7:30 to 9pm, sign up at 7 if you've come to spell. (Manhattanites can try their luck at Housing Works' offshoot bee; www.nycbee.com; they ask for a $5 donation from competitors.) All games are free, though there's a loosely enforced two-drink minimum. 709 Lorimer St., btw. Frost and Richardson sts., Williamsburg, Brooklyn. ✆ **718/302-3770.** www.petes candystore.com. Subway: L to Lorimer St.; G to Metropolitan Ave.

Rocky Sullivan's FREE   After a decade sharing the love with Murray Hill, Rocky's has fled high rents for the relatively gentle shores of Red Hook. Programming remains the same, with no- and low-cover music, readings, movie nights, and Thursday night trivia. You can show off those nimble brain cells with the prodding of a congenial host, who leads participants through music, photo, and general knowledge quizzes. Victorious founts of knowledge are rewarded with house mix CDs, fermented hops. No cover, no minimum; the game starts around 8pm. 34 Van Dyke St., at Dwight St. ℂ **718/246-8050.** www.rockysullivans.com. Subway: F/G to Smith/9th St., then B77 bus.

8 Talk It Up: TV Tapings

Why saddle yourself with those endless cable, satellite, and electric bills, when you could be watching TV for free? New York is home to a bunch of top-flight shows, many of which rely on live in-studio audiences to keep the energy levels high. In exchange for your enthusiasm (and patience), you'll get a great peek behind the curtain. Fans are always amazed at just how small the sets—and stars—really are. To make it even more worth your while, most shows employ MCs to get the crowd fired up, and often you can collect some swag in the form of T-shirts or free tickets to the MC's upcoming show.

TALKING POINTS

New York's most famous shows are incredibly popular, and waits of 6 months or longer are commonplace. Often you'll have to send a postcard or e-mail with your relevant info and preferred dates. (Tickets to a taping make a great cheap birthday present, by the way.) For those who arrive without tickets, it is possible to get standbys on the day of the show. Usually they'll only give one ticket per standee, so everyone in the party has to be assembled. Even then it's no guarantee, since standby status only kicks in if there are enough no-shows among the regular ticket holders. Of course, if you're not choosey about what you want to see, plenty of shows in New York are unpopular enough to get you in without delay. The NYCVB has more details on tapings (ℂ **212/484-1222;** www.nycvb.com), with some two dozen potential shows represented.

The Colbert Report `FREE` Stephen Colbert's nightly "news" program has reached the cult status of *The Daily Show,* which spun it off in the fall of '05. Colbert's studio is *The Daily Show*'s cramped former home, making it a harder ticket to nab than its progenitor. Comedy Central has an online ticket request system, but it's usually booked up solid. For standby seating, you can hope for a no-show by going to the studio door. Tapings are Mondays through Thursdays at 7pm, but to have a shot for a standby you should get there by 4pm. You'll increase your chances if there isn't a big-name guest on the docket. Audience members must be at least 18. No bears. 513 W. 54th St., btw. Tenth and Eleventh aves. ℂ **212/767-8600.** www.comedycentral.com. Subway: A/B/C/D/1 to 59th St./Columbus Circle.

The Daily Show with Jon Stewart `FREE` There's been no drought of mockable material in the news recently, which helps Jon Stewart's satirical news/talk show remain a water-cooler conversation staple. In addition to biting analysis of current events, if you attend a taping you'll be treated to a few minutes of personable conversation with Jon himself. Though the show is more popular than ever, it's filmed in a new and larger studio, so tickets aren't impossible to come by. Tapings are Monday through Thursday with doors open at 5pm, though they want you there an hour early. An online system will give you a shot at a seat, although it's usually booked up. You can also make a request via e-mail (requesttickets@thedailyshow.com); see the website for complete details. The minimum age is 18. 733 Eleventh Ave., btw. 51st and 52nd sts. ℂ **212/767-8600.** www.thedailyshow.com. Subway: A/B/C/D/1 to 59th St./Columbus Circle.

Good Morning America `FREE` If seeing the face of George Stephanopoulos first thing in the morning is actually an enticing prospect for you, join the live audience in ABC's studio right on Broadway. Tickets for the 7 to 9am broadcast can be wrangled by filling out the online request form. If you get tickets, plan on arriving at 6am. Sans tickets, you can try for the standby line at 6:45am, or join the throng outside the Broadway and 44th Street studio window. ***Note:*** In the summers, big-name performers come to Rumsey Playfield in Central Park for the **Good Morning America Summer Concert Series.** Those shows are free and require no tickets, running from 7 to 9am (but get there by 6am). ABC Studios, 1500 Broadway, at 44th St. ℂ **212/930-7855.** www. abcnews.go.com/GMA. Subway: N/Q/R/S/1/2/3/7 to Times Sq./42nd St.

Late Night with Jimmy Fallon `FREE`   Former host Conan O'Brien may have received some shabby treatment, but the honeymoon is still on for the likeable Jimmy Fallon. The best plan for tickets here is to call about a month in advance, and request up to four tickets. For last-minute openings, check the Late Night Twitter feed, or try for a standby. Starting at 9am outside 30 Rockefeller Plaza—the GE Building, under the NBC Studios awning on the 49th Street side, you can get one ticket per person, with no guarantee of entry. The third option is entering the Band Bench lottery (www.fallonbandbench.com). If you're rabid about a particular group, these are great seats if you get lucky (and if you just want in, enter "ANY" as your lottery code). You must be 17 to attend tapings. NBC Studio, 30 Rockefeller Plaza, 49th St., btw. Fifth and Sixth aves. © **212/664-3056.** www.nbc.com. Subway: B/D/F/M to 47th–50th sts.–Rockefeller Center; N/Q/R to 49th St.

The Late Show with David Letterman `FREE`   And the number-one hottest New York TV taping ticket is . . . yeah, it's still Letterman. Though it's not what it was in the '80s, the show has really picked it up lately, with our favorite Hoosier squeezing the most out of his regulars, and Paul and the band keeping things energetic. Tapings are Monday through Thursday usually at 5:30pm, sometimes with a second taping Thursday at 8pm. You can request tickets online (it's a lottery, and usually a 6-month wait) or you can stop by the theater in person. The lobby handles walk-ins Monday through Thursday from 9:30am to noon, and weekends from 10am to 6pm. If you're feeling lucky, you can also try calling in for a same-day standby seat. The phone line opens at 11am. Be patient and use your redial button liberally. Also bone up on your Letterman trivia because you may need to pass a test to get the tickets (which aren't actually tickets, but are spots on the standby line, should anything open up and should you have correctly identified Biff Henderson's real first name as James). You must arrive an hour and a quarter before tape time, be 18 or older, and be ready to show some ID. Ed Sullivan Theater, 1697 Broadway, btw. 53rd and 54th sts. © **212/247-6497.** www.cbs.com/latenight/lateshow (click on "Get Tickets"). Subway: B/D/E to Seventh Ave.

The Today Show `FREE`   Watching NBC's morning mainstay is free and easy; just show up outside *Today*'s glass-walled studio at Rockefeller Center, on the southwest corner of 49th Street and Rockefeller Plaza. Tapings are Monday through Friday from 7 to 10am, but if you want to be up front, 7am is way too late to be rushing over with your goofy hat and hand-painted sign. In the summer, *Today* holds a series of concerts in Rockefeller Center, generally on Friday mornings at 7am. It's always big names playing, and they attract commensurate huge crowds so don't get there any later than 6am. Southwest corner of 49th St. and Rockefeller Plaza. ℂ **212/664-3056.** www.msnbc.msn.com. Subway: B/D/F/M to 47th–50th sts.–Rockefeller Center; N/Q/R to 49th St.

The View FREE Barbara and crew chat away about cellulite, diets, calories, weight issues, and other urgent matters every Monday through Thursday at 11am. You can request online for a date at least 12 weeks in advance. Ticket holders are expected to show up by 9:30am sharp. The ticket backlog runs at least 12 months, but you can also try to nab a standby from a View Audience Associate at the studio entrance. Between 8 and 9am they'll give seats away. You must be at least 16 (bring ID). 320 W. 66th St., off West End Ave. ℂ **212/465-0900.** www.theview.abc.go.com/tickets. Subway: 1 to 66th St./Lincoln Center.

Who Wants to be a Millionaire FREE Millionaires miss out on all the fun listed in this book, but you can look on with condescending pity should anyone run the table against Meredith Vieira. Tapings are usually Monday through Wednesday at 2:30 and 4pm when the show is in production. Note that they'll want you there 2 hours early and the show can take 2 hours or longer to tape, so make sure you're fed and watered before you go in (and be warned that as posh as the set looks on television, those benches are hard). Requests for tickets can be made online; you must be 18 or older to attend. ABC at 30 W. 67th St., btw. Columbus Ave. and Central Park West. ℂ **212/479-7755.** www.millionairetv.com. Subway: 1 to 66th St./Lincoln Center.

9 Word Up: Readings

New York has always been a city of writers, and modern Gotham has no shortage of literary lights. Undiscovered hopefuls, midlist strivers, and huge names with cultlike followings all find their way to lecterns across the city. Bars, galleries, libraries, bookstores, and schools do the hosting. With eight million other stories unfolding in the Naked City, most people don't take the time to be read to, and I usually find literary events are pleasantly underattended. There are exceptions—voices of the moment and package nights that bring in a bunch of big names at once—but generally you have a better chance to see a big-time writer up-close than you'll get with any actress, athlete, or musician. And almost always you'll get to do it for free.

AT BOOKSTORES

Bookshops are good spots for getting a hit of that sweet, sweet literature, and getting it for free. Some stores offer regular readings, and some just signings, but either way on a quiet night you may get the chance to talk up a favorite author.

Barnes & Noble `FREE` The Union Square location gets the biggest names and most frequent readings. Literary stars like David Sedaris, Helen Fielding, and Michael Chabon come through to read from their works or participate in conferences and discussions. For kids, Sundays at 2:30pm is story time. The seating area is large and comfortable, but you should show up early for the best-sellers because it does get crowded. A close second is the Lincoln Center location, with its steady parade of big-shot scribes. 33 E. 17th St., btw. Broadway and Park Ave. S. (② **212/253-0810.** www.bn.com. Subway: L/N/Q/R/4/5/6 to 14th St./Union Sq. Other location: *Lincoln Center,* 1972 Broadway, at 66th St. (② **212/595-6859.** Subway: 1 to 66th St./Lincoln Center.

Bluestockings `FREE` DIY ethos is in full effect at this newly expanded communal bookstore. Frequent readings of a feminist and lesbian bent intersperse with seminars and meetings. The readings and many lectures/discussions are free; other events can ask for suggested donations of $5 to $10. The **Dyke Knitting Circle** meets the third Sunday of every month from 4 to 6pm. It's open to all levels of knitting skill; bring yarn and needles. 172 Allen St., btw. Rivington and Stanton sts. (② **212/777-6028.** www.bluestockings.com. Subway: F/M to Second Ave.; J/M/Z to Essex St.

BookCourt `FREE` For over 2 decades now, this Cobble Hill favorite has been a clean and well-lighted place for literary fans. The local authors section is comprehensive, which is impressive considering how many writers are calling the area home. In-store readings, signings, book clubs, and lectures bring in important new voices. 163 Court St., btw. Dean and Pacific sts., Cobble Hill, Brooklyn. (② **718/875-3677.** www.bookcourt.org. Subway: F/G to Bergen St., R to Court St.; 2/3/4/5 to Borough Hall.

Books of Wonder `FREE` The agenda here is books for the kiddies. Readings are schedules for Saturdays at noon, as well as select evenings and Sunday afternoons. Publication parties and multi-author extravaganzas are common. Light refreshments are often served too. 18 W. 18th St., btw. Fifth and Sixth aves. (✆ **212/989-3270.** www.booksofwonder. net. Subway: L/N/Q/R/4/5/6 to 14th St./Union Sq.

Drama Book Shop   When this venerable performing-arts bookstore relocated a few years ago, they added a performing-arts space (the Arthur Seelen Theatre) to the mix. Discussions, readings, open mics, book launches, and workshops are all part of the mix. The effort to build a community comes through clearly in events like monologue fests and headshot fests. Check online for the calendar; events can run as much as $20, but many (like Kathleen Turner giving a book talk) are offered for free. 250 W. 40th St., btw. Seventh and Eighth aves. (✆ **212/944-0595.** www.dramabookshop.com. Subway: A/C/E or 1/2/3/7 or N/Q/R/S to 42nd St.

McNally Jackson FREE   As every last retail inch of SoHo and NoLita seems primed to become a trendy restaurant or bar, the last new-comer one might expect would be a big, sophisticated bookstore. McNally Jackson (née Robinson) is thriving, however, with an inde-pendent spirit and a knowledgeable staff. A full slate of readings, dis-cussions, and signings can be found here. 50 Prince St., btw. Lafayette and Mulberry sts. (✆ **212/274-1160.** www.mcnallyjackson.com. Subway: 6 to Spring St., N/Q/R to Prince St.

192 Books FREE   This lovely newer shop brings in authors for 7pm readings (plus the occasional Sun afternoon). Night of the week var-ies, and seating is limited so call ahead for reservations, especially if it's Ethan Hawke reading Mayakovsky. (Mary Gaitskill and A.M. Homes have also graced this intimate space.) Check the website for schedule. 192 Tenth Ave., at 21st. (✆ **212/255-4022.** www.192books.com. Sub-way: C/E to 23rd St.

Revolution Books FREE   The revolution will be televised, and it will also make its way into print. Alternative viewpoints are aired during in-store readings and screenings right in the heart of The Machine. 146 W. 26th St., btw. Sixth and Seventh aves. (✆ **212/691-3345.** www.revolutionbooks nyc.org. Subway: N/Q/R or 1 to 28th St.

The Scholastic Store FREE   The retail outlet for the children's pub-lisher Scholastic has books and toys and a full schedule of in-store events. Every Tuesday, Wednesday, and Thursday at 11am is story time, plus there are book signings and special events scattered across the schedule. Most everything is free, although craft workshops can have a small materials fee. 557 Broadway, btw. Prince and Spring sts. ℂ 212/343-6166. www.scholastic.com/sohostore. Subway: N/Q/R to Prince St.

Three Lives & Company FREE Just browsing in this low-key West Village legend makes a person feel smarter and more sophisticated. Pressed-tin ceilings and exposed brick complement a classy selection. Though space is tight here, the readings and signings are worth checking out. 154 W. 10th St., at Waverly Place. ℂ 212/741-2069. www.three lives.com. Subway: 1 to Christopher St.

Unnameable Books FREE A response to a lawsuit over an innocuous former name was the inspiration behind this odd moniker. The selection here is well curated, and there are great prices on lightly used literature. (Look for the $1 bargain rack out front.) The free monthly Uncalled-For reading series is an additional draw. 600 Vanderbilt Ave., at St. Marks Ave. ℂ 718/789-1534. www.uncalledforreadings.blogspot. com. Subway: B/Q to Seventh Ave.

AT BARS & CAFES (& LAUNDROMATS)

What better way to advertise the intelligent conversation your coffee shop or booze hall induces than by associating yourself with articulate new voices? Reading series have cropped up in bars and cafes (and even laundromats) across the city, and the informal settings encourage more showmanship than a bookshop lectern. With extreme readings the latest trend, these venues are likely spots to be entertained while listening to an author intone.

Bowery Poetry Club Poetry is just the beginning here, with music, theater, and beer adding to the enticements. A ramshackle vibe pervades, with exposed brick on the walls and a communal attitude. The calendar overflows with burlesque, book parties, open mics, slams, and plenty of other forms of poesy. Covers average around $6, but many free events can be found (some with two-drink minimums). 308 Bowery, btw. E. 1st and Bleecker sts. ℂ 212/614-0505. www.bowerypoetry.com. F/M to Second Ave.; 6 to Bleecker St.

Dirty Laundry: Loads of Prose FREE With New York's perennial space squeezes, it's not so surprising that a reading series wedges itself into working laundromats. Attendees not only get scintillating prose and poesy (and the occasional musical performance), but they also come out with clean duds. Readings are sporadic and times and locations vary; check the website. Laundromats vary, check website. ℂ **917/ 501-9825.** www.dirtylaundryreadings.com.

Earshot Reading Series This bimonthly reading series provides opportunities for MFA students to be heard. Although that means less polished material, it also provides the opportunity to catch real up-and-comers. Established writers also make appearances, usually five writers in all. The show does come with a $5 cover, but then it also comes with a free drink; Friday nights, 7:30pm, at Rose Live Music. 345 Grand St., btw. Havemeyer St. and Marcy Ave., Williamsburg, Brooklyn. ℂ **718/599-0069.** www.earshotnyc.com. Subway: L to Lorimer St.; G to Metropolitan Ave.

The Half King `FREE` *The Perfect Storm* author Sebastian Junger is a co-owner of this bustling Chelsea bar. He's also a contributor to their weekly reading series, which presents writers most every Monday night at 7pm. The authors and titles selected here are excellent and all but guaranteed to provoke. On select Sunday afternoons look for free astrology readings as well. 505 W. 23rd St., near Tenth Ave. ℂ **212/462-4300.** www.thehalfking.com. Subway: C/E to 23rd St.

Happy Ending `FREE` This Chinatown lounge, whose name advertises a salient detail about the services of the former tenant (a massage parlor), is home to the city's most ambitious reading series. Monthly "In the Flesh" and "Sex Worker Literati" nights bring echoes of the space's past as writers strut their smut. Mr. Beller's Neighborhood also drops by once a month with slices of city life. Readings start at 8pm. 302 Broome St., at Forsythe St. ℂ **212/334-9676.** www.happyendinglounge. com. Subway: B/D to Grand St.; F to Delancey St.; J/M/Z to Essex St.

KGB Bar `FREE` Hidden away in a former speak-easy on the second floor of an East Village tenement, KGB has the most comprehensive reading series in the city. Sunday night brings fiction, Monday poetry, Tuesday nonfiction, and some Wednesdays feature the fantastic, in the form of sci-fi authors. Drunken! Careening! Writers! is a great monthly night, with at least one big laugh guaranteed. The bar was once the clubhouse of the Ukrainian Labor Home, and the commie kitsch adorning the walls completes the literary atmosphere. Most readings start at 7pm. 85 E. 4th St., near Second Ave. ℂ **212/505-3360.** www. kgbbar.com. Subway: F/M to Second Ave.; 6 to Bleecker St.

Pete's Candy Store `FREE`   Not content with a mere single literary evening, Pete's brings in the ink-slingers on Thursdays and Fridays. Alternating Thursdays focus on local writers, favoring fiction, with Jonathan Ames and Jim Shepard making recent appearances. Alternating Fridays are reserved for those of the poesy persuasion. Alternate Mondays you can catch Open City Dialogue, a quirky lecture series dedicated to obsessive knowledge. Readings start at 7pm, lectures at 7:30pm. 709 Lorimer St., btw. Frost and Richardson sts., Williamsburg, Brooklyn. ℂ **718/302-3770.** www.petescandystore.com. Subway: L to Lorimer St.; G to Metropolitan Ave.

Secret Science Club `FREE`   With the whole dying-planet thing going on these days, science is enjoying a resurgence in the popular imagination. This monthly series attracts physicists, mathematicians, and even Nobel Prize–winning biologists. In addition to a free lecture, there's music, Q&A's, and science-themed cocktails. The second Tuesday of the month at 8pm, doors open at 7:15pm, and the limited seats go fast. The Bell House, 149 7th St., btw. Second and Third aves., Park Slope, Brooklyn. ℂ **718/643-6510.** www.secretscienceclub.blogspot.com. Subway: F/G to Smith/9th St.; R to 9th St./Fourth Ave.

Triptych Readings `FREE`   These poetry nights evolved from the long-running Reading Between A&B series. Emerging poets are the focus, usually 3 per night. The neighborhood bar that hosts couldn't be more congenial. Every other Monday or so at 7pm. 510 E. 11th St., btw. aves. A and B. ℂ **212/982-3929.** www.readab.com. Subway: L to First Ave.

10 Big Leagues, Little Prices

It's said that it's now cheaper to be an opera fan than to follow a major league sports team, and with ticket prices racing well ahead of inflation it's easy to believe. The NFL long ago climbed into the stratosphere, and with new stadiums the Mets and Yankees seem eager to follow suit. Premium Knicks seats? Prices top out over $330. This for a team that hasn't played a second-round playoff game since the last millennium? If you're seeking an affordable sporting event, your best bet may be outside the major leagues.

The Amazing Mets   Citi Field has replaced mostly charmless Shea, but Yankee-level crowds have yet to materialize. That doesn't make this a

Playing the Horses

Horse racing has seen its bottom line repeatedly gouged by the dumb luck of state lotteries. Every year fewer and fewer fans trek out to the track, which means Belmont and the Big A will be happy to see you when you go. So happy, in fact, that they'll let you in for only a nominal charge (or no charge at all). While it's possible to lose some real money on the ponies, I have a system. Always pick the first horse off the rail that's wearing red, or any horse whose name begins with B. You can't miss.

Aqueduct Racetrack FREE Thoroughbred racing runs from late October or early November to early May. 110th St. and Rockaway Blvd., Rockaway Beach, Queens. ℂ **718/641-4700.** www.nyra.com. Clubhouse and Skyline Club admission is free, as is parking. Closed Mon–Tues. Subway: A to North Conduit.

Belmont Park When the season ends at Aqueduct (see above), the ponies run here, from May through July, and September through October. Hempstead Ave., Belmont, Long Island. ℂ **516/488-6000.** www.nyra.com. Tickets $3–$5, with free parking. Closed Mon–Tues. Train: LIRR Belmont Express from Penn Station or Flatbush Ave.

cheap ticket, but for 10 marginally compelling matchups (in the "Value" tier), the Mets will let you in for $11. The same seats are just $15 for some two dozen "Bronze" dates. Citi Field, 126th St., at Roosevelt Ave., Flushing, Queens. ℂ 718/507-8499. www.mets.com. Subway: 7 to Mets/Willets Point.

Baby Bombers The **Staten Island Yankees** have a lovely new waterfront stadium just a few steps from the ferry terminal. Running from $14 to $16, tickets are easier to come by than the Cyclones', although they're scarce when the two rivals play. Prices are up (the picnic area is now $12), but gluttons can take advantage of $18 all-you-can-eat and -drink specials. Richmond County Bank Ballpark, Staten Island. ℂ 718/720-9200. www.siyanks.com. Subway: R to Whitehall St.; 1 to South Ferry, take the ferry to Staten Island and follow the signs.

Damn Yankees The new Yankee Stadium has been derided as a "mallpark" rather than a ballpark, but there's no disputing the time and effort put into all those smooth finishes. Despite the pricey build-out (and the pricey virtual all-star squad that plays there), you can find a few ways to get in the building for cheap. Select seats in sections 201 and 239 are obstructed view and only retail for $5 a pop. The Yankees also designate nine games a season as special value nights (not the Red Sox or Met series). For these games, $5 buys you select seats in the terrace, grandstand, and bleachers. Yankee Stadium, 1 E. 161st St., at River Ave., the Bronx. (C) **718/293-6000.** www.yankees.com. Subway: B/D/4 to 161st St./ Yankee Stadium.

Knicks & Cut-Rate Seats   Ten-dollar Knicks seats are about as elusive as Knicks playoff victories. They do exist, but they're nosebleeds and they tend to sell out quickly. If you don't pick them up in September when they first go on sale, your best bet is to check the "Stub Hub" on the Knicks website, where season-ticket holders unload their spares at list after another disappointing season. (If you do opt for these cheap seats, you may be able to move down to a lower section if there are empty rows.) Madison Square Garden, 4 Pennsylvania Plaza, Seventh Ave., at 34th St. (C) **212/465-6741.** www.nba.com/knicks. Subway: A/C/E or 1/2/3 to Penn Station.

Mini Mets   No one confuses the **Brooklyn Cyclones** for dem bums of old, but the new stadium near the Atlantic Ocean and the Coney Island boardwalk has fast become a borough fave. Box seats are $13 or $16. General admission and reserved bleacher seats will only set you back $8. Though some of the sheen is off the new stadium, tickets still go quickly. MCU Park, 1904 Surf Ave., at W. 19th St., Coney Island, Brooklyn. (C) **718/449-8497.** www.brooklyncyclones.com. Subway: D/F/N/Q to Coney Island/ Stillwell Ave.

Rumble on the River   `FREE`   Practitioners of the sweet science assemble every summer on the Hudson at this offshoot of the Church Street Boxing Gym's legendary amateur bouts. There's a full-on ring and no punches pulled as a series of pugilists go three rounds apiece. The event takes place at Pier 84, usually on a Thursday night in midsummer. Pier 84, at W. 44th St. and the Hudson. (C) **212/533-7275.** www.hudson riverpark.org. Subway: A/C/E/7 to 42nd St./Port Authority. Walk toward the river.

Sweet Land of Liberty   The Liberty offers more cheap ways to get into Madison Square Garden than its male counterparts. They also play harder. Though prices go as high as $260, you can find a fair amount of upper-row seating for $10. Madison Square Garden, 4 Pennsylvania Plaza, Seventh Ave., at 34th St. (C) **212/465-6075.** www.wnba.com/liberty. Subway: A/C/E or 1/2/3 to Penn Station.

11 Into the Drink

FREE WINE TASTINGS

The intricacies of wine are endless, which is excuse enough to try as much of the stuff as possible. The wine shop tasting experience can be frustrating because you're only getting sips, but if you've come for edification and not to catch a cheap buzz, there's little chance of going away disappointed. Besides, many shops throw in free snacks for your trouble.

Astor Wines & Spirits NOHO `FREE`   Astor's ginormous space in the basement of the De Vinne Press Building usually hosts free tastings on Thursdays and Fridays from 6 to 8pm, and Saturday afternoons from 3 to 5pm, with other spot sessions scattered through the calendar. Look for artisanal champagnes, liquor, and sakés among the offerings, with the booze in question usually discounted 15%. Regular prices are great here, too, making this my top stop for stocking up. 399 Lafayette St., at E. 4th St. ✆ **212/674-7500.** www.astorwines.com. Subway: 6 to Bleecker St.; B/D/F/M to Broadway/Lafayette.

Best Cellars New York UPPER EAST SIDE `FREE`   Tastings can be found 6 days a week at this classy wine shop. Weeknights from 5 to 8pm find wine samples following a weekly theme. On Saturday afternoons from 2 to 4pm, the wine often comes with a free snack provided by a visiting local chef. 1291 Lexington Ave., at 87th St. ✆ **212/426-4200.** www.bestcellars.com. Subway: 4/5/6 to 86th St. Other location: Upper West Side, 2246 Broadway, btw. 80th and 81st sts. ✆ **212/362-8730.** Subway: 1 to 79th St.

67 Wines and Spirits UPPER WEST SIDE `FREE`   Rotating hosts walk guests through wine tastings at this shop, highlighting the fruits of a particular country or region. Tastings are usually on Friday and Saturday afternoons between 4 and 7pm. 179 Columbus Ave., btw. 67th and 68th sts. ✆ **212/724-6767.** www.67wine.com. Subway: 1 to 66th St.

Union Square Wines UNION SQUARE `FREE`   The new larger digs of this neighborhood shop just mean there's more counter space for uncorking the fruit of the vine. Tastings are held several nights a week, with as many as two dozen different wines in rotation. Look for 20% discounts on sampled vintages. 140 Fourth Ave., at 13th St. ✆ **212/675-8100.** www.unionsquarewines.com. Subway: L/N/Q/R/4/5/6 to 14th St./Union Sq.

12 Free & Cheap Pub Grub

There's nothing like a salty treat to keep the beer orders flowing: Witness the ubiquity of pretzels and peanuts in proximity to barstools. Several New York bars get more elaborate with their snacks, offering up bagels, wings, and pizza pies. Discounts can be deep—in many cases all the way down to $0—although most places expect you to spring for a drink or two, since they're running bars and all.

Alligator Lounge WILLIAMSBURG, BROOKLYN   This lounge took over a former pizza joint to exploit an existing wood-burning oven. The result is remarkably good pies, free with the purchase of a drink. That's right—a free personal pizza with your beer. Toppings run $2 for the first and $1 for the follow-ups. The pies roll from 6pm on the weekdays and 3pm on the weekends, and they don't stop until a bleary-eyed 3:30am. 600 Metropolitan Ave., btw. Leonard and Lorimer sts., Williamsburg, Brooklyn. ℭ 718/599-4440. Daily 3pm–4am. Subway: L to Lorimer St.; G to Metropolitan Ave.

The Brazen Head BOERUM HILL, BROOKLYN   Sharing a name with Dublin's oldest pub, this low-key neighborhood spot rolls out the welcome wagon with dining and drink specials. Monday nights see free chicken wings (and thighs) from 5pm on; Tuesday and Wednesday evenings there's complimentary cheese; Saturdays feature $5 barbecues; and Sunday afternoons are the time for bagels, fixins, and $5 bloody marys and mimosas. 228 Atlantic Ave., btw. Court St. and Boerum Place, Boerum Hill, Brooklyn. ℭ 718/488-0430. Tues–Sat noon–4am; Sun–Mon noon–2am. Subway: F/G to Bergen St.; A/C/G to Hoyt-Schermerhorn.

Crocodile Lounge EAST VILLAGE   This Alligator Lounge spinoff may not win any prizes for its pizzas, but it's hard to beat for price ($0) and convenience (especially for NYU students). The lure of one free pizza per drink attacts a young and hungry crowd. Crocodile kitsch and free Skee-Ball complete the atmosphere. 325 E. 14th St., btw. First and Second aves. ℭ 212/477-7747. Daily noon–4am. Subway: L to First Ave.

Croxley Ales EAST VILLAGE   This pub represents something between the death of a once-proud indie 'hood and a breath of unpretentious relief in a trendier-than-thou zone. Croxley puts games on its televisions and offers specials at the bar. If you're drinking, you're entitled to 20¢ wings on Saturdays from noon to 5pm, and all day and night on Sundays. That price goes down to 10¢ on Monday, Tuesday, and Wednesday nights from 5pm to 1am (after 7pm, select pints are just $4). Weekday happy hours run from 5 to 7pm, with $1 off of most everything. 28 Ave. B, btw. 2nd and 3rd sts. ℂ **212/253-6140.** www.croxley.com. Kitchen Mon–Sat 11am–1am; Sun noon–1am. Bar nightly until 4am. Subway: F/M to Second Ave.

The Delancey LOWER EAST SIDE   The rooftop of this lowrise bar is an oasis on the Manhattan side of the Williamsburg Bridge. Palms and fountains provide a tropical air. On select summer days, that air fills with burger and dog smoke from the grill ($5 for all you care to eat). When you've had your fill of flesh, head downstairs for free live rock. (Mon nights enjoy two-for-one drinks; recession victims can add a free shot of tequila, too, if they've got proof of unemployment.) 168 Delancey St., btw. Clinton and Attorney sts. ℂ **212/254-9920.** www.thedelancey.com. Daily 5pm–4am. Subway: F to Delancey St.; J/M/Z to Essex St.

East River Bar WILLIAMSBURG, BROOKLYN   East of the East River is the site of this paint factory turned biker bar turned casual South Williamsburg hang. Industrial chic corrugated metal adorns the outdoor patio, which holds a real, live barrel drum barbecue pit. That, and three smaller grills, provide the fire for BYOBBQ nights (as in Bring Your Own.) Call ahead to reserve charcoal space. 97 S. 6th St., btw. Bedford Ave. and Berry St. ℂ **718/302-0511.** www.eastriverbar.com. Sun–Thurs 5pm–3am; Fri–Sat 5pm–4am. Subway: J/M/Z to Marcy Ave.

Fish WEST VILLAGE   This restaurant is a decent facsimile of a seafood shack, with a lively crowd and walls cluttered with old waterfront photos and buoys. Though the sit-down prices aren't cheap, you can net a great deal at the bar. Just $8 covers a half-dozen oysters and a beer or glass of house wine. Available at all hours, 7 days a week, and perfect for date nights. 280 Bleecker St., at Jones St. ℂ **212/727-2879.** Sun–Thurs noon–11pm; Fri–Sat noon–midnight. Subway: 1 to Christopher St.; A/B/C/D/E/F/M to W. 4th St./Washington Sq.

Metropolitan WILLIAMSBURG, BROOKLYN   When the weather turns forgiving, the grill at this gay Williamsburg haunt turns to wings, dogs, and veggie burgers. The patio setting is spectacular, with lots of space beneath the creeping vines. A cheerful crowd gets even friendlier the more they're plied with cheap drinks ($7 pitchers of Bud) and free meat (or fake meat, as the case may be). Start time is around 4pm on Sunday afternoons. Also look for two-for-one happy hours and $1 PBR nights scattered through the schedule. 559 Lorimer St., btw. Metropolitan Ave. and Devoe St. (✆ **718/599-4444.** www.myspace.com/metropolitan11211. Daily 3pm–4am. Subway: L to Lorimer St.; G to Metropolitan Ave..

Papacitos GREENPOINT, BROOKLYN This ramshackle Brooklyn spot offers not one, not two, but *three* happy hours. The first runs on weekdays between 11am and 4pm, with discount tacos and $2 Tecates and Modelo Especials. At 4pm, happy hour #2 kicks in: The same cheap cans, plus two-for-one frozen margaritas, discount nachos, and other drink specials. The third happy hour fills the last hour of the night and goes by the name "$1 TACO MADNESS." You must order a drink to be eligible (and, if you've enjoyed all three happy hours, still be standing upright). 999 Manhattan Ave., btw. Huron and Green sts. (✆ **718/349-7292.** www.papacitosbrooklyn.com. Sun–Wed 11am–2am; Thurs–Sat 11am–4am. Subway: G to Greenpoint Ave.

Phebe's EAST VILLAGE When this corner was occupied by a Bowery saloon you could get a worker's lunch for 40¢. On Monday and Wednesday nights that same outlay will get you four chicken wings— they're just a dime apiece with the purchase of a pitcher. Tuesday from 8pm until midnight it's two-for-one burgers, and there are happy hour discounts from 4 to 8pm every weeknight. A recent spruce up has made for a comfortable scene, popular with NYU students and post-collegiate partiers. 361 Bowery, at E. 4th St. (✆ **212/358-1902.** Daily 11am– 4am. Subway: 6 to Astor Place; N/Q/R to 8th St.

Rudy's MIDTOWN WEST The pig that stands sentry outside this Hell's Kitchen dive is there to prime your appetite for hot dogs. *Free* hot dogs. If you're looking to diversify your diet, they've recently added fried chicken ($1) and chili with cheese ($2.50 a bowl) to the menu. Rudy's Blonde Ale is just $7 a pitcher, should you feel like luxuriating with a cold one on a duct-taped booth. 627 Ninth Ave., btw. 44th and 45th sts. (✆ **212/974-9169.** Daily 8am–4am. Subway: A/C/E/7 to 42nd St./ Port Authority.

Sip UPPER WEST SIDE This coffee shop/lounge treats its local clientele right, with half-price food on Mondays, half-price wine on Wednesdays, and free Wi-Fi all through the week. Happy hour is an even bigger draw. Free tapas like beet salad or sausage and potatoes come out for drinkers between 5 and 7pm, and again between 2 and

4am, on top of discounted libations. 998 Amsterdam Ave., btw. 109th and 110th sts. ℂ **212/316-2747.** www.sipbar.com. Daily 6am–4am. Subway: B/C or 1 to 110th St.

Spring Lounge SOHO   A profusion of stuffed sharks provides the alternative name ("the Shark Bar") for this long-running corner spot. The place dates back to the '20's and an illegal beer bucket-to-go operation. Its current iteration features a trim and mostly tourist crowd. Wednesday nights at 5pm, take advantage of free hot dogs, cooked in a beer of the week. On Sundays at noon grab a free bagel with your eye-opener. 48 Spring St., at Mulberry St. ℂ **212/965-1774.** www.springlounge.ypguides.net. Mon–Sat 8am–4am; Sun noon–4am. Subway: 6 to Spring St.; N/Q/R to Prince St.

Standings EAST VILLAGE   The EVill's evolution away from its gritty alternative status is complete enough to now accommodate sports bars. This is an amiable one, with eight plasma screens and happy hour specials that run 5 to 8pm Wednesday through Sunday, and all night Monday and Tuesday. Come on a Friday night and you'll get free pizza—they treat the entire bar starting at 8pm until it runs out. There's also a free bagel bar on Sunday afternoons (except in July and Aug). 43 E. 7th St., btw. Second and Third aves. ℂ **212/420-0671.** www.standingsbar.com. Mon–Thurs 5pm–midnight; Fri 5pm–1am; Sat, noon–1am; Sun noon–midnight. Subway: 6 to Astor Place; N/Q/R to 8th St.

13 Liquid Assets

Despite the rise of the $18 cocktail, an entire paycheck isn't required for a night on the town. Recession pressures have opened up happy hours across town, and two-for-ones and $1-off specials are ubiquitous. Even sweeter deals can be found, especially in the cheap drinker's meccas of the East Village and the Lower East Side. Just look for the happy hour deals scrawled on sidewalk signs. Or find a comprehensive list of happy hours and even open bars online—see "eHappy-Hour Harmony" at the end of this chapter.

Bar None EAST VILLAGE   For the longest happy hours in the city the choice is, without exception, Bar None. You have to wait until noon, but then you'll get $3 Bud and Bud Light pints and $4 wells and other drafts until 8pm. Stick around until 11pm and you can take advantage of Power Hour, 60 minutes of $3 Buds, Bud Lights, and well drinks.

Miscellaneous drink specials run from Sunday through Thursday evening, too. The environs are divey, but it's perfectly amiable, and the prices can't be beat. 98 Third Ave., btw. 12th and 13th sts. ℭ **212/777-6663.** www.barnonenyc.com. Daily noon–4am. Subway: L to Third Ave.

Blue Owl EAST VILLAGE   It's gotten hard to swing a cat in NYC without knocking over a tray full of fancy cocktails. Most purveyors charge up the ying-yang for their mixology, but hit up a happy hour at Blue Owl and you'll be sipping in style for just $6. The cocktail specials run weeknights from 6 to 8pm, extended to midnight on Wednesdays. 196 Second Ave., btw. 12th and 13th sts. ℭ **212/505-2583.** Sun–Mon 5pm–2am; Tues–Sat 5pm–4am. Subway: L to First or Third aves.

Doc Holliday's EAST VILLAGE   Redneck theme bars would seem to be a tough sell in cosmopolitan Manhattan, but quite a few trashy joints thrive here. Doc Holliday's plies the familiar formula, with attractive bar crews and booze priced to sell. Tuesday nights are all you can drink from 8 to 11pm. It's $7, and the beverage is Bud Light, and the surroundings are less than clean, but after a few trips to the bar, who remembers? Buy-one-get-one-free happy hours run daily from 5 to 8pm. 141 Ave. A, at 9th St. ℭ **212/979-0312.** Daily noon–4am. Subway: F/M to Second Ave.; 6 to Bleecker St.

Jeremy's Ale House FINANCIAL DISTRICT   When you need to show a tourist real New Yorkers, you can't do much better than the über-authentic Jeremy's. A mix of blue and white collars hangs out beneath a burgeoning collection of liberated ties and bras. The house is known for its huge Styrofoam cups, which hold a full *quart* of beer. A Coors is $5. After-work happy hours (weekdays 4–6pm) feature half-price well drinks, $4 Coors and Coors Light buckets, and $1.50 junior burgers. With the fish market departed from South Street there are fewer takers, but construction workers and film students can still avail themselves of "The Eye Opener," $1.75 for a bucket of Coors, available Monday through Friday from 8 to 10am. 228 Front St., btw. Peck Slip and Beekman St. ℭ **212/964-3537.** www.jeremysalehouse.com. Mon–Fri 8am–midnight; Sat 10am–midnight; Sun noon–11pm. Subway: A/C/J/Z/2/3/4/5 to Fulton St./Broadway Nassau.

Slane WEST VILLAGE   Irish conviviality and exposed brick make for a charming atmosphere in the middle of a touristy 'hood. The weekday "Beat the Clock" happy hour ticks down some great deals. From noon to 2pm well drinks are only $1. For the 2 to 4pm shift, Yuengling

What's in a Name?: Free Drinks, That's What

If you're one of those people who has a name, you can drink for zero dollars and zero cents at bars **No Idea** and **Antarctica.** There is one small catch: Your name has to sync up with the name of the night. Each bar posts a different monthly list, and although there are some oddball monikers, there are also plenty of occasions to hang out with fellow Meghans, Joshes, and Jessicas. Open-tab Name Night runs 5 to 11pm Monday through Saturday (at Antarctica Sat name night is 8pm–1am). Check www.noideabar.com and www.antarcticabar.com to see when you're up. FINE PRINT They're not running a booze charity; the idea is to drag along some friends and let them run up the tab while you hobnob with a roomful of fellow Vartans. If you show up alone they may not let you play along. *No Idea:* 30 E. 20th St., btw. Park Ave. and Broadway. ✆ 212/777-0100. Subway: 6 or N/Q/R to 23rd St. *Antarctica:* 287 Hudson, at Spring St. ✆ 212/352-1666. Subway: C/E to Spring St.

drafts take over the $1 slot. Appletinis and Cosmos for $3 take over for the 4 to 6pm shift. 102 MacDougal St., btw. Bleecker and W. 3rd sts. ✆ 212/505-0079. www.slanenyc.com. Mon–Sat 11am–4am; Sun noon–4am. Subway: A/B/C/D/E/F to W. 4th St./Washington Sq.

Verlaine LOWER EAST SIDE Finding a dive that'll hook you up with a cheap happy hour is no great sleight, but a sleek spot that'll discount you seven nights a week? Verlaine's house specials are a lychee martini, just $5 between 5 and 10pm, joined by $5 sangrias, Vietnamese bloody marys, basic cocktails, and house wine. Hops heads can knock back $3 Yuenglings. The space is a little generic, but it's stylish, and you don't have to pad yourself with cocktail napkins to avoid sticking to the surfaces. 110 Rivington St., btw. Essex and Ludlow sts. ✆ 212/614-2494. www.verlainenyc.com. Sun–Wed 5pm–1am; Thurs–Sat 5pm–4am. Subway: F to Delancey St.; J/M/Z to Essex St.

eHappy-Hour Harmony

Once the domain of the back pages of local rags, happy hours are now best found online. The following happy hour websites, Twitter feeds, and smartphone apps will match you with the boozy deal of your choice, usually at any time of day. Prices of the happy hours vary, but the sites and apps are all free.

Boozeparty.net   This site glosses rock shows and other opportunities for "getting smashed on the cheap."

Cocktail Compass   The *L Magazine* co-sponsors this free iPhone app, which will take a GPS read of your location and hook you up with the nearest happy hour, with a countdown of how long you've got left.

Coovents.com   These happy hour experts will text the cheap drink 411 right to your phone, or you can follow along online with convenient neighborhood and timeline breakdowns.

Drinkdeal.com   If you've settled on your inputs (neighborhood, night, booze selection), this site is both comprehensive and easy to navigate.

Freenyc.net   Among filtered listings for art, culture, and activism, you'll also find some nightlife giveaways here.

Happy Houred   Time, booze, and atmosphere are the filters available for this happy hour iPhone app. Go to Appsolutemedia.com/happyhoured.

Myopenbar.com   On the one hand, if this daily short list is advertised to the whole interwebs, it's going to be a full-on scrum to get to the goods. On the other hand, *free booze*.

Pulsejfk.com   Follow the Twitter feed @pulsdJFK for free tastings, drink deals, and a bunch of other cheap NYC stuff.

Coney Island is getting a modern overhaul, but the iconic Wonder Wheel will remain, as will the Cyclone Roller Coaster. See p. 302 for a full itinerary.

FREE & DIRT CHEAP DAYS

T hough New York is happy to gouge visitors for $40 bus tours and boat cruises, a person can scope out a lot of city for no money at all. It's hard to swing a cat in NYC without banging into a free daylong adventure or cheap date. The city's close quarters means you can hit a huge range of sites without putting excessive mileage on your soles. You don't even need to pack—Gotham's corner stores are already storing your provisions for you.

Itinerary 1: Coney Island, Baby

Where	Coney Island, Brooklyn.
How to Get There	D/F/N/Q to Stillwell Avenue/Coney Island. The subway ride is about 40 minutes from downtown Manhattan. You can also use the B/Q at Brighton Beach.
How Long to Spend There	It's easy to amuse yourself along the boardwalk and environs for 2 or 3 hours. Anything longer probably requires a beach towel and a page-turner.
What to Bring	If you're planning on a dip, a bathing suit and towel are the obvious needs. There are public restrooms, cabanas for changing, and showers for shedding saltwater. Even if you're going to keep to the streets, bring sunscreen because there's light aplenty reflecting off the sand and sea.
Best Times to Go	Morning's calm is nice. Midday summer days can be brutal and hectic. Late afternoons the crowds start to disperse and the light is lovely.
Related Tip	The big holiday weekends bring in special events, but they also bring the biggest crowds. If you're not in the mood for the crush, go on a weekday, or keep to the fringes, which are less populated. In the non-summer months, the amusement parks are closed and the boardwalk is almost empty, but the experience can be peaceful and replenishing.

After a few weeks or months of city living, trapped in the concrete canyons, it's easy to forget that New York City grew so far and fast because of its access to water. New York Harbor stays close to the public consciousness, but too many of us overlook the Atlantic Ocean, which is just a subway ride away. When you feel like traveling to a distant place but don't want to invest more than a couple of Metrocard swipes, Coney Island is hard to beat. In summer, the area becomes a blue-collar resort, with salsa bands and volleyball games and screaming kids on the rides. As with all of Brooklyn, it's the furthest thing from monolithic. Tourists, hipsters, and elderly immigrant residents all overlap on the beachfront benches. Giuseppe Cautela wrote in 1925, "When you bathe in Coney, you bathe in the American Jordan. It is holy water. Nowhere else in the United States will you see so many races mingle in a common purpose for a common good." Yes, there's a looming $1-billion makeover to go with the new $250-million subway terminal, but Coney is still a long ways away from shedding its diverse and gritty charm.

① The Beach

The Atlantic up close is hard to beat and the broad beaches here are a nice spot to start a tour. Get good and hot in the sun and then go for a dip. The water is not the

ITINERARY 1: CONEY ISLAND, BABY

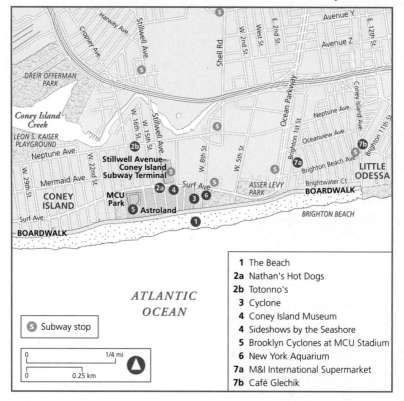

Legend:
- **S** Subway stop
- *ATLANTIC OCEAN*

Scale: 0 — 1/4 mi / 0 — 0.25 km

1 The Beach
2a Nathan's Hot Dogs
2b Totonno's
3 Cyclone
4 Coney Island Museum
4 Sideshows by the Seashore
5 Brooklyn Cyclones at MCU Stadium
6 New York Aquarium
7a M&I International Supermarket
7b Café Glechik

cleanest, but just follow the lead of the other souls out there bobbing in the waves. On a hot day it's particularly refreshing. A few blocks to the east of Astroland and the subway station, the bodies thin out quickly and you can find wide-open stretches. If you're unwilling to track sand back in your shoes, a stroll along the boardwalk offers endless people-watching entertainment.

2 Mealtime

The options for cheap beach food in Coney Island are almost limitless. Fried clams, fried dough, french fries, and soft-serve ice cream are among the highlights.

- On July 4th at high noon, hefty Americans and rail-thin Japanese fight it out in the annual Coney Island Hot Dog eating contest. For $3.25 a pop you can hold your own minicontest at **Nathan's Famous** (*(C)* **718/ 946-2202;** www.nathansfamous. com), which still sells some million dogs a year at their busy stand.

Coney Island Costs

Free	
Sun, sand, and sea	$0
Dirt Cheap	
A day at the beach + 1 museum	$1
Add-Ons for Spendthrift Millionaires	
Cyclone Roller Coaster or Wonder Wheel	$6–$8
+ Half a pizza	$8
+ Sideshow	$7.50

● As good as a meal on a picnic table just off the beach is, it's worth noting that one of New York's best pizzas is just a few blocks away at 1524 Neptune Ave. **Totonno's** (℃ **718/372-8606;** totonnos.com) is an old-school, family-run operation that serves up top pies (no slices). The fresh mozzarella and crisp crusts haven't lost a step through 85 years of operation. Small plain pies are $16.50, larges $19.50.

❸ The Legendary Cyclone
The Cyclone Roller Coaster (℃ **718/372-0275;** www.astroland.com) is the granddaddy of Coney Island amusements. Accelerating heart rates since 1927, it's the oldest and most-imitated roller coaster in the world. It's also a quota-starved insurance underwriter's nightmare, with engineering limited to a pulling chain and gravity, but still managing to get those rickety cars up to 60 mph. The supporting rails and wooden boards look mighty untrustworthy, but of course that's the thrill (and in truth, the safety record here is excellent). Rides are $8 a pop ($5 for a re-ride) for 1 minute and 50 seconds of action, so it's not exactly dirt cheap, though it's definitely memorable.

❹ The Coney Island Museum & Sideshows
The Coney Island Museum (℃ **718/372-5159;** www.coneyisland.com) stands in proud opposition to the history-shrouding changes planned for the area. The suggested admission of 99¢ provides entry to an evolving second-floor space. Funhouse mirrors, old signage, and a creepy baby's coffin (complete with baby skeleton) exemplify the collection. Rotating temporary exhibits reflect the love this organization has for Coney Island's vanished heyday. A fascinating hour-long PBS documentary screens in the main room.

The Coney Island Skyline

Parachute jumps were developed as military-training devices, but leave it to America to convert them to fun. Coney Island's parachute jump started out as a ride at the 1939 World's Fair in Queens before packing up for Brooklyn, where it served thrill-seekers until 1964. The skeletal form that remains has an unexpected elegance. A recent design contest was the first step in installing an architecturally ambitious new base, complete with a restaurant and visitor center. The jump has been designated a historic landmark and it's the pride of the local skyline, so much so that it's sometimes called the Eiffel Tower of Brooklyn.

The Eiffel Tower of Paris was the motivator for George Washington Gale Ferris, an engineer who took up the challenge for America to respond to the Frenchies' innovations in steel. The famous wheels still bear his name and Coney Island's version, the 1920s Wonder Wheel (🕾 **718/372-2592;** www.wonderwheel.com), is one of the world's tallest at 150 feet. From the ground it looks like a gentle spin, but as the cars slide on lateral rails they create a somewhat stomach-churning effect. For panoramic views of the city and sea it's worth it. The $6 cost to ride, however, is a matter of individual budgetary discretion.

Just around the corner you'll find **Sideshows by the Seashore,** run by the same people. It's the nation's last 10-in-1 freak show; step right up to see illustrated men and women, fire-eating, albino-serpent handling, and even beds of nails. The theater is small and run-down, with no air conditioning, but there's 45 minutes of entertainment for only $7.50 adults, $5 kids 12 and under. If you're patient, you may hear the barker hustle up some empty seats at a discount. Shows run from Easter through the end of September, weekends only except in the heart of summer, when there are Wednesday through Friday shows as well. Weekend and holiday shows are between 1 and 9pm, weekdays 2 to 8pm.

⑤ MCU Stadium

The return of baseball to Brooklyn certainly hasn't diminished local pride, and tickets to Mets farmhands, the **Brooklyn Cyclones** (🕾 **718/449-8497;** www.brooklyn cyclones.com), aren't that easy to come by. If the game you're aching to see sells out, keep in mind that some standby seats are made

Make a Date

Coney Island after hours is even seedier than the daylight spectacle, but that doesn't impede on the potential for a great cheap date. The sight of the dark swells of the Atlantic and the cleared-out beach is pretty grand. The only thing that could improve on it is free **fireworks,** which come around 9:30pm every Friday night from late June to late August (and also a few Saturdays, thanks to the Cyclones). After the fireworks if you've got money to burn, check out Sideshows by the Seashore's **Burlesque by the Beach.** Troupes from around the city come down to shake various body parts. Campy costumes and fire-eating round out the experience. Thursday and Friday nights at 10pm; tickets $10–$15.

On Saturday nights, the same Sideshow folk unfold chairs in the Coney Island Museum so they can project campy films (p. 304). Coney Island–themed fare and other B-movie obsessions are the norm, and it's only $5. 1208 Surf Ave., 2nd floor. ⓒ **718/372-5159.** www.indiefilm page.com. Sat 8:30pm.

available on game day outside the boardwalk stadium. Seats are pretty cheap, for professional sports, $8 to $16.

⑥ New York Aquarium
If you've really got your timing down, you can enjoy a cheap visit to the city's only aquarium: After 3pm on Fridays it's pay what you wish. See p. 106 for more details.

⑦ Bonus Round: Brighton Beach
If you want to leave America but neglected to pack a passport, there is a close-by option. A quick trip east on the boardwalk will put you in the heart of **Little Odessa** in Brighton Beach. Between the strolling Russian émigrés, the Cyrillic signs, and the clunky design on the sidewalk cafes, you'll be forgiven for thinking you've walked into a Black Sea resort town. The cafes are surprisingly pricey, but there's plenty of cheap street fare a block inland. Take a left and walk toward the El, which runs above Brighton Beach Avenue, a bustling street dotted with caviar shops and street vendors.

For total immersion in a foreign land, check out the **M & I International** (ⓒ 718/615-1011) supermarket at 249 Brighton Beach Ave. You can stock up for the trip home, or enjoy Russian pastries or smoked fish in the upstairs cafe. Prices are all outer-borough low.

To enjoy a more sit-down experience, join the foodies making a pilgrimage to **Café Glechik** (© **718/616-0494;** glechik.com) at 3159 Coney Island Ave. This petite Ukrainian restaurant is known for its dumplings, served in two supple varieties (*pelmeni,* folded like tortellini, and *vereniki,* which resemble *pierogi*). There are also excellent soups, salads, and Kabobs, and most everything comes in well under $10.

Special Events

- In mid-July, the *Village Voice* sponsors the **Siren Music Festival,** a massive rock concert. Some 100,000 indie fans show up to enjoy music on two stages from noon until 9pm. It's all free, with no tickets necessary; just show up. Main stage: 10th Street at the boardwalk. Second stage: Stillwell Avenue at the boardwalk (© **212/475-3333;** www.villagevoice.com/siren).

- With body paint and beads, plus a few strategic scraps of fabric to keep things legal, the avatars of New York's retro-culture scene transform themselves into mermaids and Neptunes at the annual **Mermaid Parade** (© **718/ 372-5159;** www.coneyisland. com/mermaid.shtml). Classic cars join the procession as it works its way east on Surf Avenue, dispersing when the participants dash down the beach to the ageless Atlantic. Saturday around the summer solstice. Surf Avenue from West 21st to West 10th streets.

Itinerary 2: From Brooklyn Bridge to DUMBO

How to Get There	To reach the Brooklyn Bridge, take the J/Z to Chambers Street or the 4/5/6 to Brooklyn Bridge–City Hall. Return from DUMBO on the F train at York Street, or walk about 15 minutes to Brooklyn Heights to catch the A/C train at High Street, or the 2/3 train at Clark Street.
How Long to Spend There	The walk across the bridge takes 30 minutes or so, and it's easy to spend an hour walking around on the Brooklyn side. Adding galleries, meals, and park time will stretch out the visit to 2 or 3 hours.
Best Times to Go	A sunny afternoon is ideal, but it's all good. Late at night it gets pretty sparse around the bridge and DUMBO. It's more disconcerting than it is dangerous, but unless you're familiar with the area I recommend against it.
Tip	If you're interested in the galleries, check in advance to see which ones have exhibits up. Note that galleries in DUMBO keep different hours than those in Manhattan; many are closed mid-week, but open on Sundays.

1 The Bridge

The Brooklyn Bridge is one of New York's great treasures, and as such it's not a very well kept secret. Tourists, bikers, joggers, and commuters jam the planks on sunny days. The dizzying rigging, stunning views, and towering Gothic charm leave a person feeling like they're within the sanctuary of an inside-out cathedral. The bridge's official romance with New York began in 1883, and from Walt Whitman through Hart Crane, the love has only grown. When you reach the first tower, stop for a while so you can admire the Manhattan views. The assorted plaques here are a mix of the ceremonial and the informative.

2 The Brooklyn Side: DUMBO & Its Galleries

On the far side of the bridge, the pathway slants downward and divides. Staying to the right takes you to Downtown Brooklyn and Brooklyn Heights, and veering to the left will put you beneath an overpass. Walk down the stairs, hang a left, and head toward the water. You'll find yourself among the cobblestones and broad-shouldered buildings that characterize **DUMBO.** DUMBO (Down Under the Manhattan Bridge Overpass) is a surprisingly well-preserved patch of old industrial New York. Artists have infiltrated the area, and their touches can be seen on and around many of the loft structures. For a closer look, check out some of the galleries. (Even if you hate the art, many of the spaces have killer views.) The **1st Thursdays DUMBO Gallery Walk** (℃ 718/222-2500; www.brooklynartproject.com) is a great way to sample the goods, augmented with free music and artists' talks.

- **BAC Gallery** FREE The gallery arm of the Brooklyn Arts Council. 111 Front St., #218, btw. Washington and Adams sts. ℃ **718/625-0080.** www.brooklynartscouncil.org. Mon–Fri 10am–5pm.

- **5 + 5 Gallery** FREE Works on paper specialist. 111 Front St., #263, btw. Washington and Adams sts. ℃ **718/624-6048.** www.5plus5gallery.com. Sun–Thurs noon–6pm.

- **DUMBO Arts Center** FREE The 3,000-square-foot gallery here offers ample space for innovative art. There's a $2 suggested donation. 30 Washington St., btw. Water and Plymouth sts. ℃ **718/694-0831.** www.dumboartscenter.org. Wed–Mon noon–6pm.

- **Smack Mellon Studio** FREE A DUMBO classic in a new home. 92 Plymouth St., btw. Washington and Main sts. Check the website for free

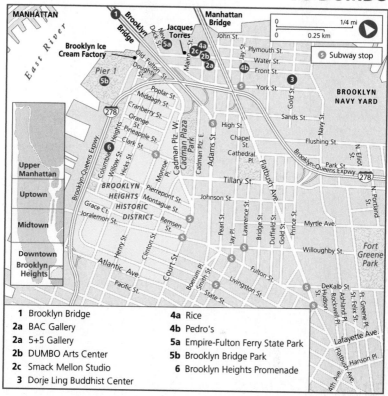

1 Brooklyn Bridge
2a BAC Gallery
2a 5+5 Gallery
2b DUMBO Arts Center
2c Smack Mellon Studio
3 Dorje Ling Buddhist Center

4a Rice
4b Pedro's
5a Empire-Fulton Ferry State Park
5b Brooklyn Bridge Park
6 Brooklyn Heights Promenade

artists' talks. © **718/834-8761.** www.smackmellon.org. Wed–Sun noon–6pm.

3 A Moment of Zen & Vinegar Hill When you've had your fill of art, walk up Front Street (keeping the water to your left). When you reach Gold Street, peek through the yellow cement blocks on the corner at #98. The compound inside belongs to the **Dorje Ling Buddhist Center** (© **718/522-6523;** www.jonang.org). When

Front Street dead-ends, take a left and enter my favorite forgotten neighborhood in New York, Vinegar Hill. The well-preserved mid-19th-century buildings are oddly juxtaposed with a field of electrical transformers. The neighborhood is only 4 square blocks, so it's a quick tour. Taking a right on Evans Street will bring you to a cul-de-sac, where you'll see an elegant white house behind a gate. Between 1806 and 1966 this is where the Navy Yard

Brooklyn Bridge/DUMBO Costs

Free	
Historic walk, art galleries, afternoon in the park	$0
Dirt Cheap	
Walk, art, park, plus an ice-cream cone or hot chocolate	$3.50
Add-Ons for Spendthrift Millionaires	
Cuban sandwich at Pedro's	$5.50
Brunch at Rice	$12

commandant hung his hat, while keeping watch over the outfitting of ships to fight everything from Barbary pirates to Nazis. The residence is now in private hands, and the Navy Yard is closed to the public. If you're interested in checking out the vine-smothered ruins of old naval housing, walk up Navy Street and turn left onto Nassau Street (it becomes Flushing Ave.), and then retrace your steps. Otherwise, double back down to Plymouth Street and walk south to DUMBO.

④ Mealtime

● Asian fusion fave **Rice** (✆ **718/222-9880;** www.riceny.com) at 81 Washington St. brings its exotic grains to Brooklyn, from Thai black to Bhutanese red. Starches are accompanied by curries, salads, and satays. Most every dish is under $11, with brunch running noon to 4pm on the weekends. There's a

Crossings Over

New York's two other East Village crossings are more utilitarian approaches to Brooklyn, but they're excellent alternatives if you've already done the Brooklyn Bridge to death. The Williamsburg Bridge is newly refurbished, with walk- and bikeways to connect Billyburg with the Lower East Side. The Manhattan Bridge's pathway is narrow and the subway can be near deafening, but the views are unimpeachable. On the Manhattan end you get ancient tenements cutting razor-sharp lines through Chinatown, at midpoint you overlook the stunning full span of the Brooklyn Bridge, and on the far side you can spy on the parks of DUMBO.

Make a Sweet Date

The Brooklyn Bridge at night is one of the most romantic spots in You can take in the Manhattan skyline, plus the shimmering ligh Brooklyn, plus the mystery of the dark water below, plied by tugs and fe ries. In the hours after dusk there's still plenty of foot traffic on the bridge so there's no menace, but it's much more secluded and sedate than at the rush hour or high noon peaks. If you've done a little planning, you can crank up the romance level a few notches by timing your visit with moonrise, creeping up over the Brooklyn skyline. Check the paper or a weather website for the exact time, and allow an extra 20 minutes or so for the satellite to clear the rooflines. If you're really organized, make the date for the full moon—it's the best free show the city's got.

After strolling along the bridge, cool down at the **Brooklyn Ice Cream Factory** (© **718/246-3963;** www.brooklynicecreamfactory. com) on the Fulton Ferry Landing Pier. The ice cream here is as pleasurable as the view, well worth the $3.50 per cone. A little more inland, chocolatier extraordinaire **Jacques Torres** (© **718/875-9772;** www. mrchocolate.com) operates a factory at 66 Water St.. Though the chocolates themselves could never be confused with dirt cheap, once they take liquid form they become affordable. Order a hot chocolate and you're basically drinking a candy bar. Opt for the "wicked" version, with its subtle hot pepper hints, and enjoy extra warmth. This rich treat is a relative bargain at $3.25.

great side garden, should the weather accommodate.

- Nearby **Pedro's** occupies a ramshackle basement that feels taken straight from a David Lynch flick. Dominican and Mexican food are served, with a big plate of pork, rice, and beans for only $8. Tables at street level allow for leisurely alfresco dining (with cheap margaritas).

⑤ Park It

DUMBO offers twin spots for the cooling of jets, the **Empire–Fulton Ferry State Park** and **Brooklyn Bridge Park.** The former was the point of departure for the Manhattan ferry, which ran until 1924 despite competition from the Brooklyn Bridge. A major refurbishment will be completed in the spring of 2011. The northern

...entire city. On the south side of the old Fulton Ferry Landing, ambitious new park construction is underway. Six industrial piers beneath the Brooklyn Promenade are being reborn as bonus open space. Check in at www.brooklynbridgepark.org for the latest developments.

6 Bonus Round: Brooklyn Heights
Just up the hill on the other side of the Brooklyn Bridge lies Brooklyn Heights. The neighborhood is staid, but the historic building stock is astounding. The fruit streets (Pineapple St., Orange St., and Cranberry St., running east-west)

are especially nice to stroll through. The **Brooklyn Promenade** along the Hudson has brilliant views of the Manhattan skyline.

Special Events

- Thursday nights in July and August, walk over the Brooklyn Bridge and then reward yourself with a free flick. The **Brooklyn Bridge Park "Movies With a View" Summer Film Series** projects in the shadow of the anchorage. (See p. 258 in "Entertainment" for a full review.)

- One weekend in late September (Fri–Sun) you can get the entire DUMBO arts scene at once. During the **Dumbo Arts Festival** (© **718/488-8588;** www.dumboartsfestival.com), galleries and artists' studios open their doors for some 150,000 gawkers. There's also live music, film, performance art, and installations adorning the streets.

Itinerary 3: The Secrets of Lower Manhattan

Where	Lower Manhattan, skirting the East River, Hudson, and New York Harbor.
How to Get There	The area is very well covered by trains; J/Z trains to Broad Street and 2/3/4/5 trains to Wall Street are good places to start.
How Long to Spend There	A straight walk can be done in an hour. To get your fill of museums add 2 more hours, and a round-trip on the ferry clocks in at another hour.
Best Times to Go	The ferry's views of downtown and the Statue of Liberty are great at night, and incomparable at dusk.
Tips	On the weekends Lower Manhattan feels deserted, with tourists the only signs of life. Quiet streets in New York are a great luxury, but many of the museums and almost all of the stores and restaurants are closed. To really get a feel for the area, hit it on a weekday.

The combination of too many tourists and too many uptight money-grubbers doesn't exactly make for an inviting scene, but the Financial District gets a bad rap. New York City's post–Native American life began here, and the oddly shaped streets attest to the patterns of ancient, organic urban planning. New York is notorious for paving over its own history, but Lower Manhattan has some unlikely survivors. The area is densely packed and even a short walk can put a person in easy reach of a host of historical sites. Ignore the $9 trillion that changes hands down here every year at the New York Stock Exchange; there are freebies aplenty for the discerning seeker.

❶ Federal Hall National Memorial

This is not an especially popular memorial, probably because the really interesting stuff happened in predecessor structures on this site. Federal Hall (© **212/825-6888;** www.nps.gov/feha) was built in 1842 to serve as a customshouse, and it's now a Park Service museum. Exhibits touch on Washington's inauguration, the drafting of the Bill of Rights, and the first stirring of rebellion against British authority, all of which occurred right here. The building itself is a preeminent example of Greek Revival architecture, with an impressive rotunda. Beyond the architecture, there's not that much to see beyond a comprehensive collection of New York brochures. The vertiginously steep stairs outside are a popular spot to spy on the chaos that surrounds the New York Stock Exchange. After enjoying a photo op, head east to 48 Wall Street.

❷ Museum of American Finance

A grand lobby, decked in marble and murals, provides the backdrop for exhibits dedicated to what the local workers manufacture—money. Historic ticker tapes share space with terror-inducing headlines from crashes past and Richter scales of recent market jitters. Don't miss the alcove dedicated to the history of money, where you'll see a dubious-looking greenback marked "Hawaii" (in 1942 the U.S. replaced standard currency on the islands, in case the Japanese pulled off a successful invasion). Get here between 10 and 11am and your visit is free (see p. 100 for more details). When you've seen enough finance, head east on Wall Street, hang a left on Front Street, and then a right onto Old Slip.

❸ The Police Museum

The Police Museum is housed in an odd fortresslike structure at the end of Old Slip that for six decades was the First Precinct

Lower Manhattan Walk Costs

Free	
Five museums, exhibits at three churches, and a round-trip ferry ride	$0
Dirt Cheap	
The museums, exhibits, ferry, and lunchtime concert	$2 (suggested donation)
Add-Ons for Spendthrift Millionaires	
Falafel sandwich	$3

Station House. The museum can be more of a shrine than a source of information, but with three floors of galleries, you're almost sure to find something of interest. I like the copper badges on the first floor (yes, that's where "cop" comes from), and the circa 1910–12 mug shots on the second floor. There is a suggested admission, but no one pays you much heed when you pass through the turnstile.

④ Meal Break

Nearby Front Street has several lunch vans to serve the worker bees from the adjoining financial and insurance offices.

● The best of the bunch is the **Veronica's Kitchen** truck (℃ **917/848-2465**), which parks at the corner of Front and Pine streets. West Indian plates are $5.50 to $8.50 (the prices include two sides), highlighted by curried goat and beef, and oxtail that's been braised for three hours. For more familiar

fare, try the **Jiannetto's** truck (℃ **917/753-0819;** jiannettos pizza.com), just down Front Street at Wall. Thick pizza slices are $2.75 and parmi-giano chicken and eggplant heroes are $7.50. The area is dotted by benches and small parks, perfect for picnicking.

● In bad weather, head over to **180 Maiden Lane,** an office building designed by I. M. Pei. The ground floor atrium is pub-lic space, and every Tuesday at 12:30pm students from the Juil-liard School present classical recitals (℃ **212/799-5000**). No food is available here; this is a good picnic spot for your street meat, however.

● There's also a hidden park right across from the Police Museum. **The Elevated Acre** at 55 Water Street has great swatches of (fake) grass and lovely river views. Come back on a Thursday night in summer and you can catch a free movie here (see p. 258).

ITINERARY 3: THE SECRETS OF LOWER MANHATTAN

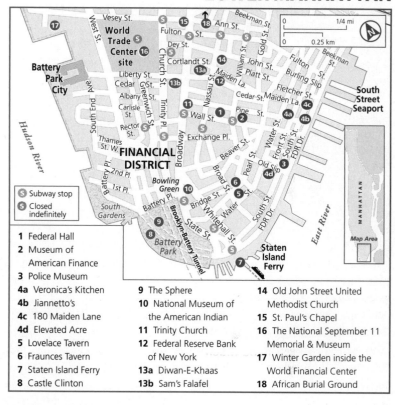

1 Federal Hall
2 Museum of American Finance
3 Police Museum
4a Veronica's Kitchen
4b Jiannetto's
4c 180 Maiden Lane
4d Elevated Acre
5 Lovelace Tavern
6 Fraunces Tavern
7 Staten Island Ferry
8 Castle Clinton
9 The Sphere
10 National Museum of the American Indian
11 Trinity Church
12 Federal Reserve Bank of New York
13a Diwan-E-Khaas
13b Sam's Falafel
14 Old John Street United Methodist Church
15 St. Paul's Chapel
16 The National September 11 Memorial & Museum
17 Winter Garden inside the World Financial Center
18 African Burial Ground

Ⓢ Subway stop
Ⓢ Closed indefinitely

⑤ Lovelace Tavern

Make your way down Pearl Street. Just south of Coenties Alley, under the colonnade of the office building to your right, you'll see a brass railing over glass flooring. Peer into the ground and you'll be looking at stones laid in 1670. During construction of this skyscraper, the foundations of an ancient tavern were discovered. You can also see the foundations of successor structures, and a support beam for the eyesore high-rise overhead. A more famous historic tavern is across the street, just to the south at 54 Pearl.

⑥ Fraunces Tavern

This is definitely an optional stop because it comes with a $10 admission charge. Fraunces Tavern (② **212/425-1778;** www. frauncestavernmuseum.org) has impressive historical credentials—the building's origins date from 1719, and George Washington gave his farewell speech to his officers in the Long Room upstairs—but multiple fires and remodels have made the current version something less than authentic. Among the more interesting relics under glass is a lock of George's hair, which will be absolutely essential when it comes time to clone the father of our country. History buffs should definitely cough up for the tariff, but everyone else has my permission to admire the building and its surreally low-rise neighbors and keep moving.

 **7 Staten Island Ferry**

You're now very close to the poor man's Circle Line, the Staten Island Ferry (℃ **718/815-BOAT** [2628]). This is one of my all-time favorite NYC freebies. From Manhattan to St. George and back again takes a little more than an hour, with inspiring views all the way. The brand-new terminal rises exuberantly over the water at the end of Whitehall and State streets. Find a seat on the right-hand side of the boat as you enter. You'll have great vantages of the downtown skyline, including the burgeoning construction at Ground Zero. About halfway through the ride, you'll spot Lady Liberty herself from the same western windows. Though there isn't all that much to do on the Staten Island side without a further bus or train

ride, if you're really organized you can catch an inexpensive minor league baseball game (p. 290), just a few steps from the terminal.

8 Castle Clinton

Back on the Manhattan side, a few steps west from the ferry is Battery Park. The park is anchored by Castle Clinton (℃ **212/344-7220;** www.nps.gov/cacl), a Napoleonic-era fort. Although this battery has undergone several renovations, from theater hall to aquarium, the original 1811 walls are still intact. Another wall of interest—recent MTA construction uncovered a 1744 halfpenny, pipe shards, and some Delft pottery—has been reconstructed inside. Free concerts are held here on select Thursday nights in summer, usually popular indie-rock bands (p. 243). The battery's now mostly used as the ticket station for the Statue of Liberty and Ellis Island ferries; fittingly, Castle Clinton once served as New York's immigration station, and one out of every six Americans can trace their ancestry through here.

9 The Sphere

As you exit Castle Clinton, pass the Hope Garden and walk toward the modern art, which is part of a small, moving 9/11 memorial. Fritz Koenig's sculpture, The Sphere, stands behind an eternal flame lit on the first anniversary of the terrorist attacks. Koenig designed The Sphere as a symbol of world peace and for 30 years it adorned the plaza at the World Trade Center. The sculpture was salvaged from the rubble and placed here, where the shoreline would have been in 1625 New Amsterdam. Though battered and abused, The Sphere is surprisingly intact. There's a metaphor in there someplace, I hope.

⑩ National Museum of the American Indian

On the far side of The Sphere you'll hit a busy intersection that marks the bottom of Broadway. The petite park across the street is Bowling Green, Manhattan's oldest public park. It was here or very close by that Peter Minuit, director general of New Netherland, traded the legendary $24 in beads with the original locals. Just a few feet away the Smithsonian maintains a museum (© 212/514-3700; www.americanindian.si.edu) dedicated to those native populations. Most of the artifacts collected by New York banker George Gustav Heye are now on the Mall in D.C., but rotating exhibits remain in three galleries. Native American craftsmanship is unparalleled, and the exhibits here are well lit and lovingly curated.

Even if the walls were bare, the building itself, the former U.S. Custom House, would be worthy of a visit. It was completed in 1907 to the specifications of Beaux Arts master Cass Gilbert (he also did the nearby Woolworth Building), and the central rotunda by Raphael Guastavino is a structural marvel. Make sure you see it before the Native Americans reclaim their title to Manhattan and the eviction notices begin.

⑪ Trinity Church

Head north on Broadway and at the intersection of Wall you'll see Trinity Church (© 212/602-0800; www.trinitywallstreet.org). Trinity has been ministering Episcopal-style on this spot since 1698. The current Gothic Revival church was built in 1846 and has a dark and somber interior. There's a small museum on-site. The churchyard is of more interest, with its ancient headstones (Alexander Hamilton is one of the bold-letter names buried here) somehow surviving in the shadow of Mammon. On Thursdays you can catch the **"Concerts at One"** program. (Mon the series comes to St. Paul's Chapel; see below.) The suggested admission is $2, which in no way reflects the high caliber of the classical performers found here.

⑫ The Federal Reserve Bank of New York

Walk up 3 blocks on Broadway and you'll hit Liberty Street. A right turn and a 1-block walk will bring you to the Florentine Renaissance hulk of the Federal Reserve Bank (see p. 90 for a full review). The American Numismatic Society (**℃ 212/234-3130;** www.numismatics.org) keeps a gallery here. Among the cowrie shells and currency you'll find the only existing 1933 Double Eagle, a gold coin now worth some 400,000 times the value printed on its face.

⑬ Meal Break

Right around the corner at 53 Nassau Street is a small shop with fresh, delicious Indian food. **Diwan-E-Khaas** (**℃ 212/571-7676**) serves rich palak paneer for $6.45 and chicken tikka masala for $7.35. Entrees include a choice of rice or naan.

Also nearby is downtown legend **Sam's Falafel,** run from a cart on Cedar Street between Trinity Place and Broadway. The long line will tip you off to the quality of the food here. Portions are huge and prices are tiny ($3 for a sandwich, $5 for a platter).

⑭ Old John Street United Methodist Church

This quiet little plot has been dedicated to Methodism since 1768, when the first American congregation began meeting in a humble chapel here. Inside a tiny, free museum (**℃ 212/269-0014;** www.johnstreetchurch.org) you'll find a wooden pulpit and altar from the original building, along with a still-working clock given by John Wesley himself. The paintings and memorabilia are on the musty side, but it's an interesting history—Harlem's Mother A.M.E. Zion Church had its origins among freed slaves here. The current church dates to 1841, as reflected in the understated Italianate sanctuary upstairs.

⑮ St. Paul's Chapel

This satellite chapel (**℃ 212/233-4164;** www.saintpaulschapel.org) of Trinity Church, completed in 1766, is the oldest continuously used public building in the city. The interior is surprisingly cheerful and colorful. Even the 9/11 exhibits have an upbeat and healing tone, although a self-congratulatory note does seep in. On the north side of the chapel you can see the pew used by George Washington when New York was the official seat of the U.S. government and not just the de facto capital. Over the pew is a 1795 painting of the Great Seal, in one of its earliest renditions. Out back is a little country courtyard, which miraculously survived the rain of debris on 9/11. Standing amid the ancient tombstones, surrounded by the Financial District's bustle and clamor, and looking out at the rising Freedom Tower, you might have the day's best opportunity for putting the long thread of the city's history into some sort of context.

🔟 & 🔟 Bonus Round: Ground Zero and Battery Park City

A recent invention, Battery Park City is a complex of offices, hotels, and apartment buildings built on fill created by the excavation of the World Trade Center's foundation in the '60s. The city has never done a better job of landscaping, and the walkways along the Hudson are ideal for strolling, or just sitting down to watch the river flow. Vesey Street, which runs along the north side of St. Paul's Chapel, will lead you past Ground Zero and straight down to the Hudson. In 2011 **The National September 11 Memorial & Museum** (© 212/ **312-8800;** www.national911 memorial.org) is scheduled to open on and around the original

footprint of the World Trade Center. Additional perspective on Ground Zero can be found from the Liberty and Vesey street walkways, and from the back of the **Winter Garden** inside the World Financial Center.

🔟 Bonus Round Two: City Hall Park and the African Burial Ground

Alternatively, a short walk north along Broadway will lead you to City Hall Park. On the far side of City Hall and the Tweed Courthouse (for tours see p. 126), at the intersection of Elk and Reade streets, is the **African Burial Ground National Monument** (© **212/637-2019;** www.nps.gov/ afbg). Unearthed during construction of the federal office building on the corner, this patch of graveyard was part of a 6.6-acre burial ground that stretched beneath New York's municipal center. Starting in the 1690s, some 15,000 Africans were laid to rest here. Undulating mounds and a granite memorial make somber markers for this occluded layer of New York history.

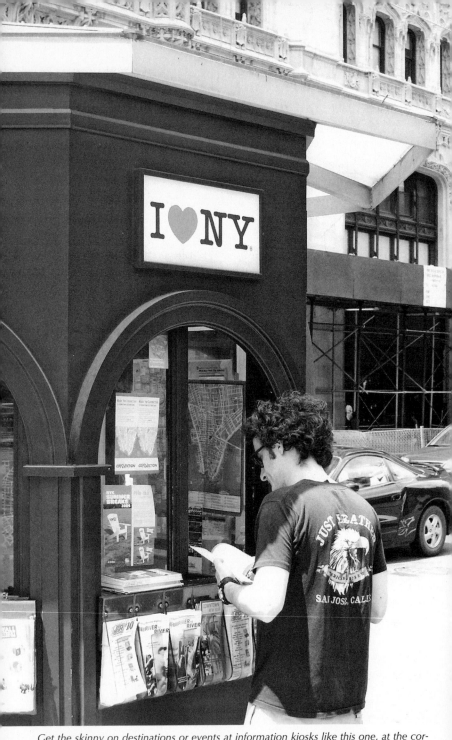

Get the skinny on destinations or events at information kiosks like this one, at the corner of Broadway and Park Row. See p. 321 for more information.

NYC BASICS FROM A TO Z

1 Information Centers

The city runs five information centers, with free maps and brochures as well as discount coupons for tourist-friendly fare. Check with ☎ **212/484-1222** or www.nycgo.com for more information.

New York City's Official Visitor Information Center 810 Seventh Ave., btw. 52nd and 53rd sts. Mon–Fri 8:30am–6pm; Sat–Sun 9am–5pm; holidays 9am–3pm. Subway: B/D/E to Seventh Ave.; N/Q/R to 57th St.; 1 to 50th St.

Gateway to America: Discover New York Harbor Visitor Information Center Federal Hall (Financial District), 26 Wall St., at Broad St. Mon–Fri 9am–5pm. Subway: 2/3/4/5 to Wall St.

Official Visitor Information Kiosk—City Hall Broadway and Park Row. Mon–Fri 9am–6pm; Sat–Sun 10am–5pm; holidays 9am–3pm.

Subway: 2/3 to Park Place; R to City Hall; 4/5/6 to Brooklyn Bridge/ City Hall; A/C/J/Z to Fulton St./Broadway Nassau.

Official Visitor Information Kiosk—Chinatown At the triangle of Canal, Walker, and Baxter sts. Daily 10am–6pm; holidays 10am– 3pm. Subway: J/N/Q/R/Z/6 to Canal St.

Official Visitor Information Center—Harlem Studio Museum, Harlem, 144 W. 125th St., btw. Lenox Ave. and Adam Clayton Powell Blvd. Mon–Fri noon–6pm; Sat–Sun 10am–6pm. Subway: 2/3 to 125th St.

Information at the Libraries New York's public libraries are founts of information, and real live librarians are on hand to answer your brief *factual* questions (this service is of little utility for existential concerns). The Bronx, Staten Island, and Manhattan residents can call ✆ **917/ ASK-NYPL** [917/275-6975], Mon–Sat 9am–6pm. You can also text, IM, or e-mail for answers. Check www.nypl.org/ask-nypl/phone-us for more numbers for specialized questions. In Brooklyn, call ✆ **718/230- 2100,** option 5 (Mon and Fri 9am–6pm, Tues–Thurs 9am–9pm, and Sat 10am–6pm). There's also a 24/7 online chat service, which the Queens Library participates in as well. The analogue Queens InfoLine is ✆ **718/990-0728** (Mon–Fri 9am–8:45pm, Sat 10am–5:15pm). Brooklyn and Queens also provide answers via e-mail.

Internet Access for Free or Cheap The city's Wi-Fi zones are constantly expanding. The South Street Seaport, Bryant Park, City Hall Park, and Penn Station are among the areas covered by free wireless connections. Many hotels have gotten onboard, and lobbies like the Ace Hotel (20 W. 29th St.; ✆ **212/679-2222**) are good spots to log in. Check **www.nyc wireless.net** for the latest news, or **www.openwifinyc.com** for an index of locations. Many public libraries are Wi-Fi friendly, in addition to the free computers they provide for Internet connections. Check online for more information (www.nypl.org in the Bronx, Manhattan, and Staten

---

Current Events

The city does a decent job of providing the latest scoop on goings-on around town. **NYC & Company** keeps a 24-hour information hot line (✆ **800/NYC- VISIT** [692-8474] or 212/397- 8222). For updated listings of music, theater, museum, and other events, check online at www.nycgo.com.

Island; otherwise www.queenslibrary.org or www.brooklynpublic library.org). Many cafes and fast food establishments also offer Internet access; the Wi-Fi connections at McDonald's and Starbucks are free and easy to access. The **ING DIRECT Café** on 45 E. 49th St. (☎ **866/692-2233;** www.home.ingdirect.com) offers free Internet-connected computers (and cheap and tasty coffee) on weekdays from 8am to 4pm.

2 Getting There & Getting Around

GETTING THERE

By Plane

New York City is served by three major airports: **LaGuardia Airport** (☎ **718/533-3400**), **John F. Kennedy (JFK) International Airport** (☎ **718/ 244-4444**), and **Newark International Airport** (☎ **973/961-6000**) in New Jersey. Newark often has the best cheap flight deals, and during high-traffic hours it can be the most accessible to and from Manhattan. For transportation information for all three airports, call **Air-Ride** (☎ **800/247-7433**).

Getting into Town from the Airports

JFK   **AirTrain JFK** has been running for over six years now, and it's by far my favorite pick for airport travel. The cost is only $5 (on top of the subway or Long Island Railroad fare to get within AirTrain range), the ride is smooth, and monorails come around often enough that you won't be in a panic over missing your flight. JFK terminals connect with the E/J/Z trains at Sutphin Boulevard/Archer Avenue, the LIRR at Jamaica Station, and the A train at Howard Beach. For the latter, make sure you catch an A to Far Rockaway, not to Lefferts Boulevard. The train runs 24/7. Allow about an hour for the subway and monorail combined once you've left Manhattan. ☎ **877/JFK-AIRTRAIN** (535-2478). www.panynj.gov.

To LaGuardia   The **M60 bus** ($2.25) serves all LaGuardia terminals, connecting to the Upper West Side of Manhattan. Bus rides from 106th Street average 1 hour to the airport, though traffic will cause that time to vary. The **Q48** also makes LaGuardia runs. For the complete schedule, call ☎ **718/330-1234** or log on to www.mta.nyc.ny. us/nyct.

To Newark The **AirTrain Newark** (✆ **888/EWR-INFO** [397-4636]) is a smooth ride, but it's a little pricey at $15 one-way. It takes 20 minutes to get from Penn Station in Manhattan to the airport monorail. The cheapest trip is to take the **Path train** from Manhattan to Newark ($1.75). At Newark Penn Station you can catch the **62 bus,** which makes several stops but will get you to the airport for only $1.50. On the downside, it's all but impossible to make that bus ride in under an hour. ✆ **800/772-2222.** www.njtransit.com.

Carpooling Alternatives God bless the interwebs for bringing people together. Two new online services will help you save money on cabs and black cars via carpool hookups. **Hitchsters** (www.hitchsters. com) specializes in airport rides, to and from Brooklyn and Manhattan. **RideAmigos** (www.rideamigos.com) takes a broader approach, opening its ride board for events and commutes on top of flights. (They also provide an environmental slant, telling you how many pounds of carbon dioxide you'll save by sharing your ride.)

BY INTERSTATE BUS

As symbols of cheap highway travel, Greyhound buses will live on in country songs, but the burgeoning **Chinatown bus** industry has stolen the hearts of Eastern Seaboard adventurers. A round-trip ride to Washington, D.C., is only $35, and the slightly longer trip to Boston is $30. There are now dozens of companies making runs, with possible destinations stretching to include places like Richmond, Philly, and Albany ($20–$60 round-trip). The difference between any two companies isn't dramatic; I choose based on who's got the most convenient schedule for me on any given trip. You can buy a ticket online, or you can just show up at the departure point and let eager touts jostle each other for your business. The buses are full size, and every driver I've ever had has been a professional.

Fung Wah Bus Service This bus line travels between Boston's South Station Bus Terminal (700 Atlantic Ave.) and New York's Chinatown (139 Canal St., btw. Chrystie St. and the Bowery). A one-way ticket is $15. ✆ **212/925-8889.** www.fungwahbus.com.

New Century Travel For the DC to NY and NY to Philly routes, this company runs a full schedule from 86 Allen St. (btw. Grand and Broome sts.). The run to DC's Chinatown (513 H St. NW) is $20 one-way and $35 round-trip, and Philly (55 N. 11th St.) is $12 each way, $20 round-trip. ✆ **212/627-2666.** www.2000coach.com.

Washington Deluxe   If DC and New York's Chinatowns aren't convenient for you, this bus company makes pickups in assorted NYC locations (Brooklyn, the Lower East Side, and Penn Station), and drops off at 1320 19th St. NW, 1015 15th St. NW, and Union Station in DC. $21 for one-way and $40 round-trip ($25 each way on Sat). © **866/ BUS-NYDC** (287-6932). www.washny.com.

GETTING AROUND TOWN

BY SUBWAY & CITY BUS

The MTA cooked its books and put the screws to subway and bus riders—$2.25 is now the price of a single ride, and they've cut back service to boot. Until straphangers are called upon for our next bloodletting, there are a couple of discounts. When you spend $8 or more on a pay-per-ride **MetroCard,** you get a 15% bonus. For 24 hours of heavy commuting you can get a FunPass—all-you-can-ride for $8.25. Unlimited rides are also available in 7-day ($27), 14-day ($51.50), and 30-day ($99 for 90 rides or $104 for unlimited) formats. Children under 44 inches tall ride free. © **718/330-1234.** www.mta.nyc.ny.us.

BY BOAT

The **Staten Island Ferry** is hard to beat for scenic satisfaction, with great views of the Statue of Liberty, Ellis Island, and Governors Island (p. 315). The boat runs 24/7, leaving from the new terminal at Whitehall, on the southeastern tip of Manhattan. On the far side you can enjoy the distractions of St. George, Staten Island (such as they are), or you can follow the boat-loading sign and circle back across the harbor. Other ferry services and the New York Water Taxi (www.nywatertaxi.com) also offer great views, but it's hard to compete with free. Staten Island ferries leave every 20–30 minutes on weekdays, less frequently during off-peak and weekend hours. Subway: R to Whitehall St.; 4/5 to Bowling Green; 1 to South Ferry.

BY CAR

New York's spectacular public transportation and surfeit of taxis should be enough to dissuade you from city driving, but I can add a few cautions. Traffic can be miserable, and at weird hours, too (mile-long backup to get across the Brooklyn Bridge at 3am, anyone?). Parking is difficult: Pay lots charge king's ransoms, and street parking can be impossible to find. If you leave your car too close to a hydrant (or commit any other infraction) you're looking at least at a $100 ticket. Driving in the city is doable, but with so much that can be accessed by foot power alone, why risk hassle?

BY FOOT

This town is built for walking. The dense clustering of neighborhoods makes for great overlaps and cultural collisions, which are best enjoyed at a pedestrian's pace. You can get a taste of the city's diversity within just a few blocks. For example, standing on the corner of Grand and Broadway, you're less than a 10-minute walk from Chinatown, TriBeCa, SoHo, NoHo, the West Village, the East Village, Little Italy, and the Lower East Side. Supplement with a train ride here or there, and you can enjoy plenty of city without resorting to more complicated (and expensive) modes of motion.

BY TAXI

My senior citizen mother gets all around the city by foot, train, and bus. She considers resorting to taxis "unsporting." Now I wouldn't think less of you for not making your way as ruggedly as a little old lady, but cabs aren't cheap, and if you're traveling at anything close to a peak hour it's much slower than zipping under clogged streets on the train. A taxi costs $3 at entry, plus 40¢ for every fifth of a mile, 40¢ for every minute of idling, 50¢ more for a night ride, and a $1 more for rush hour. If it's an odd hour, or you're in an unfamiliar place, by all means hail a cab, but it's my least favorite way of traveling.

3 Free & Dirt Cheap Resources A to Z

Disability Services The mayor maintains an office (✆ **212/788-2830**) that provides free advice to visitors with disabilities on how to get around the city. A few elevators aside, the subway system is largely inaccessible to those with disabilities, but all city buses are equipped to carry wheelchairs.

Emergencies ✆ **911** is, of course, the number for emergency police, fire, and ambulance service. For nonemergencies and just about any city government function you can think of, call ✆ **311.** Other emergency numbers include the **AIDS Hot Line** (✆ 212/807-6655), **Animal Bites** (✆ 212/676-2483), **Poison Control** (✆ 800/222-1222), **Suicide Prevention** (✆ 212/673-3000), **Traveler's Aid JFK** (✆ 718/656-4870), and **Safe Horizon** (formerly Victim Services; ℂ 212/577-7700). Among the city's 24-hour emergency rooms are **Bellevue Hospital Center** (462 First Ave.; ℂ 212/252-94571), **Beth Israel Medical Center** (First Ave. and 16th St.; ℂ 212/420-2000), **St. Luke's/Roosevelt Hospital** (425 W. 59th St.; ℂ 212/523-4000), and **St. Luke's Hospital Center** (Amsterdam Ave. and 113th St.; ℂ 212/765-5454).

GLBT Resources   The **Lesbian, Gay, Bisexual & Transgender Community Center** (208 W. 13th St., btw. Seventh and Eighth aves.; ℂ **212/ 620-7310;** www.gaycenter.org) is a meeting place for more than 400 organizations. Most of the online calendar lists events with charges, but there are a few freebies, like the free lending library and archive. GLBT information can also be found in the free monthly *Next* (www. nextmagazine.com), the free bimonthly *Gay City News* (www.gay citynews.com), and the free weekly *Village Voice* (www.villagevoice. com). You can find copies stacked up in bars, clubs, stores, and sidewalk boxes throughout town. If you don't want to risk getting a little ink on your fingertips, their websites are also good sources of information. The **Gay and Lesbian National Hot Line** (ℂ **888/THE-GLNH** [843-4564]; www.glnh.org) offers peer counseling and information on upcoming events. Open Monday through Friday 4pm to midnight, Saturday noon to 5pm. Also see p. 155 for the **Gay Men's Health Crisis;** their hot line is ℂ **800/AIDS-NYC** [243-7692].

Legal Aid   Any person familiar with cop shows knows that in the U.S., an accused person has "the right to consult with an attorney and to have that attorney present during questioning, and that, if he or she is indigent, an attorney will be provided at no cost to represent her or him." Another freebie! Also see p. 156 for **Legal Services NYC.**

Moving   On city streetlamps, "Man with a Van" signs are ubiquitous. For small moves, I find that's as good a way as any to go. For the online version of those streetlamp flyers, **www.citymove.com** is a helpful site. Movers bid against each other so you get decent prices, and movees critique the jobs so you know which companies to avoid.

Newspapers & Magazines   New York has three major dailies. The *New York Times* is the legendary paper of record, and the *Daily News* and *New York Post* are tabloid-style. Two free daily papers, *AM-New York* and *Metro,* can be found near subways in the mornings. *The New Yorker*, *New York Magazine*, and *Time Out New York* are weekly glossy magazines with extensive information on city goings-on.

Pharmacies Duane Reades are ubiquitous in NYC, with some 250 branches. Locations with 24-hour pharmacies include 1279 Third Ave. (© **212/744-2668**), 250 W. 57th St. (© **212/265-2101**), and 2522 Broadway (© **212/663-1580**). Two of the city's Rite Aids also offer 24-hour service: 301 W. 50th St. (© **212/247-8384**) and 408 Grand St. (© **212/529-7115**).

Post Offices The **Main Post Office,** at Eighth Avenue and 33rd Street (© **212/967-8585**), is open 24 hours a day, 7 days a week. Check www.usps.com for other city locations; note that New York post offices generate long lines—try to time your visit with a morning or afternoon lull, or make use of the automated machines.

Smoking Laws New York's legendary tolerance does not extend to smokers. You can light up on the sidewalks, but smoking on public transportation and in hotel lobbies, taxis, and shops is prohibited. Most bars and restaurants ban smoke as well, although their outdoor areas are generally exceptions. Buy cigarettes before you hit the city: A pack will set you back around $13 now.

Telephone Service Several small companies have come into the New York phone market, saving consumers hundreds of dollars a year versus the rates for AT&T and Verizon. Prices start low, but once the Man slaps on his $20 or so in monthly taxes and surcharges, it may not seem quite so cheap. If you're already paying for broadband, you can get around the gummint by signing up with a company like **Vonage** (www.vonage.com). Monthly rates start low: $17.99 for basic (500 free min. of local and long-distance), up to $25.99 for all-you-can-yak. Usually you can keep your existing number, too. The next broadband telecommunications wave is to turn your PC into a phone. **Skype** (www.skype.com) will let you talk free with other Skype users worldwide. You'll need a mic and headphones, but those are cheap enough, and the program downloads quickly. (For calls outside the Skype system, rates start at around 2¢ per min., and get even cheaper with subscriptions.) **Yahoo!** is another entrant into this field. Their rates start at nothing (PC to PC via Yahoo! Messenger), and vary widely for PC to phone. Long-distance starts around 1¢ or 2¢ per minute. For 60¢ a minute you can get caught up with your college buddies in Antarctica. Check www.voice.yahoo.com for the latest offer. If you're only interested in long-distance savings by traditional means, compare rates online at **www.lowermybills.com**. (The site also offers

For Further Reading

The same era that's coined the words "frugalista" and "recessionista" has also spawned a host of cheap living material on the interwebs. Our colleague **Broke-Ass Stuart** maintains a great website, with an army of columnists providing tips on how to live more for less (www.broke assstuart.com). **Cheapism** (www.cheapism.com) is almost a Consumer Reports for the price-conscious, with product overviews and sample costs. Coupon codes can be plucked from **www.retailmenot.com**, and group-rate specials are churned out daily at **www.groupon.com**. **FreeNYC** (www.freenyc.net) is chockablock with city cultural give-aways. To keep up with New York's music scene (free and not free), check out **Brooklyn Vegan** (www.brooklynvegan.com) and **Oh My Rockness** (www.ohmyrockness.com). When I'm not toiling for Frommer's, I moonlight as the NYC listings editor for **BlackBook** (www. blackbookmag.com)—check the website or free iPhone app for tons more on New York City shops, bars, restaurants, and hotels. "Free & E-Zeens" on p. 224 and "Liquid Assets" on p. 296 also have additional helpful websites.

rate comparisons on everything from cellphones to insurance to mortgages.) Also, if you're still paying for directory assistance for businesses, stop. Google now has a completely free service (✆ **800/ GOOG411** [466-4411]). There's also a text-message offshoot (send to ✆ **GOOGL** [46645]) if you want results sent straight to your cellphone.

Tipping   Despite the cheapness advocated on these pages, I consider good tipping to be essential for my financial karma. Typically in New York, we leave 20% for our waiters/waitresses/waitrons (less for poor service), 10% for food delivery guys (more if it's pouring or freezing), 10% for cab drivers, 10% or so for bartenders, around 15% for hairdressers, and $1 per bag for bellhops.

Toilets   For free public toilets, you can take advantage of the efforts of people with way too much time on their hands by logging on to **www.thebathroomdiaries.com** and browsing the lists of facilities.

INDEX

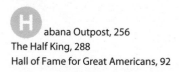